BEST CANADIAN RÉSUMÉS

by
Sharon Graham

Published By:
Sentor Media Inc.
285 Mutual Street, Suite 2401
Toronto, Ontario
M4Y 3C5
Tel: 416-924-4832
Fax: 416-924-6979
E-mail: info@sentormedia.com
Internet: www.sentormedia.com
Bookstore: www.careerbookstore.ca

SENTOR MEDIA INC.

Kevin Makra, Publisher
Sharon Graham, Author
The Design Booth, Text Layout
Ryan Snow, Cover Design
Printed in Canada by Printcrafters

Library and Archives Canada Cataloguing in Publication

Graham, Sharon —
Best Canadian résumés : 100 best Canadian-format résumés and cover letters / Sharon Graham.

Includes index.
ISBN 978-1-896324-27-4

1. Résumés (Employment). I. Title.

HF5383.G722 2007   650.14'2   C2006-906688-4

DISCLAIMER

We have made every effort to provide complete and accurate information in this book. Still, it is possible that we have not found and corrected some typographical errors, omissions, or other mistakes. This book contains information that is current only up to its printing date. This book does not provide legal or specialized counsel. Therefore, use the content as a general guideline and not the only source of your job search information.

The author and the publisher will have neither liability nor responsibility to any person or entity with respect to any loss or damage caused, or alleged to have been caused, directly or indirectly, by the information contained in this book. If you require legal advice or other expert assistance, seek the services of a qualified professional.

Table of Contents

Acknowledgements

To all the professional résumé writers who generously contributed their best Canadian résumé samples for publication, I express my gratitude. You can see a complete contact list for these highly qualified professionals in Appendix D.

A special "thank-you" goes to Career Professionals of Canada's Certified Résumé Strategist Certification Committee, Linda Schnabel (chair), Heather Erskine, Lynda Reeves, and Marlene Slawson. Your advice and support have been essential in bringing this book to life.

Thank you to Kevin Makra and the publishing team for your enthusiasm, dedication, and support in making this immense project a reality.

I would also like to express my appreciation to our clients who kindly agreed to allow us to publish their résumé. Of course, I want to acknowledge and thank the hundreds and thousands of Canadians who have put their careers in the hands of professional résumé writers. You have enabled us to develop our abilities and talents as leaders in the Canadian Career Industry.

This book is dedicated to my mother for showing me the meaning of empathy, my father for giving me the determination to succeed, and to my husband and best friend, Wayne Graham for his undying support. Most of all, thanks to God, who continues to make the impossible possible.

Sharon Graham

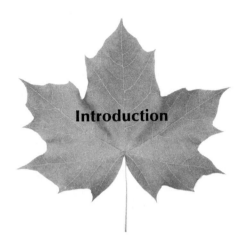

Introduction

For millions of Canadians, the résumé plays a critical role in the success or failure of a job search. The competition in our market is tough. Job seekers know that their résumé must stand apart from the rest on the recruiter's desk. Therefore, to win that all-important interview, you will require a superb résumé.

Best Canadian Résumés is your one-of-a-kind resource. It provides tools, information, and checklists to enable you to create an outstanding résumé targeted to the Canadian employment market.

This book is distinctively Canadian. The résumé samples come from unique jobs and fields that exist across Canada. The book will provide you with the language, grammar, and style rules that you should apply within your résumé. You will learn Canadian legislative requirements regarding such topics as personal information and bilingualism in certain provinces. Finally, at the back of the book, we provide a number of resources to enable you to succeed in your job search.

HOW THIS BOOK IS ORGANIZED

This book empowers you to create an effective résumé by taking you through a logical sequence of steps. The book is broken down into three main parts:

PART 1—PLANNING YOUR RÉSUMÉ

First-rate résumé writing takes planning. This section will enable you to understand your job search goal. You will uncover your pertinent qualifications and identify your job search target. Then you will create your own Value Proposition that will be the foundation for your résumé.

PART 2—DEVELOPING YOUR RÉSUMÉ

Established processes, techniques, and methods are important to learn and know. This section discusses a variety of proven formulas used by professional résumé writers across Canada. By learning how to apply these guidelines, you will build a sound foundation to write an exemplary résumé.

PART 3—SAMPLE DOCUMENTS

The largest portion of this book showcases résumés and cover letters that professional résumé writers have created for their Canadian clients. It includes some of the very best work produced by members of Career Professionals of Canada. All the samples are directly transferable to the Canadian employment market. These documents will provide you with inspiration to stimulate your thinking and creativity. A "strategic tip" box annotates each résumé sample to help you visualize and understand how to apply a specific strategy.

Although it may be tempting to skip directly to the samples, you will find that using them in conjunction with the first two parts of this book will enable you to write a unique document rather than just a copy of someone else's work.

After reading this book, you will be fully prepared to launch an effective and successful work search armed with a professional résumé, valuable insight into yourself, and the confidence that will give you the advantage in the job market.

PART 1
PLANNING
YOUR RÉSUMÉ

1
Clarifying Your Job Search Goal

Before setting out to write your résumé, you must have a good understanding of your job search goal. This requires that you know both who you are _and_ what job you are going for. Your first challenge is to create an accurate picture of yourself and your goal. Then, you must identify what type of job you are interested in pursuing and what skills this role requires.

UNCOVER YOUR QUALIFICATIONS

To create an accurate picture of yourself, you need to gain a solid understanding of what you bring to the table. You should know your _background_, _area of expertise_, _added value_, and _style_. By taking stock, you will learn just how valuable you are to your market.

Before you ever start writing your résumé, it is critical that you identify and uncover all areas of your _background_. Not only must you delve into your education, career history, and life experience, but you must identify the accomplishments that you have accumulated over the years. By bringing all your background to the forefront, you will be able to select and include the very best items for your résumé.

To know your _area of expertise_, you must have insight into your specialty—the specific subject areas where you are the expert. You must also have a realistic perception of your level, or position, within an organization's hierarchy. Finally, you need to have a keen awareness of your stature, or prominence, in the industry. For example, if you hold a highly visible political role within the Government of Canada, you would design a very different document than if you hold a supporting role. You may choose to focus on highlighting your highly public achievements rather than administrative work you have done. Conversely, if you are a strong administrative professional, you may choose to bring out and list different aspects of your technical expertise.

To really know yourself, you must dig deep and discover your _added value_. This is the unique offering that you provide to your prospective employer. Look outside the job posting and find the additional benefit that you bring to the employer. For example, you may be a customer service representative based in Ontario and the employer is looking for specific skills, which you have. In addition to this, you may offer the added value of being bilingual in English and French. This feature allows you to do much more than the average English-speaking customer service representative because you can service clients throughout Canada in the primary language of their province.

Finally, to create a résumé that reflects yourself accurately and effectively, you must know your *style*. Identify the distinctive aspects of your personality that enable you to succeed. Focus on showing the individuality that you bring, which enables you to make your role much more than just a job description. For example, you may be a very aggressive salesperson that does what it takes to "get the client" and quickly "close the deal." You would describe yourself very differently from a sales professional that specializes in developing long-term relationships. You must understand yourself to be able to express your style accurately to recruiters. Knowing your style will also help you to find a position that will be the right fit for you.

Chapter 2 will delve into your qualifications in more detail and enable you to uncover all that you have to offer your next employer.

UNDERSTAND YOUR TARGET

To be effective, your résumé must not only reflect your very best qualifications, it must also meet and exceed your prospective employer's needs. The best way to do this is to understand exactly what kind of job you are targeting so that you can focus on presenting the skills that are required.

Focus yourself on positions where you are a good fit and you can succeed. By narrowing your job search target, you will better match yourself to appropriate roles. Your goal is to enable the employer to see you as the ideal candidate for the job.

Learn what you can about the industry or career field that you are focusing on. Investigate your prospective employer and understand the requirements of the job you are targeting. In your résumé, document exactly what the recruiter is looking for. Include your added value, and leave off the rest.

Chapter 3 will help you to further focus on your target.

QUALIFICATIONS AND TARGET CHECKLIST

Complete the following checklist to determine if you clearly understand yourself and your focus. If there are areas that you feel are missing, go through Chapters 2 and 3 to fill in the gaps. Once you are sure that you have learned as much as you can, you will be able to take advantage of Chapter 4 to develop your unique Value Proposition and a focused résumé that will win you interviews.

Do you know your qualifications and your target?
❑ I know my area of expertise (speciality, level, stature)
❑ I know my background (education, experience, accomplishments)
❑ I know my added value (unique offerings)
❑ I know my style (personality, individuality)
❑ I know my target industry (career field)
❑ I know my target employer (company, products, services, culture, interviewer, supervisor)
❑ I know my target job (responsibilities, requirements, objectives)

2
Uncovering Your Qualifications

Your very first step in designing an exemplary résumé is to take a formal, in-depth look at yourself, your career history, and your employment objectives. This will allow you to identify and articulate the vast qualifications that you have to offer. By going through this process, you will uncover your hidden strengths, skills, accomplishments, and abilities. The information that you uncover will be the basis for building a powerful attention-getting résumé that represents you in a professional manner and ultimately enables you to achieve your job search goals. You will soon find out just how valuable you are to the job market.

Before you start, gather all your documentation. If you have a current résumé, keep it handy. Some other important documents that you will want to refer to are your performance evaluations, salary reviews, awards, transcripts, personal biography, published articles and reviews, and letters of reference. Also, make sure to collect a few job postings or job descriptions that interest you.

As you work through to uncover your qualifications, always keep in mind that you will be using the information to create a personalized résumé. Focus on selecting information that will be important and valuable to your next employer.

YOUR CONTACT INFORMATION

Determine all the contact information that you would like to provide to your employer. You will want to include your full name, home number, and e-mail address. Include your full street address, city, province, and postal code.

Consider listing only the very best ways to find you. For example, if you rarely have your cell phone on, you may not want to list that number. Also, be careful about listing business phone numbers and addresses. You do not want to appear as if you are doing personal business on work time. You may also want to list a facsimile (fax) number or pager if you have either one readily accessible.

Only list your website if it provides a professional synopsis, résumé, or portfolio of your background and qualifications. Personal information on a site will quickly turn off an employer.

Contact Information Checklist

- ❑ Full Name
- ❑ Home Address (Street, City, Province, and Postal Code)
- ❑ Home Phone Number
- ❑ Fax Number
- ❑ Cell Phone Number
- ❑ E-Mail Address
- ❑ Website URL
- ❑ Other Contact Information

YOUR EDUCATION

List your educational background including all applicable details. Make sure to include your education that is most related to your job objective.

In your résumé, indicate the school name, location, and program. Provide your degree or outline the level you attained. If you have achieved honours or have an exceptionally high grade point average, you may want to include this information. Most people also include their graduation date, unless they have graduated quite a while ago and they want to conceal their age.

If you are a recent graduate and you do not have much work experience, consider including the list of courses you completed, your extracurricular school activities, and scholarships.

You may want to consider additional training and professional development programs that you may have taken during the course of your life and career. If you have a list of courses, seminars, certifications, or licensing programs to include, you may want to list them in a separate section on your résumé. If you have a lack of formal education, or you are an older worker, this category may be especially important to include.

Education Checklist

- ❑ Universities
- ❑ Community Colleges
- ❑ CEGEPs
- ❑ Courses
- ❑ Seminars
- ❑ Workshops
- ❑ Trade Shows
- ❑ Certifications
- ❑ Licenses
- ❑ Courses
- ❑ Extracurricular Activities
- ❑ Scholarships
- ❑ Awards
- ❑ Special Honours
- ❑ Outstanding Grades
- ❑ Other Education Information

YOUR EMPLOYMENT HISTORY

You are now ready to provide a detailed work history. When documenting your employment history, start at your most recent position, describing one role at a time.

In your résumé, you will likely want to list the company name and location, your start and end date, and the title of the position you held. If you have been promoted, you will want to highlight that by including the titles of each of your previous positions.

In many cases, it is helpful to provide some context to your employment history by including a brief description of the organization for which you worked. List the company's industry, ranking, specialty, products, services, size, number of employees, and/or sales volume. In addition, the title of the person reporting to you may be important to discuss especially if your job title does not accurately reflect your level of accountability.

Outline your responsibilities briefly. Include the departments that you were accountable for, the number of people you supervised, and your major job functions. Quantify your responsibilities with numbers whenever possible. If you had any financial accountability, include the type of budget and dollar amount you managed. If you had a specific revenue, profit, or expense target, document it. Focus on your most pertinent employers, providing more information to the most relevant positions.

In Canada, certain information such as your salary or reasons for leaving a position is off limits. Do not discuss these kinds of topics in this section or anywhere else in your résumé.

Responsibilities sometimes referred to as "job duties," are useful in providing an overview of your job, but they are not nearly as important as what you have achieved. Rather than creating long lists of responsibilities, opt for making your résumé rich in accomplishments.

Employment History Checklist

- ❑ Company Name
- ❑ Company City and Country
- ❑ Company Description
- ❑ Your Start Date and End Date
- ❑ Your Job Title
- ❑ Other Job Titles You Have Held
- ❑ Title of the Person You Report To
- ❑ Number of Employees You Supervised
- ❑ Departments that You Oversee
- ❑ Budgetary Responsibilities
- ❑ Sales Targets
- ❑ Major Job Functions
- ❑ Other Employment Information

YOUR ACCOMPLISHMENTS

In your résumé, focus on accomplishments, rather than job duties. Highlight only the best of the best. Make it accomplishment-rich to show off your distinguishing features.

You will want to brainstorm to identify some of your achievements. Reflect on your life, education, and career experiences, and create a list of your accomplishments. Consider all areas including work, home, school, volunteer, and community life. Aim for a minimum of ten accomplishments. You may not use all of them in your résumé, but the more you identify, the better your selection. This way, you can choose the very best ones to sell yourself effectively. To uncover and quantify some of your accomplishments, answer the following questions:

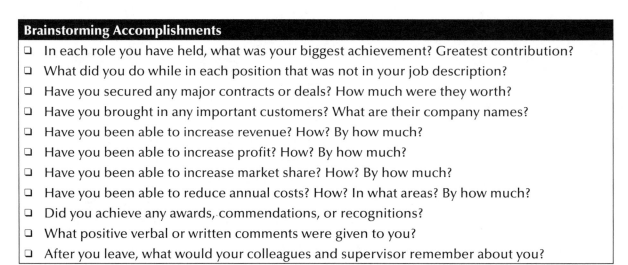

Brainstorming Accomplishments

- ❏ In each role you have held, what was your biggest achievement? Greatest contribution?
- ❏ What did you do while in each position that was not in your job description?
- ❏ Have you secured any major contracts or deals? How much were they worth?
- ❏ Have you brought in any important customers? What are their company names?
- ❏ Have you been able to increase revenue? How? By how much?
- ❏ Have you been able to increase profit? How? By how much?
- ❏ Have you been able to increase market share? How? By how much?
- ❏ Have you been able to reduce annual costs? How? In what areas? By how much?
- ❏ Did you achieve any awards, commendations, or recognitions?
- ❏ What positive verbal or written comments were given to you?
- ❏ After you leave, what would your colleagues and supervisor remember about you?

Once you have identified your very best achievements, use the *Action-Result* formula to write concise achievement stories, which you can transfer into the résumé. Break down each accomplishment into two parts: *Action* and *Result*.

In a brief phrase, outline the action you took in order to achieve the particular accomplishment you are discussing. Your action may be a one-time event, a series of activities, or routine work. Whether you performed the action on your own or as part of a team, keep focused on the role that you took. For example, you may have "Reconciled inventory by identifying and eliminating stagnant product lines."

Notice that the action phrase starts with an active past tense verb. You can see a list of high-impact action verbs in Appendix B.

Follow this phrase up with another short statement outlining the result of your actions. Talk about how your actions benefited your employer. Be specific and quantify your results using facts and figures. If there were side benefits, include these in your statement. In the previous example where you reconciled inventory, your result may be "slashed in-stock levels by 15% while maintaining annual sales of over $1 million."

The combined accomplishment sentence in the example above would sound like this: "Reconciled inventory by identifying and eliminating stagnant product lines, slashing in-stock levels by 15% while maintaining annual sales of over $1 million."

Once you have created a number of clear and concise accomplishment messages, incorporate them in a bulleted list within your résumé. You can further capitalize on your accomplishments by using them in employment interviews and throughout your career.

- The senior-level executive may have "hands-on experience creating multi-million dollar deals with Canadian industry leaders."

Complete the following checklist to determine your *added value*. Ask yourself what extra benefit you bring to your new employer.

Your Added Value
❑ Supplementary value (unique offerings)
❑ Individuality (personality, style)

PUTTING YOUR VALUE PROPOSITION TOGETHER

Your Value Proposition will be the key to your résumé, cover letter, and interview. Through it, you will be portraying your career brand.

Here is an example of how an Ontario-based Field Service Technician created his Value Proposition. First, he determined that he could resolve his next employer's *buying motivators* by decreasing the escalation of customer complaints, improving call response time, and generating sales of product upgrades. His *supporting qualifications* include his college diploma in Systems Analysis, experience providing field support to large businesses, and current computer hardware expertise. Additionally, he offered the *added value* of being able to speak in English and French and experience in providing excellent customer support.

In response to the question, "Why should I hire you?" the computer technician would answer, "I would like to advance the goals and objectives of your organization using my strong ability to decrease escalation of customer complaints by improving call response time while generating sales of product upgrades. Through my college courses, I have developed current expertise and a strong technical foundation, which will enable me to resolve issues before they escalate. I also have hands-on knowledge in providing field support to large businesses. Finally, I can provide outstanding customer support in the central Ontario region and in the outlying areas because I am fluent in both English and French.

This computer technician created the following *qualifications summary* for his résumé:

HIGHLY EDUCATED AND ACCOMPLISHED FIELD SERVICE TECHNICIAN

Top performing professional with expertise providing outstanding technical support and customer service. Verifiable experience in improving call response time, decreasing the escalation of customer complaints, and generating sales of product upgrades. Talent for supporting large businesses and implementing current computer technology. College diploma in Systems Analysis. Fully bilingual in English and French.

Now that you are ready to develop your Value Proposition, a good strategy to start is to incorporate it into your résumés Qualifications Summary. You can read more about how to do this in Chapter 5. Include details and accomplishments throughout your résumé that directly relate to your Value Proposition. Do the same with your cover letter. By the time you are finished developing your documents, you will have a strong understanding of who you are and what you have to offer. This will help you to gain confidence in articulating your value in your upcoming job interview.

4

Creating Your Value Proposition

You are a unique individual. There is no one else on earth that has exactly your qualifications. To highlight your special offerings, it is imperative that you show your prospective employer the value that you bring to the table.

Your résumé is a marketing document and you are the featured product. In order to promote yourself, you need to develop and present your "Value Proposition" to the employer.

A well-designed Value Proposition will clearly tell the employer the reason that he or she should select you for the position. It answers the employer's question "Why should I hire you?" with a consistent response that runs like a thread through your résumé, cover letter, and interview.

Your Value Proposition will comprise of three components, your employer's *buying motivators*, your *supporting qualifications*, and the *added value* you bring.

BUYING MOTIVATORS

Buying motivators are the reasons that an employer will want to hire someone. They are most often related to the "bottom-line." Companies want people who can help them to generate revenue, save money, and/or solve a problem.

You need to show the employer what you have to offer that will help the company achieve its goals. For example, if an employer's *buying motivator* is to bring in additional revenue, you might offer "expertise in building sales." This would become a key component in your Value Proposition.

Here are some other examples of *buying motivators*:

- If you are an entry-level administrative assistant, your employer's *buying motivator* may be his or her need to delegate work and focus on the more important issues. You may offer the "ability to decrease your supervisor's workload."

- If you are a mid-level professional, your employer's *buying motivator* may be the need for cost reduction. You may bring in "expertise in streamlining processes to contain costs within the organization."

- If you are a senior-level executive, your employer's *buying motivator* may be the need for more visibility and a higher presence within the market. Your offering could be "your talent for increasing market share."

Complete the following checklist to determine your response to the employer's buying motivators. Ask yourself what value you bring to your future employer.

Buying Motivators
❏ Generate revenue (increase sales, expand market share, augment profit)
❏ Save money (enhance efficiency, boost productivity, improve cash flow)
❏ Solve a problem (reduce errors, eliminate downtime, increase retention)

SUPPORTING QUALIFICATIONS

Supporting qualifications are the credentials that validate your claim to resolve the employer's buying motivator. In other words, you need to show the employer proof supporting your statement using real-life examples from your background. All your qualifications related to the *buying motivator* you identified are important to mention in your Value Proposition.

Here are some examples of *supporting qualifications* that are worth including in the Value Proposition:

- The entry-level administrator discussed previously may have "shown strong organizational skills in completing assignments in CEGEP."
- The mid-level professional may have "previously implemented technology in another organization."
- The senior-level executive may have "led a competitor to unprecedented results."

Complete the following checklist to determine your *supporting qualifications*. Ask yourself what proven credentials you bring to your future employer.

Supporting Qualifications
❏ Areas of expertise (skills, abilities, level, stature)
❏ Background (education, experience, credentials, accomplishments)

ADDED VALUE

Your *added value* illustrates to the employer the special talents and contributions that you have to offer. It creates an image of you that is unique and valuable to the employer. Your *added value* shows that you bring to the role much more than what is merely expected.

Here are some examples of added value that are worth including in the Value Proposition:

- The entry-level administrator above may have "the ability to speak, read, and write in French and English."
- The mid-level professional may have "experience developing top performing production teams."

3

Understanding Your Target

Some job seekers indicate that they are willing to take "any job as long as it pays the bills." These individuals create an open-ended résumé that covers all the bases. Anything and everything about their background is included. The problem with this strategy is that most employers will look at the résumé and may find something that they need, but they will also find many unrelated items that they do not require.

Concentrate your efforts on applying for jobs that you are suitable for and really want. A résumé that is targeted on the industry, employer, and job will produce much better results than an unfocused one. The narrower your focus, the better your results will be. Of course, realistically, you cannot create a unique résumé for every position that interests you. Instead, tighten your focus as much as you can. Match the industry, types of employers, and typical jobs you are targeting.

FOCUS ON THE INDUSTRY YOU ARE TARGETING

To write a résumé that meets your potential employer's needs, you need to know as much as you can about your job target. Learn what you can about the industry or career field that you are focusing on.

There are many ways to find out more about the industry. In Canada, many government organizations provide a wide range of career and business information. Most often, their services are provided free of charge. You can do your research in government offices such as your local Human Resources and Skills Development Canada (HRSDC) Centre, provincial and territorial ministry offices, and local chambers of commerce and boards of trade.

In this information age, the Internet has become an important job search tool. If you require access to the web, Industry Canada, through the Community Access Point (CAP) program, has put a number of computers in rural communities. These computers are installed in public places such as a libraries, schools, and town offices. They are available to the public and have internet access on them. CAP access also includes the free use of a telephone, fax, printer, and paper.

Another way to obtain industry information is by reviewing professional, trade, and business association publications in your local library.

Finally, the best way to learn about a field is by talking with people you know who work in it. Set up a brief meeting and perform an informational interview. Ask good questions to draw out valuable information about that individual's industry and career field.

FOCUS ON THE COMPANIES YOU ARE TARGETING

Investigate your prospective employer. Learn about the company, its product line, the services it offers, and the corporate culture. Find out what you can about your interviewer and your potential supervisor's background.

You can learn about companies by investigating the organization's website, marketing brochures, and any other material you can get your hands on. Obtain company pamphlets, booklets, and annual reports, if you can. Don't forget to touch base with a person who works for the company. A key informant on the inside can be your best resource to understanding the company you are targeting.

FOCUS ON THE JOBS YOU ARE TARGETING

You must know the job you are targeting. Determine the requirements and responsibilities of the job. Learn about the objective of this position. Find out what goals and targets the company expects you to achieve.

An easy way to learn the outline of a job is by studying the job posting or job description if you can get one.

For an insider's perspective, ask someone who is working in the position about his or her role. This person will be able to provide a realistic picture of the job requirements—pluses and minuses.

Research Resource Checklist
❑ Canadian Government Resources
❑ Professional, Trade, and Business Publications
❑ Informational Interviews
❑ Company Websites
❑ Company Marketing Material
❑ Job Postings/Job Descriptions
❑ Other Resources

Accomplishment Checklist

- ❑ You have come up with at least ten strong achievements.
- ❑ The first part of each accomplishment statement clearly shows your actions.
- ❑ The second part of each accomplishment statement shows quantifiable results.

YOUR TECHNICAL SKILLS

In this age of technology and computerization, it is likely that you have acquired many technical skills. Through your education, employment, and personal life, you may have developed proficiency in computer, office, mechanical, and other industry-related equipment. Identify your very best skills and make sure to focus on the ones that will matter to your next employer.

List your technical skills in a separate section of your résumé. Name any specific applications, software, hardware, platforms, protocols, and languages that may apply. Depending on how you want your information displayed, you may include your skill level and years of experience.

Technical Skills Checklist

- ❑ Software Skills
- ❑ Hardware Skills
- ❑ Mechanical Skills
- ❑ Office Equipment Skills
- ❑ Other Technical Skills

YOUR VALUE-ADDED FEATURES

You may have many value-added features to offer your potential employer. This may include your ability to speak, read, and/or write in more than one language. In Canada, many positions require bilingualism in English and French. So, if you are able to offer this valuable skill, make sure to include it in your résumé.

If you belong to any professional memberships, you will want to include your affiliations. Only list your community work or volunteer work if you believe that this information is of specific interest to the employer. Do not include extracurricular activities or hobbies unless they relate to the job you are seeking.

When determining your value-added features, be creative. For example, your added value may include your board directorship or the special commendation you received by an industry association.

If you and your outstanding work have been featured in a publication such as a newspaper, magazine, or book, you may want to include this information in your résumé. Don't forget to identify and list both the articles that you have written and the ones that others have written about you.

If you are a professional speaker, you may want to include a list of your speaking engagements. Include the location, topic, and date if possible.

During your life and career, you may have received awards, ribbons, and/or medals. If you have not, you can still consider including special commendations from your employers and associates. If there is a quote that is particularly flattering, use it in your résumé.

Value-Added Features Checklist
❑ Languages
❑ Professional Memberships
❑ Community Service
❑ Publications (Written By You)
❑ Publications (Written About You)
❑ Speaking Engagements
❑ Awards & Recognitions
❑ Other Value Added Features

YOUR UNIQUE STYLE

To create a résumé that reflects yourself accurately and effectively, you must know your style. You must be able to show your employer your differentiating features. Identify the distinctive aspects of your personality that will allow you to flourish and succeed in your new role.

Focus on showing the individuality that you bring to a job, which enables you to make your role much more than just a job description. For example, if you are a very quick learner, you may want to outline this in your résumé. Maybe you are a relationship-builder and are able to close very large deals by developing strong bonds with your clients. Alternatively, you may want to focus on your flexibility and adaptability by indicating your willingness to travel or relocate.

Once you have uncovered all your qualifications, you must determine which ones are appropriate to include in your résumé. Select items that you believe show your value to your prospective employer and leave off the rest.

Style Checklist
❑ Distinctive Personality Aspects
❑ Individuality that You Bring to the Job
❑ Other Personal Style

- Holidays that you have worked (Canada Day)
- Adjectives related to nationality (French documentation)

Due to space limitations, you will be tempted to take advantage of acronyms, initials, and abbreviations in your résumé. Generally, an "acronym" is a pronounceable word formed from the first letter or letters of a series of other words, such as *ASCII* (American Standard Code for Information Interchange). On the other hand, "Initials," such as *HRPAO* (Human Resources Professional Association of Ontario) do not form a pronounceable word. "Abbreviations" are short forms for words. We may use *Admin.* (Administration), *Prov.* (Province), and *Hi-Tech* (High Technology) to save space.

If you are using an acronym, initials, or abbreviation that is not readily known by everyone in the industry where you are applying, it is best to spell out the word or phrase in full on first usage, followed by the short form in parentheses. Then, you can use the short form throughout the rest of the document. You don't necessarily need the short form if you do not use the word again in your résumé.

There are many appropriate formats for listing provinces. The following chart provides three variations. Stay consistent with the system you select throughout your résumé.

Province or Territory	Initials	Abbreviation
Alberta	AB	Alta.
British Columbia	BC	B.C.
Manitoba	MB	Man.
New Brunswick	NB	N.B.
Newfoundland and Labrador	NL	N.L.
Northwest Territories	NT	N.W.T.
Nova Scotia	NS	N.S.
Nunavut	NU	Nun.
Ontario	ON	Ont.
Prince Edward Island	PE	P.E.I.
Quebec	QC	Que.
Saskatchewan	SK	Sask.
Yukon Territory	YT	Y.T.

Whether you are preparing a résumé for the technology sector or want to show knowledge in certain hardware and software, it is important to know the correct capitalization and hyphenation for computer terminology. Many terms such as dBase, AutoCAD, and PowerPoint commonly use a mix of capital and lower case letters within the word. We capitalize certain technology related terms such as Internet and Website. Other words that refer to "electronic" terms, such as "e-mail, e-commerce, e-business, and e-technology can all be in lower case. When in doubt, always confirm the correct capitalization and spelling of the word either in a dictionary or directly with the manufacturer of the product.

In Canada, abbreviations for academic degrees such as PhD, MBA, MA, MSc, BSc, BA, and BComm generally do not require periods, but if you decide to use periods, do it consistently. The abbreviations "Mr.," "Mrs." and "Ms." take periods. Finally, the correct way to display "for example" in abbreviated format is "e.g."

Refer to *The Canadian Dictionary of Abbreviations* (ECW Press, 1994) if you need to confirm the correct structure for English- and French-language acronyms, initials, and abbreviations commonly used in Canada.

USING PUNCTUATION CORRECTLY

In your résumé, you must show a good command of the English language. Use periods at the end of complete sentences even if they are in bulleted lists. Use commas consistently – especially when you are listing a series of items. For example if you decide to list, "planning, forecasting, and budgeting" with a comma prior to the "and," then always use that structure throughout your résumé. You can also use colons to introduce lists of items. Only use semi-colons to separate two main clauses if you need to distinguish each clause visually. When incorporating quotations in a sentence, in Canada, we place the comma inside the quotes.

If you are unsure of grammatical requirements, refer to a Canadian style handbook such as the *Globe & Mail Style Book* (McClelland & Stewart, 2003). If you still decide to make an exception to a rule, be consistent throughout your résumé.

USING NON-SEXIST LANGUAGE

In Canada, the use of non-sexist language has become standard in formal communication. Always use good judgement and choose terms that are non-gender specific, whenever possible. Instead of "chairman," use "chairperson" or "chair." Instead of "manpower," consider "labour," "human resources," "staff," or "employees." We do not say "waiter" or "waitress," rather we refer to the person as a "server." Instead of "mailman" or "postman," you can try "mail carrier." Finally, rather than indicating "spokesman," try using the term "spokesperson."

Avoid using the masculine pronoun, "he" or "his" when referring to a person in general. For example, avoid a statement like this: "Trained and oriented each new employee, ensuring that he was quickly integrated in his role." Consider "Trained and oriented new employees, ensuring that each individual was quickly integrated into the position."

Only if you are referring to someone specific, should you use the correct pronoun that defines that person. For example, a comment like this would be appropriate in a résumé: "Took the initiative to provide the senior accountant with administrative assistance during a busy tax season, which prompted an outstanding commendation from him."

6

Employing Canadian Spelling and Grammar

In Canada, we find that the issue of "Canadian English" versus "American English" comes up regularly. Although Canadian English is not exactly the same as American English, it is not British English either. We employ subtle differences in spelling and grammar, which are unique to our country. If a recruiter sees a glaring mistake, he or she may feel that you perform sloppy work and this could be just enough to eliminate you from the running. To pass the detailed review, your résumé must have no spelling or grammatical errors at all. This section explains how to ensure that your document is impeccable.

SPELLING GUIDELINES

Canadian spelling is unique and takes on influences from our British and French ancestry, with a touch of Americanism. For example, in Canada, just as in the United Kingdom, we insert "u" in colour, favour, endeavour, and labour. On the other hand, we use "z" in organize and specialize just as the Americans do. A hint of French comes out when we use "centre" instead of "center." Furthermore, instead of writing a "check" or collecting a "paycheck," we write a "cheque" and collect a "paycheque."

If you are using word processing software such as Microsoft Word, it is likely that you will find that the system will default to the American language settings. If you do not use the appropriate language settings, the system will probably assume that you are spelling words correctly even if they are wrong. So, before you start creating your résumé, change your settings to Canadian English. This will ensure that the spelling and grammar you employ conforms to Canada's standards. Before completing your résumé, make sure to do a final spelling and grammar check. If you are thorough, when readers review your résumé, they are not likely to find errors.

Even when you use your computer to screen the spelling, you still must proofread your résumé very carefully. Many Canadian words are spelled correctly when you mean to say one thing, but may be incorrect in another scenario. For example, you may want to list your "Class A drivers licence" in your résumé to show your certification authorizing you to drive a tractor-trailer. This may give you the "license," or permission to drive the vehicle in Ontario. Note in the first sentence "licence" is a noun. In the second, "license" is a verb. Your computer would not be able to catch this difference, so you must be diligent in your proofreading.

You will find a list of commonly misspelled words in Appendix A. If you still are unsure of the spelling of a word, use a good Canadian dictionary such as the *Canadian Oxford Dictionary, 2nd ed.* (Oxford University Press, 2004) to verify your work.

USING NUMBERS EFFECTIVELY

Using numbers in your résumé can be tricky. Generally, in Canada, we spell out the numbers one through nine and write larger numbers as numerals. However, sometimes it is more effective to use the numerals on a résumé, since these characters tend to stand out on the résumé. Whichever system you decide to use, stay consistent. This will demonstrate that you purposely chose that particular structure for your résumé.

In Canada, we use the dollar symbol, "$," to discuss currency in writing. There are many ways to highlight money in your résumé. For example, you may choose to structure the figure as $1.5 million or you may choose to use $1.5 M.

If you are discussing Canadian dollars, it is not necessary to point this out. For example, "$1.5 million CDN" would be inappropriate if all your values are Canadian. On the other hand, if you are discussing American dollars, then it is quite appropriate to use USD or US to let the reader know that the value is in a different currency.

USING CAPITAL LETTERS CORRECTLY

We tend to use capital letters often in résumés. Generally, use capital letters following Canadian style guidelines.

Capitalize the first letter of the main word for all titles and proper names used in your résumé. Do not capitalize articles (a, an, the), conjunctions (and, but, or, nor, for, so), and short prepositions of four letters or less (at, by, in, on).

In your résumé, you are likely to use capital letters in the following ways:

- Your headline (Highly Accomplished RCMP Officer)
- Your name (Jean Beaulieu)
- Your street addresses (123 Major Avenue)
- Company names (The Hudson's Bay Company)
- Your date of employment (January 2003 – Present)
- Job titles that you have held (Accounting Manager)
- Geographical locations (Toronto, Ontario, Canada)
- Educational institutions (University of Toronto)
- Your credentials (Bachelor of Arts)
- The program name (Human Resource Management Program)
- Courses you have taken (Accounting Principles)
- Associations (Human Resources Professionals Association of Ontario)
- Books you have written (Best Canadian Résumés)
- Days that you work (Monday to Friday)

5

**Understanding
Résumé Structure**

BASIC RÉSUMÉ FORMATS

In Canada, historically, we have seen two basic formats of résumés—Reverse Chronological and Functional. Job seekers structured their résumés in one of these two formats because that was the "norm" and traditionally accepted by most recruiters and employers.

The Reverse Chronological Résumé format focuses on career history. It lists your experience in reverse sequential order working backwards starting from the most current job and listing each previous position next. The main advantage of this format is that Canadian employers see it often and know where to find what they are looking for. If you have many unrelated positions or have gaps in your work history, the reverse chronological résumé may not be the best solution for you because it will bring attention to these issues in your career history.

The Functional Résumé format arranges your skills into major categories or headings. Under each category, you may include a list of your accomplishments related to that heading. The idea is to focus on your skills and push the chronology to the back of the résumé. This is a good option if you want to seek a career change or need to minimize issues with your employment history. However, the biggest issue with this format is that employers are unable to connect what you accomplished with where you worked.

Today, with the onset of technology and the vast array of positions available, the savvy job seeker understands the benefits of each format, but opts to use a combination or a unique style. When designing your résumé, your best bet is to highlight your value in the most effective way possible considering your individual background and offerings. Determine what obstacles you want to minimize and structure your résumé to highlight only the best of the best.

THE QUALIFICATIONS SUMMARY

The top third of the first page of your résumé is critical. This section must grab your potential employer's attention and show him or her why you are the right person for the job. It should display your Value Proposition to your employer in a strong Qualifications Summary. A well-written summary will draw the reader in and motive him or her to read the rest of your résumé.

In your Qualifications Summary, you may want to include an objective statement. If you decide to do so, be careful not to discuss what you want. Rather focus on what you have to offer to your employer. These days, many professional résumé writers opt to exclude an objective because the statement itself may seem "self serving."

A better option may be to put together a strong headline, or banner, introducing yourself to the employer. An appropriate headline will concisely state the job title for which you are applying in the form of your Value Proposition. Only use the title if it describes you and your qualifications well. For example, if you have worked as a customer support professional at a help desk and you are now applying for a technical support specialist role why not put a headline on your résumé indicating "Experienced Customer Service and Technical Support Specialist." This banner succinctly introduces you to your future employer. Just like a newspaper headline, it is a great lead-in to your complete résumé, creating focus and direction.

Once you have created your headline, continue with a strong profile to introduce your Value Proposition in a powerful sentence format. Focus on addressing your employer's *buying motivators*, your *supporting qualifications*, and the *added value* you bring. Be creative and avoid repeating your words. Appendix C will provide you with some key words and phrases that you may be able to incorporate into your profile.

ADDITIONAL SECTIONS OF THE RÉSUMÉ

Once you have sold yourself in a strong Qualifications Summary, you must support your Value Proposition throughout your résumé.

Review all your qualifications, which you have uncovered and identified. Determine what you should include and what you should leave off. Select items that you believe show your value to your prospective employer and eliminate the rest. Create section headings based on the information you want to present on your résumé and list them in the order of importance. Once you have done this you are ready to fill in each section concisely detailing the best that you have to offer.

Résumé Structure Checklist
❑ Résumé is Designed in the Appropriate Format
❑ Qualifications Summary Sells Your Value Proposition
❑ Résumé Sections are Selected and Ordered Appropriately

PART 2
DEVELOPING
YOUR RÉSUMÉ

7

Adding Creative Design Elements

Since the résumé is a marketing document, first impressions count. The first time a recruiter sees your document, he or she will probably scan it briefly. If your résumé does not look professional and appealing, the reader will pass it up. A thoughtfully designed résumé that takes advantage of creative elements will differentiate you from the rest.

ENSURE THE RIGHT RÉSUMÉ SIZE

In the past, most Canadians created one- or two-page résumés. These days, we often see longer documents from highly experienced and senior-level professionals. Your résumé is a marketing document and you have a specific amount of information to share. In some cases, this means creating a three- or four-page document. Keep in mind that "less is more." So, if you can create a résumé using fewer words and fewer pages, then do it.

No matter how many pages you use, ensure that there is lots of white space throughout the document. This technique greatly helps the look and feel of your résumé. You can use a wide outside margin and increase spacing between lines and sections to create a light and fresh look to the page.

When designing your résumé, ensure that each page has not only adequate white space, but also enough wording. If you have only a few lines wrapping onto an extra page, consider eliminating some information or redesigning your résumé to fill fewer pages.

If you are using multiple pages, only put your complete contact information on the first page. Include a short header with your name, phone number, and page number on the following pages. This will ensure that the reader will not inadvertently mix up or lose additional sheets of paper.

DESIGN A CREATIVE DOCUMENT

To produce a truly captivating résumé, you must be able to take full advantage of the features in your word processing program. Most individuals create their documents in Microsoft Word. If you do not have access to this program, or do not know it well, it is best to ask a friend or colleague to design your résumé using this application, especially if you intend to e-mail the fully formatted Word document to recruiters.

First, avoid using the templates that come with your Microsoft Word application. These templates are used so often that recruiters can easily pick them out. Imagine having to weed through a stack of résumés that all have the very same old look. An original résumé creatively crafted from scratch will always stand out in the pile.

There are many ways to add creative design to your résumé. The first is to select a font that is easy to read and that others have on their computers. Some popular and commonly used fonts are Times New Roman, Arial, Bookman Old Style, and Verdana. Depending on the font you select, 10-12 point size is usually the best choice. It is best to avoid the use of elaborate or fancy fonts because many recruiters will not have access to them or they may be difficult to follow on-screen.

STAND OUT WITH UNIQUE FEATURES

To design a unique document, take advantage of the many features that Word offers. You can create a distinctive document by emphasizing words in bold, italics, and underlines. Use this technique sparingly, though. Select only the most important things that you want to highlight to the reader. The idea is to make your résumé an attractive document and not just a mass of advanced formatting.

Decorative lines, charts, and bullets can be appropriate in the right situation. Take advantage of specialized Word features such as tables, character spacing, line spacing, tab stops, justification, text boxes, borders, and shading. Include interesting bullets, not just the standard ones that come up. Try using a clever bullet design that you can use throughout your résumé.

Use a logo, image, watermark, or monogram in your résumé only if it is appropriate and adds value to the overall look of your document. A graphic that fits in with a specific industry or field may be just what your résumé needs to make it stand out. Try to avoid quirky, colourful, or loud designs because they may detract focus from the content of your résumé. You want to appear professional—not wacky or strange.

CREATE A CONSISTENT THEME

To ensure readability, your résumé must not only be attractive, but must also be consistent throughout. When you select a "look" or "theme," stick with it. Every section that you use should look similar to the previous section. Use a comparable structure in each category that you discuss. When you select design elements such as a special format for the headers or a line separating sections, use that element every time you start a new section. Using this system will show the reader that you made an extra effort to think about the professional style and theme you want to portray in your résumé.

Creative Design Checklist
❑ Résumé includes creative design elements.
❑ Document is sized appropriately.
❑ A word processing template was not used.
❑ Résumé is unique in design.
❑ The theme of the document is consistent.

8

**Writing
Strategically**

Your résumé is a marketing document. First, it works in conjunction with your cover letter to produce a job interview. Then, it presents your qualifications for detailed review. To ensure that you capture and keep the interest of your prospective employers, you must construct a powerful document that markets your Value Proposition to the employer.

Linda Schnabel, Career Professionals of Canada's Certification Advisor, suggests, "Smart marketers operate from the buyer's perspective. Therefore, strategic résumé writing means that the focus should shift towards the prospective employer's requirements, not the candidate's needs."

A strategic résumé distinguishes you from the rest. Your goal is to highlight your specific qualifications, experience, and background in the very best way possible in light of the position you are targeting. In Canada, we tend to sell ourselves openly, so don't be afraid to discuss your best strengths. Go for it and you will see results.

MARKET YOUR VALUE SELECTIVELY

Having completed Part One of this book, you probably have discovered that you have a vast portfolio of qualifications. Only some of these qualifications are critical to market to your next employer. Your Value Proposition successfully answers the employer's question, "Why should I hire you?" Your résumé must respond directly to this critical question.

What this means is that you need to determine exactly what you want to put on your résumé that will benefit your prospective employer. Put on the recruiter's hat. Go through your complete résumé and determine if every section, sentence, phrase, and word has value to the reader. Think like an employer. The best résumés give the recruiter only the parts of the candidate that the employer wants.

For example, an accounting professional in Northern Canada happens to have lots of experience related to the mining industry. She is planning to transition out of the industry into a role based in the Greater Toronto Area. Strategically, it may be best to leave her specific mining information off the résumé. Rather, she should focus on her accounting and finance skills and accomplishments that the next employer will value.

As you write your résumé, think strategically about everything. For example, if you are an experienced professional, you are selling your experience. It is unlikely that an "objective statement" will help you. Rather, put together a powerful professional profile to show the reader who you are and what you have to offer that the others do not have.

Question every section that you would like to create. Deliberately compare your educational credentials in relation to your experience. Determine which one is more critical in terms of the type of position for which you are applying. Then arrange each category of your résumé in order of importance.

TAKE ADVANTAGE OF CANADIAN LEGISLATION

Canadian human rights legislation guards against discrimination by strictly forbidding recruiters and employers to ask for certain personal information. Companies are not allowed make employment decisions based on attributes other than a person's qualifications to perform a job. Therefore, it is not necessary for you to include your age, sexual, political, or religious orientation, marital status, health, or race in your résumé.

In addition, for your own protection, it is advisable that you never give out personal information such as bank account numbers, social insurance numbers, or credit card numbers in a résumé. Laws vary by province and territory. When in doubt about what to include, check with the Human Rights Commission.

DEAL EFFECTIVELY WITH YOUR OBSTACLES

Everyone has obstacles in their career history. Some people are starting out in their career and have no work experience. Others are transitioning out of one role into another where they have little or no background. Still others are coming back to work after a long leave of absence. Whatever obstacles you have, you must deal with them effectively.

There are many ways to minimize obstacles in your résumé. Often, this requires creativity on your part. Remember, the résumé is your marketing document. Therefore, you can minimize or leave off anything that you feel will not help you get the interview. Always maintain honesty and integrity in what you choose to do.

Be careful in deciding what to include and what to exclude. For example, if you are dealing with a large gap in your career, there are many ways to minimize the obstacle, but eliminating employment dates probably will not do. Employers are looking for the dates, so you must have them there. There is no reason that you can't restructure the format of your résumé to highlight your skills rather than the dates. Alternatively, you may list the year only, instead of month and year. This buys you time by strategically taking the focus off the exact number of months you worked. You may fill a gap with volunteer work that you did during that period. If you really cannot figure out a way to minimize the obstacle, try explaining the issue in your cover letter.

Another obstacle that many older workers run into is their age. Although Canadian legislation strictly forbids age discrimination, job seekers regularly encounter this issue. You can minimize this obstacle by going back only ten to fifteen years in your career instead of listing everything from the start. Another tactic is to leave your graduation dates off the résumé.

WRITE A UNIQUE DOCUMENT

There is nobody on earth like you. You have a unique blend of experience, skills, and accomplishments. Nobody else has exactly what you have to offer. Your résumé must be different from the rest in order to sell you effectively. Therefore, copying directly from your job description, a job posting, or someone else's résumé may sound like a great idea, but it is not likely to work. Unoriginal content tells the reader "I'm too lazy to write a creative sentence on my own, so I'll just cut and paste someone else's wording." Most importantly, plagiarism is unethical and ineffective.

Be true to yourself. Select words that you commonly use. When you walk into that interview, your vocabulary, tone, and style must be appropriate and consistent with what you have put on that résumé.

ALWAYS MAINTAIN THE HIGHEST INTEGRITY

Always choose truth over fiction. It cannot be stressed strongly enough that integrity is critical in your life and career. One white lie can destroy your chances because most reputable organizations rigorously screen candidates. In Canada, background checks often cover previous employment and academic history. Even if you are not caught lying in a job search, you will always be carrying the guilt that comes with dishonesty.

Never misrepresent yourself in your résumé by overstating your experience or skills. Even if you do not have every qualification sought by the employer, stick to the facts. Tell the truth and emphasize your qualifications. With integrity, you will earn genuine credibility, trust, and respect.

MAKE YOUR RÉSUMÉ RICH IN KEYWORDS AND KEY PHRASES

Employers often use keywords and key phrases to select appropriate candidates. Usually, these words and phrases represent knowledge, skills, and abilities required for the position. Employers derive the words and phrases from industry jargon, job titles, and job descriptions. When the recruiter is going through a stack of résumés or a database to find appropriate applicants, he or she will enter these words and phrases in a search field. Only résumés that include them will then surface.

It is critical that you include effective keywords and key phrases throughout your résumé. The words and phrases that you select should show your Value Proposition to your prospective employer and match what the recruiter is looking for. If you select the right keywords, you will greatly improve your chances for success.

You can find a list of keywords and phrases in Appendix C.

ENSURE READABILITY

If you want your résumé to be selected, the recruiter must read it. Do everything that you can to ensure that this happens. You can make it easier on the person reading the résumé by delivering your message concisely and directly. If your résumé is enjoyable to read, it is more likely that the recruiter's positive experience will produce that all-important interview.

You can strategically make your résumé more readable by using active language rather than passive language. Use words that make sense and are easily understandable to the reader. Stay away from acronyms, initials, and abbreviations unless everyone will know the terms. Be consistent in the structure of sentences and bullet points within your résumé. Avoid using "I" or "me," and always speak professionally, not colloquially.

One way to determine ease of readability is to read the completed draft aloud. Listen to the flow of the phrasing. If you have to pause to take a breath at an inappropriate place, or if something doesn't sound right, revise the wording.

PROOFREAD YOUR RÉSUMÉ

Your résumé is a tool that the recruiter may use to screen out unqualified candidates. If there is any reason to eliminate you, the recruiter will. So ensure that your document is completely error free to pass the screening process.

Before you ever submit your résumé to an employer, ensure that you proofread the document thoroughly. Proofread it on your computer screen. Perform a thorough "spelling and grammar check." Print a hard-copy and proofread that as well. Finally, give your résumé to someone else to proofread.

When proofreading your hardcopy, read the résumé aloud at least three times. This way, you are likely to find all the structural, formatting, spelling, and grammatical mistakes that may be there. Make the extra effort to fix all the issues you uncover to ensure that the recruiter does not eliminate you from the running.

FOLLOW THE EMPLOYER'S LEAD

When submitting your finalized résumé, do it in the way that the employer wants to receive it. Most Canadian employers accept applications submitted by e-mail or on-line, but some still don't. Cater to your recruiter's preference. If he or she requests a résumé in hardcopy or by facsimile, do it. When you are printing and mailing your résumé, select a high-quality white or off-white résumé stock. If you are faxing it, use black print on plain white paper.

Many Canadian employers scan résumés into a database. Scannable résumés are like traditional résumés, but with fewer design enhancements. You may want to create two versions, one in scannable format for computers and one for humans. Avoid using unusual fonts, underlines, or graphics in your scannable résumé and print it on white paper.

Some Canadian employers require a plain text (ASCII format) résumé. Others will ask you to paste your text on-line. You can convert your résumé into ASCII format by saving it as a text (.txt) document in Microsoft Word. Then, open up the new file in a text editor such as notepad. You will need to clean your document up and ensure that everything is in the right order. In addition, plain text does not have any design elements at all, so add some dashes or asterisks to separate sections and improve the look of the file.

In Canada, no matter how you submit your résumé, recruiters are likely to keep it on file for three months or longer, so any contact details you give have to remain accurate. If you need to resubmit your résumé, make sure to let the employer know in advance that a replacement is on its way.

Résumé Strategy Checklist

Résumé is…

- ❑ Selectively focused on the value proposition.
- ❑ Compliant with Canadian legislation.
- ❑ Dealing with obstacles effectively.
- ❑ Unique.
- ❑ Keyword rich.
- ❑ Readable.
- ❑ Truthful and maintains the highest integrity.
- ❑ Free of proofreading errors.
- ❑ Following the employer's lead.

PART 3
SAMPLE
DOCUMENTS

Best Résumé Samples
Entry-Level and Student

TAYLOR RED

123 A Street North ▪ Saskatoon ▪ Saskatchewan ▪ S1S 1S1
(Home) 306.555.1234 ▪ tred@careerprocanada.ca

CLIENT SERVICE PROFESSIONAL
~ Tactful ~ Organized ~ Adaptable ~

Highly energetic, enthusiastic and dedicated customer service and animal care provider. Proven ability to work in chaotic situations while maintaining composure. Animal lover with deep sense of responsibility and concern in the well-being of all breeds. Conscientious practitioner employing best practices in interaction with peers, employers and clientele.

Key attributes include:

▪ Patience & Understanding	▪ Creative Thinking
▪ Customer Service Excellence	▪ Skilled Negotiation
▪ Multi-tasking Aptitude	▪ Clear Communication
▪ Team Building Style	▪ Active Listening

WORK EXPERIENCE

SELF-EMPLOYED DAY CARE PROVIDER   Current
Saskatoon, Saskatchewan

Offer stimulating activities, nutrition and supportive care for young children. Ensure safe, meticulous environment and well-rounded experiences.
- Demonstrate consistently patient, caring attitude and sense of humour.
- Gently encourage bonding with, and respect for, 8-year old rottweiler in the home.

CLERK/CASHIER   2004
No-Name Foods, Saskatoon, Saskatchewan

Compliments received for exceeding expectations in processing of purchases while maintaining composure and outgoing, friendly manner.
- Consistently attained high level of speed and accuracy in delivery of services.
- Rapidly learned and accomplished tasks normally done by more senior staff.

CUSTOMER SERVICE, WAITRESS   1997 - 1999
Centre Inn, Saskatoon, Saskatchewan

Applauded for extraordinary service and for managing multiple sections of this high-end restaurant in busiest times.
- Awarded *Employee of the Year* for consistent keen attention to clientele needs.
- Devoted to exceptional cleanliness and thoroughness in all functions.
- Trusted with accurate cash handling and register balance.
- Recognized by cooks as *Favourite Waitress* for repeatedly defusing client situations.

Continued ⇨

Animal Control Dispatcher. This individual effectively targets her potential employer by discussing her love of animals and concern for their well-being in her profile. In her most recent position, she cleverly includes the care of a rottweiler to play down the career change.

Work Experience (cont'd)

ASSISTANT MANAGER   1994 - 1997
Julie's Donuts, Saskatoon, Saskatchewan

Provided outstanding management and client support in this fast-paced foodservice establishment. Ensured immaculate and hygienic environment exceeding all requirements.
- Assumed accountability for cash outs, bank deposits, and statement reconciliations.
- Charged with staff training, scheduling and performance reviews.
- Relied upon for coaching and remaining calm in the most chaotic of times.

ACADEMIC QUALIFICATIONS

CPR AND FIRST AID TRAINING CERTIFICATE   2001
University Health Centre, Saskatoon, Saskatchewan

SAFE FOOD HANDLING AND PREPARATION COURSE   1997
University Health Centre, Saskatoon, Saskatchewan

SECONDARY SCHOOL GRADUATION DIPLOMA   1993
Bedford Road Collegiate, Saskatoon, Saskatchewan

VOLUNTEER EXPERIENCE

VOLUNTEER TEACHER'S AIDE   2002 to Present
Special Child Preschool, Saskatoon, Saskatchewan
Pretty Heights Public School, Saskatoon, Saskatchewan

TECHNOLOGY

Familiar with MS Word, E-mail, Internet searching

"The quality of a person's life is in direct proportion to their commitment to excellence,
regardless of their chosen field of endeavour."
Vince Lombardi

GORDON CURTIS, B. Eng.
12345 Thorncliffe Drive, Mississauga, Ontario L1L 1L1
Home: 905.555.1234   E mail: gcurtis@CareerProCanada.ca

PROFILE:
Creative, patient and methodical professional with a passion for the aerospace industry. Driven by a challenge; goal and solutions-oriented. Team player, takes an active role in motivating peers to deliver in a fast-paced deadline-driven environment. Ambitious, ethical, conscientious; sets and maintains high standards. Articulate and effective communicator; builds productive rapport with persons of all levels and disciplines.

EDUCATION:

Centennial College, Toronto, Ontario — Graduate 2006
Aviation Maintenance Technician

Carleton University, Ottawa, Ontario — 2002
BACHELOR OF AEROSPACE ENGINEERING
Major: Aerodynamics, performance and propulsion

Century High School, Mississauga, Ontario — 1998
Ontario Secondary School Diploma – Honour Roll

Private Pilot's Licence training
Completed 40 hours ground school and 14 hours flying in a Cessna 152.

PROFESSIONAL EXPERIENCE:

International Alliance of Theatrical Stage Employees, Toronto, Ontario
CARPENTER'S ASSISTANT — 1996 - present
- Assist Carpenters on a call-out basis to dismantle and construct sets for feature films, TV shows and other entertainment events. Work includes:
- Reviewing blueprints, devising the most productive and cost-efficient method of constructing sets for use inside studios and outside various locations across Ontario.
- Work with various materials and operating machinery, ensuring compliance with statutory health & safety, WHMIS and other regulations.
- Fabricate items in construction shop in kit form prior to taking them to filming site for final assembly.

Key projects completed include:
- "The Highwaymen" - Contracted to build a 600 foot road tunnel in a parking lot; constructed frame using plywood, drywall and aluminium.
- "The Boss of Bosses" TV Show. Built an elevated subway line in the 1920's style.
- "Dawn of the Dead" - Demolished the internal structure of a shopping mall and rebuilt 20 stores, interiors and exteriors, according to the director's vision.
- "Evil II" - Commissioned to recreate a church interior with 100 foot ceilings.

COMPUTER SKILLS:
Computer literate in the Windows environment; highly proficient in the following programs: MS Office Suite, AutoCAD, ProEngineer and ProMechanism.

Aviation Maintenance. The résumé positions this student towards an appropriate position by leading in with education to highlight aerospace engineering. Accomplishments and projects strategically point to skills that will be essential in his new role.

JOHN FARMER

123-12 Spadina Avenue, Toronto, Ontario M1M 1M1
Phone: (416) 555-5671   E mail: jfarmer@careerprocanada.ca

STRATEGIC BUSINESS CONSULTANT

Dynamic, challenge and results-driven Management Consultant with an exemplary background of delivering growth and expanded market share in a competitive environment. Exudes energy and confidence, understands organizational excellence; visionary, thinks outside the box; acknowledged for conceiving and executing unique sales strategies. Articulate communicator; inspirational and proactive; able to succeed and deliver on key business initiatives. Core business competencies include:

• Strategic Planning	• Project Management
• Sales & Marketing Management	• Customer Relationship Management
• Change Management	• Business Development

PROFESSIONAL EXPERIENCE

Opel Energy, Basel, Switzerland   2005 - Present
CONSULTANT
- Devised strategy for the segmentation of Central and European customer base with goal of developing unique and targeted marketing strategies.

Western Life Assurance Company, Toronto, Ontario   2003 - 2005
Held the following 2 progressively responsible positions:
MANAGER, GROUP BENEFITS   2005
- Consistently grew annual business results within our territory; achieving overall growth of 45%.
- Member of national focus group that developed new product design ideas and provided strategic sales recommendations for the industry.
- Engaged as guest speaker for three regional sales meetings across the country.

MARKETING SPECIALIST, GROUP BENEFITS   2003 –2005
- Recruited due to work ethic, business acumen, ability to generate action, revenue and leadership skills.
- Rebuilt an underperforming region and achieved growth of over 30% through the development and implementation of succinct product marketing strategies.
- Created and executed a sales template designed to increase sales of a new concept in Living Benefits. It is now recognized as the number 1 sales tool for over 80 sales professionals across Canada.
- Expanded the distribution channels, solidified client relationships, and negotiated directly with key accounts.

EDUCATION

Purdue University, Hanover, Germany
MASTER OF BUSINESS ADMINISTRATION, concentration in International Business   2006
- Achieved Dean's Honour List
- Received GISMA Foundation Merit Scholarship

Brock University, St. Catharines, Ontario   2003
BACHELOR OF BUSINESS ADMINISTRATION, concentration in Marketing
- Achieved Dean's Honour List

VOLUNTEER

United Way, Toronto, Ontario   2005
CAMPAIGN COORDINATOR
- Presented with Award of Excellence

Business Consultant. Having completed his MBA program in Germany, this candidate has limited work experience, but is ready for a position in Canada. This résumé positions him to obtain an appropriate role with a strong power statement followed by his experience as a consultant and his sound Canadian accomplishments as a manager.

KEVIN KIDD

Box 1A, Middle, Manitoba ▪ R1R 1R1
(Home) 204.555.1234 ▪ (E-mail) kevin@careerprocanada.ca

IT PROFESSIONAL / PROGRAMMER

Motivated and resourceful IT co-ordinator with cross-functional computer programming and electronics expertise. Comprehensive understanding and exceptional skill in analyzing and managing information technology infrastructure, applications, solutions, and processes. Ready to tackle challenges and solve problems. Quickly identify and resolve productivity issues. Especially capable of successfully sharing complex technical terms and software applications equally well with advanced users and neophytes. Dedicated and reliable: never late, work overtime. **Strengths:**

Network Operating Systems ▪ Multiple Programming Languages ▪ Digital & AC/DC Circuits

TECHNOLOGY

Software Applications: PC – Microsoft Office Suite, Simply Accounting, Adobe Acrobat, JASC Paintshop Pro, Outlook, DreamWeaver.
Operating Systems: Win9x, Windows (NT, 2000/2000 Server, XP), Linux, Novell NetWare, DOS.
Programming Languages: Visual Basic, ASP, VBA, C/C++, Java, JS, PowerBuilder 7.0, COBOL, WSH, Assembly, Perl, Windows Script Host, HTML.
Hardware: Install power supplies, motherboards, hard drives, floppy drives, CD-ROM drives, video cards, sound cards, modems and nics cabling. Fix printers, monitors and power supplies.

SPECIALIZED EDUCATION

COMPUTER ANALYST / PROGRAMMER DIPLOMA   2004 - 2006
Red River College, Winnipeg, Manitoba
Key Courses:

- Structured Analysis & Design
- Database Management Systems
- Access Database Processing
- Internet Programming
- Microcomputers
- PowerBuilder

- Object Oriented Analysis & Design
- Electronic Commerce Concepts
- Java / COBOL / C++ / Visual Basic
- Finance / Economics / Accounting
- Business Communications
- Statistics

COMPUTER SYSTEMS SPECIALTY CERTIFICATE   2002 - 2003
Assiniboine Community College, Brandon, Manitoba
Key Courses:

- AC/DC Electronic Circuits
- Digital Electronics

- Computer Servicing Lab
- Microprocessors

- Peripheral Devices
- Networks

CAREER PATH

DIGITAL MEDIA TECHNICIAN / PROGRAMMER   2005
Red River College, Winnipeg, Manitoba
One of two professionals selected from 15 candidates to fill this contract position. When funding was slashed, other worker was declared redundant. As the sole contractor before final budget cuts eliminated position, held accountabilities for upgrading both front and back end for Business Administration Program online courses. Also relied upon to set permissions for various groups within the program. Created scripts using Windows Script Host to set new user attributes. Worked overtime and volunteered expertise after funding cuts to ensure programs were running perfectly.

Continued on Page 2 ⇨

Computer Technician. With little to no work experience, this candidate takes advantage of many techniques to hone in on the IT field. He lists his technology skills first and then follows it up with education. To "beef up" the résumé, he dedicates lots of space to the short-term contract position.

Career Path Continued...

- ❑ Architected a student information system for the Business Administration Department. Identified a method to print each student, course and director on one page. Results were twofold. This eased the Computer Services Department's capability to distribute teacher evaluation forms. It also required less than five minutes to do, unlike the former time-consuming, cumbersome and incorrectly developed database.
- ❑ Updated the department's online course selection website. Resourceful nature recognized the time saving value of utilizing a more generic design. This allowed the reuse of these templates for other courses instead of creating new ones each term.
- ❑ Orchestrated the migration of a manual student registration system to an automated process. The previous manual format required three days to set up student with all required resources. Beta tested a proprietary automated program needing just one hour to complete. Value of this program recognized by senior administrators and was considered for college-wide implementation.
- ❑ Trusted with security codes, passwords, and access to all staff and student files.

CONSTRUCTION LABOURER   2005 - Present
Construction Services, Main City, Manitoba
Retained in an interim capacity to provide support for this busy construction firm. Interface well with both unionized and non-unionized workers. Provide informal technology support. Even though waiting to relocate for the right computer position, give 100% effort and never miss a day on the job!

- ❑ Complete all tasks with a positive attitude, regardless of the project.
- ❑ Exhibit unwavering commitment to confidentiality assurance for proprietary blue prints and schematics worth millions of dollars.

▪Technical Solution Generation ▪

ELISE MAY

Box 12343, Stayner, Ontario ▪ L1L 1L1
(Home) 705.555.4321 ▪ elise@CareerProCanada.ca

EARLY CHILDHOOD EDUCATOR
~ With Interpersonal & Motivational Expertise ~

Resourceful and reliable professional offering successes by working with children and youth from all backgrounds, cultures, abilities and ages. Regarded for staying calm in times of crisis. Strong follow-through, administrative and time management capabilities. Highly articulate demonstrating excellent interpersonal skills across all levels including students, colleagues, administrators, and parents. Flexible in assuming a leadership or support role. Compassionate and caring with well-grounded decision-making capability. Eager to apply skills, education and ambition in an educational setting. **Strengths:**

☑	Conflict Resolution	☑	Workload Prioritization
☑	Musical Ability (Piano)	☑	Lesson Design & Development
☑	Confidentiality Assurance	☑	Multi-cultural Awareness
☑	Behaviour Modification	☑	Remediation & Modification

CAREER PATH

PRODUCTION ASSISTANT & VEHICLE QUALITY　　　　　　　　1999 - Present
Automotive Manufacturing Company, Ontario
Selected after intensive screening to provide assembly and installation services for this quality and safety oriented corporation. Teamed with 12 individuals to contribute to the production of 400 vehicles per shift. Adhered to personal protective equipment (PPE) policy.

- Eagerness to learn new skills recognized by being authorized to work multiple jobs within many zones. Asked by both Team Leader and Coordinator to be the Zone Trainer. Tasked to train new hires and permanent workers in equipment operation and doing the job safely while meeting exacting standards.
- Accepted for the very demanding, short term Vehicle Quality posting. Used sophisticated technical and computerized equipment for final vehicle inspection before leaving plant. Strong detail orientation served to monitor any deviation from quality standards that could impact customer satisfaction.

HAIRSTYLIST　　　　　　　　1987 - 1998
Ontario and Nova Scotia Locations
Retained by hair styling establishments and independent clients to provide cutting, treatment and styling services.

- Met customer expectations by using strong listening skills and following through with the expected results.

PUBLIC RELATIONS PROFESSIONAL　　　　　　　　1986 - 1987
Farmer's Association, Ontario
Represented this organization province-wide, for a one-year term. Seamlessly interfaced with individuals from all backgrounds, sharing agricultural knowledge. Addressed small and large groups.

- Maintained a positive, friendly and personable demeanour, regardless of the often demanding and hectic schedule.

~ Continued on Page 2 ~

Early Childhood Educator. With no experience in early childhood education, the power statement up front draws on the individual's college program. The "strengths" are pulled from her educational background and transferable skills.

EDUCATION & SPECIALIZED TRAINING

EARLY CHILDHOOD EDUCATION PROGRAM   2003 - 2006
Georgian College, Orillia, Ontario
Studies include, but are not limited to:

☑	Curriculum Planning	☑	Teaching Strategies
☑	Childhood Development	☑	Music & Movement for Children
☑	Nutrition, Health & Safety	☑	Designing Childhood Environments
☑	Early Intervention	☑	Supportive Counselling

Participated in co-op placements within private Daycares and JK/SK classes. Gained insight into children with Fetal Alcohol Syndrome, Autism and Down Syndrome. Assignments provided comprehensive experience with complete accountability for program development and implementation. Generated dynamic learning centres, altering and updating as necessary.

COMPUTER TRAINING   2003
Academy of Learning, Ontario
UPGRADING PROGRAM   2002
Georgian College, Ontario
CONVERSATIONAL FRENCH   1986
Georgian College, Ontario
HAIRDRESSING CERTIFICATION   1980 - 1981
School of Hair Design, Toronto, Ontario
SECONDARY SCHOOL GRADUATION DIPLOMA   1980
Memorial High School, Ontario

Specialized 4 – H Projects consisting of 18 Homemaking and 12 Agriculture courses.

TECHNOLOGY: Word, PowerPoint, Email, Internet Navigation and educational software.

COMMUNITY INVOLVEMENT

School's Cool Program: Authorized to volunteer for this 6-week, Ministry of Children's Services' program supporting children suspected to have special needs. Participants, ranging from ages 5 - 7, were assessed for best support measures and early intervention services. Teamed with 3 professionals to tend to 28 high needs, Simcoe County youngsters.
Dialysis Unit Support: Assisted dialysis technician at Dialysis Unit in summer 2003.
Peer Tutor: Assisted College adult student with tests and exams preparation.
Coach and Coordinator: Junior Curling Association.
Coordinator: Fair Queen Competition.

SIGNIFICANT RECOGNITION

Ontario Youth Award

Received this medal for leadership in the areas of academics achievement and excellence in the arts, business, science, labour, agriculture and sports. Cited by Ontario's Premier for "countless hours spent in selfless work which enriches the lives of others."

Kiwanis Music Festival Awards

Mario Beaumont

11 Buckhorn Ave, Richmond Hill, ON L1L 1L1
Phone: 905-555-1212   Email: mbeaumont@careerprocanada.ca

CAREER OBJECTIVE

Seeking position as Probationary Firefighter with the Markham Fire Department

PROFILE SUMMARY

- Strong educational credentials with Health and Fitness Promotion Diploma and General Business Diploma.
- Extensive background in training and fitness with over five years of experience teaching and coaching fitness and wellness benefits to a diverse clientele.
- Exceptional communications skills demonstrated through 6 years of experience increasing membership and retention rates in a health and fitness club work environment.
- Sound lifesaving credentials having achieved the Standard First Aid and Cardiopulmonary Resuscitation CPR certification in January 2006.
- Second language skills with fluency in English and French.

WORK EXPERIENCE

2004-Present   Power Citrus Ltd.   Etobicoke, ON
Logistics Coordinator
Schedule up to 30 trucks per day for transfer of goods from USA into Canada. Maintain Excel spreadsheets documenting all costs and changes to customer orders. Work as part of a team of five to ensure success.
- Negotiated rates with truck companies and ensured lowest delivery price in 90% of contracts.
- Scheduled truck pickups and delivery, meeting on-time delivery deadlines 100% of the time.

2003-2004 (240 hours)   City of Mississauga   Mississauga, ON
Temporary Labourer (Parks Department)
Worked through the winter season on various work assignments requiring physical fitness and agility.
- Developed safe working habits and zero injury rates by following safety procedures while operating dangerous equipment.
- Communicated effectively with team members and demonstrated team building skills to successfully complete work projects on time while meeting department standards.

2003-2004   Sharp Fitness   Richmond Hill, ON
Certified Fitness Consultant
Conducted one-hour fitness assessments for members to evaluate fitness levels and recommend health and wellness programs in order to reach member's individual goals.
- Improved fitness club retention rates by 15% through powerful negotiation skills encouraging and coaching members to engage in health and wellness programs.
- Achieved both a strong existing clientele and increased new business sales by 10% through strong relationship building skills.

2000-2002   Hot Fitness   Thornhill, ON
Certified Fitness Consultant
Performed as many as 12 one-hour fitness assessments per day and negotiated with clients to achieve health and fitness goals. Developed exercise programs and taught clients to use equipment safely.
- Developed, maintained, and evaluated new and existing programs for club members helping to increase retention rates by 22%.

Firefighter. The career objective quickly zones in to the target job. The profile summary adds focus by outlining the individual's *Value Proposition.*

Mario Beaumont

Phone: 905-555-1212   page 2

_____

1999-2000   Gangway Racquet and Fitness Club   Richmond Hill, ON

Certified Fitness Consultant and Personal Trainer

Scheduled and performed all fitness appraisals and personal training. Conducted weekly group fitness classes one hour in length. Toured potential members through club and sold memberships as well as personal training packages.

- Promoted as a supervisor in the evenings when the manager was unavailable.
- Created new programs and monthly promotions resulting in increased retention rates by 15%.

1997-1999   Health Centre/Star College   Cornwall, ON

Recreation Centre Supervisor

Generated business through fitness evaluations for the health center and managed personal training department to ensure monthly goals were reached.

1996   Health Centre/Drive Canada   Cornwall, ON

Health Centre Supervisor

Increased membership by 25% through a marketing and promotion program and through referrals from clients satisfied with exercise programs and ongoing fitness support.

EDUCATIONAL HISTORY

2003-2004

General Business Diploma

Seneca College, Toronto, ON

- Demonstrated ability as a team player completing numerous courses in project groups.
- Developed a strong understanding of decision-making processes through a Decision Analysis course.

1997-1999

Health and Fitness Management Diploma

St. Lawrence College, Cornwall, ON

- Developed new equipment purchase plan and marketing plans.
- Completed Interpersonal Communication Skills course and Developmental Psychology.

COMMUNITY INVOLVEMENT

Volunteer, St John's Ambulance

3 hours per week (current)

Volunteer, Special Needs Individual

5 hours per week (since 1999)

Canvasser, Cancer Society

10 hours (total)

Volunteer, L'Arche Daybreak

10 hours (total)

SOPHIA KNIGHT

17 Main Street
Simcoe, Ontario, Canada ▪ N1N 1N1
(Home) 519.555.1234
(Email) sknight@careerprocanada.ca

TOURISM & HOSPITALITY PROFESSIONAL

Enthusiastic and customer-focused travel specialist offering a definitive hospitality, 5 star waitressing and retail background. Known for professional and positive demeanour, regardless of the situation. Excellent interpersonal skills, interacting favourably with clients/staff from all cultures and backgrounds. Without question, exhibit impeccable dress, deportment and etiquette. Flexibility with respect to long and variable hours of work. *On Board* Talents include:

- ✔ Customer Relation Building
- ✔ Bartending & Wine Knowledge
- ✔ Special Events & Receptions
- ✔ Diplomatic Problem-Solving & Follow-up
- ✔ Sound Decision-Making

- ✔ Multi-Cultural / Ethnic Awareness
- ✔ First Class Service Delivery
- ✔ Hygiene Standards
- ✔ Safety Consciousness
- ✔ Sales, Merchandising & Inventories

FIRST CLASS SERVICE: SUMMARY OF EXPERIENCE

ASSISTANT WAITRESS   2004 - 2006
Queen Mary 2, Cunard Cruise Line
Retained to work aboard this well-known vessel, delivering 5 Star Service and care to discerning guests. Maintained accountability for hostessing, laundry, food service and cleaning. One of a handful of waitresses offering customers in-depth bartending and wine appreciation knowledge. As one of 1 300 employees, consistently recognized the importance of teaming to achieve a common goal and delivered exceptional service.

- Successfully completed multiple elements of rigorous White Star Academy Training. (See Education below).
- Accommodating nature; patiently and willingly tended to special requests from guests. Familiar with diverse range of international cuisines, dietary requirements and cultural specifications.

BARTENDER   2002 - 2003
Callahans Beach House Restaurant, Port Dover, Ontario
Selected to work at this popular eating establishment for two summers. Prepared drink orders for guests and staff. Held utmost regard for health and safety regulations keeping bar area neat, clean, perfectly organized, stocked and presentable.

- Revamped cleaning requirements, generating a *Daily Cleaning List* detailing duties for both the AM and PM bartenders.
- Reformatted *Drink Recipe List*. Alphabetized and rewrote it, resulting in quick and easy reference.
- Formed a *Closing Duty List* to be completed nightly for closing bartender. This ensured a clean and well stocked bar, even workload distribution, and saved the opening bartender from completing tasks from the night before.
- Relied upon to train and assist other bartenders. Facility's only employee with relevant experience and specialized training.

Continued ⇨

Hospitality and Tourism Professional. Clever graphics create a visual image of the candidate's area of expertise and interest in the tourism and hospitality sector, and particularly the cruise industry. She sprinkles this sentiment throughout the résumé with the creative use of terms such as "On Board Talents" and "First Class Service."

SOPHIA KNIGHT

SUMMARY OF EXPERIENCE CONTINUED...

RETAIL SALES REPRESENTATIVE   2003
Tropical Rebel, Port Dover, Ontario
Managed time effectively to provide sales service for this seasonal clothing retail operation while working at above location. One of four staff, meeting customer needs. Trusted with both store opening and closing procedures.

- Ensured store was in pristine shape with well-organized stock, clean floors and windows.
- Utilized strong artistic sense to decorate the facility, maximizing customer appeal.
- Initiated strategic marketing strategies to boost lagging sales of some clothing lines.

PASSPORT TO EDUCATION & SPECIALIZED TRAINING

TOURISM MANAGEMENT PROGRAM   2003
Georgian College, Barrie, Ontario
Graduated from this 3-year program earning Dean's List status during final year. Key courses included, but are not limited to:

- Bartending
- Front Office / Guest Services
- Casinos
- Conference / Event Planning
- World Destinations

- International Tourism
- Cross Cultural Communications
- Adventure Travel
- Marketing / Promotions
- Fiscal Accountability

BASIC FOOD HYGIENE SENSE   2003
SEA SURVIVAL
WHITE STAR ACADEMY CERTIFICATION
Queen Mary 2

- Cash Register Operations ▪ Room Service Professional ▪ Service Excellence ▪
▪ WHMIS ▪ Sexual Harassment ▪

SMART SERVE CERTIFICATION   2000
Fanshawe College, Simcoe, Ontario

COMPUTER SKILLS: Microsoft Office Suite, SQUiRREL, Hospitality Solutions International (HSI), Email and Internet Research.

COMMUNITY INVOLVEMENT: Participant in Heart and Stroke Foundation canvassing, Church Nursery and Operation Christmas Child for third world countries.

INTERESTS: Photography, travelling and meeting new people, reading, painting, and playing baseball and volleyball.

Christina D. Sadler

111 Omagh St.
St. John's, NL A1A 1A1

Phone (709) 555-1212
E-mail cdsadler@careerprocanada.ca

Career Target: Core Program Coordinator

*** Recipient of multiple scholarships and academic achievement awards ***

A committed human services professional offering proven work experience and extensive volunteer service within the community. A hardworking and motivated individual providing outstanding customer service and support in varied business environments. Extremely reliable and trustworthy with the maturity to work well with minimal supervision. A team builder and role model with proven communication and interpersonal abilities, and sound administrative, financial, and computer skills.

Areas of expertise:

▸ Management Support	▸ Crisis Intervention	▸ Program Development
▸ Customer Service	▸ Case Management	▸ Life Skills Training
▸ Team Leadership	▸ Counselling	▸ Administrative Support
▸ Problem Solving	▸ Behaviour Modification	▸ Word Processing

*** Honours Bachelor of Arts in Psychology to be completed in June 2007 ***

SELECTED ACCOMPLISHMENTS

▸ Supported the community through active involvement in two human service programs— the Angels Substance Abuse Awareness Committee and the Angels Heart Health Coalition.

▸ Performed a wide variety of volunteer work supporting community initiatives covering young offenders, troubled high school students, and fundraising for sick children.

▸ Catalogued and stored approximately 60 artefacts for the Angels Heritage Centre, ensuring that township journals and material were kept in impeccable order.

▸ Assisted tourists by providing exceptional community information and resources, which sparked interest and promoted the tourism industry.

▸ Created and delivered a children's heritage learning program in weekly 2-hour sessions, incorporating various resources including videos, crafts, and storybooks.

▸ Provided exceptional customer service to over 200 campers and tourists visiting the region every week, and ensured park safety while meeting visitors' needs.

▸ Received the Partners Bursary Award by the Ministry of Natural Resources for outstanding performance and service to Omagh Provincial Park.

▸ Led a team of servers at Pizza Point and exceeded customer expectations by ensuring that exceptional customer service was provided to approximately 300 individuals each evening.

Continued…

Human Services Professional. To customize this résumé, the candidate names her potential employer's job title "Core Program Coordinator" in her career target. With limited experience in human and social service, she brings all her accomplishments that are most closely related to the position to the forefront.

CHRISTINA D. SADLER

PROFESSIONAL EXPERIENCE

Service Station, St. John's, NL   2005 - Present
Customer Service Representative
Responsible for cash register operation, sales, customer service, store set-up, and merchandising. Accountable for all monetary transactions.

Pizza Point, St. John's, NL   2003 - 2005
Assistant Manager
Oversee store operations in the absence of the manager. Accountable for food production, cash transactions, dealing with complaints, organizing staff, completing paperwork, and deposits.

The Ministry of Natural Resources, St. John's, NL   Summer 2002 & 2003
Gate House Attendant, Omagh Provincial Park
Charged to greet campers and tourists and provide customer service. Accountabilities include answering questions about the region, merchandise sales, and general maintenance.

The Omagh Public Library Board, St. John's, NL   Summer 2000 & 2001
Angels Heritage Centre Assistant
Responsibilities included heritage interpretation for the general public, instituting a children's learning program, cataloguing artefacts, taking inventory, and providing library support.

FORMAL EDUCATION & PROFESSIONAL DEVELOPMENT

Memorial University of Newfoundland, St. John's, NL   Expected June 2007
Honours Bachelor of Arts, Psychology
▸ Member of Dean's Honour List.
▸ Consistently achieved scholarships every year based on academic grades.
▸ 'Orientation Volunteer' providing a one-week program for new students.

Pizza Point, St. John's, NL   2003
Management Courses
▸ Completed Basic Operations and Advanced Operations management courses.

COMMUNITY WORK
Performed various volunteer work within the community including:
▸ CARES Correctional Centre for Young Offenders, anger management and coping skills training.
▸ College Heights Secondary School, life and academic skills training for youth with behavioural problems.
▸ Jonathan's Fund, fundraising for the Hospital for Sick Children in Toronto.
▸ The Omagh Distress Centre, distress line training.

COMPUTER SKILLS
Proficient in a variety of software applications including:
▸ Microsoft Office Suite (Word, Excel, and PowerPoint)
▸ Corel WordPerfect

*** Stellar references available upon request ***

CARRIE MILLER

1 Morning Crescent • Aurora, Ontario • L1L 1L1 • 905-555-1234 • cmm@CareerProCanada.ca

FOCUS

Acceptance in the University of Queensville's Conflict Studies and Peace-Building program

SUMMARY

Culturally-sensitive and dedicated professional backed by a B.A. in International Studies, approximately 1.5 years' experience as an English Teacher in Korea instructing adults and children, and strong knowledge of International Relations and Foreign Protocol gained from extensive travel in the United Kingdom, Africa, the Middle East, New Zealand, and the Cook Islands. **Proven ability to garner trustworthiness in record time based on being picked to undertake a myriad of special projects**.

An effective communicator, able to cultivate and maintain mutually-productive ties with people of all ages and backgrounds. Hold current certification in First Aid and CPR. Computer proficiencies include Word, Excel, Corel WordPerfect, Windows XP, and Internet research. **High level of ambition to accelerate career**.

Fluent English • Conversational French & Spanish • Fundamental Russian & Korean

COMPETENCIES & CAPABILITIES

Areas of Study include: Human Rights • International Law • Canadian Foreign Policy • Theories of International Relations • Gender & International Studies • Redefining Security • The European Union • Global Resources • Contemporary International Issues • Contemporary Circumpolar North • Globalization

Added Value: Cross-Cultural Communications • Report Writing • International Relations • Team-Building & Supervision • Planning, Organization, & Follow-Through

EDUCATION

University of St. Andrews • Richmond Hill, ON   May 2001
  B.A., International Studies

KEY ACCOMPLISHMENTS

Education
- Part of a 5-person team that, upon professor's approval, travelled to California to attend a model United Nations conference lasting an entire weekend. Awarded first-class honours – out of 400+ attendees – for research and presentation on current events relating to Saudi Arabia
- Authored a paper on rape as a tool of war for "Gender" class; earned a high "A" for this well-written document
- Managed aggressive part-time employment in customer service and hospitality while carrying a full subject load

International Peacekeeper. This ambitious student targets her résumé to gain acceptance in a university program to further her studies. Even without directly relevant work experience, the résumé articulates cross-functional experience that qualifies her as a worthy candidate.

CARRIE MILLER

905-555-1234 • cmm@CareerProCanada.ca　　　　　　　　　　　　　Page Two

KEY ACCOMPLISHMENTS (cont'd)

Professional / Volunteer & Community Activity
- Repeatedly tapped to assume the role of Shift Supervisor on weekends based on demonstrated responsibility *(Aurora Co-Op)*
- Liaised between the school administrative staff and teachers because of proven ability to quickly disseminate information and resolve a wealth of concerns *(ECC Chung)*
- Regularly selected for "outside" contracts based on ability to successfully connect with students 1-on-1 *(ECC Chung)*
- Assumed extra administrative responsibilities typically held by immediate supervisor; this action helped supervisor to concentrate on product development and methods to elevate business activity *(PLC Technologies)*
- Took the initiative to adopt a defined protocol when interviewing volunteers in an effort to compose strong biographies for them *(Shepherd's Bush)*

EMPLOYMENT HIGHLIGHTS

Aurora Co-Op • Aurora, ON　　　　　　　　　　　　　　　　Sep. 2003 - present
　Bakery Utility Clerk

ECC Chung • Seoul, Korea　　　　　　　　　　　　　　Sep. 2001 - June 2003
　English Teacher – Children & Young Adults

Shepherd's Bush Conservation Authority • Aurora, ON　　　　　　　Summer 2001
　Supervisor – Northern Bear Awareness Program

PLC Technologies Inc. • Newmarket, ON　　　　　　　　　May 2000 - Mar. 2001
　Executive Assistant / Marketing Research Assistant

VOLUNTEER & COMMUNITY ACTIVITY

Aurora Food Bank • Aurora, ON　　　　　　　　　　　　　　　　　Ongoing
　Food Hamper Assembler & Delivery Person

Three Thousand Villages • Bradford, ON　　　　　　　　　　　　　　Ongoing
　Sales Associate

Aurora Theatre Group • Aurora, ON　　　　　　　　　　　May 1999 - May 2000
　Office Worker / Biography Writer

REFERENCES PROVIDED UPON REQUEST

Samantha E. Knight *BScN*

1111 New Grad Avenue
Nepean, ON
K1K 1K1

(613) 555-1234
(613) 555-0123
sam@careerprocanada.ca

CAREER OBJECTIVE

Current: Nursing position • **Future**: Emergency or ICU nursing position.

PROFILE

BS Nursing graduate with remarkable academic credentials and extensive relevant experience. Articulate and professional demeanour. Proven leadership skills: experienced in hiring, supervising and organizing. Caring and nurturing disposition; compassionate and supportive; able to maintain excellent rapport with patients while working under stressful situations:

• Emergency Department Nursing Internship • Mayo Clinic Special Care Unit •
• Autistic Child • Disabled Youths and Adults • Home Care Worker •

ACADEMIC CREDENTIALS

Bachelor of Science Nursing 2006
University of Maine • Orono, Maine, USA
Dean's List • AFUM Scholarship • Omicron-Psi National Honour Society
University of Maine Nursing Honour Society

Bachelor of Arts General Studies 2002
Acadia University • Wolfville, Nova Scotia, Canada

RELEVANT EXPERIENCE

Emergency Department Nurse

Ottawa Civic Hospital, Ottawa, ON, Canada (Feb-Apr 2006)
➢ Six-week internship, with direct patient care; excellent bedside manner recognized by positive comments received from several patients; demonstrated ability to be a strong and dependable team player.

Summer III Student Program, Mayo Clinic

St. Mary's Hospital, Rochester, MN, USA (June-Aug 2005)
Summer III Student program is an annual competition for selected student nurses across the United States who have completed their third year of nursing studies.
➢ Ten-week program at the Mayo Clinic Special Care Unit, specializing in congestive heart failure. Extremely ill patients required special care after traumatic procedures: daily dialysis, pacemaker insertion, and cardiac catheterization. Performed physical assessment; educated patients and family on healthy eating — especially sodium and fluid restriction — and on the benefits of exercising.

Respite Care Worker

Newfoundland & Labrador Social Services, Gander, NL, Canada (June-Aug 2000-2004)
➢ Organized and supervised work activities for disabled youths and adults to foster economic security, and overall self-esteem.

Nurse. A dual career objective displays this candidate's current goal and future ambition. The résumé closes with a powerful quote taken from a letter of recommendation.

Samantha E. Knight *BScN* 2

Behavioural Aide Worker

Newfoundland & Labrador Social Services, Gander, NL, Canada (June-Aug 2004)
- Assisted and cared for a disabled person in their home.
- Organized and managed social, recreational, and educational activities.
- Mentored and guided overall growth and development.

Therapist

Applied Behavioural Analysis, Gander, NL, Canada (May-Sept 2001)
- Performed ABA therapy on a young autistic child. Supervised the child's interaction with the community, and recorded the child's progress.

Coordinator for the Seed of Hope Campaign

Canadian Paraplegic Association, Gander, NL, Canada (June-Aug 2000)
- Hired and supervised high school students for the Canadian Paraplegic Association's summer fundraiser.

Home Care Worker

Community and Home Support, Gander, NL, Canada (June-Aug 1998 and 1999)
- Established a fun and friendly atmosphere for children to experience, in the community and in their home.
- Assisted foster children by easing their transition into caring, loving homes. Organized and implemented special activities to help them become self-sufficient: cooking, household chores, and art classes.

SPECIALIZED TRAINING AND CERTIFICATION

- Therapeutic Crisis Intervention Training (T.C.I)
- Non-violent Crisis Intervention (C.P.I)
- First Aid/CPR Certification, American Heart Association
- Level 1 National Coaching Certification Program, Special Olympics
- OHSA Training Certificate

EXTRACURRICULAR

- Special Olympics
- Canadian Red Cross Society Volunteer
- Canadian Red Cross MASH Fundraiser
- Community Projects Coordinator, Student Nurses Association, University of Maine

"In my opinion, based on her scholarly achievements and refined communication skills, I believe that she would make an excellent addition to your institution and I have no hesitation in recommending her..."
- John Myers, Radiologist, Grand Falls-Windsor, NL, Canada

JOHN SMITH

111 Main Street, London, Ontario ▪ N1N 1N1
(Home) 519.555.1234 ▪ (Email) jsmith@careerprocanada.ca

CERTIFIED PRIMARY CARE PARAMEDIC

Seeking entry-level medical support position within a progressive and patient-focused public health care facility. Experienced in pre-hospital emergency care via paid work and consolidation experiences. Excellent physical condition and health. Motivated to serve in a full or part time capacity in southwest Ontario.

CLINICAL & MEDICAL SKILLS

- Emergency Response
- Crisis Management
- Physical Assessments
- Equipment Maintenance
- Pharmacology Awareness

- Regulatory Adherence
- Interdisciplinary Team Relations
- Confidentiality Assurance
- Sound Decision Making
- Stress Management

EDUCATION & TRAINING

A.A.S. IN MEDICAL TECHNOLOGY   2006
Wake County Technical Community College, Raleigh, NC
Gained acceptance into this competitive program due to direct experience skill-set. Completed 450-hour placement with a Paramedic at Oxford County EMS to consolidate theory and practice. Under the direction of a qualified preceptor, responsible for demonstrating the complete range of Primary Care Paramedic functions including conducting all primary and secondary patient assessments, performing critical interventions and administering medications.

- Further, served additional 132-hour observation placements involving Air Ambulance Ride-outs, Hospital Placements and Ambulance Observation Ride-outs. Only student selected by teacher for a 799 Air Ambulance Ride-out.
- Achieved Honours Status for in-class components.
- Certified by the Wake County Health Sciences Center Base Hospital to provide Symptom Relief and Defibrillation while on preceptorship.
- Adhered to proper lifting techniques when transferring patient on/off stretchers.

PARAMEDIC CORE TRAINING CERTIFICATES   2002
Ministry of Health and Long-term Care

- First Aid Level C
- CPR
- WHMIS

GENERAL ARTS (completed one term studies including math)   2002
Fanshawe College, London, Ontario

Continued ⇨

Paramedic. Although this candidate studied and worked in the US, he is now targeting employers in Canada. He utilizes Canadian conventions in spelling and grammar to ensure that employers do not discard the résumé.

JOHN SMITH

QUALIFICATIONS IN CONTEXT

SHIPPING AND RECEIVING CLERK   2003 - Present
Wake County Technical Community College, Raleigh, NC
Managed scheduling to work part-time while studying for the A-EMCA program. Received textbook shipments from freight companies. Used formula to determine pricing.

- Accepted responsibility for monitoring and ensuring the floor was fully stocked at all times.

EMERGENCY MEDICAL ATTENDANT (EMA)   2003
Superior North EMS, Geraldton, Ontario
Selected from a competitive candidate pool in a full-time capacity responding to 911 emergency calls 24 hours a day for the Thunder Bay region. Partnered closely with 130 paramedics to respond to 911 emergency calls providing rapid patient treatment and transport to the hospital.

- Received training for ministry authorized Basic Life Support Standards, Emergency First Response Program, and semi-automatic external defibrillation.
- Met approval for operating an 80,000 ambulance, even in harsh weather conditions.
- Offered to drive long distances and be stationed from the more remote areas so the ambulance service would not become down-staffed.
- Left position after gaining acceptance to the A-EMCA Certified Paramedic Program.

FILM LIBRARY CLERK   2001 - 2003
London Health Sciences Centre, London, Ontario
Selected from multiple candidates to exercise strong administrative and organizational skills for filing, sorting, pulling and distributing x-ray patient folders for health care professionals.

- Teamed with radiologists to ensure films were quickly administered and reported.
- Fielded inquiries from patients and doctors regarding results of radiology exams.
- Demonstrated flexibility with regard to overtime and call-in availability with minimal notice.

TECHNOLOGY

Word, Email and Internet Research.

Member in Good Standing Since 2003 - Ontario Paramedic Association

Joe Smyth

123 Ottawa Dr. ◆ Ottawa, ON K1K 1K1 ◆ 613.555.1230 ◆ jsmith@careerprocanada.ca

OBJECTIVE

To pursue a career as a Police Constable with the Ottawa Police Service.

QUALIFICATIONS

CERTIFICATIONS

- Ontario Association of Chiefs of Police Certificate (OACP) – 2004.
- Safety Oriented First Aid (Standard Level), and Cardiopulmonary Resuscitation (CPR Level C) Certificate, St John Ambulance – 2004.
- Life Saving I Swimming Certificate.

COMPETENCIES

- Bilingual: English, and spoken Punjabi.
- Interpersonal skills used successfully with a diverse group of people in various working environments.
- Effectively handled difficult situations with angry customers by remaining composed, listening to their problem, analysing the situation, and implementing a solution that was mutually acceptable.
- Able to recognize a situation that required assistance: contacted security when a suspected shoplifter was identified. Remained calm, observant—gathered information required to resolve the situation—and co-operated with proper authority.
- Supervised and trained several co-op students. Delegated daily work activity. Liaised with co-op university personnel, reporting on the progress and performance of the students.
- Gifted troubleshooter, able to analyse networking problems and implement solutions; solved hardware/software conflicts.
- Sociable, dependable, and adaptable individual who uses sound judgment when facing new challenges.
- Strong belief in treating people with respect and dignity.
- Life long desire to work effectively in the community, and assist people of various backgrounds.

VOLUNTEER & RECOGNITION

- National Association of Canadians of Origins in India (NACOI).
- First Degree Black Belt in Taekwon-Do, International Taekwon-Do Federation.

> "Mr. Smyth volunteered occasionally over a period of years with NACOI. …He would bring to his work a special knowledge of East Indian Community, and the problems of young people."
>
> Steve Pearl, President, Ottawa Valley Chapter of NACOI

EMPLOYMENT HISTORY

Transport Inc., Ottawa, ON – LAN Administrator   Jan 2003 – present
Utilized strong interpersonal skills to provide exceptional software, hardware, and LAN support to more than 200 users. Supervised several co-op students—one student per four month period. Configured, tested, and deployed new desktops and laptops; repaired defective hardware; and planned computer equipment lifecycle.

Home and Garden Centre, Nepean, ON – Customer Service Representative   Nov 1999 – March 2003 (Part-time)
As a valuable and responsible team member, contributed to the efficiency of store operations by providing superior customer service, as well as handling cashier duties.

TX Inc., Ottawa, ON – IT Contractor   July 2002 (Part-Time)
Installed a variety of computer equipment, including desktops and peripherals, throughout the Ottawa General Hospital. Utilized strong troubleshooting skills to solve problems encountered during the deployment.

Office Supplies, Ottawa, ON – Office Clerk   June 1999 – Sept 1999 (Summer job)
Performed general office duties including redirecting calls, word processing, faxing, and shipping & handling mail.

Direct Computer, Ottawa, ON – Sales Associate/Technician   Oct 1998 – June 1999 (Part-time)
Interacted with customers, providing computer hardware/software advice and solutions; assembled computers; and performed upgrades, repairs, and troubleshooting.

EDUCATION

Enterprise Network Specialist, Algonquin College, 2003
Co-op program

Police Constable. To demonstrate his passion for policing, this individual emphasizes his people skills and his respect for authority. Since this is a career transition, he chooses to downplay his technical skills.

MOHAMMED TASI

44 Main Avenue ▪ St. Catharines, Ontario L1L 1L1
(905) 555-1234 ▪ mtasi@careerprocanada.ca

OBJECTIVE: COMPUTER PROGRAMMING

- Client/Server Applications
- Object Oriented Programming
- Systems Analysis
- Networking
- Database Programming
- Staff & End User Training

Computer Programming graduate with proven technical abilities and a demonstrated track record for achieving in a team environment. Highly motivated, dependable, and driven to succeed. Consistently recognized for exceptional communication, interpersonal, and problem solving skills.

TECHNICAL SKILLS

Operating Systems:	Windows (9x, NT, 2000 Pro, XP Pro, 2000 Server), Linux Mandrake 7.5
Languages:	Java, Oracle, SQL, Visual Basic 6.0, VBScript
Protocols:	HTTP, FTP, SMTP
Hardware:	Printers, hard drives, disc drives, and tower repair

EDUCATION

MCSA   TBC Summer 2006
A+ Certification   TBC Summer 2006
Computer Programming (Honours) – Niagara College, Welland, Ontario   2006

WORK EXPERIENCE

HERITAGE INNS, Niagara-on-the-Lake, Ontario
Banquet Captain   2002 – Present
First selected into new position responsible for ensuring the smooth execution of onsite and offsite banquet events. Supervised all banquet and kitchen staff, communicated directly with client, and finalized all client billing.
- Implemented a series of time-saving measures to improve service and ensure guest satisfaction.
- Recognized by General Manager, clients, and staff for commitment to excellence.

Maître D'   2001 – 2002
Hired to increase morale among staff in the dining room, coordinate staff scheduling, maintain budgeted hours for the week, and ensure guest satisfaction.
- Worked closely with staff to resolve outstanding issues and improve the work environment.

CHATEAU LAKE LOUCETTE, Lake Loucette, Alberta
Promoted through a series of increasingly responsible positions for one of Canada's most prestigious hotels. Handled the full range of service responsibilities for international clientele, with particular attention paid to courtesy and customer relations.
Fairview Fine Dining Server   1999 – 2000
Dining Room Supervisor   1997 – 1999
Dining Room Waiter   1993 – 1997

PERSONAL ACHIEVEMENTS

3rd-degree Black Belt in Karate
- Winner of 15 tournaments across Canada, including the Western Canadian Championship.

Programmer. This recent graduate leads off with his strongest qualifications – technical skills and training experience. Listing his unrelated work illustrates his maturity, which is likely to distinguish him from other candidates.

ELISE DAY BA (Hon)

18 Main Court, Oakville, Ontario ▪ L1L 1L1
(Home) 905.555.1212 ▪ (Pager) 905.555.1234 ▪ EliseDay@CareerProCanada.ca

SALES PROFESSIONAL
With Interpersonal Strengths & Medical Industry Knowledge

Motivated and people oriented individual focused on entering the pharmaceutical sales industry. Intuitive relationship builder with wide range of medical professionals. Solid communication skills with small and large groups: speaks some conversational Spanish and French. Polished and professional demeanour is complemented by a dynamic personality with a good sense of humour. Characterized by integrity, determination and resourcefulness. **Strengths:**

- Product Demonstration & Promotions
- Client Relationship Management
- Market Analysis
- Merchandising

- Administrative Detailing
- Public, Community & Media Relations
- Research & Reporting
- Sound Decision Making

EDUCATION & SPECIALIZED TRAINING

HONOURS BACHELOR OF ARTS – Psychology Major   *2006*
University of Ontario, Toronto, Ontario
- Earned Dean's Honour List (80%+) each year.
- Managed time to work at University Pre School as a Supply Teacher.

Key courses and concepts covered include, but are not limited to:
Psychology (Personality, Motivation, Social and Group Dynamics), Psychobiology Abnormalities in Children, Psychopathology, Motivation and the Self, and multiple Statistics programs.

| First Aid | CPR | Wilderness First Aid | Smart Serve Licence | Ontario Bartending Certificate |

CAREER SUCCESSES

SALES / RESEARCH ASSISTANT   *2001 to 2005 (summers)*
All-Time Auto Specialties, Concord, Ontario
Selected by President of Product Development/General VP of Plant Operations for a diverse scope of important responsibilities for this 160-employee major automotive parts supplier. Fully cognizant of complete range of sales processes from client relations and proposals to negotiations and
product delivery. Excelled in this fast-paced and demanding position.

- Conducted market research for special projects at the General VP's request. Worked with interdisciplinary team members like the Public Relations Director and administrative staff.
- Key team member; participated in drafting and revising multi-million dollar sales proposals and quotes. Further, verified and validated sales pricing catalogues. Extreme attention to detail was crucial: errors could cost company thousands.
- Trusted with privileged and confidential financial and production information regarding business transactions, sales pricing, and employee contract details.
- Relied upon to assist in the preparation for company, ISO, and QS audits and mergers.
- Delivered exceptional customer service. Front line accountabilities included answering questions and clarifying sales, orders, pricing or delivery issues.
- Flexible skill-set handled accounts payable and receivable, payroll, and multiple human resource functions.

~ Continued on Page 2 ~
~ Continued on Page 2 ~

Sales Representative. This new graduate focused her résumé to target clients in the pharmaceutical industry. Note the consistent design style used at the bottom of page one and in the closing of page two.

ELISE DAY BA (Hon)   **~ Page 2 of 2 ~**

CAREER SUCCESSES

- Project managed the annual company charity golf tournament. This required months of advanced planning. Seamlessly coordinated all advertising, sponsor sourcing, financial controls, and logistical considerations. Directed 200+ executive level players. Efforts rewarded by securing $30 000 for this one day event for the *Caitlyn Foundation*.

SALES REPRESENTATIVE   *2001*
Crayola, Hamilton, Ontario
Retained to provide in-store promotions for this popular crayon manufacturer. Monitored and reported sales figures relative to each promotion.

- Facilitated product demonstrations to small and large groups. Solid product knowledge answered a multitude of questions.
- Solicited customer responses regarding product opinion. Synthesized information and relayed data to head office.

CLERICAL ASSISTANT   *1999 to 2001*
Thorn Medical Centre, Town, Ontario
Hired for this busy emergency weekend clinic to provide extensive responsibilities in the administration of the facility's operation. Assisted physicians with medical procedures, including processing lab samples, upon request. Gained extensive familiarity with medical terms, conditions, procedures, treatments, and both prescription and over-the-counter medications.

- Coordinated patient appointment schedules and booked specialist consultations.
- Prepared examination rooms for patients as per standard procedure.
- Strong detail orientation and workload prioritization served to perform clerical duties including filing, photocopying, faxing, sorting mail, all while dealing with phones and doctors' requests.

COMPUTER SKILLS: Microsoft Office (Word, Excel), SPSS (Statistical Program), Outlook Express, Accord, MYOB Accounting Plus, and Internet Research.

COMMUNITY & VOLUNTEER INVOLVEMENT

Maternity Ward /Emergency Room   145 hours
York Country Hospital
Redefined responsibilities as a student volunteer to the absolute limits of observation and assistance to medical professionals including doctors, nurses, and non-registered staff.

- Participated in direct patient care and transfer upon request.
- Monitored inventory and replenished supplies as needed.
- Oversaw waiting room activity and individual patient requests.

Neo Natal Intensive Care   140 hours
Mount Sinai Hospital
Successfully pursued the first co-op placement opportunity in the NICU of Mount Sinai Hospital to participate in the daily care of neo-natal patients.

- Observed surgeries, standard procedures, and a holistic perspective in the neo-natal intensive care unit and neighbouring hospitals.

Energy ~ Enthusiasm ~ Integrity

COLLEEN B. HARRISON

123 SUNDOWN STREET ◆ CHATHAM ◆ ONTARIO ◆ N1N 1N1 ◆ CANADA
519 555-1234 ◆ charrison@CareerProCanada.ca

MASTERS PREPARED SOCIAL WORKER
CLIENT RELATIONS / COMMUNITY OUTREACH / RISK MANAGEMENT
A highly ethical, team-spirited, and empathetic professional with outstanding academic
training and excellent work experience in the social-services environment

EDUCATION

University of Alberta, Edmonton, AB   2006
Master of Social Work Degree, Clinical specialization

University of Western Ontario, King's College, London, ON   2004
Bachelor of Social Work Degree, with honours

Lambton College, Sarnia, ON   2001
Social Service Worker Diploma, with honours

WORK EXPERIENCE

Edmonton Counselling Centre, Edmonton, AB   2004 – Present
Social Work Intern
Provided clinical psychotherapy to a diverse population of adults and children; participated in
reflecting teams; facilitated children's groups focusing on divorce and separation issues and
behavioural difficulties; and worked with court-mandated clients through a domestic violence
initiative:

- Demonstrated ability to provide ethical and confidential psychotherapy to each client through
  compassion and empathy, utilizing an evidence-based practice framework.
- Kept meticulous records, effectively consulted with colleagues, and provided timely and
  comprehensive assessment plans to meet both client and agency goals under demanding
  deadline pressures.
- Successfully completed ninety hours of specialized clinical training.

Children's Aid Society of Perth County, Stratford, ON   2004
Summer Child Protection Worker
Worked in the *Ongoing Family Services* department, supporting children and families in crisis while
abiding by the Ministry's regulations regarding child protection:

- Provided support and assistance to 32 child protection teams; assisted within the supervised
  access program, legal proceedings and documentation, triage, and emergency systems to
  provide education and supportive services to families at risk of dissemination.
- Earned recognition from Management for ability to respond in crisis situations.

Chatham General Hospital, Chatham, ON   2003 – 2004
Field placement student, Chatham PACT team
Supported a diverse group of adults in the community suffering from severe and persistent mental
health issues ranging from Schizophrenia to Borderline Personality Disorder, as an alternative to
institutionalization:

- Gained experience in the provision of crisis intervention and case management, acquired
  knowledge in the use of psychotropic medications, and effectively worked within a multi-
  disciplinary team environment.
- Developed expertise working with multi-tiered systems, including the *Public Guardian and
  Trustee* office, hospital, and health care institutions.

Social Worker. This recent graduate exhibits her education prior to her expertise to leverage her strong academic
qualifications.

COLLEEN B. HARRISON

WORK EXPERIENCE (continued)

Community Resource Centre, Chatham, ON   2002

Summer Youth Outreach Worker

Assisted the Youth Worker to connect with at-risk adolescents in the community by developing, supervising, and maintaining outreach programs:

- Facilitated various programs, including employment counselling seminars and youth-generated community fundraisers for the *Youth Action Canada* project for high-risk youth.
- Participated in a program targeting teen mothers: developed and implemented educational materials exploring self-esteem, problem-solving, and conflict resolution strategies.

Leamington Counselling & Mediation Centre, Leamington, ON   2002

Student Field Placement Worker

Provided therapeutic counselling to both individuals and families within a for-profit agency, gaining effective assessment and intervention skills:

- Assisted clients, through psychotherapy, to identify counselling goals, consider effective solutions, and find reliable resources; followed up with clients weekly, and communicated results to team members through precise record-keeping and supervision.
- Triaged with community resources and partners on behalf of clientele.

Middlesex County Social Services, Ontario Works, London, ON   2001

Summer Caseworker

Received extensive training in *Ontario Works* social assistance policy regulations to function as a relief caseworker, managing caseloads of 90 to 130 clients, and interacting with the *Ministry of Community and Social Services* as well as community-based resources:

- Developed an ability to facilitate communication with clients, clients' families, and members of the London support and assistance community.
- Provided a linkage between clients and providers to ensure the delivery of high-quality, cost-effective services.

Sam Adams Society, London, ON   2000 – 2001

Field Placement Student

Worked in the *Alternative to Custody* program dealing with youth who were in conflict with the law:

- Effectively linked with court mandated Phase 1 young offenders, through small groups, assessing each situation independently to bring about positive change and growth through listening, empathy, and education.
- Honed problem-solving skills through active involvement, appropriate strategy selection, counselling, and reflecting.

VOLUNTEER EXPERIENCE

Volunteer: *St Francis of Assisi:* prepare and serve breakfast to 80 to 100 homeless persons, one day a week ◆ *Salvation Army of Chatham:* deliver gift baskets to the less fortunate during the Christmas season ◆ Middlesex County community fundraiser for the homeless

RELATED ACTIVITIES

Dean's Honours standing in the Social Worker and BSW Programs ◆ Training in *Non-violent Crisis Intervention, Applied Suicide Intervention Skills, Prevention and Management of Aggressive Behaviour* (P.M.A.B.) ◆ First Aid ◆ CPR

111 Kings Crescen t – Pickering, Ontario L1L 1L1 –
marianne@careerprocanada.ca

MARIANNE JACKSON
AOCAD

(905) 555-1234

COMPUTER EXPERTISE

- Adobe Illustrator
- Soilworks
- CorelDraw
- Rhinoceros
- 3D StudioMax
- AutoCAD
- Photoshop
- Mechanical Desktop
- PowerPoint
- MS Word

*Member –
Association of Chartered Industrial
Designers of Ontario (ACIDO)*

INDUSTRIAL DESIGNER

Talented designer skilled in applying innovative solutions to design challenges. Natural problem solver with a creative and holistic approach to design, taking into consideration function, user, form, style, and environment. Strong computer modelling, drafting, and model making ability. Resourceful and self-motivated – able to work well under pressure and meet deadlines. Strong communication skills. Key areas of strength include:

- Conceptual Design
- 3D-Computer Modeling
- Prototype Fabrication
- Ideation Sketches
- Computer Rendering
- Drafting

EDUCATION & AWARDS

Industrial Design Diploma, Ontario College of Design   April 2005
Design, Drawing and Rendering, DesignTek Ontario   June 2005

Awards:
Winner – Top Graduate Award for outstanding work in Industrial Design
Winner – TorComp Scholarship
Winner – Stanley Morrissey Award
Winner – Lena A. Vaughan Award
Winner – Inaugural ACIDO Rocket Competition (Ontario-wide)

NOTEWORTHY DESIGNS

Children's Toy – designed award-winning line of items to address separation anxiety in pre-school children. Creative design marries function with whimsy, appealing to children while providing practical functionality to help address emotional needs. Modelled prototypes using sterolithography (SLA). Patents filed.

Breastfeeding Chair – conceived and currently prototyping chair designed to facilitate breastfeeding training. For use in hospital and clinics, design solves a variety of ergonomic design challenges in comfortably accommodating all standard feeding positions.

Customized Wheelchair Tray – created a variety of design concepts for Ontario Hospital's Centre for Studies in Aging. Solution provided tray design to retrofit extruded aluminium arm of existing wheelchair.

PROFESSIONAL EXPERIENCE

Industrial Designer   June 2005 – Present
INDUSTRIAL DESIGN INC., Toronto, Ontario
Designed, drafted, and modelled a variety of commercial and medical products for Canadian and U.S.-based corporate clients.
- Applied conceptual and problem solving skills to design solutions to meet both functional and aesthetic requirements of product.
- Completed all ideation sketches, computer modelling, and rendering.
- Routinely liaised with client to discuss ideas and finalize designs.

Technical Industrial Designer. This résumé utilizes a layout with a "design" feel to it. The résumé shifts attention away from her lack of experience by focusing on her education and awards.

Best Résumé Samples
Mid-Level and Management

NANCY WONG, BBA

555 Cariboo Street
Vancouver, BC
V1V 1V1

Home (604) 555-1234
Cell (604) 555-2345
E-mail n_wong@careerprocanada.ca

CLIENT-FOCUSED PROFESSIONAL ACCOUNTANT

Results-oriented professional with proven experience, sound technical skills, and an impeccable work ethic. An articulate individual, who is confident and poised in interactions with individuals at all levels. Experience in performing senior accounting functions including planning and executing challenging audits. Verifiable ability to produce high quality files within time-sensitive deadlines. Outstanding leadership abilities, modelling professional and ethical behaviour for junior staff. Ability to exercise sound judgement to resolve difficult and delicate issues. Expert proficiency in a wide variety of accounting software. Willing to travel.

Areas of Expertise

▪ Corporate Auditing	▪ Risk Assessment	▪ Tax Strategies
▪ Team Leadership	▪ Profit & Loss Statements	▪ Financial Statements
▪ Data Analysis	▪ General Ledger Controls	▪ Legislative Compliance

Solid educational credentials with a Bachelor in Business Administration majoring in accounting, and the Chartered Accountant designation to be completed January 2007.

CAREER HISTORY

Roberts LLP, Chartered Accountants, Vancouver, BC   **2002-Present**

Mid-sized accounting firm with offices in major cities across Canada and 40 employees at the Vancouver location, servicing small to medium-sized private and public organizations.

Accountant

Major Responsibilities

Reporting directly to the managers and partners, accountable to prepare draft financial statements including working paper files for assurance engagements. Correspond with clients on various engagement related issues. Supervise and train junior accountants. Prepare personal, corporate tax, and GST returns. Analyze data to assist client consultation and financial planning. Maintain and administer CaseWare.

Selected Accomplishments

➡ Assigned Senior Auditor and travelled to China for five days to audit 2 subsidiaries under extreme time pressures; corresponded with overseas CPAs and clients after hours, completing the file on schedule.

➡ Developed a reputation for always showing initiative to learn and understand the big picture to ensure that tasks are performed effectively, relieving pressure from the managers and partners.

➡ Prepared financial statements for more than 150 clients per year with exceptional attention to detail, ensuring virtually zero error.

➡ Generated over 12 audit planning memos and audit programs per year, working proactively to ensure that all major projects are completed on schedule.

➡ Trained and developed 5 junior accountants, instructing them on file preparation and the utilization of various accounting software including CaseWare and Taxprep.

➡ Participated in the upgrading of the central accounting software, proactively learned the new system, and assumed the responsibility to maintain and administer templates on an ongoing basis.

Accountant. Note the consistent length of accomplishment bullets, which each wrap only two lines. This gives a clean "look and feel" to the résumé and makes the document easier to follow.

John Doe Ltd. Chartered Accountant, Coquitlam, BC   **2000-2002**

Independent accounting firm specializing in servicing owner-managed enterprises.

Accountant

Major Responsibilities

Develop working papers for compilation, review, and audit engagements, reporting directly to the owner. Prepare financial statements, personal and corporate tax returns. Perform bookkeeping services and general administrative duties.

Selected Accomplishments

➡ Prepared approximately 400 tax returns yearly, always displaying a highly positive attitude during the busy season and ensuring that every assignment was completed on time.

➡ Trained and supervised junior accounting students in a variety of functions including tax return and financial statement preparation.

➡ Performed monthly bookkeeping and payroll services and maintained a courteous and professional relationship with key clients ensuring ongoing business.

Friesen Electric Inc., Abbotsford, BC   **1998-2000**

Family-owned retailer with 30 employees, providing lighting solutions to businesses and consumers.

Junior Accountant

Major Responsibilities

Reporting directly to the Accounting Manager, responsible to provide a wide variety of duties. Enter accounts receivable and payable records. Generate daily cash and gross margin reports. Perform credit collections. Address telephone inquiries from customers and vendors. Update customer database.

Selected Accomplishments

➡ Audited daily invoices and recommended adjustments to ensure accurate recordkeeping and proper audit trail maintenance.

➡ Contacted customers on a weekly basis and successfully collected outstanding accounts receivables of up to $1000.00 per client.

FORMAL EDUCATION & CREDENTIALS

CA School of Business, Vancouver, BC   **CA Expected Jan 2007**
➡ Chartered Accountant (CA) Program, completed 'Uniform Evaluation' in September 2006.
➡ Successfully completed all six CASB modules on first attempt and received 'Competency with Distinction'.

Simon Fraser University, Burnaby, BC   **2000**
➡ Bachelor's Degree in Business Administration (BBA), Concentration: Accounting

The University College of the Cariboo, Kamloops, BC   **1999**
➡ Faculty of Business Administration (Transfer Courses), Honour Roll

COMPUTER SKILLS

Proficient in a variety of software applications including:
➡ Microsoft Office Suite (Word, Excel, and PowerPoint)
➡ CaseWare, CaseView, QuickBooks, Simply Accounting, Taxprep, NS Taxbyte

LANGUAGES

➡ Fully fluent in English and Mandarin

HELEN MATTHEWS

111 Humberline Drive • Aurora, Ontario • L1L 1L1 • 905-555-1234 • Mobile 905-555-2345

E X E C U T I V E   A S S I S T A N T

> *"In broad terms, Helen's priority is to maximize the productivity of 2 senior positions she supports. The position is largely unstructured, and the incumbent's effectiveness is heavily dependent on trust, confidentiality, discretion, maturity, good judgement, and the willingness to take a proactive approach to problem resolution and support.*
>
> *Helen possesses all of these characteristics and conducts herself with professionalism and tremendous dedication to her function and those she supports. Her self-imposed standards are of the highest order, and her output is to both her and the Company's credit.*
>
> *Helen's pleasant manner and engaging personality have allowed her to form relationships with outside parties that are important to me and to the company. Her organizational skills and professional approach to organizing schedules, etc. makes her contribution invaluable."*
>
> *-- Warren King, President/CEO, Methodux*

Customer-driven, loyal, and hard-working professional with over 15 years of experience. **Consistently goes beyond the requirements of a job in order to meet – and exceed – organizational objectives**. Demonstrated record of successfully executing day-to-day tasks in fast-paced and deadline-driven environments. Computer knowledge includes Word, Excel, PowerPoint, Outlook, and ACT! (Version 3.0). Fluent in English and German. **A sincere and genuine team player willing to do whatever it takes to ensure an organization's success.**

Areas of Expertise:

Problem-Solving & Independent Decision-Making • Workflow Planning & Prioritization
Executive, Board, Subcommittee, & Customer Liaison • VIP Relations & Communications
Appointment/Board Scheduling & Speaking Engagements • Travel & Itinerary Coordination
Documenting, Record-Keeping, & Reporting • Mail & Courier Services • Tape Transcription
Expense Tracking & Reporting • Budget Assistance • Database & File Management
Meeting, Conference, & Special Event Planning/Coordination • Minute-Taking

SIGNIFICANT CONTRIBUTIONS

- Slashed travel costs 30% per year by recruiting a new travel agent *(Methodux)*.
- Accommodated a significant increase in workload – stemming from IPO's, due diligence, mergers, and acquisitions – without the need for additional temporary or part-time staff *(Methodux)*.
- Created a comprehensive filing system to ensure that critical information could be easily retrieved *(ACC)*.

Administrative & Executive Assistant. The glowing endorsement by the President and CEO creates a strong lead-in to this résumé. It clearly outlines the individual's Value Proposition through the eyes of her employer.

HELEN MATTHEWS

905-555-1234 • Mobile 905-555-2345... Page Two

SIGNIFICANT CONTRIBUTIONS (cont'd)

- Tapped by President/CEO, after only 2 days on the job, to assume all logistical responsibilities of an extensive relocation involving Engineering, Sales, Finance, Operations, and Executive Offices. Completed this ambitious project in under 2 months *(Ace Aerospace)*.

- Averted the prospect of six-figure litigation by taking the initiative to collaborate with a corporate lawyer in President's absence during a time-critical crisis *(Methodux)*.

- Stepped in for President during his absence to provide constant interaction with – and support for – a key manufacturing account awaiting a vital order. Successfully met this challenging deadline on schedule *(Ace Aerospace)*.

- Earned reputation as the first one in and the last to leave – especially when facing important deadlines *(all)*.

- Elected as President for 2 years and served on the Executive Committee for 7 years *(PESI)*.

PROFESSIONAL HIGHLIGHTS

Executive Assistant to the President & CEO • Methodux Inc., Toronto	1995 - present
Executive Assistant to the President • Ace Aerospace, Brooklin	1993 - 1995
Executive Assistant to the President & CEO • ACC, Aurora	1990 - 1992

PROFESSIONAL MEMBERSHIP

Professional Executive Secretaries International (PESI)	1993 - present

Excellent References Furnished Upon Request

MARJORIE HILL

111 Queen's Circle, Burlington, ON   L1L 1L1

Telephone: 905-555-1212   mhill01@careerprocanada.ca

ADMINISTRATIVE & FINANCIAL PROFESSIONAL

A self-motivated professional who balances a detail-oriented approach with an eye for innovation and creativity at all stages of problem diagnosis and solving. Possesses effective oral and written communication skills along with the ability to operate with a high level of autonomy and independence. Proven knowledge and skills in the following areas:

- Accounts Receivable & Payable
- Payroll
- Customer Service
- Teamwork

- G/L
- Office Procedures/Management
- MS Word, Excel, AccPac
- Systems & Reporting

NOTEWORTHY CAREER HIGHLIGHTS

- Acknowledged by senior management for discovering costly discount error to dealers. Went beyond job parameters to investigate several systems (billing, customer database, accounts receivable) and resolved errors resulting in an annual savings of $250,000.

- Charged by senior management to research inventory overage at 225 dealers across the country. Designed a streamlined system to effectively collect monthly inventory numbers. Within twelve months achieved $500,000 reduction in paper and chemistry.

- Entrusted by senior management to establish a protocol for customer credit requests. Designed a delivery charge credit form and tracking system that significantly streamlined the process, reduced customer complaints, and reflected increased company professionalism.

- Developed and implemented a financial reporting structure for a distribution centre and seven stores. This system facilitated accurate data collection and report generation.

- Collaborated with A/P manager at US parent organization to successfully manage heavy workload of Canadian A/P counterpart during a four-month illness. Credited with reducing customer complaints through timely processing of invoices.

- Collaborated with company tax professionals to troubleshoot PST and GST discrepancies within the A/R process. Analyzed billing database to track and resolve errors.

- Resolved large overdue receivable with key customer by tracking details, settling original invoice errors, and re-issuing corrected invoice. Acknowledged by national credit manager for exceeding expectations and maintaining diplomatic relationship with customer.

- Bestowed with *Employee of the Year* award on two occasions.

Administrative and Finance Professional. With an exemplary career, this experienced professional presents her "Noteworthy Career Highlights" first. This technique shifts the focus from number of years' experience to her extraordinary achievements.

MARJORIE HILL   page 2

CAREER HISTORY

Quality Photo Labs – Burlington, ON   1997-Present
Accounts Receivable Administrator, Special Projects
- Provided daily support to the credit team located in Tulsa, Oklahoma
- Liaised with customers, co-workers, suppliers, management, and financial institutions
- Applied and deposited all monies received by Canadian labs and Head Office
- Transacted payments via dealers' credit cards and maintained confidential credit card database
- Created manual invoices (non-system A/R) and followed up for payments
- Collected on NSF, post-dated, and problem cheques
- Created and entered purchase orders as well as receipts into the A/P system
- Performed administrative duties and special projects as required

Adnil Inc. – Burlington, ON   1991-1996
Office Manager
- Managed cash flow in a dynamic sales and manufacturing environment
- Maintained G/L and A/R using AccPac software
- Prepared and reconciled payroll, T4s, and government remittances
- Supervised A/P clerk

The Mission House – Toronto, ON   1988-1990
Human Resources Administrator
- Coordinated volunteers with Mission requirements
- Administrated Employee Benefits Plan
- Recruited staff for summer camps

Computer World – Toronto, ON   1982-1987
Director of Administration
- Researched and implemented computerized accounting system
- Developed and implemented financial reporting structure for seven stores and a warehouse
- Assisted in preparation and presentation of financial proposals to financial institutions
- Reviewed all salary increases to ensure budget guidelines met
- Compiled statistics for the Management and Compensation Committee

EDUCATION

- Business Administration Certificate - (Ryerson University)
- Business Concepts Certificate - (Sheridan College)
- Work term Accounts Receivable – (Sheridan College, Jan. 1992)

CATHERINE GLENN

123 Ottawa Court ◆ Nepean, ON K1K 1K1
613.555.1234

ADMINISTRATIVE PROFESSIONAL

Sports Medicine…Health Services…Retail…Daycare…Veterinary…Government

High-calibre administrative professional, bringing a wealth of experience from various industries. Recognized for being a self-starter and taking on responsibilities in support of management. Skilled communicator, able to develop rapport with a diverse group of professionals, and promote a positive work environment. Demonstrated ability to lead projects from start to finish. Proficient in Word, Outlook, Excel, Works for Windows, ACCPAC-Bedford, and Simply Accounting.

PROFESSIONAL EXPERIENCE

Carleton University, Ottawa, ON   2001 – Present
Sports Medicine and Physiotherapy Centre – Administrator (2004 – Present)
Provide full scope of office administration including staff supervision, author job descriptions, interview and hire personnel, and provide performance reviews. Liaison between the Director and the medical staff, including associate professionals. Anticipate potential problem areas, and implement preventive measures.

- Developed a comprehensive policies and procedures manual; created a training manual to aid new staff. **Results:** well-trained personnel, reliable patient information, clear clinical direction.
- Revitalized office atmosphere, by actively engaging staff in providing solutions to office challenges, while remaining focused on the needs of a very diverse group of professionals.
- Initiated an "All Staff" meeting—now held every 4 months—which opened the lines of communication between physicians of the Sports Medicine Centre, the physicians of Health Services, and the support staff. **Results:** Office synergies improved significantly.
- Instrumental in promoting—to the physicians—use of an electronic billing system to Quebec (RAMQ), which significantly increased speed and accuracy of billing.
- Ensured all expenditures fell within budget.

Health Services – Financial and Administrative Coordinator (2001 – 2004)
Provided office administration support to Health Services at a critical time when organization became a BETA site for the OHTN (Ontario HIV Treatment Network). Implemented daily revenue balancing procedures; performed MD billing data entry to OHIP, RAMQ, and third party insurance companies; performed bookkeeping functions, including A/P, A/R, petty cash, and bank deposits. Planned special company functions, including Christmas festivities, yearly retreats, and team-building events.

- Accountable to the Director: booked travel arrangements, organized demanding agenda, prepared expense reports, and scheduled business meetings.
- Performed CIS (Clinic Information System) troubleshooting to ensure MD billing to the Ministry of Health transmitted accurate information into accounting software (Simply Accounting).
- Collaborated with Health Promotion Manager on organizing a large-scale conference for the Ontario College Health Association.
- Organized and scheduled monthly administration meetings, bi-monthly physician meetings, and semi-annual staff meetings, which provided venues to discuss and improve office cooperation.
- Assisted in the conversion of Payroll and Accounts Payable to electronic payments; collaborated with hired consultant in the development of an HR Employee Policies and Procedures manual.

Administrative Professional. The immaculate "look and feel" of this résumé portrays this candidate as a highly professional and proficient administrative specialist.

Civic Hospital, Ottawa, ON   2000 – 2001
Patient Registration Clerk

Ensured efficient patient admission. Dependability, versatility, and ability to learn quickly led to broadened duties in multiple locations, including childbirth, ambulatory care, and emergency. Ability to work independently eased supervisor's workload. Performed multiple tasks with accuracy and confidentiality. Interacted professionally with all medical staff.

Canadian Tire, Ottawa, ON   1999
Office Manager

Charged will full scope of office administration, including payroll, accounts payable, inventory, cash balancing, and banking issues management.

Home Daycare Provider, Ottawa, ON   1997 – 1999
Owner/Caregiver   1984 – 1995

Provided quality, secured, and structured in-house childcare. Communicated tactfully with parents to resolve sensitive issues. Managed all aspect of a home-based business.

- Member of the Board of Directors for the Child Care Providers Association of Ottawa-Carleton.
- Network Leader, organized workshops dealing with the business aspect of starting a daycare: contracts, bookkeeping, tax requirements, and addressing parent concerns.

Perfect Framing Supplies, Ottawa, ON   1996 – 1997
Office Manager

Handled office administration, including customer service, inventory, and bookkeeping using Business Visions II and ACCPAC-Bedford.

ADDITIONAL WORK EXPERIENCE

Kanata Veterinary Services, Ottawa ON ◆ Bookkeeper
Children's Clothing Store, Ottawa ON ◆ Bookkeeper
Teck Corporation, Ottawa ON ◆ Office Clerk
Atomic Energy of Canada Limited, Ottawa ON ◆ Administrative Assistant

EDUCATION & SPECIALIZED TRAINING

Hospital Patient Registration Specialist ◆ Career Canada College, Ottawa, ON 1999
"Dealing with Difficult People" training ◆ Career Canada College, Ottawa, ON 1999
"Cultural Diversity" seminar ◆ Career Canada College, Ottawa, ON 1999
Business Administration: Major in Accounting ◆ Algonquin College, Ottawa, ON 1976

COMMUNITY INVOLVEMENT

Ottawa Urban Inline Skating Club ◆ Board of Directors, Certified IISA Level 1 Coach
Rideau Skating Club ◆ Board of Directors – Treasurer, Recreational Programme Director
Child Care Providers Association of Ottawa-Carleton ◆ Board of Directors
Dorack Drive Park Association ◆ President
Atomic Energy of Canada Limited ◆ Head of Social Club Committee
Cancer Society ◆ (former) Canvasser

Jason Bell

111 Raven Road	Tel: 905-555-1234
Glendale, Ontario	or 905-555-2345
L1L 1L1	jbell@careerprocanada.ca

Ambulance Attendant • Care Assistant • Team Player

Ambulance Attendant with two years of experience and a further four years in customer-focused, time-sensitive driving and security roles. Committed to career progression within the ambulance service and to professional development through training and experience.

Proven to be focused and reliable in high-pressure, team-oriented environments that require the highest standard of personal and professional integrity and professionalism. Earned reputation for ability to communicate at all levels and for enthusiasm to provide courteous and empathetic patient care.

Key Skills

- **Driving Qualifications:** Commercial driver's licence since 1999. Safe driving record with no accidents or incidents.
- **Driving Experience:** Patient Transfer Vehicles (PTVs), flat bed trucks, armoured vehicles, people carriers, vans and cars.
- **Driving Theory:** Scored 100% on both the Road Rules and Road Signs exams.
- **Teamwork:** Proud to contribute to the team effort in order to give excellent care and service to patients who rely on our ambulance service.
- **Professional Development & Training:** Pursuing career goal to become a Paramedic. Take the initiative to learn new skills in Ambulance Aid, driving and Sign Language (including self-taught finger signing).

Experience

Ambulance Attendant   *12/02 – Present*
Glendale Ambulance Service, Huronbank Depot
P/T evening shift. 30 hours per week plus approximately 7 hours of overtime.

Work as part of a 2-member crew and communicate with various medical staff. Transport patients and provide supportive care and handling, including those with medical and/or mobility difficulties. Work overtime at various stations.

- Ensure patient transfer vehicle is safe and roadworthy. Check medical supplies and equipment. Maintain a high level of health and safety for crew and patients.
- Use training and excellent driving skills to provide smooth and comfortable ride.
- Attend non-urgent calls, as required by Emergency Room Control.
- Receive positive feedback from patients who appreciate helpful and friendly approach to meeting their needs.

Page 1 of 2

Ambulance Driver. The strong profile statement highlights this candidate's personality and clarifies his intention to seek a promotion within his company and secure a place on a highly sought-after training course for paramedics. The "Additional Information" section at the end of the résumé successfully displays his added value.

Experience continued

Driver / Security Guard   *04/99 – 12/02*
SecurityPlus Ltd., Glendale
F/T morning shift

High security position replenishing and maintaining ATMs at business premises. Ensured all monies transferred and delivered safely. Accurate paperwork.

- Built excellent relationships with customers through good communications.
- Conducted daily vehicle checks (mechanical, security and body).
- Drove a variety of vehicles (vans and trucks), abiding by provincial and federal regulations.
- Worked within tight security and time constraints.
- Commended by Area Manager for calm and professional conduct in accordance with company policy during high-risk incident involving a man brandishing a knife.

Driver / Baggage Handler   *09/94 – 04/99*
AirControl Handling, Glendale Airport
P/T shift work

High security and physically demanding position, working within a team environment with tight time constraints.

- Drove flat bed truck to load and unload baggage from aircraft, ensuring that critical deadlines for aircraft turnaround were met safely and efficiently. Drove various vehicles, including tugs, within the airport.

Education & Training

Ambulance Aid Study Group   *Ongoing*
Since December 2002, attend bi-monthly classes given by
Paramedic Paul Stevens at Glendale Community Hospital.

High School Diploma   *1994*
St Augusta High School, Glendale

Additional Information

Sign Language Training – Currently studying at the Deaf School, Glendale.

Sports Coaching – Junior Baseball League Coach for the Glendale Panthers.

Computing – Troubleshooting PC problems; use MS Word, Internet and email.

MONICA THORNTON

12 Windermere Court
Vancouver, British Columbia
V1V 1V1

Home (604) 555-1234
Cell (604) 555-2345
E-mail mt@careerprocanada.ca

EXPERIENCED APPLICATION PROGRAMMER & ANALYST

Results-driven professional with advanced proficiency in JAVA software development and extensive expertise in Graphical User Interface (GUI) design principles. Verifiable accomplishments in the full development lifecycle from needs assessment through to implementation and support. A talent for problem solving, applying logical and creative approaches to implement effective solutions. An approachable individual with outstanding interpersonal and communication skills. A quick learner who has been consistently cited for the ability to adapt easily to advances in technology. Willing to travel. Proven achievements in:

▸ Full Lifecycle Programming	▸ Project Management	▸ Software Installation
▸ Object-Oriented Development	▸ Data Modelling	▸ Customer Service & Support
▸ Analysis & Design	▸ Problem Solving	▸ Technical Training
▸ Database Development	▸ Technology Documentation	▸ Demonstration & Presentation

*"Monica's organizational skills lead to quick development cycle times
...her work is virtually error free when turned over to the users."*
- X-Tech Performance Review

TECHNICAL SKILLS

Operating Systems	Microsoft Windows 95, 98, 2000, XP, NT, UNIX
Programming	Java, PowerScript, C, UNIX Shell
Development Tools	WebSphere (WSAD), Visual Age Java (VAJ), PowerBuilder, S-Designor
Databases	Oracle (7, 8i, 9i), Sybase, MS SQL Server, dBase
Internet	Netscape, Internet Explorer, Outlook, Lotus Notes
Office Applications	Microsoft Office Suite (Word, Excel, PowerPoint, and Project), ReportSmith, JetForm

CAREER HIGHLIGHTS

▸ Led a major project to convert existing work tracking systems from PowerBuilder into a Java based environment; successfully completed the migration without disrupting the end-user working environment.

▸ Acted as IT team lead for a project to automate the bulk release printing process in two business locations; analyzed needs and designed the application, which virtually eliminated human error and waste.

▸ Designed and implemented a procedural change in the OE system that resulted in a major performance improvement and slashed processing time from 5 minutes to 10 seconds per 1000 orders.

▸ Created numerous technical documentation and user manuals including release memos, system descriptions, and extended PowerPoint presentations.

▸ Selected to demo the work tracking and administration systems of international locations including the Australian Lab, due to a comprehensive understanding of the complete system from beginning to end.

▸ Designed and developed a major security system enhancement for a Strategic Human Resource Management application.

▸ Earned a reputation for providing exceptional technical support, by being available to provide timely assistance to end-users.

▸ Aggressively promoted and assigned to large-scale project leadership roles, directly as a result of quickly acquiring an advanced technical proficiency and an overall business knowledge.

Application Programmer. This candidate highlights quotes from her performance reviews to draw attention to her talents. She neatly lists her technical skills early in the résumé to ensure that recruiters easily find her specific areas of expertise.

MONICA THORNTON

PROFESSIONAL EXPERIENCE

X-Tech (a wholly owned subsidiary of the ABC Group), Vancouver, BC   **2004 – Present**
http://www.x-tech_abcgroup.com
World leading organization offering extensive range of services and technologies for the Theatrical, Television, and Home Entertainment industries, with 2000 employees in the Toronto and Hollywood Locations.
Java Programmer/Analyst (2000 – Present)
PowerBuilder Application Developer (1999 – 2000)
Reporting directly to the VP of Information Technology, responsible for the full scope of software design and analysis in the Canadian and US operations. Implement, maintain, and enhance the work tracking and order entry systems. Perform user training and demonstrations. Lead and participate in projects as required.

▸ Took a lead role in automating the release printing process by building up a communication protocol, which reduced operator intervention and minimized waste and human error.
▸ Integrated two business locations by producing a flexible, re-configurable design, enabling both offices to utilize the same software system.
▸ Maintained full responsibility of X-Tech Work Tracking System in Toronto and Hollywood Labs including full implementation of enhancements due to business process changes.
▸ Created an individual Project Reporting System that provides a clear overview of expenses and company budget.
▸ Played a significant role in a major enhancement of the administration system to improve the billing process.

XYZ Metrix Inc., Vancouver, BC   **2002 – 2003**
http://www.xyzmetrixinc.com
Internationally recognized provider of strategic human resource management systems for many of the largest and most successful public and private organizations.
Programmer/Analyst
Responsible for program design and development in PowerBuilder. Develop and maintain custom-made Human Resources applications. Discuss system features and enhancements with clients. Design and create flexible reports for custom data analysis.

▸ Supported key clients, including American Express and Red Engineering, customizing systems to meet their HR needs.
▸ Migrated applications coded in PowerBuilder 4.0 to later versions and extended single-user applications to a multi-user mode.

Previous Positions Held
▸ BC General Assurance, Programmer/Analyst
▸ XYZ Cable Television Ltd., Programmer/Analyst

FORMAL EDUCATION

Gabor Denes Technology and Information Science College   **1997 – 2000**
▸ Computer Science Degree
SZAMALK Computer Technical Educational Centre   **1994 – 1997**
▸ Computer Programming Diploma

PROFESSIONAL DEVELOPMENT

Actively committed to continuing education via various courses and workshops:
▸ Java Programming, IBM
▸ PowerBuilder Programming
▸ Rational Unified Process (RUP)
▸ ReportSmith

"Monica's advanced proficiency in JAVA, comfort in learning new technology, and ease in training others have greatly benefited the department and the organization as a whole."
- XYZ Metrix Performance Review

MOIRA NAMGREB
1111 Galaxy Avenue
Oakville, ON L1L 1L1
(905) 555-5431
mnamgreb@careerprocanada.ca

AutoCAD Drafting Technologist
Architectural Draftsperson

PROFESSIONAL COMPETENCE

AutoCAD Draftsperson/Architectural Technician with over 7 years of experience in technical drafting. Create architectural drawings for design development, presentations, tendering, and detailing of residential villas, warehouse and commercial projects. Estimate project completion time for new drawings. Produce drawings and revise existing ones while guaranteeing quick turnaround time. Possess a thorough understanding of Ontario building codes and by-laws and extensive knowledge of materials, methods and machineries involved in commercial and residential construction.

- Strong technical and administrative skills in supporting both designers and project managers in design development, specification and detailing, contract documents and bidding.

- Detail-oriented and innovative individual who has accomplished many assigned tasks/projects in a timely manner, even under pressure and with limited supervision.

- Experienced in preparing and releasing engineering change notices.

- Strong interpersonal, analytical and problem solving skills; capable of intense concentration.

- Skilled in computer applications: AutoCAD 2004, Windows XP and MS Office Suite.

PROFESSIONAL EXPERIENCE

SELECTED ACHIEVEMENTS

- Successfully negotiated 3 contracts valued at **$250,000** within **8 months** after joining firm.

- Developed and prepared engineering drawings, plans, and elevations from sketches for more than **100** projects (villas, commercial buildings and a warehouse).

- Prepared tender documents for **20** projects including special and general specifications. Company secured contracts for **15** of those projects. Estimated value: **$106 million**.

- Assisted senior drafters with verification, technical accuracy and quality of drawings to enable site engineers to complete projects on time and within budget guidelines.

Architectural Draftsperson. This candidate inserts key phrases defining possible job titles in both the header and the profile. When an employer searches a database for any of these job titles this résumé will come up: "AutoCAD Drafting Technologist," "Architectural Draftsperson," "AutoCAD Draftsperson," "Architectural Technician."

CAREER PROGRESSION

Architectural Draftsperson
- Sentinel Consulting Engineers Ltd., Toronto   1998–Present

Trainee Draftsperson (Summer Internships)
- Sentinel Consulting Engineers Ltd., Toronto   1995–1998

Engineering/Administrative Assistant
- ROCME Technical Services, Mississauga   1992–1994

EDUCATION & MEMBERSHIP

Architectural Technology Certificate
- Canadian Institute of Technology, Brampton   1994–1997

AutoCAD Certificate
- Canadian Institute of Technology, Brampton   2004

Computer and Internet Applications Certificate   2002
- BDI College, Windsor

Member, Association of Architectural Technologists

PAULINE COULSON, BA
111 First Street SW, Edmonton, Alberta T1T 1T1

Phone: 780.555.1234	E mail: pc@CareerProCanada.ca	Cell: 780.555.0123

BEAUTY PRODUCTS SALES PROFESSIONAL

Ambitious, charismatic, challenge and results-driven sales professional with an exemplary record of moving a territory into profit. Confident, articulate, tactful and diplomatic negotiator. Impressive closer capable of working with person of all levels, cultures and backgrounds. Customer focused; listens to clients' needs and drives the competitive advantage. Patiently and methodically sources and secures new business opportunities in a defined environment, steers the path to success.
Core expertise includes:

- Sales
- Branding Products & Sales
- Product Management
- Marketing

- Business Development
- Business to Business (B2B)
- Product Launch
- Category Management

PROFESSIONAL EXPERIENCE

Dermskin Care Canada Inc., Edmonton, Alberta   2003 – present
REGIONAL DEVELOPMENT MANAGER
- Recruited by the Toronto-based exclusive hair care manufacturer to develop the underperforming Alberta, Saskatchewan and Manitoba territory.
- Researched potential opportunities within a limited market, prepared a business plan and established relationships with salons to secure their business, resulting in the signing of 17 additional contracts and doubling the client base in Alberta with an average initial sale of $5,000 per account.
- Accredited for an impressive 25% to 50% growth in existing accounts within one year.
- Provided 39% growth in territory business YTD October 31, 2004 versus same period in 2003.
- Facilitated interactive product training with hair technicians, aestheticians and business owners with the intention of optimizing revenue generated per salon customer.
- Worked in partnership with salon management to develop and implement a strategic business plan and loyalty incentive program customized for each location.
- Acknowledged for providing outstanding support and guidance to accounts in sales, business development and product enhancements, achieved through advertising, public relations and in-house events.
- Boosted revenue in one account by 85%, achieved through hands-on customer-focused training.
- Play a key role in tabulating and customizing special programs based on points for incentives to entice sales.

L'Oreal Professional – L'Oreal Canada   1997 – 2002
Held the following four progressively responsible positions:
KEY ACCOUNT MANAGER, Toronto, ON   2002
- Moved to reposition the products by sourcing and securing an additional 25 distributorships to expand the products' reach and minimize administrative costs.
- Instrumental in elevating the product knowledge at the distributor representative level by providing interactive coaching and sales training strategies.
- Penetrated the Ontario region, garnering 125 new permanent hair colour accounts obtained through aggressive research and cold calling, providing a 32% increase in sales.
- Consistently outperformed company-mandated sales quotas.
- Prepared and delivered special sales training sessions for hair stylists on how to optimize hair colour product sales.
- Captured a London salon from the competition which generated $65,000 in year one.

Beauty Product Sales Manager. Clear branding in the headline and throughout this résumé easily target sales management positions within the beauty products industry.

L'Oreal Professional...continued

BUSINESS DEVELOPMENT MANAGER, Calgary, AB   2001 – 2002

- Seconded to Calgary to realign underperforming business operations at the distributorship level, performed a business analysis and prepared and executed a viable plan to turn the territory around resulting in an unprecedented 38% per quarter average growth.
- Coached and trained distributorships to actively target new accounts and develop partnerships with potential clients through business plans.
- Assigned 12 account prospects, securing 6, which generated in excess of $2,000 per opening with a potential for $45,000.
- Conceived and organized a PR event and press breakfast, recruited L'Oreal make-up artist to use products resulting in significant print media coverage.
- Accredited for boosting the products carried per account from 2.5 to 4 brands per client.

PRODUCT MANAGER, Toronto, ON   2000 – 2001

- Launched the innovative demi-permanent colour line cream in a competitive business segment, positioned the product to gain significant interest in the grey hair market.
- Controlled the cross-promotion of other products working in tandem with the demi-permanent colour cream.
- Created and delivered marketing, advertising, packaging, forecast, distribution and competitive analysis strategies for all brands.

KEY ACCOUNT REPRESENTATIVE, Toronto, ON   1997 – 1999

- Parachuted into the vacant downtown Toronto territory experiencing significant image and client service problems. Worked with existing and potential clients to appease them and amicably address concerns, resulting in an elevation in sales from -35% to +39% in 15 months.

Canadian Cosmetics Magazine, Toronto, Ontario   1995 - 1997

MANAGING EDITOR/ADVERTISING SALES

- Recognized for outstanding work and the ability to perform; promoted from **Assistant Editor** to **Managing Editor** within a few weeks.
- Accredited for conceiving and initiating unique strategies to halt a declining subscription base, subsequently resulting in a significant increase in readership and attracting new advertisers allowing the publisher to increase the size of the bi-monthly magazine from 32 to 64 pages.
- Scripted feature articles and news stories, edited contributors' articles and played a role in coordinating the magazine production.

Holt Renfrew, Toronto, Ontario   1994 – 1996

SALES ASSOCIATE

- Interacted with wealthy clientele purchasing footwear; developed a reputation for exemplary customer service.

Toronto Life, Toronto, Ontario   1991 – 1994

SALES REPRESENTATIVE/PRODUCTION COORDINATOR

- Played a significant role in elevating sales by 34% for the prestigious society magazine.

EDUCATION

University of Toronto, Toronto, Ontario   1990

BACHELOR OF ARTS

Major-Mass Communications, **Minor**-Advertising, Public Relations & Journalism

Ryerson Polytechnic University, Toronto, Ontario   1995

CERTIFICATE - MAGAZINE JOURNALISM

GEORGIA STAPLETON
111 Wellington Street, Hampton, NS B1B 1B1
902.555.1234 (H) gstapleton@careerprocanada.ca 902.555.0123 (C)

SALES MANAGEMENT / BUSINESS DEVELOPMENT

Organizational /Team Leadership   *Building Strategic Networks*
Market Positioning & Territory Development   *Sound Time Management*
Customer-focused Service   *Negotiating /Closing Skills*

"developing sales teams and increasing market share"

PROFESSIONAL EXPERIENCE

FELICITY MARKETING, INC. Hampton, NS

Sales Manager   2001– Present

Implemented company goals and objectives through maximizing sales potential of a skilled and motivated staff, surpassing monthly revenue targets. Increased market penetration, identified and secured new corporate accounts, and introduced innovative products and support services.

- hired and trained additional sales staff, cost effectively increasing sales from $336,000 to $921,000 annually
- coordinated new promotional methods, accelerating market infiltration by 23%
- earned President's Management Award, National Division, 2003

FURNITURE TEXTURES, INC. Hampton, NS

Sales Account Executive   1998 – 2001

Optimized marketing strategies highlighting company profile, products and services. Developed proactive relationship with clients, and creatively initiated solutions to meet customer needs. Established and maintained key accounts, significantly increasing sales and marketing penetration within short time frame.

- multiplied customer base from 50 to 175 accounts within three-year period
- achieved closing ratio at 150% higher than industry average
- increased sales from $68,000 to $156,000 annually

EDUCATION / PROFESSIONAL DEVELOPMENT

Bachelor of Business Administration, Marketing Major
Ontario State University, Halifax, NS 1998

Vice-President, Chamber of Commerce
Hampton, NS 2001

Computer Applications
Torgate Technical College, Halifax, NS 2000

Business Development Manager. This succinct résumé clearly delivers the *Value Proposition* developing sales teams and increasing market share" in the headline and in concise accomplishment statements.

Mr. Kevin Davidson

Westwood Estate, Toronto, ON M1M 1M1 ❖ Tel: 416.555.1234 ❖ kevindavidson@careerprocanada.ca

Household Manager ❖ Professional Butler

Fifteen years of experience in organizing every facet of running a large-scale household. Effectively oversee entertainment and special events, manage finances and yearly budgets, hire and fire staff, supervise buildings and grounds maintenance, develop and implement programs, policies and procedures, as well as provide vision and long-range plans.

Excellent references are available that attest to friendly personality, reliability, and above all, to professional and caring attitude in fulfilling duties.

Experience

01/91 – Present **The Tomlinson-Parker Family**, Westwood Estate, Toronto

04/98 – Present **Household Manager & Head Butler**

- Report directly to Sir William Tomlinson-Parker.
- Manage 12 household staff (housekeeper, cleaning staff, valet, and kitchen staff), as well as contractors, suppliers, and other service providers.
- Accountable for budget of $500,000 and keeping household accounts.
- Recently organized upgrade of security systems and massive renovations to outbuildings and gardens.
- Orchestrate fine eating experiences, champagne receptions, large outdoor parties and other functions.
- Originally hired as the Assistant Butler. Subsequently promoted three times to positions of increasing challenge and responsibility.

Education

1990 **Professional Butler & Household Administrator Diploma**
London's International School for Butlers and Administrators
Oxford Street, London, England

1988 **Diploma in Tourism Management**
Islington Community College, Toronto

Butler. With only one employer in his career, this professional takes advantage of a one-page format. He adds prestige by incorporating an elegant "Edwardian Script" font and name-dropping his famous employer.

SOPHIA LIGHT

1 Main Road
Village, Ontario N1N 1N1

Res: 519.555.1234
Email: slight@careerprocanada.ca

BUYER / PURCHASER
With A Medical Industry Focus

Client-focused entry-level purchasing specialist motivated to serve in a healthcare setting. Advanced ability to research and investigate suppliers, negotiating favourable agreements and contracts. Adept at identifying and resolving inefficient procedures and resource allotment. Establishes plans, goals, and processes assuring strategies are competitive, effective and protective of long-term success. Consistently demonstrates advanced organizational, administrative file maintenance, and time management skills. Values team-based environments. Accepts role as assigned and strives for excellent results.

Strengths Include:

- Vendor Sourcing
- Procurement Strategies
- Warehouse Operations
- Customer Relations

- Administrative Detailing
- Inventory Planning
- Regulatory Compliance
- Price Negotiations

- Process Optimization
- Distribution Management
- Team Building
- Materials Management

QUALIFICATIONS IN ACTION

NURSE'S AIDE   2002 - Present
Good People Nursing Home, Village, Ontario
Retained to provide daily living care for elderly and physically challenged residents in this 70-bed accredited facility.

- One of two professionals tasked to deliver care for 35 assigned patients.
- Provided resident-centred care in cooperation with multi-disciplinary team.
- Maintained a positive and caring disposition, regardless of workload or time constraints.
- Cited for being…*"conscientious about work responsibilities."*

SUPPLY TECHNICIAN   1989 - 2001
Canadian Forces Bases Edmonton and Trenton - Department of National Defence
Managed multiple inventory processes in adherence to the stringent DND policies and procedures. Received rigorous supply trades training. Scope of responsibilities were diverse, including receipts issues, repair and disposal, customer service, sourcing, procurement, stocktaking and supply repair parts. Trusted with "confidential" security status.

- Tenacious nature and dedicated work ethic improving operational efficiency by revamping a multitude of administrative / record keeping systems, and backlogged high-end recalls.
- Expedited the receipt, handling and preparation of items for shipment.
- Drafted customer invoices, shipping documentation. Followed through with tracking all accounting and financial records.

Continued ⇨

Buyer. To enable this individual to transition back to a buyer's role after a short period as a nurse's aide, this document reflects her most marketable attributes in the power statement. Under the "Qualifications in Action," she dedicates the most space to the supply technician (buyer) role to make it stand out.

SOPHIA LIGHT

QUALIFICATIONS IN ACTION Continued...

- Project managed United Nations supply coordination functions for an international Peace Keeping Force in Golan Heights, Israel. Awarded with UN Peace Keeping medal.
- Recognized for displaying versatility towards constant situational changes and applying sound judgment while executing assigned duties.

COMPUTER SKILLS

Word/ Outlook/ Access/ Excel/ SAP/ DND Supply Management Software/ Internet Research

EDUCATION & SIGNIFICANT TRAINING

- ✔ Apprentice and Journeyman Supply Technician
- ✔ Practical Nurse Program (Completed 15 course components) – Norquest College
- ✔ Understanding & Managing the Challenges of Dementia – Seneca College

✔ Warehouse Safety	✔ Back Care
✔ Hazmat	✔ First Aid / CPR
✔ WHMIS	✔ Racism Prevention
✔ Fire Safety	✔ Diversity / Harassment

CERTIFIED TO OPERATE

Forklift up to 10 tonne/ Extended Boom/ Rough Terrain Forklift/ Military Pattern Vehicle

"Sophia is an extremely intelligent individual who eagerly responds to direction with unconditional loyalty and dedication to her job... She ensured all tasks were completed in a conscientious, competent manner and was always willing to assist coworkers and customers with professionalism and courtesy."
- performance appraisal comments.

ANDREW P. PATTEN

1111 Greenwood Ave, Angus, Ontario ▪ L1L 1L1

(Work) 705.555.1234 ext 2000 ▪ (Home) 705.555.2345 ▪ (Email) ap@CareerProCanada.ca

COMPUTER CRIME SPECIALIST
With F.B.I., O.P.P. & Military Training

Respected and focused policing professional motivated to contribute to investigative techniques for search and seizure of illegal computer data. Expert at handling multiple, technologically intricate and time critical tasks. Follow through with qualified recommendations and administrative detailing. Clear and concise communicator and instructor, interfacing easily with others from all levels and backgrounds. Speaks Mandarin. Especially capable of conveying complex technical terms and software applications equally well with experts and neophytes. Trusted with "Top Secret" clearance. Motivated and ready to share expertise. **Core Competencies Include:**

▪ Cyber Crime & Intelligence	▪ Analysis & Problem Solving	▪ Systems Security
▪ IT Forensics	▪ Investigations & Interviews	▪ 24-7 Data Recovery
▪ Confidentiality Assurance	▪ Research & Reporting	▪ Community Relations
▪ Presentations & Training	▪ Sound Decision Making	▪ Legislative Knowledge

TECHNOLOGY

Software Applications: EnCase FTK, Access Data, ILook Investigator, WebCT Administrator and Design e-learning systems, Public Key Infrastructure system, Microsoft Office, (Word, Outlook, PowerPoint, Excel Level 3, Access Level 3), Photoshop and Internet Research.

Operating Systems: Windows 95/98/2000/XP/NT4 Workstation, DOS and Novell.

WEB: HTML Coding Language, FrontPage and Dreamweaver.

Networking Operating Systems: Windows NT4 Server, Windows 2000 Server/Advanced Server, Banyan Vines and Open VMS.

Networking Topologies: LAN/MAN/WAN, TCP/IP, DNS, WINS, DHCP and SNMP.

CAREER PATH – Department of National Defence

CHIEF INSTRUCTOR for CRIMINAL COMPUTER INVESTIGATIONS and SECURITY   2002 - Present

Canadian Forces Base Newton

Solid industry expertise serves to instruct 3 courses, including Officer Training. Trusted to execute all aspects of Computer Forensics, Physical Security, IT Security, and Military Police Criminal Investigator courses. Advise and support 3 subordinate instructors for program delivery.

- One of 2 individuals selected, Forces-wide, to participate in the *International Criminal Investigative Best Practices Symposium* in alliance with the Ottawa Carleton Police.
- Refined writing skills draft Standard Operating Procedures, subordinate performance appraisals, and generate all pertinent reporting for internal and external use.
- Since 2003, solely accountable for senior level candidate training.
- Strategized to expand the functionality of instructional format and course resources. Used Web CT to develop complete Physical and IS Security online training. Well received by DND: currently rolling out programs system-wide.
- Appointed by Commandant to represent the Police Academy and Military Police Branch interests of the DND Distance Learning Network steering committee. Subject matter expert, contributing to the development of distance and online training.

Continued ⇨

Computer Crime Specialist. This professional showcases his military expertise in criminal computer investigations through key phrases and a detailed technology section. To detail his extensive education, he invites the reader to review a separate addendum.

ANDREW P. PATTEN

CAREER PATH – DND Continued...

COURSE MANAGER & INSTRUCTOR / INFORMATION SYSTEMS SECURITY   1998 - 2002
SUPERVISOR / MP CRIMINAL INVESTIGATOR
Canadian Forces Base Newton
Coordinated and conducted training for Military Police recruits. Accountable for program delivery, supervising other instructors and assuming duties of Warrant Officer during times of absence. Further, as the sole qualified professional on Base, relied upon to deliver the advanced, 6-month Qualification Level 5 and 6 courses.

- Researched and rewrote entire curriculum, lesson plans and exams, ensuring adherence to DND guidelines and subject matter depth.
- Exceptional work performance rewarded with promotion to sergeant's rank.

MILITARY SECURITY GUARD   1998
Canadian Embassy in Beijing, and all Asia
Led physical security measures while maintaining Canada/ China partner-focused relations.

- Upon initial assignment, recognized shortfalls of security pass methods required to meet the threat of operating in a hostile intelligence environment. Authorized with a $10 000 spend to project manage the design and implementation of a better structure. The former, antiquated Polaroid photo glued to a card was completely replaced. Employed sophisticated revamping methodologies. Purchased software and created Access database. Processed new cards for each well-screened candidate. Improvements included: digital photographs, fingerprinting, designated security clearance, colour coding and holographic imaging, all embedded onto a plastic card.
- Spearheaded efforts to revitalize morale while channelling money to local charities. Created a 5 star fundraising ball.

MILITARY POLICE OFFICER / COMBAT ENGINEER   1984 – 1990
CF Bases Winnipeg, Chilliwack and Vancouver
Requested to team with 6 other officers to provide 24-7 physical security for the Canadian Ambassador to Haiti. Accountable for the protection of the Ambassador, staff, residence and grounds during this period of military coup.

- Granted *Commissioner for Oaths* status in Manitoba.

SPECIALIZED EDUCATION (See attached addendum)

PROFESSIONAL AFFILIATIONS

High Technology Crime Investigation Association (HTCIA)   2001 - Present
Yellow Kings International Law Enforcement Motorcycle Club, Inc   2000 - Present

SIGNIFICANT RECOGNITION

Canadian Forces Decoration – Cited for 12 years Good Conduct while serving Canada.
Letter of Appreciation – Noted for providing leadership during Armed Forces Day Weekend.
Bravo Zulu – Received for launching and organizing Unit's morale boosting social activities.
Reference Letter – Personally prepared by Canada's Ambassador to Beijing.
125th Anniversary Medal – Awarded for consistent and exceptional community service.

KATE BELLERA, BEng.

1-11 Hopewell Circle
Brampton, Ontario • L1L 1L1
(905) 555-0123 • kbellera@careerprocanada.ca

ADMINISTRATION AND CUSTOMER SERVICE PROVIDER

Responsible, focused and highly adaptable professional with broad-based experience. Well regarded team player; proven record of excellent work performance and reliability both in groups and independently. Quality detail, thoroughness, and precision consistently evident in report generation, data management, and administrative procedures. Tactful response and dedicated follow-through handling client needs efficiently and within tight timelines.

Core strengths include:

- Customer Service
- Technical Aptitude
- Written & Oral Communication
- Creative Solutions

- Detail Orientation
- Team Building
- Process Improvement
- Procedure Documentation

WORK HISTORY

CUSTOMER SERVICE PROVIDER, AUTO DETAILER   2003 - 2006
Car Interiors By Design
Burlington, Ontario

Delivered top-notch service standards in this busy automotive detailing business. Motivated team members, accurately coordinated appointments and work schedules, and frequently assumed all functions of a professional detailer.

- Quoted on average 20 complex service packages per day for specialized needs. Offered suggestions and recommendations, which were consistently well received.
- Assumed additional responsibility covering reception and invoicing. Appreciated by peers, owners, clientele, and vendors for genuine care and clear communications.
- Provided high quality detailing and top-of-the-line finished product with minimal training, often ahead of schedule.
- Devised a diluted formulation of cleaners to ensure safe yet effective application for the unique requirements of antique automobiles.

ASSISTANT SUPERVISOR, NETWORK SYSTEM ADMINISTRATOR   1999 - 2002
Engineering Unlimited
Scarborough, Ontario

Promoted quickly from administrative role to supervisor in this Canadian company which supplies independent inspection and testing operations for the construction industry. Led and trained team members in laboratory procedures. Provided health and safety instruction according to standards. Noted for patience and care in ensuring staff thoroughly understood all processes.

- Performed office administration including reception, data entry, technical report writing, and daily communications with clients.
- Created a Laboratory Quality Manual to meet ISO 9002 standards. Structured a detailed review of office and laboratory procedures from the quotation stage to the delivery of service and test results to those retaining services.
- Updated and maintained the company's Windows operating and networking system as well as several company databases.
- Enriched data entry forms for laboratory test results. Provided clear and logical flow particularly essential and appreciated by staff with English as second language.

Continued ☞

Customer Service Professional. This résumé maintains a businesslike look and feel, which is essential for a professional with an administrative slant.

KATE BELLERA, BEng.

DOCUMENTATION AND DATA ENTRY PROVIDER   *1998*
All Options Electric Company
Toronto, Ontario

Chosen from among numerous university students for part-time role in the Toronto plant of this international manufacturer of welding machines and related consumables. Applauded for rapid requirements comprehension, data entry accuracy, and formatting enhancements.

- ♦ Organized a company database using Microsoft Access. Provided documentation and maintenance instructions for ongoing application.
- ♦ Consistently met ISO 9002 standards by liaising with Manufacturing, Quality Assurance, and Purchasing Departments in the procurement of information.
- ♦ Performed precise data entry, filing and formal formatting tasks for Quality Assurance and Engineering Departments.

TECHNICAL SKILLS

MS Word, Excel, PowerPoint, Access, Explorer, Digital Image Pro 10, Email, and Internet Searching; and Computer Assisted Processing for Laboratory Results

Proficient in server tools including local and wide area networks.

EDUCATION

Administrative Assistant Program   **2003**
Skills Development Centre
Burlington, Ontario

Program achievements:

- ♦ Enhanced skills, completed career assessments and interviewed contacts in the administrative assistant field.
- ♦ Performed notable behavioural style interviewing process and presented results to the group for discussion and evaluation.
- ♦ Completed insightful career and personality assessments including Myers-Briggs, SkillScan, Self-Employment Profile, and True Colors.
- ♦ Gathered labour market information through diligent research, from topics addressed by guest speakers, and through liaison with fellow students.

BACHELOR OF ENGINEERING   **1999**
Ryerson Polytechnic University
Toronto, Ontario

♦ Dedication ♦ Determination ♦ Dependability ♦

Elise Sutton

1111 Ledge Street ▪ Nepean, ON K1K 1K1 ▪ 613.555.1234

DENTAL RECEPTIONIST

A successful dental professional with over 15 years' experience working with general dental surgeons, orthodontists, periodontists, and oral surgeons. An energetic, motivated, and independent individual with a proven record for increasing practice productivity; able to work as part of a team, and to lead and motivate co-workers; multi-task oriented, capable of prioritizing, delegating, and staying focused on providing superior patient care.

Industry Software
Abel ▪ Dentrix ▪ Oasis

SKILLS & ACCOMPLISHMENTS

❖ Excelled as a Treatment and Recall Coordinator—created and maintained contact lists. Efficient patient scheduling led to **increased productivity**.

❖ Prepared and forwarded patients' pre-treatment plans to insurance company; kept abreast of approval status by communicating regularly with insurance company; contacted patients for follow-up treatment and booked outstanding work.

❖ Courteous and pleasant professional demeanour, making patients of all ages feel welcomed – from young children's first visit to the elderly.

❖ Strong **communicator** and **educator**; adept at explaining required procedures to patients in simple, understandable language.

❖ Implemented procedures which **lowered the rate of short notice cancellations**—mailing reminders one month before the appointment, calling patients a few days earlier to remind them of upcoming appointment, and utilizing patients available for short notice cancellations.

❖ Experienced in **establishing and promoting** a new practice—distributed referral pads to bigger offices, put business cards in daycares, talk to schools, and send out new patient packages to new residents of the community, welcoming them to our office.

❖ Contributed in the implementation of a payment plan enabling us to **significantly reduce** the office AR; processed post-dated cheques, extensive treatments charges, insurance plan coverage, regular treatment payments.

❖ Adaptable to change, which includes a willingness to pursue continuous education; capable of working well under pressure; resourceful when dealing with difficult situations.

PROFESSIONAL HISTORY

Dental Receptionist ▪ Dr. Steven Johnson, Mayfair Corner Dental Care, Mayfair, VT   2003 - 2005
Dental Receptionist ▪ Western Dental Centre, Ottawa, ON   1999 - 2001
Dental Receptionist/Assistant ▪ Meriwood Dental Centre, Ottawa, ON   1992 - 1998
Dental Receptionist ▪ Haven Mills Dental Centre, Nepean, ON   1989 - 1992
Dental Assistant ▪ Dr. George Richmond, Richmond Dental Centre, Nepean, ON   1988 - 1989
Dental Receptionist ▪ St-John Dental Centre, Ottawa, ON   1986 - 1988

EDUCATION

Certificate Examination ▪ Ontario Dental Nurses and Assistants Association, 1987
Dental Office and Chairside Assisting Diploma ▪ Career Canada College, 1986
H.A.R.P. ▪ Commission-approved course in Dental Radiography, 1986

Dental Receptionist. To minimize this individual's out of country experience and a small gap in employment, the résumé focuses on her skills and accomplishments, rather than highlighting her employment history.

Steve Champion

schampion@careerprocanada.ca
123 Main Drive ▪ Ottawa, ON K1K 1K1 ▪ 613.555.1234

ELECTRICAL PROJECT COORDINATOR

Supervisor ▪ Trouble-shooter ▪ Facilitator ▪ Safety Rep

Licensed Commercial Electrician with significant background in all aspects of electrical design, installation, and maintenance. Skilled journeyman, known for being well organized, successful in executing multiple tasks and in **managing/mentoring** apprentices on several large-scale projects. General RCMP security clearance. Strengths include:

- Expert trouble-shooter, able to identify problem areas and devise/implement cost saving solutions.
- Facilitated information flow between various tradesmen, architects, engineers, and general contractor to ensure smooth completion of projects.
- Enforced safety concerns—hazardous working conditions or unsafe equipment—as Safety Rep, between the workers, general contractor, and the Ministry of Labour.

PROFESSIONAL EXPERIENCE

COMMERCIAL ELECTRICIAN ▪ XYZ Electric, Ottawa, Ontario   2004 - Present
Coordinate, delegate, supervise apprentices' daily activities, ensuring work adheres to Electrical Code, and mentoring/teaching when facing new challenges. Analyze architectural/engineering blueprints and develop "material take-off" required for the projects. Lead with enthusiasm, positive outlook, and exemplary work ethics.

Significant Project: Home Depot (Barrhaven)

- Installed Class A Simplex fire alarm system: devised a practical solution for the system to release the outside magnetic locks; implemented a superior approach of monitoring the emergency generator. **Results**: labour/cost savings.

COMMERCIAL ELECTRICIAN ▪ PowerTech Electric, Ottawa, Ontario   2000 - 2004
Head Safety Rep for 170 tradesmen during the Cognos Headquarters project. Taught weekly safety classes to subordinates. Supervised daily activities of apprentices.

Significant Projects: Cognos Headquarters ▪ Ottawa International Airport ▪ Nortel Skyline ▪ CMPA
                                      All Saints High School ▪ New National Defence Building ▪ MBNA Headquarters
                                      240 Sparks Street

- Electrical and control equipment expertise include: DC power plants for OC192 fibre optic switches, Class A and Class B fire alarm systems, low voltage building automation, pumps, motors, emergency generators, and transfer switches.
- Skilled in several types of testing and metering equipment/troubleshooting techniques, and the installation of all varieties of cable tray.

COMMERCIAL ELECTRICIAN ▪ Black's Electric, Ottawa, Ontario   1998 - 2000
Built foundation of expertise in the installation, maintenance, and troubleshooting of all types of electrical and control systems.

Significant Projects: War Memorial Restoration ▪ JDS Fitel Headquarters ▪ Famous Players Theatre

CERTIFICATION

Certificate of Qualification: Electrician (Construction and Maintenance) Red Seal, May 2004
WHMIS Certification ▪ Fall Protection Certification ▪ Quebec Safety Certification ▪ OCA Safety Certification

EDUCATION

Algonquin College of Applied Arts and Technology, Ottawa, Ontario, 2004
ELECTRICIAN CONSTRUCTION MAINTENANCE ▪ Graduated with Honours

---

Electrical Project Coordinator. The interesting design of headers effectively separates sections on this one-page résumé. To transition this electrician into a management role, the headline and keywords focus on project leadership.

KRYSTYN SMITH

555 Main Street
Bell River, NWT X1X 1X1
(867) 555-1234

EXECUTIVE ASSISTANT

PROFESSIONAL…DEDICATED…RESULTS-ORIENTED

PROFESSIONAL PROFILE

DEDICATED AND HIGHLY SKILLED PROFESSIONAL combining comprehensive executive administration and support skills with superior project management and planning expertise. Consistently recognized for ability to take initiative and complete tasks to highest standards. Forward thinker with the ability to effectively anticipate needs and avoid obstacles in the management of all high-level executive concerns. Highly organized with outstanding communications skills – able to represent office with highest degree of professionalism and support to all levels of internal and external contact. Particularly well suited to special project work. *Key strengths include:*

☑ Executive Office Management	☑ Executive Calendar / Scheduling	☑ Executive Correspondence
☑ Travel Planning & Itineraries	☑ Client Relations	☑ Special Projects
☑ Event Planning	☑ Records Management	☑ Minutes & Agendas
☑ Proposals & Reports	☑ Office Efficiency	☑ Supplier Negotiation

Computer proficiencies include:

☑ MS Word	☑ MS Excel	☑ MS Outlook
☑ MS PowerPoint	☑ Corel WordPerfect	☑ Lotus
☑ Windows 95/98/2000	☑ Internet Research	☑ Website Design

EXECUTIVE ADMINISTRATION & SUPPORT

EXECUTIVE ASSISTANT TO MAYOR, TOWN MANAGER, COUNCIL, AND COMMITTEES   2000 – Present
TOWN OF BELL RIVER, NWT
Provided primary administrative support for the Mayor's Office, Town Manager's Office, and supporting officials and executives. Scope of responsibilities encompassed full range of administrative, communications, and project management.

- Maintained executive calendars, scheduled appointments, and managed confidential correspondence, meetings, and records keeping.
- Prepared and maintained a wide variety of documentation, including council meeting reports and minutes, business correspondence, project proposals, and inter-office memoranda.
- Represented Mayor's office in communication with Territorial government officials, routinely liaising with offices of the Premier, Ministers, and Deputy Ministers.

Achievements and special projects include*:*

- ➢ Website Revitalization – enhanced online presence through complete redesign of town website. Worked closely with Webmaster in overall design and usability and coordinated full project life cycle through implementation.
- ➢ Smart Communities Project – key player on team submitting first of only two proposals throughout NWT. Coordinated with Town Manager and external IT representative on concept and proposal development.
- ➢ Union Negotiations – worked with Mayor, Town Manager, and Director of Finance on successful negotiation of renewed public services contract.

…2

Executive Assistant. The professional profile dedicates considerable space to the breadth of skills that this candidate offers. She positions herself with added value by drawing out her volunteer experience under the "Social Services Leadership" heading.

EXECUTIVE ASSISTANT TO THE VICE PRESIDENT AND CFO   1996 – 2000
NWT POWER CORPORATION, Bell River, NWT
Hired to coordinate and complete all executive administration and support functions for VP and CFO of territorial corporation providing power generation throughout the NWT.

- Maintained executive calendars, coordinated all travel arrangements, drafted correspondence, and scheduled all appointments, conference calls, and meetings.
- Managed operating budget for building and maintained telephone system.

  ➢ Initiated, coordinated, and implemented new records management system that dramatically improved records keeping and data management company-wide – coordinated with staff and external consultant on software selection and managed project through implementation.
  ➢ Coordinated upgrade of telephone systems throughout corporation – oversaw implementation and trained employees on system functions and operability.

SOCIAL SERVICES LEADERSHIP

CHAIRPERSON   1999 – 2002
BELL RIVER COMMUNITY HEALTH BOARD, Bell River, NWT
Appointed by Town Council to chair local health board overseeing smooth operation of all community health and social services. Oversaw 8-person Board of Directors and represented board interests in communication with Health Board CEO.

- Leveraged strong leadership and communication skills to ensure integrity of board operations.
- Coordinated with Health & Social Service Department in all matters of policy and strategic direction.

  ➢ Spearheaded acquisition and selection of Speech Pathologist for community.
  ➢ Additionally served as Board Trustee with NWT Health Care Association and Bell River Regional Health Board.

EXECUTIVE DIRECTOR   1997 – 1998
BELL RIVER WOMEN'S RESOURCE CENTRE, Bell River, NWT
Selected to revitalize all program operations for local women's shelter. Full strategic and operations accountability, including management of $500,000 budget. Hired, trained, and supervised 5 full-time and 13 casual employees.

- Improved existing policies and procedures through close coordination with the Board of Directors and enabled improved programs and support through sound financial planning and increased funding.
- Worked closely with Territorial and Federal government offices for all funding, contracts and proposals.

  ➢ Successfully negotiated $80,000 in additional funding for shelter activities and programs.
  ➢ Led development and implementation of well-received "Keep Kids in School" program for teens at risk – secured funding and coordinated program development and delivery with local schools.

Previous positions include:
PROGRAM COORDINATOR – 1994 – 1997
PROJECT MANAGER (Contract) – 1994

PROFESSIONAL DEVELOPMENT / EDUCATION

- Writing for Results
- Managing, Shaping, and Maximizing Your Role (Administrative Assistants)
- Effective Listening Skills
- Effective Communication skills
- Building Teamwork within Organizations
- Facilitator/Trainer (Boards/Communities That Get Results) – NWT Health Care Association
- B.S.W. (Social Work) – University of Manitoba, Winnipeg, Manitoba (ongoing)

Mickey Pramas

123 Augusta Gate ▪ *Pinehurst, Ontario L1L 1L1*
Home: (905) 555-4433 ▪ *Cell: (416) 555-2211*

FASHION INDUSTRY PROFESSIONAL
Stylist / Stylist Coordinator / Fashion Events Planning

Diesel ▪ **Guess** ▪ **Nike** ▪ **Parasuco** ▪ **Indian Motorcycle**

Talented, detail-oriented professional balancing exceptional fashion sense, a strong eye for visual style, sound fashion event planning, and project management skills. Outgoing and personable with strong communication, negotiation, and problem resolution skills. Strongly motivated to "get the job done" and exceed expectations.

- **Styling Expertise** – experience and skill working within a wide range of fashion styles, from urban casual (Diesel, Guess, Indian Motorcycle) to sportswear (Nike). Exceptional skills coordinating clothes, accessories, hair, and makeup.

- **Fashion Event Planning & Vision** – able to stage both simple and elaborate shows for any size of audience, fit the show and all particulars to available space, and develop all details to fit theme and tone. Experienced in both public and corporate fashion events.

- **Creativity & Vision** – creative outlook capable of styling the most eclectic apparel, staging innovative shows, and envisioning dynamic event themes to showcase products and generate audience excitement

- **Communication & Leadership** – skilled in communicating with all models, staff, catering, security, and volunteers to ensure all members of the event team are on track and fully engaged

- **Media & Event Details** – experienced coordinating media, food, music, floral, lighting, props, and other special needs to create a cohesive look and feel to all visuals.

- **Industry Knowledge** – additional expertise includes talent scouting, modelling, sales, and model training. Extensive industry contacts.

RELATED EXPERIENCE

Assistant Stylist Coordinator
TNT Entertainment, Toronto, Ontario ▪ *January '01 – Present*

Played key roles in the planning, styling, and staging of major events for a fashion consultancy coordinating fashion shows and special events throughout the Greater Toronto Area. Coordinated critical process and logistics details for major public and corporate events attended by 400-600 people. Major clients include **Nike**, **Diesel**, **Guess**, **Indian Motorcycle**, and **Parasuco Jeans**.

- Coordinate all clothes and accessories with available models to present products in the best possible light, taking into consideration the show theme and tone as well as the label's branding strategy.

- Organized upfront logistics to ensure all event details and processes are in place – communicate theme and details to models, dressers, makeup, and hair specialists.

- Oversee lighting, props, camera placement, and audience seating to ensure open sightlines and an attractive and professional presentation.

- Control backstage by coordinating sequencing and timing between models and themes.

Additional industry experience includes positions in model scouting and sales, modelling and model training (John Casablanca)

.../2

Fashion Stylist. This career-change résumé transitions the individual from a corporate environment into fashion. The stylish format suits the industry. Even with limited experience, page one is entirely focused on fashion. The profile exhibits areas of expertise and brand names.

CORPORATE EXPERIENCE

Major Accounts Service Representative
clearNET, Toronto, Ontario ▪ December '99 – March '01

Personally selected by VP Sales and Marketing to provide elite-level account service for major corporate clients and Fortune 500 companies. Responsible for managing 12 major corporate accounts, resolving all client issues, ensuring account retention, and upselling on new service offerings. Client accounts include **Xerox**, **Coca-Cola**, **Dynamex**, **Loomis**, **Netricom**, **University of Toronto**, and **Durham Regional Police**.

Mike Commercial Senior Accounts Representative
clearNET, Toronto, Ontario ▪ July '97 – December '99

Provided single point of contact in the resolution of billing, credit, and collection issues for a client portfolio of up to 3000 accounts (dealer, consumer, and commercial). Worked effectively with coordinating areas, including Client Care, Dealer Care, Credit, and Activation, to resolve common issues.

Process Coordinator
clearNET, Toronto, Ontario ▪ March '96 – June '97

Finalized financial month-end for 6 branches – supervised client care representatives to ensure proper procedures and processes were followed, reconciled accounts to keep accurate financial records, and liaised with team leaders to ensure consistently high quality of client care.

COMPUTER SKILLS

- Proficient in all MS Office applications, including **Word**, **Excel**, **Outlook**, and Explorer – particularly strong developing and presenting **PowerPoint** presentations
- Additional experience using Corel WordPerfect, AccPac, and specialty applications including Boss 1-2, BSCS, Clarity, AFP Viewer, DSS, and BOA

EDUCATION

Broadcasting – Radio & Television, *Seneca College*   1992
Business Management, *Ryerson University*   Ongoing

REFERENCES

Outstanding professional and personal references can be provided upon request.

JOANNE RADFORD MBA, CFA

111 Main Street
Vancouver, BC V1V 1V1

jradford@careerprocanada.ca

H: 604.555.1234
B: 604.555.6789

SENIOR FINANCE & INVESTMENT SPECIALIST
Portfolio Management • Treasury & Reserve Management • Risk Management

International Capital Markets / Foreign Exchange / Fixed Income / Large & Multi-Asset Class Portfolios
Monetary Policy Development / Compliance & Reporting / Relationship Management / Staff Leadership

Accomplished professional with over 15 years' senior finance and investment experience. Rich mix of technical and industry knowledge — global market perspective, skilled in monetary policy development at the highest levels, and experienced in developing sound short- and long-term investment strategies. Recognized as a motivating leader and trusted advisor with exceptional communication, relationship building, and institutional liaising skills. Thorough and precise with demonstrated analytical skills synthesizing large amounts of complex data into meaningful forecasts and reports. Published author (*Bank of Canada Review*). Member of the Vancouver Association of Business Economists. Fluent English and French.

CAREER EXPERIENCE

ABC INVESTMENTS, Vancouver, BC

Fixed Income Portfolio Strategist – ABC Dominion Securities   2004 – 2006

Senior financial strategist providing key advisory services on global financial markets to over 1500 ABC Investment Advisors. Supported all aspects of over $40 billion in fixed income assets under management.

- Provided consultative expertise to Advisors on portfolio structure, composition, sector weightings, trade timing, and switch recommendations — personally designed and built more complex portfolios (up to $500 million) for individual clients, corporations, and foundations.
- Analyzed US and global economic data and distilled/extracted investment dealer strategies on interest rates, sector weights, and credits — prepared and distributed daily, weekly, quarterly, and annual reports in both English and French
- Established excellent relationships with Investment Advisors throughout Quebec — called upon to manage communications and PR surrounding Montréal office closing and ensured a seamless conversion.

REGIONAL MUNICIPALITY OF NANAIMO, Nanaimo, BC

Manager, Treasury & Reserves   2000 – 2003

Recruited into this new leadership position overseeing all aspects of the Region's $750 million treasury. As first incumbent in position, challenged to build structure around the function and raise the return on the Region's reserves. Additional accountabilities include all cash management, banking arrangements, and the management and development of 3 full-time staff. Earned highest internal audit results (Dec. 2000).

- Consistently outperformed the Region's fixed-income benchmark, raising the rate of return an average of 25 basis points.
- Developed a much-needed framework and reporting mechanism to provide senior management with timely information on the Region's reserves and long-term financial position.
- Oversaw and secured $28 million in financing to support the Lucida Waste Water Plant Project — established the process, completed all due diligence, and conferred with lawyers and banking officials.
- Recognized inequities and inflexibility in the BC Municipal Act regarding eligible investments and capital financing options — proposed and successfully lobbied amendments allowing for more flexibility in dealing with major capital projects, based upon Region's ability to absorb risk.
- Formalized the capital budgeting process, establishing a formal link between annual budgets and long-term capital budgeting.

Finance Portfolio Strategist. A "no-nonsense" résumé for a senior finance and investment expert outlines her accomplishments in a neat, quantifiable manner.

BANK OF CANADA, Vancouver, BC

Senior Analyst – Financial Markets & Economic Liaison (Vancouver)   1997 – 2000

High-profile position liaising directly with large domestic and international institutional investors on critical financial market issues. Working on behalf of the Bank of Canada, discussed proposed changes on issues involving government debt programs, monetary policy, market transparency, etc.

- Established ongoing relationships with top corporate and institutional executives, garnered and synthesized feedback, and reported findings directly to Governing Council of the Bank of Canada – results positively impacted Canadian economic/monetary policy and regulatory/governance issues.

Senior Analyst – Foreign Exchange Operations (Victoria)   1992 – 1997

Resident FX specialist and key contributor driving the BOC's shift from an exchange rate focus to an interest rate and inflation focus. Completely redesigned Canada's foreign exchange intervention policy and created an operating framework to manage Canada's foreign exchange reserves.

Analyst – Canada Savings Bond Program	1991 – 1992
Analyst – Reserve Management	1990 – 1991
Analyst – Treasury Management	1989 – 1990
Analyst – Canada Savings Bond Program	1986 – 1989

In key analyst roles, led the development of alternative government retail debt instruments and developed both short-term and long-term debt strategies on the federal government's debt structure.

PUBLISHED ARTICLES

"Corporate Bonds in Canada" – *Bank of Canada Review*, Summer 1997
"Canadian Foreign Exchange and Derivatives" – *Bank of Canada Review*, Fall 1995

EDUCATION / PROFESSIONAL DEVELOPMENT

Chartered Financial Analyst (CFA)	1994
MBA – University of Toronto	1986
BA, Economics – Université Laval	1984

Financial Risk Management – Rotman School of Management	1998
Options & Futures Markets – Rotman School of Management	1997
Canadian Options & Futures	1986
Canadian Securities Course	1984

COMMUNITY LEADERSHIP

WEST COAST DAYCARE & CHILDREN'S FACILITES, Vancouver, BC

President	2003 – 2006
Treasurer	1998 – 2000; 2001 – 2003
Secretary	2000 – 2001

Elected board member for a 4-location full-time daycare facility generating over $1 million in revenue, employing 45 staff, and serving over 250 children. Directed the successful transition from founder-oriented to decentralized professional management, and strategized, coordinated, and directed resources and activities impacting the corporation's budgeting, policy making, procedures, operations, and reporting.

ROBERTA W. WHITE

555-555 Main Street
Vancouver, BC V1V 1V1
E-mail rw@careerprocanada.ca

Home (604) 555-1234
Cell (604) 555-2345
Fax (604) 555-3456

FINANCIAL SERVICES CONSULTANT

Resourceful professional with formal education and experience in general accounting and financial services. Demonstrated ability to prepare, analyze, report, and present financial data. Highly organized with excellent research and auditing skills working directly with clients to obtain information, assess data, and present results to stakeholders. Outstanding communication skills used to deal effectively with individuals at all levels. Trustworthy and discreet with the maturity to work well both independently and in a team environment. Decisive and objective with well-earned reputation for taking initiative to achieve corporate goals. Proficient in Microsoft Office Suite and a wide variety of accounting software. Willing to travel and/or relocate.

Relevant Skills:

▶ Accounts Receivable (A/R)	▶ Data Analysis & Reporting	▶ Financial Statements
▶ Accounts Payable (A/P)	▶ Database Management	▶ Journal Entries
▶ Workflow Planning	▶ Business Writing	▶ Tax Planning
▶ Management Support	▶ Proofreading & Editing	▶ Bank Reconciliation

Awarded a certificate in Financial Management from the British Columbia Institute of Technology with a Bachelor's in Technology and Accounting to be completed in 2007.

PROFESSIONAL EXPERIENCE

Howard Duke Chartered Accountants, Calgary, AB   **2003–Present**

Financial consulting service offering a wide variety of assistance to small businesses, including start-up, business plan development, business structure, and tax advice.

Consultant, Client Support Services

Responsible to assist the principal, Robert Orr and to support the firm's clients. Accountable to perform research, analyze contracts, develop and present reports, and respond to client inquiries. Responsibilities include managing incoming correspondence, proofreading final drafts, performing bank deposits, handling accounts receivables, and expense costing.

▶ Analyzed a potential $2 million client acquisition, identified pricing issues, and recommended against the sale, ultimately enabling the client to achieve $4 million revenue in the following year.

▶ Wrote a Private Placement Memorandum (PPM) and successfully raised $1 million in funding in 3 months for a client organization by working closely with the CEO to target potential contributors.

▶ Provided clients with informed responses to capital structure issues, effectively using current accounting principles to analyze data objectively.

Regent Financial Group, Vancouver, BC   **2003**

Financial services firm and investment house with over 600 employees and 5000 independent advisors across Canada with $4.6 billion total assets under administration.

Office Manager

Responsible to manage the sales office covering the Western Canada region. Accountable to respond to client, broker, and claimant inquiries. Administrative responsibilities include performing data entry of quote requests for medical, dental, and life insurance policies and managing office expenses.

▶ Revamped the insurance policy filing system consisting of 7000 client files and created an efficient data centre enabling files to be located immediately.

▶ Backed up 4 employees and performed job duties during their vacation leave, building an environment of teamwork and cooperation.

Financial Services Consultant. The reader will notice the bolded company names and job titles even at a glance. In this résumé, the names and titles support the headline "Financial Services Consultant," and therefore are prominent.

ROBERTA W. WHITE

PROFESSIONAL EXPERIENCE (CONTINUED)

Top Capital Management, New York, NY   **2000–2001**

New York based hedge fund asset management organization with 2 managing partners and a staff of 4 traders.

Analyst Internship

Reporting directly to a managing partner, responsible to research companies, analyze trading sheet data, and pick stocks that will produce strong returns.

▸ Contributed to an annual 35% return in 1999 by performing fundamental (top down and bottom up) and technical (historical trends and transition points) public company analysis.

FORMAL EDUCATION

British Columbia Institute of Technology

▸ Bachelor's in Technology and Accounting, expected completion 2007

▸ Certificate in Financial Management, Professional Accounting Option, completed 2005

▸ Relevant Courses: Cost Accounting, Quantitative Analysis, Financial Accounting, Finance, and Auditing

PROFESSIONAL DEVELOPMENT & CERTIFICATIONS

Actively committed to continuing education via certification, courses, and seminars:

▸ Canadian Securities Certificate (CSC), expected completion 2005

▸ Certified Management Accountant (CMA), currently enrolled in Fast Track Program with BCIT

COMPUTER SKILLS

Proficient in a variety of software applications including:

▸ Microsoft Office Suite (Word, Excel, and Access)

▸ Accounting Software (Simply Accounting, ACCPAC, and QuickBooks)

EXTRACURRICULAR ACTIVITIES

▸ Leisure activities include Current Events, Stock Market, and Future Trends in Finance.

Outstanding references available upon request

SOPHIA DAYRE, B.A., B.Ed.
40 Main Drive, Milton, Ontario • L1L 1L1
(Home) 905.555.1234 • (Email) sday@careerprocanada.ca

TEACHER

Highly respected, motivated and resourceful educator offering a commitment to enhancing the quality of education and the dignity of the profession. Champion for supporting all students, in particular the underserved and at-risk populations. Manage conflict, mediate dispute, and assist in reaching consensus. Meticulous regard for detail and accuracy. Strong follow-through skills. Highly articulate demonstrating excellent interpersonal skills across all levels including students, peers, administrators, and parents. Member in Good Standing: Ontario College of Teachers. Energized by new challenges. **Core competencies include:**

☑ Junior-Intermediate	☑ Co-curricular Enhancement
☑ Remediation & Modification	☑ Rubric Development
☑ Multi-cultural Awareness	☑ Confidentiality Assurance
☑ Special Education Part 1	☑ Expectation-based Tracking
☑ Assessment & Reporting	☑ Classroom & Student Management

CAREER PATH

GRADE 6 CORE TEACHER   1999 - Present
Bury Middle School, Toronto District School Board
Selected to serve in the junior division of this inner city, special needs school with 500 pupils. Assigned grade 6 Core, and grade 6 / 8 Drama studies. Serve on Literacy Curriculum and School Staffing committees. Prepare dynamic and interesting lessons and units, incorporating all pertinent Ontario Ministry of Education Curricula expectations. Express a personal commitment to life-long learning, while modelling the same attitude for the benefit of students.

- ❏ Utilize rubric-based assessment, and expectation-based tracking methodologies.
- ❏ Foster student appreciation and acceptance for multi-ethnic and cross-cultural idiosyncrasies. Strategically incorporate travel experiences from 13 countries and 4 continents into class dialogue. Recognize the value of having pertinent speakers. Invite select guests appropriate to address school's Native issues.
- ❏ Team with division peers to discuss student issues, grade events, effective resource allotment and for long term planning.
- ❏ Demonstrate commitment to maximizing student success by creating weekly *Homework Club,* in concert with maintaining an open door policy reinforcing *I'm here for you.*
- ❏ Contribute substantial amount of personal time for coaching basketball teams, and serving as Student Council Teacher Advisor. Enrich student experiences by co-creating and offering a Drama Club.
- ❏ Organize field trips and excursions with direct curriculum applicability (Toronto Zoo, Ontario Science Centre, Forest Valley Outdoor Education Centre, Kortright Centre).
- ❏ Reinforced optimal study skills and goal attainment as part of *Teacher Advisor Group.*

RESIDENCE DON   1996 - 1998
University of Waterloo, Ron Eydt Village, University of Waterloo
Managed time in concert with fulltime university studies to supervise residence students from all religions, cultures and socio-economic backgrounds. This position demanded significant leadership, motivational and organizational strengths, overseeing 50 first year young women. Accepted role for a second year, overseeing 50 first year co-ed students. Positive and approachable demeanour served to counsel others and mediate dispute during times of stress.

- ❏ Initiated and coordinated weekly educational and social programs for first year students.
- ❏ Chaired monthly floor meeting to discuss events, concerns and address queries.

Continued on Page 2 ⇨

Grade School Teacher. Note the final quote from the principal of the school that demonstrates the candidate's personal character in the closing of the document.

PROGRAM DIRECTOR 1996 -1997

Camp Chapleau, Old Brewery Mission, Montréal, Quebec

Retained to coordinate a flexible program of daily activities targeting needy, inner-city mothers and children. Charged with devising, scheduling and delivering fun and safe programs for three separate entities: the girls', boys' and main camps. Trusted to hire, supervise, evaluate, and schedule staff. Acted in a resource support capacity for counsellors. Spearheaded the drafting of camp's first staff training manual, and introduced a counsellor pre-camp training program.

- ❏ Reviewed needs of junior/ intermediate/ senior girls, and mothers. Strategized to offer esteem building and fun activities in an environment free from ridicule, poverty and physical or emotional risk.

EDUCATION & ONGOING PROFESSIONAL DEVELOPMENT

BACHELOR OF EDUCATION (Summa Cum Laude Graduate) *University of Ottawa* 1999

- ☑ Focused on ESL and Cultural Studies.
- ☑ Awarded *Support Staff Undergraduate Prize.* Cited for demonstrating a willingness to improve teaching practice over the practicum period.
- ☑ Pre-service placements...Toronto: grade 5, and Ottawa, grades 7 & 8. Program Director notes, *"Sophia has developed a superior array of teaching skills that gives her an unusual versatility in all subject areas…(with) personal qualities of openness, warmth and humane intelligence."*

BACHELOR OF ARTS *University of Waterloo* 1998

- ☑ Major: English Literature, Minor: Speech Communications.
- ☑ Earned *Presidents Circle Award* for Volunteerism.
- ☑ Drafted proposal and selected to speak at *Lean on Me* Residence Life Conference at York University during final year. Presented *A Little Cup O'Culture*, outlining the necessity for cultural awareness and creating an inclusive environment within residences.

See *Addendum* for ongoing professional development.

COMPUTER SKILLS: PC and Mac platforms: MS Office, PowerPoint, Word, Excel, Paint, Kid Pix, MS Publisher, eTeacher, and Independent Education Plan.

COMMUNITY INVOLVEMENT

- ❏ Village Charity Outreach Campaign from 1996 - 1998 and Executive Co-Chair for one year of Waterloo's Food Bank drive and MS Society. Coordinated multiple fundraising. events, volunteers and ensured media coverage. Secured $15 000+ and food items.
- ❏ English, Math and ESL Tutor for student with learning disability and new immigrants.
- ❏ ESL Tutor - Keatsway Public School, Waterloo, Ontario.
- ❏ University of Waterloo: PALS - Peer Help Crisis Phone Line Participant, Volunteer for Advisory Council Committee, and Placement Officer - Student Employment Centre.

"Sophia exemplifies warmth, sensitivity, advocacy and commitment to student success. Not surprisingly, her students reciprocate with attention and respect. Her students see integrity and sincerity in her challenges and responses toward them. She thrives on new knowledge and challenges and continues to demonstrate tremendous commitment and energy."

R. Goldenrod, Principal
Bury Middle School

Leanne Falk

100 Main Drive ◈ Saskatoon, Saskatchewan S1S 1S1
(306) 555-1234 ◈ leannefalk@careerprocanada.ca

GRAPHIC DESIGNER
Packaging Design ◈ Pre-Press Production

PROFILE

◈ Talented graphic designer balancing imagination and creative design sense with solid technical skills and printing expertise

◈ Proficient in trapping, image setting, fixed type flow correction, film proofing, and dyluxs – additional experience working with scanners (flatbed and drum) and Misomex sample cutting tables

◈ Hands-on experience and training in packaging design and pre-press for major corporate clients

◈ Extremely self-motivated and organized – able to work both independently and as part of a team and multitasks effectively in high pressure deadline-driven environments

◈ Proficient with the following design and graphics programs:

MAC: QuarkXPress, Adobe Illustrator, Photoshop, INposition
PC: Corel Draw, AutoCAD Designer Workbench, Artios, Spaceman Merchandiser

PROFESSIONAL EXPERIENCE

MAC Operator   2002 - Present
SASKTECH IMAGING, Saskatoon, SK
Provided a variety of end-to-end pre-press functions on major advertising projects for high-profile corporate accounts.

◈ Received files from corporate clients and design houses, checked all image and document formats, and completed all client changes as required.

◈ Completed trapping, set or replaced images, fixed type flow errors, established printing parameters, prepared film proofs and dyluxs, and output film to image setter.

◈ Paid close attention to detail and ensured that work is of highest quality and goes to film error-free.

◈ Set up scans for drum scanner (reflective and transparency).

◈ Major client projects include **Bank of Montreal**, **Ford Motors**, **Kodak**, and **LogiTech**.

Structural Designer   Summers 2000, 2001
Litho-Press Incorporated, Saskatoon, SK
Worked exclusively on merchandising display and packaging projects for **Shoppers Drug Mart**, **Wal-Mart**, and **Business Depot**.

◈ Based on basic product design, created a wide variety of eye-catching flip trays, end caps trays, and floor standing displays for use in national merchandising campaigns.

◈ Designed plan-o-grams using Spaceman Merchandiser, designed and created fillers using Designer Workbench, and operated Misomex sample cutting table to create end-product.

◈ Consistently received positive feedback from clients and superiors for creativity, technical proficiency, work ethic, and consistent commitment to ensuring a quality product.

Other experience includes:
Sales Clerk – John's Retail Warehouse, Saskatoon, SK   (P/T) 1998 – 1999
Waitress – Desserts Desserts, Saskatoon, SK   (P/T) 1997 – 1998

EDUCATION

Formal Education:
Package & Graphic Design - Diploma   Saskatoon Community College, 2002

Packaging Training:
AutoCAD Artios Certification (1 week)   Norampac Lithotech, 2001
Retail Spaceman   A/C Neilson, 2001

References and portfolio available upon request.

Graphic Designer. With only two years of experience, a visually unique and compelling design in a strong one-page format effectively displays this Graphic Designer's background. To add impact, she highlights big name clients.

BARBARA BURNHAM

12 Millpond Way • Aurora, ON • LIL ILI
905-555-1234
Email bb@CareerProCanada.ca

GOAL

Qualified for **Photolab Specialist opportunities** where the following would be of value:

- Over 15 years of progressive and well-rounded experience at grocery store level with demonstrated proficiency in Elvis, Telxon, MS Outlook, Excel, Sweda, and BDR software applications.
- Sound knowledge of grocery store operations that include customer service, Photolab, lottery, tobacco, video rental, and cash office departments.
- The ability to build, lead, motivate, and develop customer-focused teams who strive to deliver exceptional performance.

BACKGROUND SUMMARY

Customer-focused and highly-motivated professional with a **history of contributions that have grown revenues, produced high-performing teams, contained operational costs, and instituted policies and procedures to foster repeat clientele.** Fast-tracked promotions in earlier career at a local established supermarket, with accountability for Cash, Deli, and Customer Service areas. Sincere and honest with a high level of personal and professional integrity. Trained in First Aid tactics. **Able to articulate a shared sense of purpose to inspire staff to further important business goals.**

KEY COMPETENCIES

Leading-Edge Photolab Technology & Industry Trends • Employee Coaching & Mentoring • Policy & Procedure Compliance • Problem-Solving & Trouble-Shooting • Budgeting & Operational Cost Controls • Fiscal Management & Accounting Principles • In-Store & POS Promotions • Inventory Shrinkage Prevention • Buyer Awareness • Cash Office & Credit Operations • Customer Service & Satisfaction • Low Employee Turnover • Merchandising Techniques • Product Ordering & Planogram Compliance • Sales & Labour Forecasting • Staff Recruitment, Training, Orientation, & Discipline • Tactical Planning & Execution • Team Building & Department Leadership • Union Relations • WHMIS & Safety Training • Workflow Planning & Prioritization

CAREER HIGHLIGHTS

Boisvert's Grocery, Aurora ... 1996 - present

2000 - present: Photolab Manager

Promoted to direct all day-to-day activity involving 4 departments that encompass Lottery, Tobacco, Customer Service, and Photolab areas. Attractively set up merchandise in an effort to entice customers to buy a range of products. Specific accountabilities include store opening and closing, budgeting, fiscal honesty, Photolab equipment maintenance, and payroll processing. Supervise between 7 and 15 direct reports, depending on seasonal demand.

Selected Achievements:

- Realized strong and sustainable revenue gains of 30% over a 42-month span.
- Boosted and preserved employee morale by modelling a positive attitude and high levels of respect to staff.
- Continue to avert costly production downtimes by applying a proactive mindset toward maintaining intricate Photolab equipment.
- Launched a bevy of policies and procedures to minimize losses, enhance efficiencies, and strengthen overall accountability in Tobacco, Lottery, and Customer Service areas.
- Coached inexperienced staff who went on to hold responsible and vital positions throughout the store.
- Met surge of competition from a well-known retailer renowned for customer service by emphasizing top quality and personalized attention
- Selected by current owner to take on the role of Cash Office support for 6 months prior to assuming the role of Photolab Manager.
- Introduced a wealth of policies and procedures to maintain high levels of business activity.

1997 - 2000: Assistant Photolab Manager

Promoted after only 6 weeks as a Cashier to support Photolab Manager in running the 4 above-mentioned areas.

EDUCATION & TRAINING

Completed **Fuji Photolab Technician** and **8-month Business Software** coursework
Queen's College, Aurora • **Diploma in Office Administration** *(With Honours)*

Grocery Manager. Strong photolab expertise and progressive experience combined with a focus on achieving operational objectives positions this candidate as a highly qualified specialist.

SIDNEY LEE

111 Second Avenue • Ottawa, Ontario K1K 1K1
(613) 555-1234 • slee@careerprocanada.ca

OCCUPATIONAL HEALTH & SAFETY / HUMAN RESOURCES

Motivated and dedicated professional with diverse HR and OHS experience in the telecommunications and medical industries. Credited with major contributions to Ottawa Regional Hospital's successful response and emergency preparedness during the 2002 SARS outbreak. Personable and professional with reputation for positive attitude and superior communications/consulting skills. Decisive with strong organizational and time management skills. Creative, innovative, and resourceful. Value-added corporate partner able to:

☑ **Promote and implement Health and Safety / HR programs**
☑ **Create and maintain the Health and Safety infrastructure to safeguard life, health, and corporate property**
☑ **Ensure compliance with both Provincial and Federal legislation**
☑ **Review injury and HR statistics to develop appropriate policies, programs, and reports**
☑ **Develop, apply, and track risk assessments, loss prevention, and safety training programs**

Canadian Registered Safety Professional (ongoing)
CHRP Designation (Spring 2005)

AREAS OF EXPERTISE

Health and Safety:

- Policies & Procedures
- Emergency Preparedness
- Safety Program Design
- Accident Causation & Analysis
- Occupational Health Act
- WSIB / WHMIS

Human Resources:

- Policies & Procedures
- Change Management
- Training & Development
- Cultural Change Programs
- Job Analysis & Job Posting
- HR Management

PROFESSIONAL EXPERIENCE

OTTAWA REGIONAL HOSPITAL, Ottawa, Ontario

Health and Safety Coordinator / Human Resources Generalist   2002 - Present

Recruited to join the HR department with a focus on completing job analysis and cultural change exercises supporting the hospital's 3000+ employees. Quickly given responsibility for Occupational Health and Safety programs in response to the SARS outbreak, and successfully turned an underdeveloped series of OHS programs into a structured and integrated OHS function capable of identifying and addressing risk in key areas.

OHS Contributions:

- Developed the hospital's first Respiratory Protection Program – researched legislation, CSA standards, infection control best practices, and developed all communication materials provided to managers throughout the hospital.
- Coordinated the outsourced Fit Testing of respirators for 3000+ employees and oversaw the staffing of all points of entry during SARS outbreak.
- Analyzed current practices and injury statistics in proposal of the No Manual Lift Pilot Project.
- In response to a Ministry mandate, researched and introduced a Heat Stress Program including all new policy development and communications.

cont...

Health & Safety Coordinator. With only two jobs to his credit, this résumé presents the individual's "Areas of Expertise" in a separate section after the profile, taking a full two-thirds of the first page. The approach packs two complete pages with value.

OTTAWA REGIONAL HOSPITAL (*cont*)

- Analyzed and upgraded the existing WHMIS system, introduced the first sustainability plan, and developed communications and online training solutions to bring staff up to speed.
- Designed and delivered the Emergency Preparedness and WHMIS training components to the new employee orientation program.
- Member of the Occupational Health and Safety Committee, Emergency Planning Committee, and Emergency Preparedness Sub-Committee.

General HR Contributions:

- Created job descriptions for 57 distinct positions and introduced the first standardized job posting/professional development process for on-staff nurses – model is currently being implemented in other hospital areas.
- Established the hospital's first official Code of Conduct program introducing a corporate-wide expectation of behaviour – developed and implemented the program and trained over 1000 frontline staff.

TELCO COMMUNICATIONS (*formerly Sudbury TelcoSystems*), Sudbury, Ontario

Health and Safety Coordinator   1999 - 2001

In response to an unfavourable Work Well audit, personally selected to assume new position as Health and Safety coordinator for this small telecommunications firm with 300 employees. Specifically challenged to identify deficiencies, develop the required policies and SOPs, and position company for successful follow-up audit.

- Developed key components of a Health and Safety Program that contributed to a passed audit and a 12% savings in annual WSIB premiums.
- Researched, created, and introduced new OHS programs, policies, and procedures to ensure compliance with both Provincial and Federal legislation.
- Injected renewed focus and structure as a key member of the Joint Occupational Health and Safety Committee.
- Trained over 260 employees in the new OHS policies and procedures.

Previous employment includes senior positions in video production – award-winning Producer and Production Editor on numerous 30-60 minute programs.

EDUCATION & CERTIFICATION

Canadian Registered Safety Professional	BC Institute of Technology, TBC 2005
CHRP Designation	HRPAO, TBC 2004
eLearning Development Program	Northeastern Ontario Medical Education Centre, 2004
Human Resources Management (Post Diploma Program)	Cambrian College, 2002
Journalism Diploma	Cambrian College, 1991

COMPUTER PROFICIENCY

Advanced computer proficiency includes **Microsoft Office, Excel, FileMaker Pro, WHMIS, Adobe PhotoShop,** and **PageMaker**.

SIMONE A. DUCHARME

555 Joseph Street, Guelph, Ontario N1N 1N1 ◆ Phone (519) 555-1212 ◆ simone.ducharme@careerprocanada.ca

EXPERIENCED HEALTH & SAFETY SPECIALIST

A results-driven professional, with a background spanning Occupational Safety, Human Resources, Administration, and Finance. Exceptional educational credentials including a Masters of Science and Programs in Environmental Health, Safety, and Wellness. Skilled at managing multiple tasks in an analytical, organized, and decisive manner. Proven expertise in designing, documenting, and auditing programs. Demonstrated ability to prepare, analyze, and report data. Confident communicator adept in training employees, managing meetings, and promoting teamwork. Fully proficient in MS Office.

Areas of Expertise:

- Safety Orientation & Training
- Health & Safety Compliance
- Workplace Inspections
- Technology Training

- Data Analysis & Reporting
- Database Management
- Financial Administration
- Budget Management

- Senior Management Support
- Departmental Liaison
- Document Development
- Policy & Procedure Manuals

HEALTH ◆ SAFETY ◆ WELLNESS

PROFESSIONAL EXPERIENCE

McMaster University, Hamilton, Ontario   **2001 - Present**

Health & Safety Coordinator/Administrative Secretary (2004-Present)
Classroom Planning Coordinator (2002-2004)
Operations Assistant (2001)

Directly recruited and promoted to full responsiblity for coordinating and delivering Health and Safety programs, managing technical training initiatives for new employees and faculty, and liasing with other departments. Responsibilities for Human Resources and Financial support tasks include maintaining confidential files, reconciling salary reports, and performing month end procedures. Accountable for researching, analyzing, and reporting on technology, expenditures, and statistics.

Accomplishments

- Chosen to work with management to develop the first Local Joint Health and Safety Committee, which included instituting a formal plan outlining membership selection criteria and associated duties.

- Performed over 25 workplace safety inspections, over the course of four years, which resulted in significantly improved departmental safety.

- Produced and implemented a new employee health and safety orientation program with adherence to university policies and the Occupational Health and Safety Act.

- Selected to serve on the joint University Classroom Planning and Operations Committee, which directly resulted in improved communications between four independent departments.

- Coordinated the renovation planning process for 105 classrooms by compiling appropriate data, effectively analyzing results, and reporting recommendations, which were implemented by university management.

- Wrote a comprehensive operation manual and delivered training for an automated equipment reservation system using Information Mapping® principles, which are essential to new employee orientation.

- Performed accurate budget adjustments for departmental financial reporting by utilizing linked, multi-layered MS Excel workbooks.

Previous positions held
Rocky Mountain School Inc., Guelph, Ontario, Presenter
ABC Inc., Guelph, Ontario, Assistant

HEALTH ◆ SAFETY ◆ WELLNESS

Health and Safety Specialist. A tight listing of progressive experience within the university points to multiple promotions and long-term loyalty. Accomplishments selectively focus on competencies required for a professional in health and safety.

EDUCATION

Occupational Health and Safety Certificate Program   **Present**
Conestoga College, Guelph, Ontario

Master of Science   **2000**
University of Guelph, Guelph, Ontario

Honours Bachelor of Science   **1997**
University of Guelph, Guelph, Ontario

PROFESSIONAL DEVELOPMENT

Information Mapping® - Developing Procedures, Policies & Documentation
Communicare, Toronto, Ontario

Environmental Health, Safety and Wellness Programs
McMaster University, Hamilton, Ontario
◆ Workplace Hazardous Materials Information System (WHMIS)
◆ Hazard ID Through Workplace Inspection
◆ Accident Investigation
◆ Electrical Safety and Awareness

COMPUTER SKILLS

Advanced proficiency in a variety of computer technology and software including:
◆ Microsoft Word, Excel, PowerPoint, and Access
◆ University Electronic Financial Systems (FRS and ADI)

VOLUNTEER EXPERIENCE

Campus Child-Care Cooperative, Hamilton, Ontario
Serve on Board of Directors as Secretary and Treasurer

HEALTH ◆ SAFETY ◆ WELLNESS

Dorothy Mee, BA

1234 White Cedar Drive, Pickering, ON, L1L 1L1 · 905-555-1212 · e-mail d_mee@careerprocanada.ca

PROFILE

Experienced Human Resources generalist with extensive background in the full scope of human resource management practices and exceptional educational qualifications. Customer focused, highly organized, solutions driven professional, with knowledge and training in conflict resolution, problem solving, planning, and decision-making. Over 6 years of achievements and promotions demonstrating expertise in:

- Recruitment, Selection, and Orientation
- Workplace Health and Safety Programs
- Employee Relations
- Conflict Resolution
- Performance Management

- Leadership, Training, and Development
- Policy Management
- Team Building and Employee Retention
- Budgets and Inventories
- Retail Operations Management

Education: Human Resources Management (HRM) Graduate Certificate, a Bachelor of Arts (BA), and the Certified Human Resources Professional (CHRP) accreditation in progress.

PROFESSIONAL EXPERIENCE

Retail Operations Manager/Human Resource Management   1996 - 2006
Mega Shop Ltd., Toronto, ON

Directly managed over 50 employees and oversaw human resources requirements supporting 150 employees. Implemented training programs for new hires and refresher programs for existing staff.

- Recruited several hundred sales associates over a 6-year period, which produced consistently excellent employees and resulted in reduction of turnover by 60%.

- Coordinated and managed both local and regional recruitment fairs, which resulted in the hiring of a minimum of 20 new employees per annum for the Toronto stores.

- Conducted store staff performance reviews for merit increases and promotions, building a team environment and producing an 80% improvement in staff satisfaction surveys.

- Trained over 300 new regional-level Sales Associates in operational policies and procedures over a 12-month period. Awarded corporate 'Training Star' recognition for this contribution.

- Successfully resolved performance, morale, and shrinkage issues within a three-month period at a North Toronto location at the request of the District Manager.

- Initiated and managed an associate recognition program to increase employee morale and performance, resulting in customer surveys exceeding customer satisfaction standards.

- Promoted to Store Administrator within four months of hire and advanced to Customer Service Manager within one year.

Human Resource Generalist. A well-balanced profile clearly outlines this candidate's competencies in a readable format. The modified job title and transferable accomplishments shift focus to the human resources aspects of the Retail Operations Manager role.

Dorothy Mee   Page 2

EDUCATION

Human Resources Management Graduate Certificate, Seneca College   2006
President's Honour List   2005

Bachelor of Arts, Sociology, York University   1998

TRAINING

Leadership Development, Recruiting and Hiring   2002

Leadership Development, People and Performance Management   2001

Workplace Safety and Insurance Board, Basic Certification and First Aid Training   1999

ADDITIONAL SKILLS

- Proficient in Microsoft Excel, Word, PowerPoint, and Outlook.
- Working knowledge of HRIS (Super-HR).
- Experienced in the use of SMARTS and Vista data management programs.

VOLUNTEER EXPERIENCE

York University Women's Centre   1994
- General Office Administration

RICHARD DeSOUZA, BA, CHRP

123 Thorn Street, Calgary, Alberta T2T 2T2
Phone (403) 555-1234 ◆ Cell (403) 555-2345 ◆ E-mail rdesouza@careerprocanada.ca

HUMAN RESOURCES MANAGER

People are our most important asset...working together we can attain infinite success!

A collaborative, creative, and conscientious generalist with a well-earned reputation for taking initiative to achieve corporate goals. Outstanding interpersonal skills, with the ability to interact with employees at all levels, generating trust and rapport. Demonstrated experience spearheading corporate change initiatives by designing and instituting progressive policies, procedures, and programs. A confident communicator, offering high-calibre presentation and facilitation skills.

Core Competencies:

◆ Organizational Effectiveness	◆ Recruitment & Selection	◆ Training & Development
◆ Change Management	◆ Rewards & Recognition	◆ Legislative Compliance
◆ Performance Management	◆ Compensation & Benefits	◆ WSIB/LTD Management

Exceptional educational credentials including a Bachelor of Arts and the National CHRP designation.

EMPLOYMENT HISTORY

Mirrors Inc., Calgary, Alberta **2002 to Present**
Canada's top mirror manufacturer with over $30 million revenue.
Human Resources Manager
Reporting directly to the President, responsible for the overall HR support to 125 employees. Responsible for providing a complete range of HR services including payroll, recruitment & selection, health & safety, training & development, and organizational development. Accountable to institute processes to improve corporate culture and organizational health.

- Served as the catalyst for an organizational culture change, moving from a "top-down" structure to a decentralized model, which empowered employees and significantly improved teamwork and morale.
- Slashed employee turnover and absenteeism by over 70% by instituting progressive hiring, orientation, performance management, and recognition programs.
- Implemented a broad-banded, market-driven, performance-based compensation and profit-sharing program, which improved internal equity without increasing overall compensation costs.
- Designed, customized, and delivered front-line management training on a variety of topics, including progressive discipline, quarterly performance reviews, employee motivation, and coaching.
- Reduced lost-time injuries by over 70% through the implementation of modified work programs and other claims management strategies.

Textile Group of Companies, Calgary, Alberta **2001 to 2002**
Textile manufacturer located in Toronto with five divisions with $8.5 million revenue.
Human Resources Coordinator
Reporting to the President, responsible for overseeing strategic and administrative HR functions supporting all five divisions with 150 employees in Calgary and Ontario. Accountable to create formal HR programs, provide management training, oversee group benefits and pension plans, and manage WSIB and LTD claims.

- Improved employee relations by instituting internal communications and focus groups, which resulted in positive comments by employees and senior management.
- Managed the downsizing of the Calgary operations, instituted an outplacement program, performed terminations, and developed a retention strategy for five key employees within a 5-day window.
- Implemented Early and Safe Return to Work programs and appeals process, improving cost containment and reducing overall number of days lost by 25%.
- Controlled WSIB and LTD costs by effective claims management and increased yearly rebates to the company by more than 40%.
- Implemented various safety initiatives including awareness programs, signage, and machine safety; achieved the lowest accident rate in the industry, 1/10th of the industry average.
- Researched and established a new group benefits carrier, which provided cost effective and comprehensive employee coverage.
- Championed the Employment Equity program and met the Federal Contractors' Program requirements, successfully completing the project in less than 2 months.

Human Resource Manager. This candidate draws attention to the strong credentials after his name and at the close of his power statement. Italicized company information adds context for potential employers in other industries.

RICHARD DeSOUSA, BA, CHRP

EMPLOYMENT HISTORY (continued)

Previous positions held:
- Rock Insurance Company, Human Resources Administrator
- ZYX Canada, Orientation Program Developer

EDUCATION

College of Applied Arts and Technology, Calgary, Alberta   2001
- Human Resources Management Post-Graduate Certificate Program, Dean's List

McMaster University, Hamilton, Ontario   2000
- Honours Bachelor of Arts, Labour Studies and Political Science

PROFESSIONAL AFFILIATIONS

Human Resources Institute of Alberta (HRIA) Edmonton, Alberta
- Certified Human Resources Professional (CHRP) designation (2005)

Manufacturing Industry Safety Council (MISC), Calgary, Alberta
- Council Committee Member

PROFESSIONAL DEVELOPMENT

Active participant in a variety of seminars and workshops:
- Privacy Law Seminar, Crawford, Chondon and Andree LLP
- Privacy Law and Employee Benefits, Johnson-Schock and Associates
- Annual Employment Law Update, Gowlings, Smith, Lyons LLP
- Joint Health and Safety Committee Certification, Parts 1 and 2, Safer Workplaces
- "Surviving the Workwell Audit", Industrial Accident Prevention Association (IAPA)

TECHNICAL SKILLS

Proficient in a variety of computer applications on various platforms:
- Microsoft Office Suite (Word, Excel, PowerPoint, Project, Publisher)
- Corel WordPerfect Suite (WordPerfect, Lotus)

People are our most important asset…working together we can attain infinite success!

Raymond D. Duncan, BAA - Interior Design
1234 Rue Maurice, Montréal, Quebec H1H 1H1
Phone (514) 555-1234 ● Cell (514) 555-2345 ● E-mail rdd@careerprocanada.ca

Interior Designer & Space Planner
...with extensive experience in the commercial and corporate office environment.

Highly creative professional, with a talent for conceiving and developing appropriate solutions for office environments and commercial space. Demonstrated expertise spearheading large-scale projects, from inception to completion, with dedicated attention to technical considerations, construction, finishes, millwork, and detailing. Dynamic leader, with expertise in managing employees and overseeing cross-functional project teams. Proficient in strategic, business, and financial planning to optimize operational efficiency and profitability. Exceptional interpersonal skills used to interact with, and inspire the confidence of, clients. Areas of Expertise:

● Strategic Planning	● Project Management	● Technical Documentation
● Team Leadership	● Estimating & Budgeting	● Design Concepts
● Formal Presentations	● Construction Supervision	● Floor Plans & Layout
● Contract Negotiation	● Planning & Scheduling	● Furniture Selection

*** *Canada Constructs Speaker* ***
Presenting the National Banking Industry's Office Standards Program.

Career Highlights

Interior Design

- Planned and designed a 45,000 sq. ft. office space, and effectively relocated Canada Post facilities, consolidating 200 employees at one location.

- Designed and presented working drawings for 20 executive units within a 6-month period to meet the unique décor and layout needs of the Montreal Olympic Stadium.

Space Planning

- Analyzed and optimized space for the Montréal Science Centre, effectively restructuring the existing premises to facilitate 10% anticipated growth of the operations.

- Completed a formal needs analysis and 3-year strategic space planning study for the consolidation and integration of International Bank office facilities, saving $3 million in real estate costs.

Project Management

- Facilitated the relocation and consolidation of 1000 staff into a new 250,000 sq. ft. facility for Bank of Montreal Operations and Systems Division.

- Overhauled and integrated in-house project management processes, systems, and documentation for a high-profile design firm.

General Management

- Oversaw and managed a team of 26 designers. Facilitated business development and client relations, working closely with the sales team to improve services.

- Managed a busy Facilities Support department of a Furniture Dealership and oversaw 12 employees, ensuring the timely and accurate specification and layout of systems furniture for clients.

Interior Designer. The layout of this résumé offers a creative design, while keeping a professional image, which is appropriate for commercial and corporate clients. The italicized opening and closing lines of the power statement focus the reader on the candidate's area of specialty – the office environment.

RAYMOND D. DUNCAN, BAA - INTERIOR DESIGN ● Phone (514) 555-1234   Page 2

CURRENT PROFESSIONAL EXPERIENCE

Sophisticated Space Planning & Design, Montreal, Quebec   1999 - Present
Independently owned and operated space planning and design consultancy.
Planning & Design Consultant, Managing Director
Responsible for the full scope of design, planning, and project management for corporate interior projects. Conduct client presentations, prioritize work, and monitor scheduling. Perform strategic forecasting, feasibility studies, building analysis, and standards programs. Manage business operations, budgeting, and administration.

- Effectively completed projects for various high-profile design groups and clients including Bell Canada, Canada Post, The Olympic Stadium, and International Bank.

Vanier College, Montreal, Quebec   2003 - Present
Educational institution providing post-secondary and degree programs to 15,000 students.
Instructor
Provide "Partial-Load" daytime adult education in a classroom scenario.

- Successfully taught courses in "Drawing" and "Manual Drafting."

OTHER PERTINENT CONTRACT & LONG-TERM EMPLOYMENT

- **Manager, Space Planning,** Rich Business Interior   1998 - 1999
- **Senior Designer,** Wow Design Ltd.   1996 - 1998
- **Design Manager,** Yes Design Interiors   1993 - 1996

PARTIAL CLIENT LIST

- **Financial Institutions-** Royal Bank of Canada, National Bank, Bank of Montreal, and Scotia Bank.
- **Insurance Companies-** Royal Insurance, Hudson Insurance, Royal Life Insurance, and Sun Alliance.
- **Miscellaneous-** Montreal Olympic Stadium, West Island Super Mall, and Montreal Science Centre.

FORMAL EDUCATION

- **Bachelor of Applied Arts, Interior Design,** Ryerson Polytechnic University, Toronto, Ontario
- Actively committed to continuing education via ongoing CEU courses

TECHNICAL SKILLS

Proficient in a variety of software applications including:

- Microsoft Office Suite (Word, Excel, PowerPoint, Project)
- Corel WordPerfect
- AutoCAD R2000i

PROFESSIONAL AFFILIATIONS

- Interior Designers of Canada (IDC)
- International Facilities Management Association (IFMA)

LANGUAGES

- English and French

Client references available upon request.

Raymond D. Duncan, BAA – Architecte d'interieur
2360 Rue Maurice, Montréal, Québec H1H 1H1
Téléphone : (514) 555-1234 ● Cellulaire : (514) 555-2345 ● Courriel : rdd@careerprocanada.ca

Architecte d'interieur et specialiste en amenagement de l'espace
...avec une grande expérience dans les milieux de bureaux d'affaires et d'entreprises.

Professionnel extrêmement créatif, avec un talent particulier pour la conception et la mise en oeuvre de solutions adaptées aux besoins des bureaux et des espaces commerciaux. Expertise reconnue dans la direction de projets de grande envergure, de leur création jusqu'à leur exécution, il prête une attention particulière aux aspects techniques, la construction, les peintures, la menuiserie et les finitions. Dirigeant énergique, avec des compétences en gestion du personnel et en supervision d'équipes de projets inter-fonctionnelles. Expert en planification financière, stratégique et d'affaires afin d'optimiser la profitabilité et l'efficacité opérationnelle. Habileté exceptionnelle en communications interpersonnelles pour communiquer et inspirer la confiance des clients. Domaines d'expertise :

- Planification stratégique
- Direction d'équipes
- Présentations officielles
- Négociation de contrats

- Préparation de devis et budgets
- Gestion de projet
- Supervision de la construction
- Établissement du calendrier

- Études conceptuelles
- Documentation technique
- Plans et schémas d'étages
- Choix de l'ameublement

*** *Orateur pour Le Canada construit*
Présentation du programme des normes de bureaux de l'Industrie bancaire nationale

Points forts de carriere

Architecture d'intérieur

- Planification et conception d'un espace de bureaux de 45 000 pi^2 et déménagement réussi des locaux de Postes Canada, réunissant 200 employés dans un même endroit.
- Conception et présentation de dessins d'exécution de 20 bureaux pour cadres supérieurs sur une période de six mois pour répondre aux besoins spécifiques en terme de décors et de schémas d'étages du Stade olympique de Montréal.

Aménagement de l'espace

- Analyse et optimisation de l'espace pour le Centre des sciences de Montréal, restructuration efficace des locaux existants pour faciliter une croissance des opérations prévue de 10 %.
- Complétion d'une analyse officielle des besoins et d'une étude stratégique d'aménagement de l'espace sur 3 ans pour effectuer la consolidation et l'intégration des bureaux de la banque internationale, économisant ainsi 3 millions de dollars en coûts immobiliers.

Gestion de projet

- Assistance pour la réinstallation et la consolidation de 1000 employés dans de nouveaux locaux de 250 000 pi^2 pour la Division des systèmes et des opérations de la Banque de Montréal.
- Révision et intégration de la documentation, des systèmes et des processus internes de gestion de projet pour une entreprise de conception réputée.

Gestion générale

- Supervision et gestion d'une équipe de 26 concepteurs. Facilitation de la prospection et des relations avec la clientèle, en collaboration avec l'équipe des ventes pour améliorer les services.
- Gestion du département de soutien d'une concession de meubles de grande activité et supervision de 12 employés, s'assurant que les spécifications et les schémas des systèmes d'ameublement pour les clients soient corrects et dans les délais prescrits.

Architecte d'intérieur. La mise en page de ce CV offre une conception inédite, tout en gardant une image profession-nelle, ce qui est approprié pour les clients commerciaux et d'entreprises. Les lignes d'introduction et de conclusion en italique de la déclaration des facultés attirent l'attention du lecteur sur les domaines d'expertise du candidat, les espaces de bureaux.

RAYMOND D. DUNCAN, BAA – ARCHITECTURE D'INTERIEUR ● Téléphone : (514) 555-1234   Page 2

EXPERIENCE PROFESSIONNELLE ACTUELLE

Sophisticated Space Planning & Design, Montréal, Québec   1999–Présent
Cabinet de conseil en architecture et aménagement d'espace indépendant
Consultant en conception et planification, Directeur général

Responsable de la gestion complète des projets, de la planification et de la conception des projets de locaux d'entreprises. Présentations aux clients, établissement des priorités de travail et contrôle du calendrier. Réalisation des prévisions stratégiques, des études de faisabilité, des analyses de construction et des programmes de normes. Gestion des opérations de l'entreprise, du budget et de son administration.

● Complétion réussie de projets pour plusieurs clients et groupes d'architectes réputés, y compris Bell Canada, Postes Canada, le Stade olympique et la banque internationale.

Collège Vanier, Montréal, Québec   2003–Présent
Institution d'éducation offrant des programmes de diplômes post-secondaires à 15 000 étudiants.
Instructeur

Donne des cours d'éducation « charge partielle » dans des classes pour adultes pendant la journée.

● Enseignement réussi de cours en « Dessin » et « Dessin technique manuel. »

AUTRES CONTRATS ET EMPLOIS A LONG TERME PERTINENTS

● **Directeur, planification d'espace,** Rich Business Interior   1998–1999
● **Chef architecte,** Wow Design Ltd.   1996–1998
● **Architecte principal,** Yes Design Interiors   1993–1996

LISTE PARTIELLE DE CLIENTS

● **Institutions financières** – Banque Royale du Canada, Banque nationale, Banque de Montréal et Banque Scotia.
● **Compagnies d'assurance** – la Royale, Hudson Insurance, la Royale Vie et SunAlliance.
● **Divers** – Stade olympique de Montréal, West Island Super Mall et Centre des sciences de Montréal.

ÉDUCATION

● **Baccalauréat ès arts appliqués, Architecture d'intérieur,** Université Ryerson, Toronto, Ontario
● Suivi actif de l'éducation continue par cours réguliers CEU

COMPETENCES TECHNIQUES

Très compétent dans plusieurs logiciels d'applications y compris :

● Suite de Microsoft Office (Word, Excel, PowerPoint, Project)
● Corel WordPerfect
● AutoCAD R2000i

ASSOCIATIONS PROFESSIONNELLES

● Designers d'intérieur du Canada (IDC)
● International Facilities Management Association (IFMA)

LANGUES

● Anglais et français

Références de clients disponibles sur demande.

Mary Ann Lancaster

1111 Evergreen Avenue, Toronto, Ontario M1M 1M1
Phone: 416.555.1234
E mail: mlancaster@careerprocanada.ca

Early Childhood Educator

Resourceful, innovative and dedicated educator with the ability to design and deliver stimulating age-appropriate lesson plans. Energetic and enthusiastic, actively promotes values and traditional teaching practices coupled with the introduction of technology into the classroom. Articulate, communicates effectively with students, parents, peers and other stakeholders. Well-travelled, culturally sensitive; assesses students with respect to their personalities; committed to building self-esteem and motivation and creating a relaxed and harmonious environment. Recently appraised by parent with the following testimonial:

"Miss Lancaster has provided inspiration, guidance and support to my son; we have been highly impressed with her ability to enrich his life with her wisdom, caring and sharing…
She is a true teaching professional and we wish her well in her new teaching appointment."

Professional Experience

Pine Point Elementary School, Burloak, Ontario   2001 – Present
KINDERGARTEN TEACHER
- Designed and facilitated an interactive and theme-based curriculum focusing on monthly calendars to senior and junior kindergarten students.
- Utilized diverse instructional methods and resource materials to emphasize individual learning capabilities.
- Oversaw, with assistant and parent volunteers, two physically challenged students with cerebral palsy and spina bifida requiring extra support and attention.
- Acknowledged by Principal for actively contributing to staff meetings and other school activities and encouraging parents to take on a more responsible role in supervision during critical financial restrictions.

Education

McMaster University, Hamilton, Ontario   2001
MASTER OF EDUCATION – Early Childhood Education

D'Youville College, Buffalo, New York   1999
STUDENT TEACHER
TEACHER'S CERTIFICATE

Completed the following modules: August – December 1999:

Methods of Elementary Reading and Writing, (A)	Meeting the Needs of Exceptional Learners, (A)
Elementary School Strategies, (A)	Curriculum Planning, (A)
Major Themes in Early Childhood Education, (B+)	Theories of Learning, (B+)

Assigned student teaching positions include the following:
Wilfred Laurier School, Burlington, Ontario   March – May 1999
- Developed curricula, assembled teaching materials, prepared goals and agendas, created lesson plans, and taught Grades 1 & 2.

Chelsea School, Hamilton, Ontario   January – March 1999
- Prepared and delivered programs encompassing stories and crafts including a Valentine's Day theme.

University of Western Ontario   1998
BACHELOR OF ARTS – History

Kindergarten Teacher. This candidate effectively markets herself by bringing together a strong profile, sound experience, and outstanding academic credentials in one page. The thoughtful use of fonts and graphics contribute to a theme that clearly says, "Early childhood education is my calling."

MARY GILBERT

123 Main Street ◈ Ottawa ON K1K 1K1 ◈ 613.555.1234 ◈ mgilbert@careerprocanada.ca

LIBRARY TECHNICIAN

meticulous researcher…effective communicator…outstanding customer service

Computer skills: DB/Textworks, MEDLINE (using Ovid and PubMed), Word, WordPerfect, Outlook, Internet.

PROFESSIONAL EXPERIENCE

Canadian Medical Association (CMA), Ottawa ON

SENIOR LIBRARY TECHNICIAN (1983 – 2006)
ACTING MANAGER, LIBRARY AND RESOURCE CENTRE (2001 – 2003)

As Senior Library Technician, provided first-rate technical and clerical client service—researched, compiled, and delivered clinical, scientific, practice management, and general information—to members of the Canadian Medical Association (a vibrant organization of 16,000 members). Skilled in all functional library operations and services, including computerized cataloguing; serial acquisition, collection, and maintenance; selection and acquisition of texts, videos, and CD's; and interlibrary loans (ILL). Trained and supervised Library Technicians and Library Clerks.

As Acting Manager, full scope of responsibilities included budget management, staff supervision, text and journal acquisition, inquiry assistance, and liaison with various CMA departments. Reported to Director, Membership and Professional Services.

SIGNIFICANT ACHIEVEMENTS

- Initiated and assisted Canadian Institute of Scientific and Technological Information in implementing the National Library of Medicine (NLM) DOCLINE system. **Results**: DOCLINE provided national and international library access to CMA's specialized journal collection; supplemental income realized through interlibrary loans (ILL).
- Demonstrated impeccable research capabilities to ensure accuracy of solicited material from members of the Canadian Medical Association, in support of providing appropriate patient care.
- Originated the idea of *Medical Teamwork*, a quarterly newsletter for medical personnel, focusing in effective management of medical practices.
- Researched, organized, and provided informational material published in various periodicals: *Journal of the Canadian Medical Association* (JCMA); *Medical Teamwork; Communiqué* newsletter.
- Represented Canadian Medical Association at annual provincial and national industry conventions. Hosted CMA's booth; built rapport with various medical industry professionals; promoted the benefits of the CMA Library.
- Collaborated with CMA Librarian in designing library segment of the Canadian Medical Association's website.
- Restored indexing to the monthly *Journal of the Canadian Medical Association* (JCMA), which significantly improved material retrieval.

EDUCATION

Library Technician Diploma ◈ Algonquin College, Ottawa ON 1983

COMMUNITY INVOLVEMENT

Volunteer ◈ Meals on Wheels
Volunteer ◈ Jewish Family Services of Ottawa-Carleton
Library Committee, School Committee ◈ Temple Israel
Past President and Membership Chairperson ◈ Hadassah-WIZO (Ottawa local chapter)
Past Council Vice-President (representing all Ottawa chapters) ◈ Hadassah-WIZO

Library Technician. A concise one-page résumé can work for a candidate with 20 years experience. The precise wording included here clearly targets her area of expertise.

YVES GEORGES MARTIN

555 West End Road
Mississauga, Ontario L1L 1L1

Contact (647) 555-1234
E-mail y_m@careerprocanada.ca

EXPERIENCED MANUFACTURING OPERATIONS MANAGER

Operational Enhancement ▪ High Growth Environments ▪ Multi-Site Operations

Results-oriented professional with 10 years' experience and demonstrated achievements in manufacturing, project management, and quality assurance for industry leaders. A strategic thinker with a talent for proactively optimizing operational efficiency through business process redesign and change management. Dynamic leader and mentor, developing highly motivated teams and fostering an environment of continuous improvement. A diplomatic communicator and relationship builder with a career long record of negotiation and strategic alliance building to improve quality and reduce costs. Willing to travel if required.

Areas of Expertise:

- Budgeting & Forecasting
- Cost Estimations
- Customer Service
- Vendor Management

- Feasibility Analysis
- Policy Development
- ISO 9002 Implementation
- Quality Improvement

- Organizational Leadership
- Team Building
- Training & Support
- Employee Retention

CAREER HIGHLIGHTS

Manufacturing Management:

- Established a satellite manufacturing division from the ground up, completing the project on schedule and within budget; the division now produces $1.7 million revenue and serves as a backup facility.

- Participated in a corporate acquisition and led the integration of two manufacturing organizations, establishing one standard operating procedure.

Process Improvement:

- Developed business requirements and functional specification documents compliant with ISO 9002 guidelines to streamline internal procedures.

- Instituted a formal operations problem and change management process, which significantly improved awareness and internal communications, and ultimately slashed system downtime to virtually nil.

Logistics & Distribution:

- Championed a project to enable manufacturing equipment to perform multiple diverse jobs, which eliminated bottlenecks and slashed production time by 30%.

- Re-engineered logistics processes and implemented new policies to improve operational efficiencies, resulting in a head count reduction of 7 FTE with a 17.5% increase in output.

Team Leadership:

- Acquired expertise on the product manufacturing lifecycle, created user manuals, trained team leaders on equipment, and provided staff with direction in ongoing usage of systems.

- Mentored, coached, and developed employees to align their personal goals with the organization's vision, which resulted in improved morale and increased retention.

Manufacturing Operations Manager. Areas of expertise highlight key phrases that may be of interest to recruiters. The headers in the career highlights section take advantage of another technique to incorporate key phrases for recruiters that may glance at the résumé.

116

YVES GEORGES MARTIN

Contact (647) 555-1234   Page 2 of 2

PROFESSIONAL EXPERIENCE

HI-PRO LOGISTICS, Georgetown, Ontario   2005 – 2006
Privately owned logistics company with 45 employees, sorting and re-distributing 2 million packages annually.
Operations Consultant
Major Responsibilities:
Responsible to assess various distribution lines and suggest operational, system, and process improvements, reporting directly to the President. Oversee teams of up to 6 employees. Accountable to perform cost analysis and improve overall efficiencies.
Selected Accomplishments:
- Improved processes, assessed staffing, and implemented individuals with appropriate skill sets, enabling the organization to reduce headcount by 25% while maintaining the same level of output and service.
- Streamlined pricing processes and implemented a cost matrix sheet, slashing errors in customer invoicing by over 20%.

TOPCARD CORPORATION, Mississauga, Ontario   1993 – 2004
Leading Canadian manufacturer with 150 employees offering a one-stop solution for card production services.
Manager, Operations and Transitions
Major Responsibilities:
Progressively promoted to oversee the full scope of technical manufacturing operations. Responsible to supervise a team of 8 operators, developers, and support staff. Oversee equipment set-up, configuration, servicing, machine module upgrading, and sample product production. Assess client needs and determine manufacturing requirements. Strictly adhere to financial institutions' requirements, ISO standards, and quality assurance. Accountable to sign off on Credit Card specifications prior to production.
Selected Accomplishments:
- Established recognition and accountability as the technical 'Subject Matter Expert' for the product manufacturing lifecycle due to extensive knowledge of all equipment, systems, and ISO standards.
- Designed and set-up a satellite card manufacturing facility in Vancouver to improve services to the Asian market and produce an additional $2.8 million revenue.
- Championed a formal manufacturing process improvement to eliminate duplicate runs of production batches, which reduced stock usage, slashed turnaround time, and produced 37% cost savings.
Previous Positions Held:
- Manager, Data Operations
- Lead Equipment Operator

FORMAL EDUCATION

DEVRY INSTITUTE OF TECHNOLOGY, Mississauga, Ontario   1996 – 1998
- Diploma in Computer Programming for Business (Continuing Education)

PROFESSIONAL DEVELOPMENT

Actively committed to continuing education through courses, seminars, and workshops:
- Management Skills and Techniques, Canadian Management Centre
- Communicator/Facilitator, Negotiation, Project Management, and Behavioural Interviewing

TECHNICAL SKILLS

Proficient in a variety of software applications on various platforms including:
- Microsoft Office Suite (Word, Excel, PowerPoint, Project, Access, and Visio)
- Voiceover ATM, Voiceover IP, Cisco, Nokia, ACD, PBX, IVR, LAN, WAN

Sameer Khan

11 Stonehill Court, Unit 11
Toronto, ON M1M 1M1

Phone: (416) 555-1212
Email: skhan@careerprocanada.ca

EXPERIENCED MARKETING MANAGER

Top performing professional with over 5 years of experience in the full scope of marketing and advertising:

- Strong educational credentials with a Marketing Administration Diploma, a Bachelor in Business Administration, and a Certificate in Professional Management in-progress.

- Outstanding experience creating advertising copy, managing budgets, monitoring a distribution network, and building strong client relationships.

- Demonstrated communication skills include liaising with senior editors, suppliers, clients and employees, and developing strong partnerships with publication suppliers.

- Expertise in planning, organizing, analyzing, implementing, and marketing advertising campaigns.

- Proven ability to achieve revenue targets on advertising sales to both internal and external clients.

- Proficient in Microsoft Office, Photoshop, Act, and Lotus Smart Suite.

PROFESSIONAL EXPERIENCE

Marketing and Advertising Manager   1997 to 2006
Magna Newspaper, Greater Toronto University, Toronto, ON
(Magna Newspaper is the largest student newspaper in North America, publishing 23,000 copies bi-weekly.)

Overall responsibility for developing internal and external partnerships, managing budgets, maintaining quality of newspaper, and creative advertising. Accountable for distribution network.

- Created and recommended advertising strategies to department heads, which increased student awareness of university services by 15%.

- Achieved and exceeded annual advertising sales and revenue targets established by Magna Newspaper Board of Directors.

- Developed and maintained partnerships with such clients as Altoids, Blue Jays, and CFL, and managed client accounts for high profile 'Frosh' week.

- Communicated on an ongoing basis with printing suppliers and developed strong relationships to maintain and ensure that print deadlines were met 100% of the time.

- Increased readership by 10% through redesigning and monitoring over 150 distribution points.

- Maintained high quality employee skills by organizing and coordinating networking opportunities with internal clients such as university department heads and external clients, such as The Toronto Star, reducing costly errors by 5%.

- Recommended and provided team leadership on the successful development of online advertising. Monitored and measured success by number of online hits showing an increased readership by 25%.

Continued…

Marketing and Advertising Manager. Strong accomplishment bullets clearly quantify the individual's results with lists, amounts, and percentages.

Sameer Khan
Phone: (416) 555-1212

Sales Associate (part-time)   1994 to 1998
Hudson's Bay Company, Toronto, ON
(Queen Street is the Hudson's Bay Company's flagship store.)

Responsible for communicating with customers, responding to enquiries on products and services, and increasing sales through excellent customer service skills.

- Selected as Sales Representative for 4 corporate special events per year.
- Completed Hudson's Bay Retail Computer Courses and over 10 training seminars on sales and customer service.
- Created creative displays on a daily basis to maximize point of purchase impulse buys.

EDUCATION

Bachelor of Business Administration   Expected completion 2007
York University, Toronto, ON
Project Highlights:

- Created and implemented the development of a product with major emphasis on marketing.
- Produced print advertising as well as radio and television ads.
- Conducted product research on competitors and customers as part of market research.
- Analyzed and interpreted financial statements to forecast budgets.
- Developed a questionnaire for market research purposes.

Certificate in Professional Management   2006
York University, Toronto, ON
Project Highlights:

- Worked in teams to create reports on budgeting and forecasting.
- Presented findings with analysis and recommendations to professors.

Diploma in Marketing Administration   1994 to 1997
Seneca College, Toronto, ON
Achievements:

- Designated Vice President of External Affairs for the Marketing Association at Seneca College.
- Graduated with High Honours.

MARY COCHRANE

111 Lynden Street, Brantford, Ontario N1N 1N1   Phone: 519-555-1111   Email: mc@careerprocanada.ca

*A conscientious **Marketing and Sales Professional** with an extensive knowledge of brand management.*

Expertise includes:

➢*Advertising*   ➢*Merchandising*   ➢*Trade Marketing*   ➢*Strategic Planning*   ➢*Market Research*

CAREER ACHIEVEMENTS

SENIOR BRAND MANAGER   1999-2006
Sara Lee Household & Body Care Canada – Cambridge, ON

- Championed international project to develop new strategy to reinforce the Tana brand's leadership position in specialty trade for implementation in 19 countries.
- Developed new international look based on an architectural hierarchy to make it easier for consumers to shop for shoe care for entire product range (100+ skus).
- Created and implemented industry leading business-to-business model - s.t.e.p.s. (**S**pecialty **T**rade **E**nhanced **S**upport **P**rogram) for specialty trade retailers.
- Established annual retail sales associate contest among pillar accounts, which resulted in 25% sales increase.
- Led cross-functional team to create new Tana website for consumers and retailers only s.t.e.p.s. section.
- Launched new self-serve specialty merchandising racks to display Tana shoe care products in shoe stores.

MARKETING MANAGER   1998-1999
Germiphene Corporation – Brantford, ON

- Established Joint Sales agreement with Follare Oral Pharmaceuticals that provided Germiphene the right to sell COP products in Canada resulting in increased profitability.
- Implemented new monthly promotional program that allowed territory managers to increase customer base by 15% and sales by 39%.

BRAND MANAGER   1993-1998
Dow Brands Canada, Inc. – Paris, ON

- Achieved record profit levels for four consecutive years.
- Led project team to launch Fantastik Antibacterial in record time after obtaining government approval.
- Re-launched new & improved Handi-Wrap with lower product costs. Increased market share after several years of decline.
- Repositioned wraps under Ziploc umbrella for profit optimization.
- Co-ordinated and managed consumer focus groups and usage/attitude study. Utilized research findings in development of strategic plan for wraps.
- Increased profitability 10% through packaging redesign on Stretch'n Seal.

Marketing Brand Manager. Rather than a comprehensive profile, this résumé leads in with a short headline and some areas of expertise. It lets the uppercase bolded job titles speak for themselves. The strong quantifiable accomplishment bullets add value to the candidate's offering.

MARY COCHRANE...page 2

CAREER ACHIEVEMENTS...*continued*

SENIOR BRAND MANAGER   1987-1992
United Distillers, Canada Ltd. – Toronto, ON

- Implemented marketing and sales program for company's two largest brands in declining market. Grew market share nine share points over four years. Increased profitability by 55%.
- Led the industry in the development of integrated, innovative merchandising programs. Generated significant sales increases of 25%.
- Arrested share erosion of three established brands by developing and executing offensive brand strategy.
- Trained assistant brand manager to assume brand manager responsibilities.
- Proposed and spearheaded national continuous consumer research tracking study.

BRAND MANAGER   1981-1987
Gilbey Canada Inc. – Toronto, ON

- Relaunched three priority brands with new brand positioning, packaging change, new advertising campaign, and promotional activities. Programs resulted in increased market share and profitability.

EDUCATION & PROFESSIONAL DEVELOPMENT

- Master of Business Administration, McMaster University
  Co-op Program, Marketing Major

- Bachelor of Applied Science in Consumer Studies (Honours), University of Guelph

- Leadership Effectiveness, Leadership for Change, Kepner Tregoe (Project Management), Dale Carnegie – Effective Speaking & Human Relations, New Product Development, Finance for Non-Financial Managers

- Proficient in Office 2000 Applications, Cognos, A.C. Nielsen

CURRENT COMMUNITY VOLUNTEER INITIATIVES

- School Council Chair
- Guide Leader

ELISE MAYER

11 Street Crescent, Newton, Ontario • N1N 1N1
Home 519.555.4567 • Email elisemayer@CareerProCanada.ca

MEDICAL PROFESSIONAL
With Training & Time Management Strengths

Dedicated, patient-focused individual offering comprehensive experience in clinics and offsite locations. Meticulous regard for detail and accuracy with strong follow-through and administrative skills. Maintains composure, and makes decisions in fast-paced, unpredictable and stressful environments. Interfaces seamlessly with individuals from all backgrounds and levels. Respected leader and trainer. Resourceful in perceiving and resolving problems. Clear articulate communicator in both one-to-one and group settings. Accepts role as assigned and strives for excellent results. Without fail, projects a polished, positive and professional demeanour.

Core Competencies:

- ✔ Direct Patient Care
- ✔ Diagnosis & Treatment Care Planning
- ✔ Charting & Patient Documentation
- ✔ Instructing & Supervising
- ✔ Interdisciplinary Team Relations

- ✔ Administrative Detailing
- ✔ Confidentiality Assurance
- ✔ Sound Decision Making
- ✔ Workload Prioritization
- ✔ Stress Management

QUALIFICATIONS IN ACTION

MEDICAL TECHNICIAN/ ASSISTANT/ INSTRUCTOR　　　　　1990 - Present
Canadian Armed Forces Reserves

As a fully qualified medical professional, relied upon to serve in a variety of medical functions nationwide and globally. Solid experience in front-line unit section tasks like medical care and the education of military personnel and other trainers has resulted in multiple assignments. Senior designate to facilitate training measures for up to 150 military personnel from varying ranks for First Aid and CPR. Works effectively both on site and in remote locations.

- Supervised and mentored other instructors and medical staff, giving support and guidance. Followed through with drafting performance evaluations.
- Generated detailed lesson plans, ensuring the most current and applicable data is included and disseminated appropriately. Created summation notes and performed PowerPoint presentations. Provided extra help to maximize student learning.
- Provided immediate medical service in numerous settings. Conducted triage, took and recorded vitals, performed oxygen/IV therapy, gave immunizations, and partnered with physician to tend to any treatments. Prepared lab requisitions, accident reports and patient records.
- Called upon to provide important logistical and field support for emergency situations like the Ottawa Ice Storm and the Winnipeg Floods.
- Maintained accurate supply tracking records for accountability and effective resource allotment.
- Gave up personal time readily and consistently to volunteer for providing medical services and guidance at various public events and activities.
- Selected to fill duties in South West Asia as Medic. Instrumental in organizing hundreds of medical supplies and training operational professional staff for four ships. Trusted to fulfill the duties of a more senior ranking official on a regular, rotational basis.
- Cited as a professional who "ensures taskings are completed to the highest possible standard by constant checking and applying her excellent supervisory skills" and as "a self- directed individual who demonstrates a high degree of professionalism and problem-solving ability."

Continued ⇨

Medical Technician. This candidate converts specialized military medical training to a non-military setting by carefully altering terminology to civilian language.

ELISE MAYER

QUALIFICATIONS IN ACTION continued...

Managed time to work part time in these assignments, often balancing three roles at once...

INSTRUCTOR – FIRST AID/ CPR/ BABYSITTING COURSE	1996 - Present

St. Albert's Ambulance, Newton, Isaactown, and Parsons locations, Newtonville

HOME SUPPORT WORKER – PALLIATIVE CARE	1996 - 1997

St. Angela Nurses' Association, Newton and Isaactown locations, Newtonville

SPECIAL NEEDS WORKER	1996 - 1997

Isaactown Association for Community Living, Isaactown, Newtonville

HEALTH CARE AIDE	1995 - 1996

Newton Manor Nursing Home, Newton, Ontario

EDUCATION & SPECIALIZED TRAINING

As a **Medical Technician** and **Medical Assistant,** received multiple, progressively advanced military trades training modules.

EMERGENCY MEDICAL ASSISTANT	2001

Justice Institute of Newton, remotely via Isaactown campus, Newtwonville

PARAMEDIC PROGRAM	1999

Newton College, Isaactown, Newtonville

HOME SUPPORT WORKER 3, Palliative Care – Comfort Measure	1996

Apple College, Isaactown, Newtonville

HEALTH CARE AIDE CERTIFICATION – 240 hours of hands-on training	1995

Newton Vocational School, Isaactown, Newtonville

- Community Coaching
- First Aid Instructor Trainer
- First Aid & CPR Instructor
- First Responder
- Valid Standard First Aid & CPR
- Wilderness First Aid
- Sexual Harassment & Racism Prevention
- Suicide Intervention
- Lifeguard I, II, III
- Restricted Radiotelephone Operator

TECHNOLOGY: Word, PowerPoint, Outlook, Excel, Access, Medical Data Base H-task and Internet Research.

SIGNIFICANT RECOGNITION

Canadian Decoration - Awarded for Good Conduct throughout DND career.
Southwest Asia Medal - Noted for efforts during SW Asian tour.
Letters of Appreciation - Numerous congratulatory letters noting job proficiency, volunteer initiatives like Mess Committee President and advanced instructional capabilities.
Certificate of Recognition - Issued from the Mayor of the City of Hamilton for delivering generosity and compassion during the ice storm relief for Eastern Ontario and Quebec.

COMMUNITY INVOLVEMENT

- Treasurer of Simcoe County Ladies Soccer League 2004.
- Team manager of both CFB Borden's Mens and Ladies soccer teams 2004, and Ladies 2002.
- President of Intersection Soccer 2004.
- Sports representative for Junior Ranks Mess 2003.
- Vice-President of Simcoe County Ladies soccer 2002.
- Team member of CFB Borden Lasers soccer 2002.
- Team member of CFB Volleyball team 2003.

CARMITA MENDEZ
1234 Edenbrook Avenue
Mississauga, ON L1L 1L1
PH: (905) 555-0000
Email: carmita21@careerprocanada.ca

I have the experience; give me an opportunity
Tengo la experiencia; déme una oportunidad
J'ai l'expérience; donnez-moi une opportunité

HIGHLIGHTS OF QUALIFICATIONS

- More than 10 years of combined experience in **Office Management**, **Customer Service** and **Data Entry**.

- Fluent in English, Spanish and French.

- A take-charge individual willing to take on challenges and learn new skills.

- Excel at communicating and consensus building within and outside the Company.

- Independently oversaw day-to-day management of office, including supervision of staff and juggling competing priorities.

- Consistently exceeded monthly personal sales targets of **$40,000**, which resulted in winning numerous travel and incentive awards year after year.

EXPERIENCE

Travel Office Manager
El Lugar de Viajes
1234–123rd Avenue, Queens, NY, 11111   Jan '95 – Nov '03

Recruited to oversee the day-to-day activities of this 4-person office with a loyal clientele of approximately 300. Persuaded owner to become one of the first small-service firms to introduce and orient clients to use e-tickets.

- Served clients in Spanish, English and French.

- Made transportation and accommodation reservations using computerized reservation and ticketing system.

- Provided travel information to clients regarding destinations, transportation, tourist attractions, foreign currency, customs, accommodation options and travel costs.

- Planned and organized vacation travel for individuals and groups.

…continued

Office Manager. A creative banner headline gives no doubt that this candidate is trilingual.

- Successfully cultivated amicable relationships with other travel agencies and airlines resulting in extensive two-way referrals.
- Aggressively marketed destinations and tour packages to Mexico, Dominican Republic and St. Maarten, which accounted for **75%** of gross sales each year.
- Continuously sourced new travel destinations, hotels and other facilities and attractions to give clients a wider menu of choices.
- Supervised staff and made recommendations for pay increases and incentive awards.

Data Entry Operator

Exavier Data Services   Dec '93 – '95

(a subsidiary of A Major Airline)

1234 Conklin Drive, Brooklyn, NY 10123

- Quickly and efficiently keyed data into Sabre ticketing system, regularly receiving weekly error-free stroke reports.
- Managed a variety of databases, cruise line and passenger lists, and telephone contacts.
- Developed and maintained company's electronic filing system, reducing paper filings by **50%**.
- Recipient of prestigious Customer Service Award for contributions to Company's success for 1994 and 1995.

EDUCATION

- *Travel Agency Management* Certificate
  Elite Travel Careers Inc., Manhattan, NY 12345   Aug '01

- *Travel Consultant* Certificate
  Elite Travel Careers Inc., Manhattan, NY 12345   Nov '95

- *Conversational French*
  The Language Institute, Brooklyn, NY 10123   Apr '02

VERA SHORE

111 Denver Drive, Burlington, ON   L1L 1L1
Phone: 905 555-1111 • versa@careerprocanada.ca

PROCUREMENT/INVENTORY CONTROL MANAGER

An organized and reliable professional with a successful career history gained in packaged goods, manufacturing, and food industries. Behavioural flexibility, task orientation, and hands-on approach add value to overall profile. Areas of expertise include:

- Sourcing & Vendor Negotiations
- Inventory Analysis
- Warehouse Supervision
- Cross-Functional Projects
- Health & Safety Management

- Budget Development & Containment
- Production Planning
- Traffic & Logistics
- Supply Chain Management
- Leadership & Team Building

CAREER HISTORY & NOTEWORTHY ACHIEVEMENTS

KENSINGTON HOME CARE PRODUCTS - KITCHENER, ON   1993-Present
Purchasing/Safety Manager – 2002-2003
Logistics Manager/Safety Director – 1993-2002

- Procured 250 to 700 sku's with expenditure of over $20MM annually. Known for successful sourcing and productive vendor negotiations.

- Led a distribution team to move entire inventory ($2MM) from Burlington to Kitchener over a 12-week period without affecting picking, shipping, and customer service demands. Ensured full compliance with National Fire Protection Act due to large inventory of aerosol products.

- Consolidated processes to accommodate merger of Tallman Inc. with Kensington, which involved quickly learning new product and distribution differences. Within first 3 months, switched from 6 regional couriers to a major contract with Purolator, which reduced distribution costs by $200,000 annually. Maintained 2.1 to 2.3 variable freight factor over 9-year tenure.

- Assisted in the implementation of a Warehouse Management System; gathered weights and dimensional data for 600+ sku's, and laid out order picking process. Improved system and reduced warehouse head count by 25%.

- Liaised with sales and marketing to evaluate systems and recommend the implementation of an economical and flexible forecast management system. Solid background in product knowledge, principles of inventory control, and an appreciation for customer service added strength to cross-functional planning activities. This has subsequently evolved into a full-blown SO&P system.

- Increased inventory turns in 2002 from 2.8 to 3.9, increased customer order fill rate from 84% - 95% and reduced the inventory by $1MM.

- Wrote Safety Manual that included emergency plan and individual safety programs as required by Occupational Health & Safety Act. Experienced no lost time accidents in 11 years.

Procurement Manager. This résumé is rich in accomplishments. Care is taken in each bullet point to quantify the achievement whenever possible with dollars, percentages, and other numbers.

VERA SHORE   page 2

DEVONSHIRE MEDICAL PRODUCTS – OAKVILLE, ON   1989-1993
Warehouse Supervisor – 1991-1993
Production Planner – 1990-1991
Inventory Analyst – 1989-1990

- Led a logistics team to implement an automated replenishment system to reduce customer order turnaround of offsite warehouse goods from 48 to 24 hours. Worked closely with IT to develop replenishment report by overcoming inventory discrepancies and product expiry issues.

- Reduced lost shipping days from 5 to 1.5 for physical inventory count by pre-printing 10,000 plus inventory tags in logical counting pattern.

- Planned and improved overall layout and operation of warehouse through more efficient staging of raw materials and finished goods. Successfully reduced the amount of materials handling, which made it easier for personnel to access raw materials during off-hours.

- Planned production to meet requirements of domestic market needs and North American export customers. Oversaw 10 production lines with a daily output of 2.2 million surgical gloves daily.

- Procured 4,000 sku's annually with full responsibility for $15MM inventory.

TALLMAN INDUSTRIES – BURLINGTON, ON   1985-1989
Purchasing Agent

- Selected vendors and negotiated pricing and procurement of approximately 250 – 300 sku's annually.

- Developed flawless work record and excellent reputation that resulted in recruitment back to the company in 1993 when consolidation with Kensington Canada occurred.

EDUCATION

MCMASTER UNIVERSITY – HAMILTON, ON
Bachelor of Applied Science in Consumer Studies

PMAC (PURCHASING MANAGEMENT ASSOCIATION OF CANADA)
Principles of Production Inventory Control
Principles of Transportation
Principles of Buying

ONTARIO HEALTH & SAFETY
Certification (2nd level) Warehouse Safety
Current First Aid Certificate (1st level and CPR)

John Smith

123 Main Avenue ◆ Ottawa, ON K1K 1K1 ◆ 613.555.1234 ◆ jsmith@careerprocanada.ca

TECHNOLOGY

VB ◆ SQL DML & DDL ◆ ASP ◆ ActiveX ◆ MQSeries ◆ VBA ◆ Crystal Report ◆ Clipper
NT ◆ 2000 ◆ XP ◆ TCP/IP ◆ XML ◆ HTML
OS/400 ◆ RPG/ILE ◆ CL ◆ Query ◆ SEQUEL ◆ J-Walk
MS Word ◆ Excel ◆ Outlook ◆ Internet Explorer ◆ PC Anywhere

STRENGTHS

- Over 13 years' programming experience on various platforms—VB on NT/SQL platform, OOP using Clipper, RPGLE on the iSeries.
- Demonstrated ability to learn and excel with new technologies; in-depth knowledge of VB, and excellent understanding of VB/.NET concepts.
- Very strong foundation of Object Oriented Programming and Design, and database normalization techniques.
- Skilled in identifying problem areas, recognizing the impact on the business and users, and prioritizing the implementation of appropriate solutions.
- Established leadership and training capabilities.

PROFESSIONAL EXPERIENCE

Your Discount Stores Ltd., Ottawa, Ontario   1994 to Present
Technical Lead ◆ Senior Programmer Analyst ◆ Senior Technical Support ◆ 3rd Line Support
Provide development and support of business applications, including Retail Sales, Warehousing, Distribution, Buying, Marketing, Payroll, and Accounting. Apt at solving technical challenges; easily identifies business benefits (needs versus desires). Promoted to positions of increasing responsibilities.

- Supervisor comments: *"Learned VB/SQL at an extremely fast pace… Very strong problem solving skills…Resolved Sybase database corruption problem…Good job in meeting deadlines…Strong leadership…Strong people skills… Excellent communications."*
- Technical leader of the POS Store System, including application architecture and database design using VB and SQL.
  - POS Store System back-office functionality: AS/400 to PC data interchange, Buying, Purchase Orders, Receiving, Sign printing, Accounting, Payroll & Scheduling, and various process oriented and analytical reports.
  - Mentored developers, contractors, and consultants on becoming proficient with VB.
- Recommended that MQSeries replace an old, obsolete store polling system, which would provide improved AS/400 to VB inter-communication. **Results**: recommendation was approved.
  - Experienced with various cross-platform data sharing technologies, from the use of flat files, to transactional messaging systems such as MQSeries.
- Demonstrated ability to code lower-level APIs, which allowed VB to interact with the NT operating system—NT and NT Server.
- Provided a working VB prototype—within 2 hours—to a team of developers, for POS Store System to interact with a third-party C language application running as a server.
- Developed a Purolator Transaction Management application. **Results**: approximately 20 hours per month was saved for users to dedicate to other tasks.
- Designed and coded a Staff Scheduling and Payroll Analysis application.
  - Generated a 3-5% staff scheduling efficiency for the stores—significant annual savings when applied company wide for 2,000+ employees.
  - Instrumental in guiding the store managers/owners in scheduling allocatable payroll hours as a correlation to sales.

Programmer Analyst. This résumé leads in with a list outlining technology expertise. The candidate then dedicates a great amount of space to his foremost employer. This technique emphasizes this individual's experience and accomplishments.

- Trained Help Desk in network maintenance, and in troubleshooting systems and applications.
- Authored numerous business documents, technical analysis documents, and quality assurance plans, as part of the overall development process of new systems.

Canadian Government, Ottawa, Ontario   1991 to 1994
CS-2 Programmer/Analyst
Provided end-user support of third-party applications, and developed several in-house applications.

- Developed strong Object Oriented Programming knowledge using CLIPPER.
- Authored a Payroll Audit application. **Results:** Auditors had a powerful tool to help them identify discrepancies in employee/employer EI/CPP contribution. Application precision was critical as the data could be used in a court of law.
- Designed and programmed an application to track Duplicate CPP/QPP postings—challenged with requiring the application to communicate between similar programs at Health & Welfare Canada and Régie des Rentes du Quebec, at a time before the use of the Internet facilitated such endeavours.
  - Built telecommunication interface.
  - Created a process to share data between disparate systems.
  - Designed and implemented data security, ownership, and reconciliation.

ADDITIONAL WORK EXPERIENCE

Conceived, designed, authored, and sold a PC-based Inventory application to J.D. Fine Papers.
- Application benefited J.D. Fine Papers for over 13 years before being ported to their AS/400.

EDUCATION

Pursuing *Computer Information Systems/Computer Programmer Diploma*, Algonquin College, Ottawa, Ontario.

Additional Courses: Active Server Pages, Database Architecture, Java, Business Statistics, and Business Math.

- References available on request -

ELISE DAYE, BFA, MA

11 Gloucester Street, Toronto, Ontario ▪ M1M 1M1
Home 416.555.4321 ▪ E-mail edaye@careerprocanada.ca

COMMUNICATIONS SPECIALIST
~ Specializing in Public Relations and Medicine ~

Highly motivated and respected professional with strengths in writing, presenting within a cross-functional context. Passionate interest in medicine, health care and personal wellness. Valued for consistently exhibiting a calm and positive demeanour, regardless of the situation. Clear, refined and diplomatic communicator, both oral and written. Interact favourably with others from all levels, cultures and backgrounds. Sincere and honest with a high level of personal and professional integrity. Balance demands from multiple stakeholders. **Core competencies include:**

~ Community Relations	~ Writing & Editing
~ International & Cultural Experience	~ Stress Management
~ Public & Media Relations	~ Workload Prioritization
~ Presentations, Training & Speeches	~ Confidentiality Assurance
~ Research & Reporting	~ Board Relations

EDUCATION & SPECIALIZED TRAINING

MASTERS OF ARTS   2006
University of Toronto, Toronto, Ontario
Studies included:

☑	History of the Profession	☑ Canadian Psychiatry
☑	Canadian Health Care	☑ Canadian Social History
☑	Canadian Medicine	☑ Material Culture

Thesis: *The History of Psychiatry in Ontario*

PROFESSIONAL DRAMA STUDIES   2003
School of Drama, England
THE SECOND CITY CONSERVATORY PROGRAM (2 year program)   2003
Second City Review, Toronto, Ontario
BACHELOR OF FINE ARTS   1999
York University, Toronto, Ontario

☑	Vocal Training	☑ Advanced Improvisation
☑	Voiceover Technique	☑ On Camera Scene Study
☑	Comedy Writing	☑ Improvised Singing

CAREER PATH

TRAINING FACILITATOR & SUPERVISOR   1999 - 2003
                                                           (Sabbatical in 2004)

Coffee Company, Toronto
Skill-set relied upon to serve dual roles with this busy specialty coffee chain. Proficient in the "hands on" role of Barista, training corporate executives, managing staff performance, customer relations, and all administrative functions.

~ Continued on Page 2 ~

Public Relations Specialist. This candidate pulls together a wide range of positions by centering her power statement on communications and public relations. She follows this up with her Master's degree to drive the focus towards the health-care industry.

Career Path Continued...

- One of 10 Canadian Training Facilitators. Train professionals from all levels within the Eastern Canada Region. Ensure all coffee company employees have the fundamentals of product preparation in conjunction with customer service.
- Trusted with store keys, alarm codes, and handling cash deposits of $10 000.
- Create in-store message boards. Present new promotions, products and corporate objectives for teams of 12.

STAND UP COMEDIAN   1997 - 2006
Greater Toronto Area
Retained to provide entertainment for multiple comedy clubs and cabarets. Scouted for television shows and festivals, commercials and live theatre. Performed these activities in addition to daytime responsibilities. Distributed press kit including news releases, biography, photos and performance history.

- Received special recognition for *Best New Female Comic* at Yuk Yuk's talent search.
- Opened for Adam Sandler at the *Laugh Resort*. Worked with Canadian talent like Mike Bullard, Ron James and Colin Mochrie.

THE SECOND CITY EDUCATION PROGRAM INSTRUCTOR   2005
Second City Training Centre, Toronto, Ontario
Conducted workshops for both elementary and secondary school students. Required to prepare and implement programming adhering to *Ontario Curriculum* guidelines. This was not a comedy class, rather, a structured program addressing the following concepts:

☑ Team Building	☑ Group & Interpersonal Relationships
☑ Listening & Comprehension	☑ Leadership Divergent Thinking
☑ Communication & Presentation	☑ Focus & Concentration
☑ Risk Taking	☑ Improvisation

ADMINISTRATIVE PROFESSIONAL   2000 - 2001
Graphic Arts Support, Toronto, Ontario
Selected to administer office managerial functions for this recruiting agency for registered graphic designers. Sourced leads and addressed phone enquiries. Generated accounts payable.

- Revamped supply and inventory methods increasing operational efficiency.

TECHNOLOGY

Windows, Word, PowerPoint, HTML, Dreamweaver, Outlook and Internet Research.

COMMUNITY INVOLVEMENT

- Mentor for Toronto University's 2005 on-line program for 10 History high school students.
- Special Olympics 1999 volunteer for athlete hospitality and food services.

"Elise has a wonderful ability to deal with people, to radiate kindness and friendliness and good humor in an entirely unaffected and uncalculated way. It is what one calls a "mega-watt personality." She would be well suited for any position involving dealing with the public or where positive, upbeat relations with co-workers are at a premium."
Kevin Kidd PhD. FRSC
Faculty of Arts, Toronto, Ontario

DEAN R. DOBSON

30 Princess Drive
Winnipeg, Manitoba, R1R 1R1

Phone (204) 555-1234
E-mail drd@careerprocanada.ca

EXPERIENCED QUALITY ASSURANCE MANAGER

Results-oriented professional with demonstrated achievements in quality assurance, manufacturing, and customer support for industry leaders. Dynamic team leader with strong communication and interpersonal skills, combining innovation with polished execution to ensure operational excellence. Effective negotiator, with a talent for fostering successful supplier relationships, resulting in improved quality and reduced costs. Highly responsive to change, with the proven ability to excel in a fast-paced environment. A customer-focused individual, capable of prioritizing, delegating, and coordinating tasks to meet critical deadlines.

Areas of Expertise:

✦ Engineering Support	✦ Supplier Management	✦ Leadership & Team Building
✦ Technical Documentation	✦ Parts Sourcing	✦ Training & Support
✦ Cost Estimation	✦ Tooling Maintenance	✦ Process Re-engineering
✦ Technical Troubleshooting	✦ ISO 9002 Implementation	✦ Best Practices

CAREER HIGHLIGHTS

QUALITY MANAGEMENT

- ✦ Achieved ISO 9002 Certification for ABC Air Ltd. by documenting and coordinating the application of quality specifications and standards.

- ✦ Reviewed non-conformance reports, authorized the release of over 1000 parts, and jointly resolved concerns with engineering, as a member of both the Material and Tooling Review Boards.

PROJECT MANAGEMENT

- ✦ Instituted best practices and amalgamated worldwide metrology procedures, as the company representative to the Corporate Metrology Systems Committee.

- ✦ Investigated and selected a strategic partner, and outsourced the calibration functions, maintaining quality standards despite company downsizing.

SUPPLIER MANAGEMENT

- ✦ Conducted formal surveys auditing prospective tooling suppliers, interpreted the results, and recommended first-rate suppliers for program inclusion.

- ✦ Resolved supplier quality issues by actively meeting suppliers at their location and assisting them with corrective action plans.

Quality Assurance Manager. The career highlights section cleanly outlines this candidate's three major areas of interest with associated accomplishments. The résumé closes with a snappy tagline.

DEAN R. DOBSON, Phone (204) 555-1234   Page 2

PROFESSIONAL EXPERIENCE

XYZ Construct Inc., Winnipeg, Manitoba   **2003 - Present**
$2.8 billion global manufacturer of a broad range of construction, infrastructure, and mining equipment.
Quality Assurance Supervisor
Responsible for all aspects of quality management, working closely with the engineering department. Accountable to qualify suppliers and manage ongoing relationships. Responsibilities include verifying incoming and outgoing quality, solving line problems, and recommending improvements to engineering.

+ Instituted a formal quality system based on ISO principles, which resulted in significant purchasing cost savings and a 15% reduction in defective parts entering production.
+ Assigned and took on the increased responsibility to assist the engineering department in creating computer designs in Solid Works 2004, which augmented engineering output 15%.
+ Identified and eliminated shortcomings with existing engineering processes, ensuring that tolerances on drawings are 100% accurate and parts being received are to drawing specifications.

ABC Air Ltd., Mississauga, Ontario   **1986 - 2003**
Global market leader in aircraft manufacturing with $40 billion revenue.
Quality Assurance Manager (1996-2003)
Quality Assurance Supervisor (1986-1996)
Responsible for all aspects of quality assurance. Provide leadership and support to a staff of 16. Ensure the efficient flow of work through the Tool Inspection, Machined Parts Inspection, and Metrology departments. Ensure that calibration of inspection, measure, and test equipment meets national standards. Provide technical support to Engineering, Fabrication, and Assembly departments to resolve production issues. Qualify and manage supplier relationships. Accountable to manage budget, manpower, and actual costs.

+ Played a key role in achieving ISO 9002 Certification and ensuring compliance with government and regulatory requirements by developing, implementing, and maintaining written quality procedures.
+ Appointed as the member delegate to the National Conference of Standard Laboratories, and represented ABC Air at international meetings.
+ Assigned additional responsibility of managing the tool room which housed manufacturing and repairing tools used in the construction of airplane wings and components.

FORMAL EDUCATION
Sheridan College, Mississauga, Ontario
+ Quality Assurance Program (completed courses in Statistics, Probability, Finance & Management)
General Technical College, London, England
+ National Certificate, Engineering
+ City and Guilds Certificate, Engineering

PROFESSIONAL DEVELOPMENT
Actively committed to continuing education via courses, seminars, workshops, and trade shows:
+ Certified Tool & Diemaker

PROFESSIONAL AFFILIATIONS
+ Federal Aviation Administration (FAA), Designated Manufacturing Inspection Representative (DMIR)
+ Canadian Department of Transport (DOT), Designated Airworthiness Inspection Representative (AIR)

TECHNICAL SKILLS
Proficient in a variety of software applications including:
+ Microsoft Word and Excel, Solid Works, and Unigraphics CAD

QUALITY...INNOVATION...SERVICE

CATHERINE WESTBROOK

12 Masters Road, Winnipeg, Manitoba R1R 1R1 • Home: (204) 555-1234 • Cellular: (204) 555-6789 • Email: cw@careerprocanada.ca

PROFESSIONAL PROFILE

Dedicated **Real Estate Law Clerk** with over 14 years professional experience, distinguished by continuous advancement, professional achievement, and solicitor/client commendation. Knowledgeable and proficient in all Acts applicable to Real Estate Law. Outstanding written, interpersonal, and organizational skills.

PERSONAL STRENGTHS AND EXPERTISE

- Project Management
- Problem Solving
- Multi-tasking
- Client Relations
- Negotiation
- Process Redesign / Improvement

Computer proficiencies include Corel WordPerfect, MS Word, Excel, Lotus 1-2-3, SoftDocs, Teraview 4.0 – POLARIS, Teraview 4.0 – Writs, E-mail, Windows Scheduler, and Calendar.

PROFESSIONAL EXPERIENCE

Law Clerk   *1999 – Present*
CITY OF WINNIPEG, Corporate Services Dept., Real Estate Div.   *Winnipeg, Manitoba*

- Support 5 real estate solicitors by accurately completing all supporting research and documentation for up to 50 concurrent municipal conveyances, requiring extensive knowledge of Real Estate Law and applicable acts, and ability to multi-task under extremely tight deadlines.
- Research and prepare all related documentation including correspondence, memoranda, requisitions, agreements, easements, undertakings, deeds, letters of credit, land transfer tax affidavits, and statements of adjustment.
- Confer with all levels of staff in all departments, as well as external solicitors and general public.
- Identify and resolve title and/or conveyance problems to secure title, and alert solicitor as required.
- Conduct remote title searches, *Registry Act* searches, and *Land Titles Act* searches.

Improvements Made:

➢ Negotiated with Finance Department to streamline the processing of *Municipal Tax Sales Act* documents, resulting in a 50% reduction in turnaround time.
➢ Created cross-referencing system for Agreement information, a solution implemented by all municipalities in the greater Winnipeg area..
➢ Arranged access to Property Database for all law clerks, significantly streamlining process.

Noteworthy Projects and Accomplishments:

➢ Successfully drafted all requisite documentation for extensive Empress condominium land exchange, involving over 35 registered documents and extremely tight deadlines.
➢ Researched and drafted all documentation for complex tri-party exchange involving 5 council authorities.
➢ Granted approval authority by Deputy City Solicitor for all releases and Municipal Tax Sales Act documents.

.../2

"Catherine is one of the most dedicated, hard working employees I have had the privilege to work with. She works well independently and is very disciplined. As a result, she always meets deadlines. Perhaps Catherine's greatest skill is her ability to learn quickly. She was selected for promotion over many of her peers with much longer tenure."

J.A. Wilson
Real Estate Manager
Corporate Real Estate Div.
Winnipeg Hydro

"We have continued to give Catherine new and more difficult challenges and each time she has responded beyond our expectations. The clear strengths of Catherine not only lie in her 'leading edge' law clerk skills but also in her superior behavioural skills of project management, client relations and open communications."

Michael Callaway
Real Estate Manager
Corporate Real Estate Div.
Winnipeg Hydro

Real Estate Law Clerk. The unique format of this résumé emphasizes the candidate's tremendous references. She makes a compelling presentation by displaying a blend of noteworthy improvements, projects, and accomplishments that directly relate to her area of expertise.

Employee Relocation Assistant   1995 – 1999
WINNIPEG HYDRO, Corporate Real Estate Division   *Winnipeg, Manitoba*
- Coordinated successful employee relocations, completing all documentation in accordance with policy and procedures, as well as arrangement of advances on equity, employee legal fees, and moving details.
- Conferred with employees, human resources, legal department, and external moving companies to ensure successful transition.

Improvements Made:
➢ Co-authored Augusta Hydro employee relocation manual for province-wide use.
➢ Created Lotus spreadsheets to accurately complete and streamline accounting functions.

Title Searcher / Conveyancer   1990 – 1995
WINNIPEG HYDRO, Corporate Real Estate Division   *Winnipeg, Manitoba*
- Researched, reviewed, interpreted and drafted real estate agreements and supporting documentation for both corporate and residential real estate transactions across Ontario.
- Required thorough understanding of real estate law, applicable acts, and Hydro Electric Commission of Ontario Act, as well as the ability to work effectively and accurately in deadline-driven environment.

Improvements Made:
➢ Recommended and implemented computer-based process to streamline transfer of documentation between regional offices throughout Ontario – travelled to regional offices to provide training.
➢ Negotiated with external law firms to settle legal fees, effectively reducing fees by 25%.

Accomplishments:
➢ Personally selected by Real Estate Manager to assume duties of Land Transfer Supervisor, managing a staff of 11 professional and clerical employees and monitoring job performance, workload, and scheduling.

Junior Conveyancer   1985 – 1988
WINNIPEG HYDRO, Corporate Real Estate Division   *Winnipeg, Manitoba*
- Reporting to Title Searcher/Conveyancer, drafted and prepared supporting documentation for real estate transactions throughout Ontario.

EDUCATION AND PROFESSIONAL ACCREDITATION

B.A. – Criminology, University of Winnipeg   1988
General Business Diploma – Legal Assistant, Winnipeg College   1985

Commissioner of Oaths   since 1990

DOUG MOFFATT, R.M.T. (Registration #M123)
11 Birchbark Way • North York, Ontario • M1M 1M1 • 647–555–1234

QUALIFICATIONS OVERVIEW

Enthusiastic, dedicated, sensitive, and proactive **Registered Massage Therapist** offering the benefit of 6 years' experience detecting and releasing the deep, underlying restrictions associated with — and stemming from — motor vehicle accidents, sports injuries, work-related stresses, musculoskeletal disorders, fibromyalgia, Multiple Sclerosis, Cerebral Palsy, and Parkinson's Disease. **Proven ability to expand an operation's bottom line based on ability to earn client trust and build strong client relations**. Sincere and honest with a high level of personal and professional integrity. Certified in C.P.R. and First Aid. Fluent in Polish with conversational ability in Czech. **Passionate about maintaining own fitness and health levels — as well as enhancing clients' overall quality of life — based on earlier experience as a Soccer Coach for 7 years and as a Physical Education Teacher for 1 year**.

Key Massage Therapy Competencies:

Regulatory Compliance • Client Needs Assessment • General Full Body & Regional Massage

Joint Play & Mobilization Swedish Massage Techniques • Remedial Exercise Programs

Cold & Hot Hydrotherapy • Friction & Trigger Point Therapy • Strain/Counterstrain Therapy

Manual Lymph Drainage • Therapeutic Additive Usage • Soft Tissue Injury Treatment

Key Management Capabilities:

Business & Market Development • Financial Management • Problem-Solving & Decision-Making

Staff Productivity Improvement • Strategic Alliance Formation • Tactical Planning & Execution

SELECTED PROFESSIONAL AND ACADEMIC ACHIEVEMENTS

- Consistently increased revenues by as much as 300% — and enhanced overall corporate operations — by gaining a reputation for growing customer base *(all)*

- Catalyst behind the development of a program that promoted ergonomic improvement and boosted overall staff productivity *(Active Health)*

- Repeatedly hailed by supervisors and patients alike for maintaining better-than-average customer satisfaction levels *(Active Health and Antibes)*

- Introduced gift certificate incentive programs designed to expand patient traffic *(Active Health and Antibes)*

- Part of a multi-person Massage Therapy Team that participated in the following sports events: (1) Canadian Karate Championship, Mississauga; (2) Professional Beach Volleyball Tournament, Toronto; (3) 10-K Marathon, Toronto; and (4) Canadian Swimming Championship, Toronto *(Dawes Road)*

Registered Massage Therapist. This résumé strongly highlights the candidate's technical competencies. It features concrete examples of stellar service in his "Selected Professional and Academic Achievements," which places him head-and-shoulders above other applicants.

DOUG MOFFATT, R.M.T. (Registration #M123) • 647–555–1234   **Page Two**

EDUCATION AND PROFESSIONAL DEVELOPMENT

Neuromuscular Integration & Structural Alignment • Advanced Sports Massage: The Runner •
Sports Massage Certificate • Summerhill Wong Clinic, Toronto   2006
Therapeutic Ultrasound & Interferential Current/TENS • Institute of Well-Being, Toronto   2005
Completed 5-Hour Course on Accommodating MVA Referrals & Marketing • CMTO, Toronto   2004
Completed "Law and the Health Profession" course • The Miller Institute, Toronto   2003
Certificate in Lymph Drainage Therapy • The Uplands Institute, Toronto   2002
Matrix Repatterning • Wellness Systems Inc., Toronto   2002

R.M.T. Diploma • Dawes Road College, Toronto   2000–2002
Successfully completed 2,200 hours of training, which included – in addition to **Key Competencies** above
  – Anatomy, Physiology, Pathology, Human Sciences, and Myofascial Work. Also earned Board / License
  Examination

EMPLOYMENT HIGHLIGHTS

Registered Massage Therapist, Active Health Conglomerate, Toronto   2 years and ongoing
Registered Massage Therapist & Manager, Doug Moffatt Massage Therapy, Toronto   1.5 years
Registered Massage Therapist, Antibes Chiropractic Clinic, Toronto   1.5 years
Registered Massage Therapist, The Manor Community Centre, Toronto   1 year
Assistant to Physiotherapist (part-time), Healthy Body Fitness Club, Toronto   2 years

CLINICAL EXPERIENCE

Dawes Road College, Toronto   2000–2002
  Completed over 200 clinical hours assisting patients suffering from motor vehicle accidents, sports
  injuries, and work-related impairments.

PROFESSIONAL MEMBERSHIP

Member, International Association of Healthcare Educators

REFERENCES PROVIDED UPON REQUEST

JANELLE MASON
University of Victoria Collaborative Nursing Program

1234 West 11th Avenue
Vancouver, BC V1V 1V1

jmason@CareerProCanada.ca

daytime (604) 555 7777
mobile (604) 555 9999

OBJECTIVE: A Registered Nurse position in a major hospital facility.

PROFILE: Extensive experience as a Licensed Practical Nurse. Very broad range of clinical assignments. Highly regarded by-supervisors and strongly recommended for a career as a Registered Nurse. Outstanding academic success and professional credentials.

ACADEMIC and PROFESSIONAL ENDORSEMENTS:

Ms. Mason is a valuable member of the interdisciplinary care team... an asset to this facility."
- Bev O'Doul, RN, BSN

"...a caring and devoted LPN...excellent skills...an informed participant... goes that 'extra step'... wonderful sense of humour...always a pleasure to work with her... It is a privilege to recommend her for the RN programme..."
- Geraldine Hart, RN

"Janelle demonstrated many responsible behaviours... She is extremely well-organized and incorporates new information and skills quickly... I enjoyed her eagerness to learn"
- E. Gail Thomas, RN, BSN, MSN

"Shares her knowledge and helps out peer students"
- Heather Tompkins, RN, MSN

EDUCATION:

Bachelor of Science in Nursing (nearing completion, April 2006)   2003 - Present
University of Victoria, Victoria, BC

Licensed Practical Nurse (LPN)   1992 - 1993
Vancouver Community College, Vancouver, BC

REGISTRATIONS and CERTIFICATIONS:
- Registered Member, College of Licensed Practical Nurses of BC   1993 - 2005
- Student Representative, Registered Nurses Association of BC
- Additional certification in CPR and training in telemetry (St. Paul's Hospital)

PRACTICA:

Burns and Plastics Preceptorship   Dec 2005 – Feb 2006
Vancouver General Hospital   (400 hours)
- Cared for patients with major burns and tracheotomies.
- Participated in burn showers and debridement.
- Monitored central venous catheters, arterial lines, fluid and electrolyte balances.
- Practiced reverse and standard isolation procedures.
- Made up and applied sterile burn dressings.

Cardiac Surgery Preceptorship   Sep 2005 - Nov 2005
St Paul's Hospital   (411 hours)
- Cared for a full load of 4 to 5 pre- and post-operative cardiac patients.
- Administered oral, subcutaneous, and intravenous medications. Applied post-operative dressings and removed staples and sutures. Conducted septic workups. Monitored blood work.
- Completed nursing assessment forms for pre-operative patients. Taught patients during the discharge process. Participated in a Code Blue.
- Took a telemetry course. Improved upon patient teaching skills. Consulted with physicians and the other team members. Participated in rounds.

Public Health Nurse's Assistant   May 2005 - Aug 2005
New Westminster Public Health Unit   (78 hours)
- Delivered health care and education to maternity wards, private homes, secondary schools, and colleges.
- Assisted with vaccination clinics for infants, toddlers, children, and adults.
- Facilitated "Baby Talk" sessions conducted by the Pregnancy Outreach Program.
- Visited speech and language pathologists and assisted at the Needle Exchange.

Page 1 of 2

Registered Nurse. This résumé conveys a large amount of specific medical information in a compact space. The left-hand side of an attractive dual-column format features glowing "Academic and Professional Endorsements."

Résumé of Janelle Mason (continued)

Public Forum Organizer   Jan 2005 - Apr 2005
Evergreen Community Health Centre   (78 hours)
- Assisted service providers in a Community Health Area with identifying food security problems in the surrounding neighbourhoods.

Care Coordinator's Assistant   Sep 2004 - Dec 2004
Victory House Residence   (180 hours)
- Cared for 48 patients with various forms of mental illness in Vancouver's impoverished Downtown Eastside.

Surgical Floor Practicum   Jun 2004 - Aug 2004
Surrey Memorial Hospital   (108 hours)
- Provided post-operative care to patients with conditions such as colostomies, appendectomies, hernia repairs, and stomach banding.
- Assisted patients whose conditions included endocarditis, cellulitis, bowel obstruction, and angina.

Medical/Surgical Floor Practicum   Jan 2004 - Apr 2004
University of British Columbia Hospital   (180 hours)
- Medical ward: 90 hours. Patient conditions included unstable angina, exacerbation of congestive heart failure, stroke, brain tumour (provided palliative care), query pulmonary embolism and exacerbation of lupus.
- Surgical floor: 90 hours. Provided post-operative care to patients with bowel resection surgery, femoral-poplitial bypasses, surgically repaired leg fracture, jaw surgery, and trans-urethral prosthetic resections.
- Intensive Care Unit: 7.5 hours, angiocathether laboratory: 7.5 hours.

Obstetrics and Maternity Practicum   Oct 2003 - Nov 2003
Richmond General Hospital   (90 hours)
- Provided care to mothers and newborns.
- Labour and delivery: 7.5 hours; special care nursery: 7.5 hours.

EMPLOYMENT HISTORY:

Care Aid   Nov 2003 - Present
St Alban's Hospital (Trevor Adams Pavilion) Extended Care Ward
- Duties as per previous LPN position (LPN positions were reclassified).

Licensed Practical Nurse   Sep 1994 - Nov 2003
St Alban's Hospital (Trevor Adams Pavilion) Extended Care Ward
- Carried out catheterizations, dressing changes, daily living activities and patient assessments.
- Prepared the hospital for accreditation in nursing standards and patient care.
- Preceptored 4 LPN students.
- Participated in care issues and multidisciplinary meetings.

Licensed Practical Nurse   Dec 1993 - Sep 1994
Shaughnessy Hospital
- Assisted in the medical, surgical, spinal cord and extended care wards.

ROBERT SEATON

One Rogers Court
Barrie, Ontario • L1L 1L1
705-555-1234 • Messages: 705-555-0123
Email R-Seaton@ CareerProCanada.ca

RETAIL MANAGER

Profile

"Customer-first" professional with nearly 10 years of increasingly responsible experience selling an assortment of products to individuals from all demographic and economic backgrounds. **Can be entrusted by senior management to take on – and complete – extra duties, all the while striving to exceed customer and company expectations.** An effective communicator, able to foster and maintain positive ties with clients, staff, and management from all walks of life. WHMIS certified. Computer knowledge includes in-house programs, Word, and Windows XP. **Strives to apply unique blend of flexibility, high energy, and maturity in order to inspire employees to achieve bottom-line success.** Willing to relocate.

Areas of Strength:
Customer Relationship-Building, Loyalty & Retention • Buyer Awareness
Diplomatic Compliant Resolution • Closing Techniques • Employee Scheduling
Goal-Setting & Incentive Planning • Inventory Control • Loss Prevention
Mass-Merchandising Techniques • Opening & Closing Procedures • Warehousing Operations
Problem Resolution & Critical Decision-Making • Senior Staff & Vendor Relations
Staff Training & Team-Building • Till Set-Up & Reconciliation • Competitive Analysis

Professional Experience

Tires R Us, Port Elgin   2005 - Present

Assistant Store Manager

Recruited to collaborate with store manager in running entire operations – consisting of 3 departments – spanning 9,800 sq. ft. Specific accountabilities included store opening and closing, managing shipping / receiving / warehouse departments, and addressing a myriad of customer concerns.

Achievements:

- Tapped to reorganize all aspects of store – including stockroom, sales floor, exterior grounds, and shop – that had not received proper attention since store opening in Year 2000. Completed this ambitious project in only 3 months.

- Eliminated all metal throw-aways by contacting a local recycler who could haul away such material; also recouped an extra $500 that the recycler was happy to pay.

- Took the initiative to instruct staff on proper up-selling techniques; as a result, consistently exceeded revenues based on previous year's performance.

- Successfully identified, organized, and sold "discontinued" merchandise valued at $20,000 – a first at this location.

- Instituted a ruling whereby staff would electronically log off at the end of their shift, thereby easing the end-of-day closing process.

Retail Store Manager. The bold arrow graphic easily captures the reader's attention. The first third of the résumé is laden with powerful key words, and the bona fide results are sure to motivate prospective employers to invite this accomplished manager in for an interview.

ROBERT SEATON

705-555-1234 • Messages: 705-555-0123
Email R-Seaton@ CareerProCanada.ca

Page Two

Professional Experience (cont'd)

Pasco Furniture, Newmarket   2002 - 2005

2003 - 2005: Senior Sales Consultant / Acting Manager

Promoted – based on history of "repeatedly going the extra mile" – to assume broader level of responsibilities such as staff training, solving an array of problems as they arise, and selling product from entire floor consisting of audio/video, furniture, and appliances departments.

Achievements:

- Credited with generating highest revenue levels for 3 consecutive months in Audio / Visual and Appliance departments.
- Repeatedly persuaded vendors to prioritize repairs for customers based on top-notch commitment to customer satisfaction.
- Hand-picked by Store Manager to serve on the store-wide Health & Safety Committee consisting of managers and non-managers.
- Tapped both by Store Manager and District Manager to travel to Quebec for 2 weeks and open 2 new stores; specific accountabilities included staff support, management, sales, warehouse operations, and customer service.
- Awarded an incentive (out of 45 employees) for exceptional Electronic Product Knowledge.

2002 - 2003: Sales Consultant – Audio/Video and Appliances

Tires R Us, Aurora   2001

Installer

Performed minor repairs and basic service (e.g., oil changes and tire rotations), picked up and delivered customers to specific areas, maintained neatness and orderliness in work area, and oriented new hires.

Achievement:

- Captured extra revenues 85% of the time by seizing the opportunity to "sell up" related products and services.

Precision Detailing, Aurora   1997 - 1999

Automotive Detailer

Achievements:

- Chosen by President – due to ability to meet time-critical deadlines – to work on dealership cars; specific tasks included shampooing and polishing.
- Repeatedly commended by owner of local dealership for commitment to top quality; "Warlock" cars were always sold within 7 days.

ELLIOT COLLINS

111-222 Cardinal Street
Burlington, ON L1L 1L1
Phone: 905-555-1235
ec@careerprocanada.ca

SALES & CUSTOMER SERVICE PROFESSIONAL

An extroverted, confident, and assertive professional with a ten-year track record that has produced strong skills and significant results in the following key areas:

- Account Management
- Customer Satisfaction & Support
- Staff Training & Development
- Leads Generation & Sales Performance
- Customer Relationship Management
- Teambuilding

CAREER HIGHLIGHTS

Global-Con Controls – Oakville, ON   **2003-Present**
ACCOUNT EXECUTIVE

- Established 20 new accounts and revived 10 dormant accounts in 12 months through persistent cold calling and tenacious follow-up.

- Developed strong level of expertise to sell and support highly technical and specialized automation devices. For example:
  - Liaised with a major packaging company to design and implement a safer production line that satisfied Ministry of Labour's stringent requirements;
  - Spearheaded and facilitated "lunch & learn" sessions to customer firms. Prepared lively presentations that effectively conveyed difficult product information to groups of 20 participants.

- Built cohesive relationships with existing clients by *going the extra mile.* For example, personally delivered orders to clients in emergency situations, which minimized their downtime and raised Global-Con's standard for customer service excellence.

- Directed a team of 4 to accurately complete $150K year-end inventory.

- Played a key role in the design, shipping, set-up, and management of out-of-province trade show booth. Gained acknowledgement for innate ability to interact in a professional, yet gregarious way that disarms customer objections and builds common ground for ongoing follow-up.

Saturn Worldwide – Toronto, ON   **1998-2003**
SALES MANAGER (2000-2003)
SALES CONSULTANT (1998-2000)

- Set record for highest sales (35 vehicles) in first 2 months as consultant. After 8 months, was acknowledged as top selling and grossing salesperson. Continued #1 status led to fast-track management promotion.

- Logged an extensive list of satisfied, and often repeat, customers through superb relationship management. Consistently assessed buyers accurately, created an atmosphere of comfort, and extended value-added support to develop win/win scenarios.

Sales Professional. This résumé uses the reverse chronological approach to show the individual's career progression in sales.

ELLIOT COLLINS P_{age} T_{wo}

CAREER HIGHLIGHTS..._continued_

- Sharpened soft skills through active participation in sales and team-building training at Saturn Head Office in Tennessee.

- Oversaw a team of 10 to successfully liaise with community stakeholders in the financing and building of a school playground as part of a corporate _give back to the community_ initiative.

- Analyzed daily customer traffic and ongoing business results in order to build long-term business development strategy. Developed and implemented log for tracking sales process.

- Implemented consultant standards to ensure benchmark for performance, accountability, and identification of high performers. Recognized as a fair, approachable leader who favours a democratic management style.

Bramlea Electric Supply, Brampton & Burlington, ON **1995-1998**
ASSISTANT MANAGER (1998)
OUTSIDE SALES REPRESENTATIVE (1997-1998)
INSIDE SALES REPRESENTATIVE (1995-1997)

- Learned to cold call, open new accounts, and quote on price and delivery. Built strong sales and customer service approach that reflected an understanding of corporate demands as well as the ability to meet and exceed them.

- Recognized as diligent, self-directed worker, which resulted in consistent role progression and increased responsibility.

EDUCATION & PROFESSIONAL DEVELOPMENT

UNIVERSITY OF GUELPH – Guelph, ON

- Bachelor of Arts – History

- Bachelor of Arts (Honours) – Sociology

SATURN, HEAD OFFICE – Tennessee, USA

- In-house sales/customer service/teambuilding/leadership training

Louise Gagné   111 Dunsdale St. ● Toronto, ON M1M 1M1

Home: (416) 555-1234 ● Email: gagne@careerprocanada.ca

Professional Objective

A career as an Adjudicator

Background Qualifications

➢ Established professional with over 15 years of experience in Social Services and Child Welfare.

➢ <u>Proven analytical and strong decision-making skills</u>:
  ✓ Interviewed and assessed eligibility of applicants for subsidized child care services.
  ✓ Assessed, motivated and counselled Ontario Works clients toward training programs, education, and employment.
  ✓ Assessed children's needs, and coordinated protective care placement.

➢ Ability to stay focused under pressure while successfully **managing a caseload** of up to 200 clients.

➢ Strong **team player**, well respected by peers; ability to **work independently**.

➢ Authored **complex documentation**: childrens' court documents, fraud reports, and protection case reports.

➢ <u>Exceptional communication skills</u>:
  ✓ Served as liaison with police, schools, hospitals, psychiatrists and lawyers.
  ✓ Advocated on client's behalf with educational and training agencies.
  ✓ Advocated for children and adoptive families at the Adoption Resource Exchange in Toronto.

➢ Languages: English with fluency in oral French.

➢ Proficient with **Microsoft Windows and Office**.

"…Louise's strengths were her organizational skills, high energy, communications/facilitation skills and ability to solve problems."

Janet Woods, Manager, Operational Resource Management Unit

Professional Experience

City of Toronto People Services   Toronto, Ontario
Child Care Services Case Coordinator   1999 to Present

From June 2001 to Dec 2001, held position of SDM Trainer (Service Delivery Model) with the Business Transportation Project. Trained social assistance employees throughout the province on the new system. Commendation letter for exceptional work ethics received from management.

<u>Other Positions</u>: R2D Case Worker   1997 to 1999
                    Welfare Worker   1993 to 1997

Social Services Adjudicator. To address this candidate's career shift from casework to adjudication, she selected only "Background Qualifications" points that relate to the new position.

Children's Aid Society   Kingston, Ontario
Adoption Worker   1990 to 1993

Managed all aspects of children adoption, including interview and assessment of couples/individuals; prepared and completed adoption home studies; pre- and post-adoption counselling sessions; supervised the placement of children during the adoption probation period; preparation of court documents.

Other positions: County Intake Worker   1988 to 1990
                 Foster Care Support Worker   1987 to 1988

Children's Aid Society   North Bay, Ontario
Foster Care Coordinator   1983 to 1987

Directed all phases of foster parent recruitment, including training potential foster parents; training foster care staff; maintaining foster care statistics; developing suitable alternatives to foster care; and implementing the Foster Parent Association within the agency.

Education

Northern College of Applied Arts & Technology   Timmins, Ontario
Social Services Diploma

Commendation Letters & References Available

NGOC (NICK) TRAN, MBA

123-12 Dodd Street, Calgary, Alberta T2T 2T2
Phone (403) 555-1234
E-mail ntran@careerprocanada.ca

LARGE-SCALE BUSINESS SYSTEMS CONSULTANT

Results-oriented professional with over 15 years' experience and a proven record of accomplishment in systems implementation, technology alignment, and project management. Senior level experience enhancing business systems. Specific expertise in financial services and high-technology industries. Demonstrated track record in full-life cycle implementation of large-scale business processes. Verifiable achievements in database design, development, and maintenance. An articulate communicator and presenter, with the ability to convey technical feedback in user-friendly terms. Proficient in English and French.

Core Competencies- Leadership & Business Management

Business Planning ▪ Feasibility Studies ▪ Cost Benefit Analysis ▪ Budgeting & Forecasting
Global Best Practices ▪ Productivity Improvement ▪ Vendor Management ▪ Presentations & Negotiations
Team Building & Leadership ▪ Program Management ▪ Cross-Cultural Communications

Core Competencies- Technology & Project Management

Technology Gap Analysis ▪ Performance Measurement ▪ Technology Alignment ▪ Project Tendering
Project Implementation ▪ Software Installation ▪ Technical Troubleshooting ▪ System Methodology
Database Development & Administration ▪ Data Modelling ▪ Capability Maturity Modelling

CAREER HIGHLIGHTS

- **Implemented structures to support new channels** for life, money market, investment, mortgage, and credit cards, which included completing comprehensive assessments and formulating enterprise architecture.

- **Created and supported a global suite of applications** designed to capture, archive, and analyze data, enabling a safety consultancy to offer customers an add-on to their services.

- Developed a technology framework to **consolidate business reporting,** which resulted in a formal cross-border exporting and outsourcing strategy.

- **Planned and migrated 300 WAN applications,** which included implementing regional intranet and a 24-hour Help Desk, and handing over the technology to 6 countries within a period of 10 months.

- Instituted a **500-person Customer Care Centre** supported by a sophisticated regional cross-business customer database to analyze sales and generate marketing leads.

- **Established an infrastructure** in India and Singapore, including the customization of Life and Group systems to local business conditions, setting up data centres, and instituting local MIS in over 5 cities.

- **Re-engineered processes for a model office,** instituting workflow/imaging integrated with e-mail and legacy systems.

- **Implemented B2C and B2B in Hong Kong and Sri Lanka** and increased profitability through web-based campaigns.

- **Executed $80 million invested capital in technology** while maintaining operational costs at less than 0.8% of revenues.

- **Developed a data warehouse with capability for multi-dimensional analysis** of client limits, exposure, and risk.

- **Won a 3-year program to build a financial system** that effectively manages service delivery and rosters for 2,000 staff.

- **Led a team of 6 to develop dealing screens for money market and foreign exchange** for Inter-Nation Banking Corporation.

Systems Consultant. This individual combines and lists all his accomplishments in one extensive career highlight section. He separates each bullet point in the long list with extra white space to ensure readability.

PROFESSIONAL EXPERIENCE

ROCK Systems Inc. 2000-Present

Independent technical services firm providing global Internet technology consulting and support to small and medium enterprises (SME).

Business Systems Consultant

Responsible for providing the full scope of technology solutions, from proposal to implementation. Accountable to contact clients, identify needs, propose solutions, and budget projects. Responsibilities include designing, executing, and supporting systems.

Big-Five Consulting Corporation 1995–2000

$20 billion organization providing a full range of business advisory services to leading global, national, and local companies with more than 100,000 employees worldwide.

Senior Manager, Data Administration & Technology Services

Project Manager, Management Consultant

Team Leader

Responsible for assessing clients' technology capability against new business needs. Accountable to design, implement, test, and perform quality assurance on business systems. Responsibilities include organizing and executing client engagements.

FORMAL EDUCATION

- Candidate Doctor of Business Administration, Tech Graduate University
- Executive Master of Business Administration, North-western School of Management
- Master of Sciences, Major Applied Physics, Minor Robotics, Euro Tech College

CERTIFICATIONS

- Canadian Securities Certificate, Canadian Securities Institute (CSC)
- Java 2 Enterprise Architect, SUN Microsystems
- Microsoft Certified Professional (MCP), Microsoft
- Microsoft Certified Solution Developer (MCSD), Microsoft
- Microsoft Certified Database Administrator (MCDBA), Microsoft
- Microsoft Certified System Engineer (MCSE), Microsoft

TECHNICAL SKILLS

- Operating Systems- UNIX, Windows NT/2000
- Database Applications- Java, C/C++/C#, Visual Basic, MS SQL Server, MS Access
- Software Applications- Microsoft Office Suite (Word, Excel, PowerPoint, Project, Publisher)

PUBLICATIONS

- A Process Theory on Technology in the Financial Services (Thesis, Tech Graduate University, 2003)
- Flexibility in Technical Implementation a Literature Review (Thesis, Tech Graduate University, 2002)

John Perkins

111 Ottawa Avenue, Ottawa, ON K1K 1K1
jperkins@careerprocanada.ca • Home (613) 555-1234

Objective

A career as an MS.Net Programmer/Analyst.

Profile

Seasoned VB professional with over 10 years' PC programming experience in business applications for the retail industry, including more than 7 years as a VB developer in an MS NT/SQL environment. Expertise includes Retail Sales, Warehousing, Distribution, Buying, Marketing, Payroll and Accounting. Successful project leader, database designer and accomplished technical troubleshooter. Quick thinker who is skilled at resolving issues and implementing solutions. Ability to lead, train and be part of a team. Background is strengthened with 4 years' programming experience on the AS/400. Bilingual in English/French.

PROFICIENCIES

Operating Systems: NT, 2000, XP, OS/400.
Programming Languages: Visual Basic v6.0, SQL (statements and procedures), Active Server Pages, Crystal Reports, ActiveX, Clipper, RPG/ILE, CL, Query, SEQUEL, J-Walk.
Software: MQ Series, MS Word, Excel, VBA, Outlook, Internet Explorer, and PC Anywhere.

Professional Skills

LEADERSHIP & TRAINING
- Project leader of the Z-Mart Store system, including application architecture and database design in VB and SQL.
- Technical Lead in the integration of a third-party point-of-sale system into the Z-Mart Store system.
- Technical troubleshooter for all store systems.
- Guided developers in understanding the business deliverables and the application of tools and techniques appropriate for the needs of the project.
- Trained Help Desk staff in the areas of network maintenance, and troubleshooting systems and applications.
- Performed on-site training to payroll auditors while at Revenue Canada (across various Canadian cities).
- Recommended that SQL and MQ Series become part of the standard development process, in an effort to follow the industry trend, but also to improve the development cycle and cost.

SOFTWARE DEVELOPMENT
- Analysed, designed, coded, tested, and implemented many business processing and analytical systems using appropriate tools.
- Authored numerous business documents, technical analysis documents, and quality assurance plans, as part of the overall development process of new systems.
- Converted a Retail Back Office system from Clipper to VB and SQL on a Windows NT platform.
- Developed a PC-based Inventory Tracking system to manage off-site inventory.

Employment History

Senior Systems Analyst	Z-Mart Store Inc., Ottawa, Ontario	1994 to Present
CS-2 Programmer/Analyst	Revenue Canada (CCRA), Ottawa, Ontario	1991 to 1994

Education

Algonquin College, Ottawa, Ontario
ASP, Database Architecture, Java, Business Statistics, and Business Math.
Computer Information Systems/Computer Programmer Diploma (Ongoing).

Systems Developer. This self-taught candidate chooses to highlight his technical and leadership skills in this succinct résumé. He minimizes his lack of formal credentials by discussing individual college courses that he has completed.

Mary-Anne Stevenson

110 Rowntree Gardens
Hamilton, ON L1L 1L1
Tel: 905.555.1234

Profile

Outgoing and patient educator with three years of classroom teaching experience and five years of office experience. Enjoy working with children at school and within the community. Team player who assists and supports colleagues and administrators.

Proven ability to relate to pupils and to manage a classroom effectively by creating an atmosphere of mutual respect and open communication. Able to identify and meet student's individual needs, including skill levels and learning paces.

Education

1993 – 1996   **Diploma in Teaching – Secondary Education**
Specializing in General Science and Religious Education, with complementary course in Guidance and Counselling. Work Experience: Classroom assisting and teaching (3+ months). Thesis: Experiential approach to religious education.
National Teacher's College, Point-a-Pierre, Trinidad

2004   **Dr. Campbell MacArthur - MacArthur Parenting Program**
(Concerning special needs children), Daniel Baxter Centre (10 weeks)

2002   **Certificate of Achievement for "Sickle Cell in the Community" course**
Hartford Community College, Hartford ON (12 weeks)

1988 – 1990   **Certificate in Personnel Administration (Merit)**
University of the West Indies, Trinidad

Experience

09/94 – 12/98   **Junior High School Teacher**
Greenacres Primary and Junior High School, Port of Spain, Trinidad
- Led classroom instruction and wrote and taught lesson plans for Science, Religious Education, Family Life Education, and Social Studies.
- Guided students who had special needs and required extra help.
- Responsible for administering and organizing First Aid at the school.
- As a Coach, was in charge of the school's winning entries in the highly prized National Family Planning Competition. Liaised with the Family Planning Association, used networking contacts at the Red Cross and contributed to media events, including radio broadcasts.

09/89 – 09/94   **School Secretary**
Greenacres Primary and Junior High School, Port of Spain, Trinidad
- Managed the office and handled all administration work, including filing, registering pupils, assisting teachers with photocopying and preparing classroom materials. First point of contact for parents' inquiries.

Community Work

Red Cross: Awarded plaque in 2002 for outstanding contribution to the HIV prevention project. As a Link Patron and Trainer, travelled nationwide teaching young people and adults.

Charity Club: As a chartered member, organize and actively participate in events and activities to benefit youth organizations and senior citizen care homes.

Teacher's Assistant. With a large gap in work experience, this candidate indicates her education up front. Rather than listing the information in reverse chronological order, she emphasizes her most important credential – her teaching diploma – first.

PETER BROWN, CCIE

123 Hawking Blvd.
Oakville, Ontario L1L 1L1

Phone: 905.555.1234
E mail: pbrown@CareerProCanada.ca

Leads the Organization into Tomorrow

SENIOR DESIGN ENGINEER □ TECHNICAL ARCHITECT

Detail and task-oriented professional with an exemplary background in conceiving and developing unique initiatives to propel technology to the limit and optimize performance. **Capable of tackling the most challenging networks and delivering results.** Creative and visionary, recognized for keeping on the leading edge of technology and utilizing the latest applications and hardware. Results and performance-driven, thrives in an environment of constant challenge and diversity. Articulate, breaks the technology barrier down, acts as the conduit between customer and technical experts. Industrious, exudes energy and confidence, motivates and mentors team members to succeed and deliver quality work within strict specifications, time lines and budgets. *Core competencies include:*

• Project Management	• Routers & Switches
• Routing Protocols	• Internetworking, TCP/IP Services
• Cost Benefit Analysis	• Presales Technical Support
• Enterprise Architecture Development	• Systems Documentation

TECHNICAL ENVIRONMENTS

Operating Systems:	MS Windows 9X, 2000, NT, Novell, OS2
Cisco Routers & Switches	1600, 2500, 2600, 3600, 4000, 7500, 1900, 2900, 3900, 4900, 5000, 6000, 8500, 10000, 12000 Internet Series
Routing Protocols	RIP, IGRP, EIGRP, OSPF, IPX EIGRP, IPX RIP, BGP IS-IS
Routed/Bridged Protocols	IP, IPX, Netbios, SNA
Telco	ISDN, Frame Relay, X25, ATM, T1, Dark Fibre, ASDL
Other Tools	Sniffer Pro, Network General Sniffer, Netview (SNMP), DNS, HTTP

PROFESSIONAL EXPERIENCE

Can Tele-Communications Inc., Toronto, Ontario   2001 – present
Held the following 2 progressively responsible positions:
SENIOR DESIGN ENGINEERING SPECIALIST, Level II   2002 – present
SENIOR DESIGN ENGINEERING SPECIALIST, Level I   2001 – 2002

- Played the key leadership role in conceiving and delivering a National Multi Protocol Laboratory Switching (MPLS) network for a high-value contract with numerous Government of Ontario ministries secured by Can Tele despite fierce competition from Bell Canada.

Process included:

- Developing the complex system, detailing equipment to be utilized to create the customized and aggregated services, devising the proof of concept to be accepted by client.
- Working with the Program Manager to define a business case to capture $9 million in funding to complete the prestigious project, one of the top 5 projects in Can Tele.
- Placing component orders with Cisco to purchase numerous switches and routers; responsible for monitoring the expenditures.
- Acting as the team lead, tasked with pre-staging the equipment and configuring prior to shipping to geographically disparate offices for rollout.

Technical Design Engineer. The by-line "Leads the Organization into Tomorrow" displays a progressive Value Proposition. This design engineer lists his technical environments early in the résumé to clarify his expertise.

Can Tele-Communications, MPLS Project....continued

- Working with the space/power/racking group to ensure the power support was adequate.
- Partnering with the transport team to optimize the long haul connectivity over SONET.
- Scrutinizing documentation with the Last Ride Access Designers to establish the processes for commodity devices.
- Directing the knowledge handoff to local Tier I & II designers acting as the main troubleshooter providing support to all Tier III network professionals.
- Interacting with vendor to iron out bugs. Initiative now providing a very high SLA for the Government of Ontario.
- Acted as the lead engineer during the complex process of moving an MPLS project for the TD Bank from pre-sales to post-sales. Involved in the Custom Solution Group to validate the functionality of services delivered to TD Bank. Designed and delivered final product, dispatched to local design engineers to implement the product on the Can Tele network allowing a complete end-to-end solution for TD Bank. Project recognized as the highest level initiative undertaken by Can Tele.
- Provided design engineering and custom solutions for clients, interacted with cross-functional personnel to complete diverse projects according to mandates.
- Reported to Manager, National Service Fulfillment; consistently appraised by manager with the highest ratings and given financial remuneration for work.
- Recipient of the 2002 "President's" award for being the *Leader of Tomorrow*.

Bell Systems Incorporated, Mississauga, Ontario   2000 – 2001
SENIOR TECHNICAL ANALYST
- Played a key technical advisory role during the office and systems move from Montreal, Quebec to Mississauga, Ontario; designed new system's environment work flow and completed transfer without business interruption.
- Moved the Bell Systems Data Centre from a layer II network building to a layer III solution enabling Bell Systems to stabilize network operations and allow for expansion.

SystemsInTel Services, Toronto, Ontario   1999 – 2000
TECHNICAL LEAD
- Contracted by the Toronto Catholic District School Board to install and rollout the Windows 2000 network across 50 schools. Project recognized by Microsoft Canada as one of the first dozen production networks in Canada.
- Developed and implemented new desktop software system for the TCDSB.

EDUCATION

Ryerson Polytechnic University, Toronto, Ontario   1994
BACHELOR OF BUSINESS MANAGEMENT – Accounting

CISCO CERTIFIED INTERNETWORKING EXPERT (CCIE #21567)

Strong proponent of continually updating skills and keeping on the leading edge. Attended numerous courses, workshops and seminars including:

Cisco Secure Pix Firewall Advanced (CSPFA)	Cisco Secure Virtual Private Network (CSPVN)
Implementing Cisco MPLS (MPLS)	Advanced Cisco Router Configuration
NetGun Masters	Expert CCIE Prep
Cisco Internetworking Troubleshooting	Designing Cisco Networks
Designing Windows 2000 Networking Services	C-Level Systems Integration
Configuration Management for Windows 2000	Windows 2000 support

TONY BOYD

1111 Armstread Circle
Toronto, Ontario, M1M 1M1 Canada

(416) 555.1234
tonyboyd@CareerProCanada.ca

IT / NETWORK MANAGER

Microsoft Specific Networking • IP Networking • Cisco Router Configuration • Routing Protocols

Global Networking & Security Infrastructure Specialist

Results-oriented, quality-driven, business-savvy professional with broad IT exposure. Multi-faceted expertise in identifying, developing and executing cost-effective, technologically-advanced IT/networking solutions to meet challenging multinational business demands. Shrewd communicator and negotiator, with proven ability to gain cooperation and build consensus among diverse groups with conflicting business objectives to successfully achieve win/win outcomes. Participative leadership and management style, encouraging collaboration toward the common goal. Expertise in:

- Cost Forecasting & Expenditure Control
- Product Requirement Analysis & Procurement
- Vendor Relations & Competitive Negotiations
- Project Planning, Management & Fulfilment
- Procedure Development & Execution

- Strategic Planning & Development
- Team Building & Performance Growth
- Help Desk Support & Leadership
- Performance & Productivity Improvement
- Process Redesign, Turnaround & Optimization

TECHNOLOGICAL INVENTORY

Operating Systems:	Microsoft Windows (all versions including 2003 server) • VMS • UNIX • Cisco IOS (routers)
Programming:	Shell Scripting for MS Windows as mentioned above • KSH/CSH on UNIX • DCL on VMS • WSH on Windows
Applications:	Microsoft Office Applications • MS FrontPage • Photoshop
Other:	Internet LAN routing/switching VLANS • Firewalls (several obscure versions plus CheckPoint Firewall-1/VPN-1NG).

PROFESSIONAL DEVELOPMENT

Advanced CheckPoint Firewall-1NG Management • Introduction & Advanced Cisco Routing • Team Leadership
OSF/1 System Manager • VMS System Manager • UNIX System Manager • UNIX Internals & Tuning
Introduction to Project Management (MS Project)

PROFESSIONAL EXPERIENCE

ARLIC MEDIA CENTRAL   1995 to Present

Leading supplier of editorial, advertising and CRM publishing software servicing prestigious newspapers, magazines and online publishers on an international scale.

Network Technical Lead

Multi-faceted role challenged to overhaul, revolutionize and maintain a secure global network to facilitate enhanced communication between nationally- and internationally-based staff and clientele.

- **Revitalized entire WAN/LAN infrastructure with optimal security on an international level**, using advanced technologies to drive aggressive transformation of previously inept system. Decreased turnaround on security-related issues from days to hours/minutes; improved internet connection logging/monitoring; and decreased resources access time from days to instantaneous.

- Sourced, assessed and forged key alliances with **ISPs/other telecommunication vendors** continually negotiating competitive deals that secured **average cost reductions of $40K/year. Slashed an outstanding $80K in costs for one year** following a change in vendor.

Continued…

Technology Network Manager. This candidate is rich in accomplishments that spill over to page two. The accountabilities box creatively breaks up the list and highlights areas of expertise.

TONY BOYD

- **Architected internal website to document VPN connectivity** for high-profile clients with contracts **totalling $10.5M in revenue** including Hong Kong Imail, Gulf News, News Ltd., New Zealand Herald, Wilson and Horton, Shepparton News, New Straits Times, South West Printing & Publishing.

- **Spearheaded recent negotiations with ISP capturing unlimited connection vs. $/MByte**, set to underpin corporate culture change and revitalize the nature of business operations to a quality rather than a quantity gain, with internet now an exploitable resource rather than a cost.

- **Headed remote integration of new offices in Singapore/Bedford** with minimal downtime after merger, despite challenges involving complex routing procedures, challenging requests of local management, and having to gain the trust and enthusiasm of existing technical staff.

- Influenced, overcame challenges, and secured client buy-in to **establish an extensive VPN based Extranet** that harnessed several technologies. Accelerated Internet connection and immediate response/problem resolution by client support teams; minimized total of varying technologies; enhanced security/client satisfaction.

- **Circumvented loss of public IP address space** during hostile divestiture by conceiving legally sound initiatives and negotiations. Attained flexibility in changing ISPs; eased extranet connection with clients/partners; enhanced issue logging; and made staff more accountable for their actions through ease of tracking.

- **Managed complex business relocation project** from concept to fruition overcoming many issues requiring in-depth research, planning, and negotiation with contractors / management / previous tenant to drive successful move of 150 staff within only two days.

- Sent to Nottingham UK office and **managed seamless transition from GEAC NT based domain to Windows 2000** environment of approximately 75 PCs within a 24-hour shift including email and servers and establishing standard security infrastructure.

Accountabilities:
- Manage & maintain internal/Internet facing Network Infrastructure
- Oversee WAN, ISDN, VPN links to clients/external offices
- Global Firewall Infrastructure Management
- Manage & Maintain Communications Equipment
- Corporate-wide Access Points Security
- Customer Liaison & Consultations
- Team Leadership, Building & Support

- **Attended Boston office and launched strategic turnaround solutions** to boost stagnated office relocation project. Overcame hostile environment, installed updated firewall, fixed security holes, devised operational standards, and trained local staff in procedures/basic router configuration.

- Installed AMC's system at Bangkok Post transforming the organization into a technically sophisticated operation despite communication barriers with local technical staff.

- **Optimized performance and productivity of entire Internal Help Desk/IT** during two-year assignment as Team Leader. Streamlined and established best-practice operations by devising procedures/standards for routine tasks and initiating projects within team.

- **Minimized outlay by integrating low-cost VOIP solution with Lucent PABX**; enhanced security by using firewall logs/network monitoring to reverse-engineer security requirements.

SEAGATE TRANSPORTATION, INC.   1992 to 1994

System Programmer

Maintained full system operability through performance tuning and support of VMS/UNIX infrastructure, pathworks implementation, and ongoing troubleshooting.

References available upon request

KEVIN DARY M.Ed.

22 Martin Way, Angus, Ontario ▪ L1L 1L1
(Work) 705.555.1234 Ext 1000 ▪ (Home) 705.555.0123 ▪ (Email) kevin@CareerProCanada.ca

CERTIFIED TRAINING & DEVELOPMENT OFFICER
Specializing in Adult Education

Versatile and resourceful instructor generating powerful learning opportunities. Balanced skill-set capably instructs academic, professional and technical courses. Highly articulate, demonstrating excellent interpersonal skills across all levels regardless of background. Regarded for delivering innovative lecture techniques and motivational teaching strategies. **Core competencies:**

- Curriculum Design & Development
- Performance Evaluations
- Cross Cultural Communications
- Recruitment & Retention
- Peer Support & Team Building
- Public & Corporate Relations
- Sound Decision Making
- Time Management

TECHNOLOGY: Windows, Word, PowerPoint, Excel, E-mail, Internet, audiovisual equipment.

QUALIFICATIONS IN ACTION

CHIEF INSTRUCTOR   1997 - Present
Canadian Forces Training Development Centre, Newton, Ontario
Relied upon to co-ordinate the organization and conduct of all Canadian Forces instructional technique courses for senior training officers and civilians. Supervise, motivate and support six instructors, each from different operational and support occupations, to facilitate 75 training courses per annum. Continually assess curriculum, ensuring content is current, reflective of ever-changing industry needs. Consistently ensure instructional excellence and accountability, combined with optimal resource allocation. Achieved rank of Captain.

- ☑ Balance the scheduling of classes, instructors and courses (on and off site) with different start dates, on a year round basis. Recently spearheaded the offsite training initiative (from coast to coast) to improve course accessibility and streamline costs.
- ☑ In addition to all administrative responsibilities, instruct *Basic and Advanced Instructional Techniques*, *Instructor Supervisor*, and *Training Analysis and Design* courses. Average class size is 20 students, comprised of military, non-military emergency response personnel and pertinent civilians.
- ☑ Senior source, trusted to train key contacts from external agencies (Environment Canada, Toronto Police Force, Greater Toronto Airports Authority Firefighters).
- ☑ Sole Canadian Forces representative requested to attend the restructuring efforts for Hungary's Defence Staff training procedures. Teamed with other expert NATO members, offering the best practices at this focused summit in Budapest.

SENIOR STANDARDS OFFICER OF TRAINING   1994 - 1997
Canadian Forces Nuclear, Biological, Chemical Defence School, (NBC) Newton, Ontario
Handpicked to train national and international Advanced Officers for current NBC requirements in a year round capacity. Supported two instructional development staff.

- ☑ Co-ordinated the restructure of all Canadian Forces NBC, radiation safety, and nuclear emergency response training.
- ☑ One of two DND members selected as Canadian task force representatives to overhaul NATO's NBC training protocols. Brainstormed with key players from 19 other countries to establish the most effective training methods, ensuring Canadian concerns were addressed.

Continued on Page 2 ⇨

Training and Development Officer. This résumé targets educational institutions, by focusing on adult instruction in the tagline, profile, and strengths.

SPECIAL PROJECTS AND ADMINISTRATIVE OFFICER 1992 - 1993
Western Recruiting Zone Headquarters, Edmonton, Alberta
Accountable for providing leadership and staff guidance for the recruiting units within the Western Recruiting Zone. This was a considerable task, given the region was massive (BC, AB, SK, MB, YT and northern ON). Subject matter expert, tasked to support other Zone staff officers.

☑ Project managed a detailed review of orders and directives of the recruiting system, collating applicable ones into specific policy statements. Recommendations accepted as the Department of National Defence's system-wide framework for Recruiting Directives.

CAREER COUNSELLOR 1989 - 1992
Canadian Forces Recruiting Centre, Sydney, Nova Scotia
Directed and supervised the operations of this busy recruiting centre. Relied upon to counsel, interview, assess and evaluate potential officer and non-commissioned officer recruits. Co-ordinated staff schedules and presentation dates. Delivered enticing mobile recruiting and elementary/secondary school, and college/university presentations. Utilized time management and organizational skills to meet demanding schedule. Conducting 26 presentations within 21 days was not uncommon.

☑ Developed and maintained a network of key contacts to facilitate the recruiting process throughout Nova Scotia and Cape Breton Island operating area.
☑ Efforts rewarded by earning the top ratio in Canada for securing new recruits. Surpassed established enrolment quotas by 50%.
☑ Updated, streamlined and personally monitored applicant processing. Applications that formerly took months to complete, were (and still are) taking just days to finalize.
☑ Voted Eastern Canada's *Top Career Counsellor* for outstanding overall performance.

EDUCATION & SPECIALIZED TRAINING

MASTERS OF EDUCATION 2003
Nipissing University, North Bay, Ontario
ADULT AND CONTINUING EDUCATION CERTIFICATION 1996
University of Manitoba, Winnipeg, Manitoba
BACHELOR OF ARTS (Major - Psychology) 1992
University of Manitoba, Winnipeg, Manitoba
BUSINESS ADMINISTRATION DIPLOMA 1984
Grant MacEwan Community College, Edmonton, Alberta

CERTIFIED TO INSTRUCT:
- Training Development Officer
- Basic Instructional Techniques
- Advanced Instructional Techniques
- Instructor Supervisor
- Training Analysis, Design & Evaluation
- Distributed Learning

AWARDS

☸ **Canadian Decoration** - Awarded for Good Conduct throughout DND career.
☸ **Special Services Medal** - Received recognition for successfully completing Tour of Cyprus.
☸ **Queens Jubilee Medal** - Cited for outstanding and exemplary service to Canada.

COMMUNITY INVOLVEMENT

☑ Elementary and Secondary Parent Council committee member.
☑ Minor Baseball coach, filling multiple executive roles, within county leagues and Base.
☑ Introduced Borden community to new initiatives like a gardening club and travel group.

KEVIN DAYLE

79 Main Street, Village, New Brunswick ▪ E1E 1E1
(Home) 506.555.1234 ▪ (Email) kevin@careerprocanada.ca

PROFESSIONAL PROFILE

A positive and people-oriented individual offering a host of skills after serving our country. Trustworthy and reliable: authorized with "Secret" security clearance. Works effectively and makes sound decisions under pressure in fast paced and unpredictable environments. Accepts role as assigned and strives for excellent results. Strong problem-solver with capabilities in organizing, prioritizing, and managing multiple projects with competing deadlines. Physically fit and healthy: eager for new challenges.

Core competencies include:

- ✔ Confidentiality Assurance
- ✔ Training & Leadership
- ✔ Punctual & Reliable
- ✔ Cross-Cultural Awareness
- ✔ Team Player Approach
- ✔ Community Relations

"(Kevin) Dayle's extensive experience and natural organization abilities make him a very strong and skilled administrator...He possesses a charismatic leadership style and positive demeanour...He never counts the amount of time or energy he has to give in order to achieve the objectives." 2003 performance appraisal

---

CAREER PATH Department of National Defence (1983 - 2006)

INSTRUCTOR   2002 - 2006
Oromocto, New Brunswick
Regarded as a reserve subject matter expert. Selected to coordinate all aspects of a 36-member program and 16 support professionals. Accountable for every single course component, from vehicle requisitions and specialized personnel, to training areas and in-class materials.

- Provided extra assistance, resources and time to ensure all participants understood course concepts and were able to meet rigorous organizational standards.
- Although assigned a leadership role, never hesitated to aid peers and subordinates, regardless of the task.
- Ensured all administrative functions were accurately completed on time.
- Exercised sound decision making capability: Cited for "being able to find quick, logical and common sense solutions to the course's everyday problems."
- Key team member of soccer team. Earned position at the national finals.

BATTALION INTELLIGENCE OFFICER   1994 - 2001
Kapyong, Winnipeg
Assigned this important role to provide clear and accurate situational briefings on the world's hotspots to the Base's most senior staff and groups of interest. Organized and used slides and PowerPoint when presenting. Handled questions and comments from attendees, both subordinate and more senior in ranking.

Continued ⇨

Training Instructor. This professional is transitioning into a civilian role after a strong military career. The résumé relays his transferable skills and focuses on strengths such as integrity and reliability.

KEVIN DAYLE

- Seamlessly balanced administrative and tactical requirements of delivering training, leadership and support to a team of 30.
- Heavily involved with organized sports in addition to working commitments.

TRAINER   1990 - 1994

Wainwright, Alberta

Relied upon to educate new recruits to the Infantry Division. Achieved a high pass rate of the Force's newest members who were technically sound and demonstrated the right attitude for a team-based career.

EARLIER CAREER EXPERIENCE   1983 - 1990

After basic training, secured progressive positions requiring the positive skills, attitude and knowledge base to support a 20+ year tenure dependent on rational decision-making and team cohesiveness. Fostered an understanding of multi-cultural idiosyncrasies as they relate to social, political and tactical issues. Set the standard for the balance of rewarding DND assignments.

TECHNOLOGY

Windows MS Office Suite, PowerPoint, Internet Research and Email.

EDUCATION & SPECIALIZED TRAINING

Infantry Section Commanders Course
Sergeant (6B) Course
Senior Leaders Course
Former St John Ambulance and CPR Instructor

▪ Integrity ▪ Reliability ▪ Results ▪

KAREN MORLEY B.ENG.

123 Main Road ▪ Mississauga, Ontario L1L 1L1
Phone: (905) 555-1234 ▪ kmorley@careerprocanada.ca

TRANSPORTATION ENGINEER / PLANNER

Transportation Planning Studies … Traffic Operations & Impact Studies … Preliminary Design … Transit Planning
Parking Assessments & Design … Environmental Assessments … Sustainable Transportation & TDM
Travel Demand Forecasting … Transportation Modelling … Intersection Capacity Analysis
Level of Service Analysis … Traffic Planning Reports

Highly motivated, hard working civil engineer with hands-on experience completing transportation studies to determine access and parking requirements, assess transportation impacts of proposed developments, and optimize traffic flow through critical corridors. Additional experience in preliminary and detailed design work. Balances strong technical skills with recognized team, interpersonal, and communications skills. Excellent research and report writing ability with extensive experience referencing the Ontario Traffic Manual (OTM), TAC Geometric Design Guide, and ITE Trip Generation Manual.

Member – Professional Engineers Ontario (EIT Status)

EXPERIENCE

TERA-PLAN CANADA, Markham, Ontario

TRANSPORTATION ENGINEER   August 2003 – August 2006

Competed and participated in a wide variety of transportation planning and design projects for this speciality engineering consulting firm. Project variety includes short- and long-term studies for residential, institutional, and mixed use developments. Clients and project sponsors include residential and commercial developers, the Greater Toronto Airport Authority, Toronto Port Authority, and the municipalities of Toronto, Mississauga, Aurora, Markham, Burlington, Windsor, and Leamington.

- Served as a key member of individual project teams – specific contributions include traffic operations and impact studies, parking studies, transportation modelling, TDM planning, capacity analyses, and technical content and diagrams for final reports.

- Took initiative to request exposure to design assignments to further develop skills – completed work includes design of signage for residential developments and preliminary road design for the Highway 9 & County Road 26 contract.

- Worked effectively with all project stakeholders, including environmental engineers, divisional managers, project managers, and team members.

(See partial project list that follows)

EDUCATION & TRAINING

Bachelor of Civil Engineering, Ryerson University   2003

In-house seminars include ***Environmental Assessment Processes***, ***Airport Engineering***, ***Construction Issues***, ***Structures***, ***MTO/Consultants Relationship Quality Control System***, and ***Basics for Designing Bus Lanes or HOV Lanes***.

TECHNICAL PROFICIENCY

- AutoCAD
- CCGCalc
- MS Word

- TransCAD
- HCS
- Excel

- Synchro
- CorelDraw
- PowerPoint

Transportation Engineer. This compelling document gives a clear idea of the individual's expertise through a one-page résumé with an addendum listing her projects.

KAREN MORLEY B.ENG.

123 Main Road ▪ Mississauga, Ontario L1L 1L1
Phone: (905) 555-1234 ▪ kmorley@emailz.ca

PARTIAL PROJECT LIST

TRAFFIC OPERATIONS & CORRIDOR STUDIES

Contributed traffic modelling and operations simulations to major master plan studies, including:

- Greater Toronto Airports Authority – Highway 401 Access Study
- City of Waterloo – Transportation Master Plan, Waterloo, Ontario

ENVIRONMENTAL ASSESSMENTS

Examined traffic operations and assisted in the evaluation of future capacity requirements and recommendation of mitigative measures to optimize traffic flows:

- Hurontario Road Corridor Study – Kitchener, Ontario
- Town of Uxbridge – Traffic Operations Study
- Airport Road Operations Study, Yankee Drive to Airport Road – Mississauga, Ontario
- Greater Toronto Airports Authority, Lester B. Pearson International Airport – Terminal 1 Access Study, Mississauga, Ontario

DEVELOPMENT IMPACT STUDIES

Completed and assisted in a series of traffic impact and saturation flow studies, including:

Commercial Developments:

- Greater Toronto Airports Authority, Areas 3A/3B – Mississauga, Ontario
- Toronto Port Authority – Proposed Ferry Terminal, Pier 12
- Tribeca Development Group – Proposed Commercial Development, Lawrence Avenue/Yonge Street

Institutional Developments:

- Greater Toronto Airports Authority, Lester B. Pearson International Airport – Traffic Impact Study, Mississauga, Ontario
- CanadaPharm Expansion, Ottawa, Ontario

Residential & Mixed Use Developments:

- Torus Development Inc. – Sullivan Lands Residential Development, Uxbridge, Ontario
- Torus Development Inc. – St. Alexis Sideroad Residential Development, Uxbridge, Ontario
- Pimento Communities (Toronto) Inc. – Springlawn Property, Uxbridge, Ontario
- Insurance Group of Canada – Mid-Town Mixed Use Development, Scarborough, Ontario
- The Gallery, London, Ontario

PARKING STUDIES

Completed parking assessments for proposed developments:

- Chang-Ling Church Apartments – Parking Study, Mississauga, Ontario
- Toronto Eastern Community Church, Ajax, Ontario

PRELIMINARY AND DETAILED DESIGN

Completed preliminary road design using AutoCAD and designed signage using the Ontario Traffic Manual (OTM) Book 5 and 6 for proposed residential developments:

- Region of Niagara – Wentworth Road widening and Class EA, City of Welland, Ontario
- Torus Development Inc. – Sullivan Lands Residential Development, Uxbridge, Ontario
- Pimento Communities (Toronto) Inc. – Springlawn Property, Uxbridge, Ontario
- Quantity Calculations for Rossland Road – The Regional Municipality of Durham

Best Résumé Samples
Senior-Level and Executive

Jeremy Allen

1234 Abbey Lane, Oakville, Ontario L1L 1L1
Phone: 905-555-1234 Cell: 416-555-0123 E mail: jallen@CareerProCanada.ca

Station Manager

Resourceful, highly productive and efficient airline executive with a diverse management background encompassing all facets of airline station management. Articulate; strong negotiator; approachable; builds productive rapport with persons of all levels, cultures and backgrounds. Coach; motivator; hands-on leader; provides staff with the tools to succeed and deliver. Industrious, exudes energy and confidence, thrives on challenges and driven by deadlines. Solutions-oriented and customer-focused; thorough, patient and methodical.

Core business expertise includes:

- Resource Management
- Crisis Management
- Ramp & Baggage Operations
- Canada Customs

- Customer Service, Operations & Cargo
- IATA Regulations
- P&L Management
- Labour Canada

Professional Experience

Air Canada, Lester B. Pearson Airport, Toronto, Ontario   1996 – present
Held the following four progressively responsible positions:

MANAGER OPERATIONS – Cargo Control   2002 - present

- Acknowledged for boosting customer confidence in shipping packages with Air Canada, achieved by harmonizing customer interaction and displaying a high level of customer care.
- Worked in partnership with a unionized work force to open up communications at all levels and provide positive reinforcement for work assignments.
- Played a pivotal role in labour relations, a tenuous task during recent uncertain economic conditions. Acted as the company's sounding board during all communications between the management and union; patiently and methodically worked with them to elevate potential labour issues. Recognized by Air Canada management for establishing trust with the leaders of the IAMAW.
- Directed a successful Six Sigma project to enhance the operations and speed up transfer of cargo transitioning through the Toronto hub. Conducted an extensive analysis into all the variables, facilitated time studies, conducted work groups, analyzed flow design and process flow. Prepared a detailed recommendation to management to make significant process changes which have resulted in a noticeable improvement in cargo flow and elevated customer confidence with 10% growth.
- Oversaw the complete cargo operations during shift with approximately 140 staff, with an average daily cargo load of 600,000kg & 40,000kg mail. Shipments included all allowable packages according to IATA regulations including live animals.
- Acted as the conduit between the company and Canada Customs to maintain strong relationships, alleviate problems and expedite shipments.
- Recognized by peers and staff for continually reviewing processes for improvement, operational excellence and cost reductions.

MANAGER RESOURCES & ADMINISTRATION   1999 - 2002

- Spearheaded the position's mandate to significantly reduce staff during the acquisition of Canadian Airlines by Air Canada in 2000 and as a result of terrorist activities in 2001, without service interruption. Process included: reviewing each position's relevance to business operations, analyzing performance and making prudent decisions on eliminating managerial staff and assisting with severance packages.
- Reduced the labour and non-labour workforce by 20% and facility costs by 33% during Q4 2001.

Airline Station Manager. This résumé is rich in accomplishments, focusing on the manager's area of expertise in the airline industry. Attention is drawn to the large number of promotions through the italicized statement "Held the following…progressively responsible positions."

MANAGER RESOURCES & ADMINISTRATION, Air Canada......continued
- Interacted between two unionized corporate cultures to enhance relationships and instill confidence to work towards a common goal.
- Was instrumental in leading the cargo operation through a major facility change from one side of the airport to a centralized purpose-built location. Process involved detailed planning with cross-functional personnel internally and externally.
- Established strong relationships with other stakeholders including the Peel Regional Police, IAMAW, GTAA, Labour Canada and Canada Customs.
- Selected to act as the Terminal Manager on an interim basis during a turbulent period in the airline's history.

CUSTOMER SERVICE MANAGER CARGO   1997 - 1999
- Successfully developed and implemented a new handling process for key account, Canada Post, to minimize delay and increase service levels during the transit of their bags through the hub.
- Oversaw 60 personnel charged with processing high volume of cargo, responsible for staffing, safety compliance, attendance issues and interaction with customers and the airport group.

BAGGAGE HANDLER & RAMP STATION ATTENDANT   1996 – 1997

J. Allen Custom Homes, Toronto, Ontario   1988 – 1996
PRINCIPAL
- Acted as the main contractor for building custom homes across the Rosedale and Leaside areas of Toronto, ranging from 3,200 to 12,000 sq. ft.
- Met with demanding high-worth clients and architects to provide a detailed contract price including materials and labour costs.
- Retained ownership on certain items during the construction process including painting, door and cabinet installation and trim work.
- Worked with diverse labour personnel and municipal staff to ensure projects' mandates and completion were met.

Air Canada, Lester B. Pearson Airport, Toronto, Ontario   1973 – 1988
Held the following three progressively responsible positions:
CUSTOMER SERVICE AGENT Cargo   1981 - 1988
- Acted as the frontline customer service representative for cargo; patiently and methodically worked with angry clients to amicably resolve issues.
- Handled a multitude of items from valuables and live animals to firearms.
- Acted as supervisor during absence of management and facilitated training modules for peers.

CUSTOMER SERVICE AGENT – Baggage   1979 - 1981
- Worked in partnership with customers to obtain descriptions and trace their misdirected baggage. Acknowledged for a high recovery rate.

RAMP SERVICES – Terminal 2   1973 - 1979
- Utilized various heavy machinery in a time-sensitive environment to meet aircrafts' mandatory turnaround time.

Continuing Education

Six Sigma – **GREEN BELT**   2003
Canadian Professional Logistics Institute – **PROFESSIONAL MEMBER**   2000
Completed numerous courses, workshops and seminars in the following subjects:

Labour Relations	Safety & Accident Investigation
WHMIS & Dangerous Goods	360 Management Process
Change Management	Leadership

ALEXANDER BAUER

555 Salmon Street
Campbell River, BC V1V 1V1
E-mail ab@careerprocanada.ca

Phone (250) 555-1234
Mobile (250) 555-2345
Facsimile (250) 555-3456

SENIOR AQUACULTURE DIRECTOR
Visionary Leadership ♦ Government Relations ♦ Strategic Partnerships

A seasoned general manager with 20 years' experience and proven achievements in aquaculture farm management and board directorships. Excellent reputation within the industry and government circles acquired by leading high-profile appointments with objectivity, integrity, and sensitivity. Proficiency in the full scope of livestock production, processing, and marketing with a career-long record of combining innovation with teamwork to create operational excellence. A confident spokesperson and influential negotiator with the ability to connect with people of diverse backgrounds and levels of authority. Extensive experience developing mutually beneficial relations with the First Nations Communities. Willing to travel.

Areas of Expertise:

- Entrepreneurial Leadership
- High-level Negotiation
- Consensus Building
- Policy Development

- Profit & Loss Management
- Leadership & Team Building
- Efficiency Improvement
- Global Best Practices

- Business Development
- Alliance Development
- Relationship Management
- Emerging Markets

Recipient of Achievement Award for Long-Term Recognition from the Aquaculture Awareness Club

CAREER HIGHLIGHTS

- **Nurtured long-term constructive relationships with provincial and federal government** leaders and various environmental related non-government organizations in BC.

- **Participated in the development of various regulations related to aquaculture**, including the current BC Salmon Aquaculture Waste Regulations and the Escape Prevention Regulations.

- **Played a significant role in lifting the moratorium on new salmon aquaculture sites** in BC, as the President of the BC Salmon Farmers Network (BCSFN).

- **Reached out to coastal First Nations to improve relations,** create dialogue, and develop business opportunities, resulting in a reduction of the unemployment rate by 50% in some communities.

- **Developed the current Best Management Practices and Code of Practice** for Salmon Aquaculture Operations in BC as a key member of the development team.

PROFESSIONAL EXPERIENCE

Aqua Consulting Ltd., Campbell River, BC   **2003-present**
Independent firm providing consultative services to the government and aquaculture industry.

President & General Manager
Acting consultant responsible for providing leadership and advice to a variety of federal government and private clients. Responsible to develop client relations, establish contracts, undertake work, write reports, and hire subcontractors as required. Full P&L accountability.

- Researched and developed a report for regulatory reform for the Federal Government; recommendations were adopted by the Department of Fisheries and Oceans in Ottawa.
- Advised a BC fishing company in the negotiation of a multi-million dollar service contract with a major aquaculture organization in Canada.
- Provided consultative advice to an aquaculture company, identifying suitable areas for the expansion of their existing business.
- Initiated a customized training program and curriculum for a local college to prepare coastal First Nation students embarking on a career in aquaculture.

Aquaculture Director. This highly experienced professional outlines his professional affiliations and memberships. Highlighting of awards and quotes throughout the résumé strategically reminds the reader of his many board appointments and directorships.

ALEXANDER BAUER

"Throughout the time that we worked together, I was truly impressed with Alexander's collaborative style, patience, and commitment to sustainability – he certainly served the interests of the aquaculture industry well."
-Robert Hatch, Director General, Department of Fisheries and Oceans

PROFESSIONAL EXPERIENCE (CONTINUED)

Top Salmon Inc. (formerly Salmon Inc.), Campbell River, BC   **2000-2003**
North America's leading marketer of Atlantic Salmon, a subsidiary of the $50 billion Agrishare Conglomerate.

Manager of Strategic Development (2001-2003)
Responsible for the strategic development and business growth in three geographical regions within BC. Accountable to participate in the development of budgets.
- Gained the respect of top management within the parent company by developing highly effective policies, procedures, and business strategies.

Fresh Water Manager (2000-2001)
Responsible for overseeing the Fresh Water Division with 5 hatcheries and 55 employees. Accountable to achieve a $17 million budget. Responsibilities include directing managers of the production facilities, ensuring that strategic goals are met, interacting with customers, negotiating contracts, and developing business.
- Redesigned production procedures and methodology, ensured access to appropriate resources for employees, and negotiated contracts to achieve targets.

Previous Positions Held
- West Salmon Farms Ltd. President and General Manager (1989-1990)
- Marine Farms Ltd., President and General Manager (1986-1989)

PROFESSIONAL AFFILIATIONS & BOARD APPOINTMENTS

BC Salmon Farmers Network (BCSFN)   **1986-present**
- Director (1986-present)
- President (1998-2002)

Aquaculture Research & Expansion Program (AREP)   **2001-present**
- Member, Pacific Steering Committee (2001-present)
- Member, National Steering Committee (2001-2004)

International Salmon Farmers Commission (ISFC)   **1995-2003**
- Representative for Western Canada

Salmon Aquaculture Advisory Board (SAAB)   **2000-2002**
- Committee Member

Coastal Economic Development Association (CEDA)   **1998-2001**
- Active Member

FORMAL EDUCATION

Government Forestry College, Steinkjer, Norway
2-year Forestry College Degree

"Alexander Bauer has done an excellent job representing BCFSN.
I have enjoyed our work together to help advance the industry."
- Roberta Fish - Assistant Deputy Minister, BC Services

ROBERT T. DUKE, MBA

55 Top Performer Drive Toronto, Ontario M1M 1M1
Phone (416) 555-1234 • E-mail r.t.duke@careerprocanada.ca • Cell (647) 555-2345

TOP PERFORMING ADMINISTRATIVE EXECUTIVE

Chief Administrative Officer • Executive Director • Director of Corporate Services

Seasoned strategic, tactical, and operational professional with extensive expertise leading the full scope of Finance, Information Systems, Human Resources, and Facilities Management. Impeccable business acumen with outstanding financial qualifications and verifiable experience overseeing multi-million dollar budgets. Talent for leading mergers, restructuring organizations, and managing change to deliver enterprise excellence.

Highly collaborative leader inspiring superior performance by developing, coaching, and mentoring employees. Articulate communicator and negotiator with a career-long record of working effectively through committees and presenting corporate information at the board level. A relationship builder, uniting cross-functional teams and organizations to build consensus and achieve corporate objectives. Willing to travel and/or relocate.

Areas of Expertise:

➡ Financial Planning & Control	➡ Government Relations	➡ Organizational Integration
➡ Budgeting & Forecasting	➡ Board of Directors Interface	➡ Reorganization & Revitalization
➡ Leadership & Team Building	➡ High-Level Negotiations	➡ Change Management
➡ Participative Management	➡ Consensus Building	➡ Efficiency Improvement

PROFESSIONAL EXPERIENCE

Northern Ontario Community Centres, Barrie, Ontario   1998 - Present

Provincial government funded organization providing a wide range of health services through over 30 contracted agencies. In 2003, the North-East and North-West organizations became co-managed under one Executive Director. The two organizations merged in 2003.

Director of Administrative Services

Oversee Finance, Information Systems, Facilities, Procurement, and Human Resources functions, supporting an organization of 230 employees. Senior financial officer overseeing an operation budget of $57 million. Lead and manage 7 direct reports, perform strategic planning, lobby government for resources, and effectively manage overall corporate costs.

- ➡ Established the highly effective Corporate Services organization within Northern Ontario Government Services (NOGS).

- ➡ Launched a shared-services model for the Finance, Information Systems, Facilities Management, and Procurement units, improving service levels and reducing annual costs by $700k.

- ➡ Consolidated two finance departments incorporating business process reengineering and quality improvement approaches, slashing costs by $50k while simultaneously enhancing service levels.

- ➡ Conceived, designed, and instituted the first formal 3-year human resources plan to achieve organizational strategic initiatives.

- ➡ Spearheaded the development of innovative technical software applications that facilitated the more efficient and effective delivery of services, resulting in a projected headcount reduction of 15%.

- ➡ Played a key role on joint committees overseeing the acquisition and implementation of a new Financial and Statistical Reporting System for operations across Ontario.

- ➡ Reduced the number of bargaining units from 2 to 1 and led negotiations of first and second collective agreements, resulting in improved employee relations and affordable settlements.

Chief Administrative Officer. Abundant content in the power statement is broken down into two paragraphs to create white space and improve readability. This executive assembles his experience in distinct sections to exhibit company context, responsibilities, and accomplishments separately.

ROBERT T. DUKE, MBA

PROFESSIONAL EXPERIENCE (CONTINUED)

Maritime Regional Health Department, St John, New Brunswick   1993 - 1998

Municipal government health department providing a wide variety of public health and homecare services, with 200 employees and 7 sites across the region.

Director Administration & Information Services

Oversee the Finance, Information Technology, and Facilities organizations. Accountable for administering a $15 million budget. Perform strategic planning, budgeting, and financial reporting. Oversee, develop, and mentor employees. Lead cross-functional project teams.

➡ Negotiated with the Provincial Government, Maritime Regional Health Department (MRHD), and Regional Health Board (RHB) and orchestrated the merger and transfer of the MRHD organization into RHB.

➡ Initiated a shift from incremental to program budgeting for the Health Department providing meaningful information to decision-makers; the highly successful program became the standard across Canada.

➡ Chaired the steering committee overseeing the design and construction of a $4.9 million health unit; co-ordinated the acquisition, construction, and operation, completing the project on time and under budget.

➡ Orchestrated the expansion of the wide area network to all major health units (5 sites) and implemented an in-house training program, ensuring the successful adoption of the innovative technology.

Prior Positions Held

➡ Northern Manitoba Institute of Technology, Assistant to VP Finance & Administration; Promoted from Budget Manager as a direct result of outstanding achievements and the attainment of an MBA.

➡ Manitoba Recreation & Parks, Financial and Contracts Co-ordinator; Recruited to oversee and institute financial controls within the $250 million Manitoba Parks Development Project.

FORMAL EDUCATION

Masters of Business Administration (MBA), University of Western Ontario
➡ Focus of studies: Finance, Human Resource Management, and International Business

Bachelor of Commerce (B. Comm.), University of Manitoba
➡ Major: Finance

PROFESSIONAL DEVELOPMENT

Queen's University, Kingston, Ontario
➡ Executive Program

University of Toronto, Rotman School of Management, Toronto, Ontario
➡ Advanced Program in Managing Strategic Change
➡ Advanced Program in Human Resource Management

University of British Columbia, Vancouver, BC
➡ Planning a State of the Art Financial Information System

PROFESSIONAL AFFILIATIONS

➡ Human Resources Professional Association of Ontario (HRPAO), Active Member
➡ Health Care Planning Group, Advisory Committee Member

Michael Tobin

111 Main Street, Halifax, Nova Scotia B1B 1B1
Cell: 902 555 1234 Email: mtobin@careerprocanada.ca

"One of Atlantic Canada's Top 50 CEO's" (*Atlantic Business Magazine*)
- Specialist in Internet, Mobility, & Wireless Industries -

10-year leadership career demonstrating accelerated growth in executive achievement. Founder and CEO of two successful technology companies earning over 8 prestigious industry awards for corporate excellence and innovation. Combines strategic and tactical ability to develop and execute corporate vision. Talented leader with a track record for building and leading teams to peak performance.

Areas of Demonstrated Expertise:

- Strategic Planning
- Sales & Marketing
- Capital & VC Financing
- Industry Presentations

- Growth & Development Strategies
- Business Processes
- Financial Stewardship
- Commercialization Strategies

- Start-Ups & Turnarounds
- Corporate Governance
- Leadership & Staff Development
- Entrepreneurship

Awards & Industry Recognition

"One of Atlantic Canada's Top 50 CEO's" – *Atlantic Business Magazine*	2004
"Canada's Hottest Start Up's" – *Profit Magazine*	2002
"Canada's Top 50 IPS Companies" – *Branham Group*	2002
"East Coast Research and Development Award"	2002
"Canada's Top 25 Up and Coming IT Companies" – *Branham Group*	2000
"Atlantic Canada's Fastest Growing Companies" – *Atlantic Progress*	1999
"Atlantic Canada's Fastest Growing Companies" – *Atlantic Progress*	1998
"Canada's Top 25 Up and Coming IT Companies" – *Branham Group*	1998
Silver Award – *Metro Halifax Chamber of Commerce Business Awards*	
Nominee – *Metro Halifax Chamber of Commerce Business Awards*	

Career Development

TECHNOLOGY SOLUTIONS INC.   Halifax, Nova Scotia
Professional IT solutions firm providing customized e-commerce and content delivery solutions to medium and large-scale enterprises throughout Canada and the U.S.

➢ **CEO / President**   2002 – Present; 1996 – 1999

Founded and currently direct a successful IT solutions firm. Hold full strategic planning, P&L, sales and marketing, operating, technology, and administrative leadership responsibilities. Identified market demand, secured all up-front capital financing, and led the strategic and tactical development of the company to award-winning growth and industry recognition.

Returned in 2002 to salvage operations and revitalize lagging revenue levels. Re-strategized product delivery and injected new vigour into business development efforts.

Performance Milestones:

- Tripled revenues and doubled staff each year for first 4 years
- First in Eastern Canada to establish foothold in wireless content delivery and secure e-commerce technology
- Following return in 2002, turned company around to realize highest profit margin in company history by 10x for fiscal 2004.
- Voted "One of Canada's Top 50 IPS Companies" by the *Branham Group* (2002)
- Voted "One of Canada's Top 25 Up and Coming IT companies" by the *Branham Group* (2000)
- Voted "One of Atlantic Canada's Fastest Growing Companies" by *Atlantic Progress* (1998 & 1999)

Chief Executive Officer. The quote at the top of the résumé positions this executive in a separate class right out of the gate. This résumé artistically addresses a return to his job after a brief absence by the statement "Returned in 2002 to salvage…" His "Performance Milestones" creatively list tangible career highlights.

Michael Tobin – *Page 2*

E-NOW   Halifax, Nova Scotia
IT development firm providing state-of-the-art enterprise applications for telecommunications and field service industries throughout North America.

> **CEO / President**   1998 – 2002

Identified market opportunity and temporarily left Internet Solutions to build new technology firm specializing in wireless POS transactions. Conceptualized product, established a commercially viable business model, and secured multi-million VC and angel funding. Led all strategic planning, business development, and technology development efforts.

Performance Milestones:

- Led firm through all rounds of financing to a total of over $5 million
- Grew company to industry-leading status and a total complement of 35 – recruited all senior management, board, and development staff
- Featured speaker at international CeBit Conference in Hanover, Germany (2002)
- Voted "One of Canada's Hottest Start-Ups" by *Profit Magazine* (2002)
- Voted "One of Canada's Top 25 Up and Coming IT companies" by the *Branham Group* (1998)
- Winner of the Metro Halifax Chamber of Commerce Silver Award
- Awarded the CANARIE Canadian Research and Development Award (2001)

EAST COAST SECURITIES   Halifax, Nova Scotia
Corporate security firm specializing in the provision, installation, and service of leading-edge security technologies.

> **Partner / Business Development**   1992 – 1995

Brought in to orchestrate an aggressive new growth phase, with a focus on targeted business development, sales, and marketing. Identified and successfully secured larger corporate accounts and generated year-over-year revenue growth.

Industry Affiliations & Contributions

TECHNOLOGY EXECUTIVES OF NOVA SCOTIA (TENS)
> **Vice President**   2003 – Present
> **Director**   2001 – 2002

NOVA SCOTIA CENTRE FOR ENTREPRENEURSHIP (NSCE)
> **Director**   2000 – Present
> **Advisor** – Entrepreneur's Forum   2000 – Present

EASTCOAST IT ASSOCIATION
> **Commercialization Committee**   2001 – Present

PREMIER'S ADVISORY COUNCIL ON TECHNOLOGY (Nova Scotia)
> **Council Member**   2003

TELECOM RESEARCH SYMPOSIUM
> **Member**   2003

METRO HALIFAX CHAMBER OF COMMERCE
> **IT Committee**   2002

Education

Bachelor of Commerce (Marketing / Economics) – Mount Allison University, New Brunswick   1992

JOE SCOLARI, B.COMM.

11 Bloor St. East, Toronto, Ontario M1M 1M1
905-555-1212   joseph-scolari@careerprocanada.ca

FINANCIAL TURNAROUND SPECIALIST

◆ Financial Strategies ◆ Target Identification ◆ Strategic Planning ◆ Contract Negotiations ◆ Government Compliance	Results-driven financial professional with proven capability to turn around negative company performance through implementation of cost-savings and revenue generation strategies. Known as a *change agent* who makes tough decisions for the benefit of the company's future stability. Fluent in three languages: English, French, and Italian.

EXPERIENCE

Central Modified Equipment Ltd.   2000 – Present
Chief Financial Officer

- Guided and assisted board of directors in the development of corporate strategies and goals to reverse negative sales trend of 25% per year for two years, to produce profits of $6.8M in first year.

- Mapped out staff compensation and succession, allowing for retention and attraction of exceptional talent, and creating strong team of powerful performers who produced over $35M in sales in 2001.

- Negotiated contracts with key suppliers and bank to reduce debt load over a longer term, at a lower interest rate, saving the company $67K in interest charges and late fines.

- Realized a cost saving of $250K through the negotiation of outsource contracts to provide non-core business services across Canada and in the US.

- Strengthened lease agreement conditions to ensure secure and timely payment, and reduce contract breach rate from 12% to 2% per year, saving a minimum of $128K per year.

- Provided expert advice and assistance during the winding down of company in 2006, exceeding government requirements while protecting shareholder interests.

Canadian Revenue Generation Corporation   1998 – 2000
Director, Finance, Operations, and Compliance (1999 – 2000)
Senior Manager, Finance (1998 – 1999)

- Oversaw $75B worth of registered plans, bringing company into legal compliance, and creating documentation flow process to ensure timely and accurate processing of information.

- Negotiated settlement of high-risk files through pro-active disclosure of potential problems, averting potential legal ramifications in excess of $2.5M, and arranging payment plans for amounts owing.

- Reduced time spent during product launch by up to 3 months through the development of communication process and information sharing amongst stakeholders and executive management.

- Developed and introduced strict adherence model and compliance protocol for newly introduced lines of service, resulting in reduction of product rejection rate by 10%.

- Analyzed company financial projections, comparing current performance with historical data, to forecast accurate sales, operational, and financial performance during expansion into global markets.

Continued...

Chief Financial Officer. This individual's *Value Proposition* is evident throughout the résumé. With a focus on turnaround, this executive clearly has expertise in taking companies from negative to postive results. This expertise is demonstrated in the profile and in the accomplishments.

JOSEPH SCOLARI, B.COMM.
905-555-1212

Financial Time Ltd.   1996 – 1998
National Operations Manager

- Systematized process for order taking and distribution of national trade magazine, focusing on maximizing delivery times while minimizing costs.

- Lowered undeliverable rates by 15% in first year through database management and creation of promotional campaign; solidified additional 20% in subscriptions.

- Defined and intensified market penetration into northern Canada, increasing sales in region by 25%; negotiated lowered delivery pricing to remote access areas, resulting in 10% reduction in costs.

- Proposed business model and assisted in the strategic implementation as part of a senior management team initiative to meet aggressive growth projections of 45% in one year.

- Generated favourable support from key lenders to contribute funds for associate marketing campaign that generated over $1.2M in additional revenue, and expanded brand awareness for all partners.

Brown's Credit Canada Limited   1992 – 1996
Financial Analyst

- Achieved double-digit savings year over year through the implementation of sales tracking and purchasing forecasting software, reducing annual inventory costs from $120K to $90K in one year.

- Conducted complete audit for company's previous five-year performance, identifying potential areas at high risk for government fines; negotiated with government officials to eliminate fines of $35K.

- Increased lease completion rates by up to 15% through the design and development of accurate approval rating system, allowing company to assess high-risk applicants accurately before approval.

EDUCATION

Bachelor of Commerce (B.Comm.)   1989
McMaster University

"Transformational Leaders offer charismatic inspiration.
They display high values and ethics and build a common purpose within teams.
When teams come together with focus and inspiration, companies can move mountains."

MICHAEL WALKER

111 Fuchsia Way, Toronto, Ontario M1M 1M1
Phone: 416.555.0123   Cell: 416.555.0000   E mail: mwalker@CareerProCanada.ca

CHIEF INFORMATION OFFICER

Acts as the conduit between IT and Business Operations

Highly successful, industrious hands-on senior IT executive with an exemplary record of realigning underperforming IT departments. Conceives and implements unique strategies to optimize business operations, elevate productivity and boost revenue. Delivers solutions; change agent, visionary and forward thinking, capable of critically evaluating and responding to diverse information technology issues. Thrives in a fast-paced environment of continuous challenges. Proactive leader, coach and mentor; gains employee confidence and utilizes their talent and knowledge. Shrewd business strategist, tenacious, exudes energy and confidence to excel and deliver. Core business competencies include:

• Executive Leadership	• Change Management	• Solutions Delivery
• Matrix Management	• Business Continuity	• Yield Management
• Web Based Technology	• Project Management	• Sarbanes-Oxley
• Mergers & Acquisitions	• Strategic Direction	• Business Transformation

PROFESSIONAL EXPERIENCE

M.B. I.T. Consulting, Toronto, Ontario   2003 - present
MANAGING DIRECTOR
Provide IT leadership, direction and support in the following core business areas: outsourcing, IT and business infrastructure, realignment, strategic delivery and Sarbanes-Oxley Act.
Key contracts have included:
Reed Bailey & Associates
- Researched and compiled the Project Charter relating to the Sarbanes-Oxley Act for a Fortune 500 company.

Canadian Media, Toronto, Ontario   2002 - 2003
GROUP VICE PRESIDENT – Information Technology (CIO)
Recruited to implement a corporate Information Technology Strategic Plan for the broadcast (CTV), print (The Toronto Tribune) and Internet (TTI) divisions and to boost financial performance.
- Secured approval for an $11 million automated newsroom system to replace obsolete technology for The Toronto Tribune, maintaining their advantage in a competitive environment.
- Conceived and executed a capital requirement cost reduction strategy, reducing expenditures by 50%. Prioritized capital projects based on benefits, cost, flexibility/investment and risk.
- Reduced project costs by 57%; achieved by eliminating projects, establishing standards, promoting reuse and streamlining common services.
- Played the lead role in renegotiating supplier contracts across all areas: telecommunications, software, hardware and consulting, leveraging the company's purchasing power.
- Co-represented Avalon Media in consultations with PriceWaterhouseCoopers to establish process controls for the implementation of Sarbanes-Oxley, ensuring risks were mitigated and achieving full compliance.
- Instrumental in reintegrating two primary business units during a massive restructuring plan to improve financial performance.
- Accountable for devising and monitoring a $30+ million operating budget, $15+ million base capital budget and leading 180 employees, tasked with supporting 4,400 customers in Canada and abroad.

Chief Information Officer. This headline works well with the tagline, "Acts as the conduit between IT and business operations." This reveals the individual's *Value Proposition*, which is then supported throughout the résumé through his achievements.

MICHAEL WALKER   **Page Two**

CTV Television Network (ATV), Division of Canadian Media, Toronto, Ontario   2001 - 2003
VICE PRESIDENT - Information Technology
- Directed a complex integration of TWin and CTV IT departments after a recent acquisition; using best practices of modern organizational design. Refocused the new unit to function as an external professional service, reversing a negative perception of the IT department.
- Designed, developed and implemented the technology relocation for 650 TWin employees into the CTV facilities without business interruption.
- Reduced a spiralling IT operating budget by 10% each year during the integration of CKCC, CKCY and BORTv.
- Partnered with the V.P. Sales Operations to consolidate 3 advertising support revenue systems, saving $4.5 million and enhancing productivity and customer service.
- Charged with selecting 70 employees and sourcing external consultants tasked with building a $44 million, 15-year business case. Secured approval from senior management team; selected and negotiated agreement with international vendor. Established a unique joint venture with BlockStar, CTV's largest competitor during the final stages of the business case project.

Dragon Communications, Toronto, Ontario   1997 – 2001
CHIEF INFORMATION OFFICER & VICE PRESIDENT
- Recruited to realign an underperforming and disjointed business unit after significant senior level terminations. Hired skilled replacements, refocused IT to prioritize projects and acquired additional funding to sustain positive business contributions.
- Appointed as TWin key representative to the CTV Integration Team with representation from external consultants. Ensured TWin's technology, process and human resource requirements were addressed.

British Broadcasting Corporation (BBC), London, U.K.   1980 – 1997
Held the following progressively responsible **Directorships**:

DIRECTOR - Corporate IT Planning	**DIRECTOR - Regional IT Support, Overseas Dept.**
DIRECTOR - Corporate Telecommunications	**DIRECTOR - National Data Centre**
DIRECTOR - Applications Development & Support	

Selected accomplishments include:
- Played the pivotal IT leadership role during a complex 3-year corporate rightsizing, meeting the mandated 30% target.
- Reduced the 1994 IT operating budget by 37%, while increasing values to core business units.
- Worked with Deloitte Consulting to plan, acquire and implement a new SAP corporate finance system to meet cost-reduction initiatives and Year 2000 compliance.
- Consistently acknowledged for the ability to break down the communication and technology barrier, enhance the perception of IT and work with all stakeholders to optimize technology, boost productivity and reduce costs.
- Contracted and oversaw numerous external suppliers to assist with IT operations and keep pace with the corporation's need for cost constraints. Drove the importance of IT as an integral and valuable entity across the Corporation.
- Managed teams appointed to design and implement multi-million dollar IT projects to gain competitive advantage.

EDUCATION

University of Waterloo, Waterloo, Ontario   1979
BACHELOR OF COMPUTER SCIENCE

Strong proponent of continuing education. Completed numerous technical and leadership programs.

MATALADO MACHADO, MBA

1234 Winding River Road
Oakville, Ontario L1L 1L1

Residence: (905) 555-1234
mmachado@careerprocanada.ca

RESULTS-ORIENTED EXECUTIVE

Resourceful and enterprising professional and innovative leader of Finance, Information Technology and Human Resource teams in fast-paced, high growth international environments. Respected for dynamic, personable approach and integrity – traits further distinguished by an ability to seamlessly amalgamate people, processes and systems for operational efficiencies across organizations. Readily appreciated and relied upon for insight, direction, enthusiasm and follow-through in process improvement, barrier removal and mergers and acquisitions. **Core strengths include:**

- Strategic Planning
- Operations & Technology Improvement
- Project Management

- Exceptional Communication
- Decision-Making & Delegation
- Change & Transition Facilitation

PROFESSIONAL EXPERIENCE

IT-FXSYSTEMS, Oakville, Ontario   1998 - Present
International personal computer distribution company headquartered in Canada with revenues of $60M, sales in over 90 countries, and 130 employees in Canada, US, the UK, Barbados and Denmark.

Earned the following positions of increased stature and accountability:

Chief Operating Officer   2002 - Present

Promoted to this position, reporting to the CEO, to drive organizational effectiveness and introduce leading edge systems while reinforcing company culture, goals and confidence boosting initiatives. Created resilient relationships with banking partners while negotiating scalable financing for growth. Maintained and revitalized infrastructure to foster future expansion, succession and management development.

- Oversaw system design and customization of e-commerce real time order entry website including online credit card processing, fraud prevention and freight quoting. Within 6 months, channelled 30% of all orders and 8% of revenue.
- Spearheaded specialized paperwork generation, automatic purchase order creation, integration with FedEx, electronic transmission of invoices and the elimination of yearend physical counts; produced $160,000 in savings in 2004.
- Redesigned and implemented US and Canadian employee benefits programs; achieved 50% savings in ongoing US benefit costs while sheltering existing staff.

Vice President, Operations   2000 - 2002

Set operational direction for IT-FXSystems worldwide - with accountability for human resources, distribution centres, and information technology, in order to support 20% year-over-year sales growth. Recruited and mentored key middle managers. Championed and organized three worldwide conferences for all employees resulting in improved morale and communication.

- Established IT-FXSystems' enterprise information system, to provide sales lead management, order entry, radio-frequency scanners, invoicing, collection and financials.
- Partnered with FedEx in first installation of a logistics service between Canada and the US, which substantially improved customer service, reduced brokerage and freight costs, created savings of $125,000 in 2002, and led to a new service offering by FedEx one year later.
- Secured 99% on time shipping in 3 centres and 50% year-over-year volume increases.
- Relocated 2 distribution locations, each over 30,000 square feet, to larger premises with no operational downtime.

Continued Page 2 ➢

Chief Operating Officer. This résumé neatly runs through the executive's career progression, highlighting his extraordinary promotions. He bolsters each position with strong accomplishments and quantifiable results.

MATALADO MICHADO, MBA   PAGE 2

Vice President, Finance & Administration 1998 - 2000

Oversaw all finance and business controls for IT-FXSystems, following an entrepreneurial start-up. Led reporting, budgeting and payroll. Enhanced financial management and analysis for on-time audited statements to all business partners and key information for corporate expansion decisions.

- Forged the first corporate strategy document and formal business plan, which facilitated the approval for a 50% increase in financing capacity.
- Maintained key associations with the bank, auditors, legal counsel and insurance providers affording a smooth transition during the unexpected departure of a minority shareholder.
- Charted an effective revenue recognition and transfer pricing strategy to meet taxation compliance and optimize worldwide tax costs.
- Executed HR processes including an Employee Performance Management System and recruiting strategy to support 30% headcount growth, health & safety compliance and policy guidelines.

CANADIAN BANK AND TRUST, Toronto, Ontario   1991 - 1998
Canada's sixth largest banking institution with over 40,000 employees servicing Personal & Commercial Banking, Wealth Management and Investment Banking markets. CB&T is known for its lean structure, focus on employees and innovative approach to discount brokerage.

Promoted steadily through management and executive positions including:

Senior Manager, Employee Development 1996 - 1998

Coordinated bank-wide succession planning and Corporate Resource Program with senior executives and high potential candidates throughout North America.

- Prepared Board of Director presentations for recommended appointments of titled bank officers; automated the process and cut preparation time in half.
- Enabled a leading edge, Internet-based, $2M career self-development program – the first fully integrated system of its kind in Canada.

Commercial Account Manager   1994 - 1996

Relationship manager for mid-market commercial borrowing accounts. Accountable for credit adjudication, sales growth, fee revenue, cross-selling, asset quality and structuring of credit facilities.

Manager, Personal Credit   1991 - 1994

Administered personal financial planning including credit and investments. Directed teams in both branch and divisional offices. Key player in credit due diligence as part of the acquisition of Central Trust.

SYSTEMS ANALYST / CONSULTANT ROLES:
The Mutual Group	1989 - 1990
Waterloo Information Systems	1989 - 1989
University Of Waterloo	1987 - 1989

EDUCATION

Charter Financial Analyst, Level 2, CFA Program	1999
Master of Business Administration, Wilfred Laurier University, Waterloo, Ontario	1995
Canadian Securities Course, CSC Program	1991
Honours, Bachelor of Mathematics, University of Waterloo, Waterloo, Ontario	1991

Just being honest is not enough. The essential ingredient is executive integrity.
Philip Crosby, Reflections on Quality

RANDALL SINGH

222 Main Crescent
Toronto, Ontario M1M 1M1

Phone: (416) 555-1234
Email: rsingh@careerprocanada.ca

EXECUTIVE PROFILE

★ *Recipient of the highest corporate distinction for commitment to excellence* ★

Award-winning professional combining top quality strategic, operational and management expertise. Distinguished 20+ year career providing high-level information security solutions designed to safeguard technology investments, services, facilities, and databases. Dynamic and results-oriented leader with outstanding communication, consulting, and team building skills. Recipient of distinguished Wall of Winners Award for excellence.

Information Security & Disaster Recovery

- Expert in Information Security, Disaster Recovery, and Business Continuity
- 20+ years expertise planning and implementing enterprise-class security and recovery solutions to ensure integrity and protection of all critical corporate data and technology services
- Expert in mainframe and enterprise LAN/WAN technologies (Alpha, VAX, HP, Novell, and Unix)

Vendor Management & Contract Negotiations

- Outstanding contract procurement and negotiation skills – proven ability to secure comprehensive, top-quality, cost-effective vendor agreements
- Particularly skilled in managing long-term vendor relationships in a consistent and professional manner

Team Leadership & People Management

- Reputation for building and leading strong high-performance teams
- Ability to create high team morale, and motivate teams to consistently meet and exceed corporate and departmental objectives
- Recognized for ability to create a positive and productive environment that effectively reduces staff turnover

---

PROFESSIONAL EXPERIENCE

CANADIAN RETAIL CORPORATION, Toronto, Ontario
Rapid advancement through senior technology and information security positions on the strength of advanced strategic planning, team leadership, process improvement, cost control, and vendor negotiation and relationship management capabilities.

CHIEF TECHNOLOGY OFFICER - INFORMATION SECURITY   1999 – Present
Senior technology position charged with the strategic planning, maintenance, implementation, administration, and interpretation of all Information Security policies, standards, guidelines, and procedures across the organization to safeguard the corporation's vital technology services, facilities, and databases. Concurrently tasked with managing key technology projects and vendor negotiations. *Achievements include:*

- Revitalized the integrity of all security privileges, and established comprehensive security and disaster recovery protocols that exceeded all audit security recommendations.
- Mandated disaster recovery procedures and offsite storage solutions for the midrange and distributed systems (Alpha, VAX, HP, Novell, and Unix).
- Successfully renegotiated major outsource printing contract with Xenon Canada, securing over $800,000 in savings for Canadian Retail over the term of the agreement, and further identifying a $125,000 cost avoidance opportunity for Xenon.
- Renegotiated critical ComDo disaster recovery contracts resulting in cost savings of over $600,000, improved client coverage, and the additional elimination of all 6% annual contract increases.
- Successfully managed implementation of a new fibre ring designed to re-route voice and data traffic in event of failure to the primary fibre option.

...2

Chief Technology Officer. The three headings within the profile distinguish this consultant's areas of expertise. Stars enclose a magnificent by-line that positions him as an award-winning leader.

RANDALL SINGH   (416) 555-1234   Page 2

MANAGER – Disaster Recovery, Data Centre Security   1997 – 1999
Challenged with safeguarding all enterprise technology services, security, and data in the event of a physical disaster. Included comprehensive planning and coordination of all network and mainframe recovery testing, physical security of computing facilities, environmental controls, and executive transportation to recovery site.

- Established infrastructure and procedures to ensure network connectivity to all business clients within 48 hours of disaster, and relocation of corporate executive to recovery site in Bergen, NJ within 3 hours.
- Spearheaded implementation of SAE, effectively reducing erase time by 66% and resolving outstanding audit security issues.
- Successfully audited five corporate computing facilities to ensure integrity of environmental and employee safety controls, including fire alarm systems, air conditioning, environmental alerts, and use of UPS/diesel generators.
- Reduced mainframe and network recovery times by 25% and card authorization (Stratus) recovery by 50%.
- Re-evaluated and/or eliminated card access to secured areas, and initiated weekly and monthly audits, reporting, and procedures to ensure security issues.

MANAGER – Program Delivery   1995 – 1997
Selected to build and manage key Project Management Team and coordinate multiple ongoing enterprise initiatives on time and within budget. Direct management of five Project Managers and resource pool of 40 technical specialists.

- Built and maintained an efficient and highly regarded professional unit through solid team leadership, process improvement, and priority management skills.
- Effectively controlled staffing costs through judicious training and redeployment within the resource pool.

MANAGER – Network Planning and Support Data & Voice   1993 – 1995
Coordinated all planning, support, and applicable outsourcing for enterprise telecommunications, voice (BPX), and WAN services across the corporation.

- Recommended technology improvements and outsourcing opportunities that allowed for significant cost savings while improving level of service.
- Effectively managed seamless crossover to outsourced voice services.
- Managed ongoing support of newly implemented SpaceTel satellite communications system throughout all Associate stores and Express Auto Parts facilities.

MANAGER – Spacepac Satellite Information Systems   1992 – 1993
Concurrently seconded by Senior Technology Team to lead strategic planning and implementation of Spacepac satellite system across 400+ Associate Dealer network. Challenged to establish entire infrastructure and manage cycle through pre-installation, installation, training, and ongoing support.

- Doubled senior management mandate by signing all 400+ Corporate Associate Dealers in first year (met expectation of 200 signed orders within 6 months).
- Successfully managed all hardware and software installations without disruption to day-to-day operations.
- Established key service level agreements with corporate sponsors and associated vendors.

MANAGER – Computer Operations / Disaster Recovery   1987 – 1992
Coordinated all online computer services, computer planning, disaster recovery, and system development throughout the organization. Additionally accountable for all negotiation and relationship management with 3rd party vendors and technology partners. Managed 42-person team with 7 direct reports.

- Successfully instituted a number of industry and corporation firsts, including the first online automated cartridge system in Canada, the largest Amdahl single image processor in Ontario, and a new Data Centre Help Desk.
- Replaced and renegotiated over 50% of current vendor relationships unable to meet business needs, resulting in significant cost savings and service improvements.
- Renegotiated all Micrographics contracts to reduce annual costs and turnaround first profit of $500,000 for Operations department.

EDUCATION

Business Administration – Marketing, Centennial College, Toronto, Ontario

BRAD NORTHRUP, B.Comm (HONS)

111 Mohawk Ave.
Toronto, Ontario M1M 1M1

416-555-1212
brad.northrup@careerprocanada.ca

CORPORATE SECURITY EXECUTIVE

Visionary and dynamic corporate security leader with an extensive portfolio of clients in the private and public sectors. Capacity to deal with high priority security issues to minimize risk of information manipulation and exposure of intellectual property. Possesses a well-rounded knowledge in global operations, marketing, compliance, and finance. Able to negotiate powerful strategic alliances through open communication and a "win-win" attitude. Key government alliance partner.

CAREER HIGHLIGHTS:

≈ Played key role in expanding contract bid opportunities, acting lead executive on security compliance project with the *Government of Canada* leading to top security level accreditation and $42M worth of new contracts.

≈ Landed key account contracts worth $21M+ within a two-year period, and increased revenues by 400% through diligent compliance with government security criteria and clear communication of directives.

≈ Turned around negative performance in key customer account from negative 10% sales to generate an additional 15% revenue stream worth in excess of $12.5M.

≈ Facilitated implementation of new sales and marketing program; oversaw process and procedure development, training design and delivery, and roll out in each province.

PROFESSIONAL HISTORY

HyperText Solutions Inc.
2003 - Present
New company start-up offering high-end on-line marketing solutions to small to mid-sized companies across Canada, the United States, and Europe.

CHIEF EXECUTIVE SECURITY OFFICER
Senior Executive position with budget in excess of $27M, oversees all national and international operations, and corporate security issues.

≈ Awarded top security level clearance for Government of Canada; positioned company as industry leader in security auditing and response agent of choice in both Canada and Europe.

≈ Developed strategic business alliances with offshore and European internet security providers, allowing company to expand into global market, resulting in $12.5M in initial two-year period.

≈ Clarified company's core competencies and assisted in the development of a strong corporate vision, identifying and pro-actively targeting key revenue generating products; produced over $23M in first year.

≈ Forged relations with elite network administration delivery partner to provide offshore facilities, reducing operational costs by 16% and streamlining service to expanding customer base.

≈ Designed expansion model and succession matrix for the strategic planning for company to expand over a five-year period; assessed projections within 2% accuracy.

≈ Coached client services team to provide exceptional customer care services, assuring the turnaround of a key account from a decline of 10% in year over year sales to produce an additional 15% ($12.5M).

≈ Executed ambitious business plan for company rollout, achieving a ten-fold increase in business between year 1 and year 2; provided input and advice to management team for growth management and performance.

Continued...

Clear Communication ≈ *Innovation* ≈ *Government Compliance* ≈ *Precision and Detail*

Corporate Security Executive. This executive's *Value Proposition* is rich in added value. As the profile suggests, in addition to being a security expert, he brings to the table extensive contacts, government alliances, and global operations expertise. Career highlights are used to strategically break the bullet points into smaller, more readable chunks.

E-BIZ Strategies Inc.
1998 - 2003

Canadian owned and operated on-line data processing firm, with key customer portfolio of Fortune 500 companies worth over $87.5M.

EXECUTIVE DIRECTOR, NATIONAL BUSINESS DEVELOPMENT

Reporting to President, responsible for the profitable operations within the Sales and Marketing division to expand market share and drive national sales.

≈ Strengthened company position in market by personally securing 16 key accounts long-term accounts, securing income of just over $52M each year for a 5-year term in first year.

≈ Exceeded company sales plans for new business by up to 35% year over year starting in year 2, while maintaining touch with established customer base to grow those sales by an additional $12M.

≈ Led creative and innovative sales and marketing team in the development and implementation of strategic marketing initiatives to acquire company account in all 9 provinces and 3 in the US.

Outlook Creative Solutions Inc.
1995 - 1998

Outsource services provider in the e-business sector, servicing Fortune 500 clients in Canada, the US, and Europe since 1991. Clients include Government of France, Belgium, and Portugal, as well as other international interests.

BUSINESS DEVELOPMENT MANAGER

Responsible for new business development for Fortune 500 companies in the North American market to provide suite of e-Business solutions.

≈ Targeted select vertical market within automotive sector to sell customized e-business solutions to companies such as GM Canada, Toyota, and Nissan; contracts worth over $11.2M in first year.

≈ Won lucrative contract ($18M) with major banking institution; partnered with them to create, develop, and oversee implementation of new e-business initiative for their Canadian operations in 9 provinces.

≈ Brought decision makers to the table for several executive level negotiations to increase new business opportunities and expand brand awareness to key prospects within industry market.

Exact Importers Ltd.
1989 - 1995

Privately owned and operated retail and mail-order enterprise, providing computer systems, parts, and software across North America.

PRESIDENT

≈ Developed business model to provide high quality personal computer systems to small business owners, developing steady customer base of 250 local and regional customers in first two years.

≈ Increased sales between 1989 and 1991 by over 500% by aggressively targeting select home office market and creating ambitious marketing plan to grow sales from $86,000 to just over $430K.

≈ Opened second location in Toronto, Ontario in 1992, augmenting company revenues by an additional $250K in the first year, while maintaining seamless operations at both locations.

FORMAL EDUCATION

B. Comm. Program, Honours, Montreal University   1989

PROFESSIONAL DEVELOPMENT

Creating Strong Brands in Business, Top School of Business   2005
Marketing and Sales Coaching System, Performers Edge Coaching and Consulting   2005
Landmark Forum, Landmark Education   2002

Clear Communication ≈ Innovation ≈ Government Compliance ≈ Precision and Detail

KEVIN BEDAY

111 Amain Street, Victoria, British Columbia ▪ V1V 1V1
Res 250.555.1234 ▪ Bus 250.555.0123 ▪ Email kevinbeday@CareerProCanada.ca

SENIOR ENGINEERING OPERATIONS MANAGER

Focused and decisive leader offering a comprehensive blend of time sensitive, unpredictable, fast-paced and fiscally accountable engineering and technical project management successes. Recognized for intuitive and diplomatic interpersonal abilities used to quell team dysfunction and build cohesiveness. Effectively motivates multi-disciplinary civilian, unionized and military professionals to performance excellence; reputation for solid leadership talents and for serving as a change agent. Highly developed technical proficiency with full range of engineering and project management software. Entrusted with *Top Secret* security status. **Core Competencies:**

- Operations Management
- Electrical Engineering
- Staff Development & Leadership
- Crisis & Emergency Response

- Safety & Compliance Management
- Confidentiality Assurance
- Resource Analysis & Allocation
- Budgeting & Report Generation

QUALIFICATIONS IN ACTION - Department of National Defence   (1996 - Present)

CONFIGURATION and CHANGE MANAGEMENT OFFICER   2003 - Present
Canadian Forces Base, Esquimalt, British Columbia
Assigned to lead the Systems Engineering Group of Base Information Services. Oversaw the complete configuration of the MARPAC Information Technology (IT) infrastructure, including 3 networks ranging from designated to secret classification levels and servicing 5000+ users distributed over the Vancouver Island, the Lower Mainland and on deployable Naval Vessels. Relied upon to serve in 3 additional roles: General Safety Officer, Risk Management Officer and Personnel Evaluation Reports Standards Officer.

- Introduced the notion of a long overdue and neglected Configuration Management Office, complete with an organization-wide IT Infrastructure Library (ITIL) initiative. Conducted an operational assessment and presented compelling evidence to receive $20 000 for funding. Project managed all database configurations, staffing, logistical, supply, safety, budgeting and conceptual elements. Researched and aligned optimal configuration management policies from DND, Maritime Pacific Commander's Mandate and best engineering practices. Launched rigorous 3, 6, 12 and 24-month goals: identified job requirements and drafted position descriptions; developed a comprehensive training plan allowing the seamless introduction of Configuration Management (CM) to an IT environment. Efforts rewarded by a transparent Request For Change process with life cycle tracking and the responsive process meets 99% of its posted timelines for 70+ requests monthly. Formed a motivated, technically advanced and fiscally responsible core configuration management team.
- As the Unit General Safety Officer, tasked to design and implement a safety program. Ensured regulatory compliance with Canada Labour Code Part II. Revamped accident and investigation reporting, workplace inspection protocols, safety training, and equipment storage. Conducted weekly safety briefs. Results: a permanent program that promotes safe workplace practices, reducing accidents by 50% and increasing legislative adherence.
- Risk Management Officer duties entailed ensuring the environmental program and systems operated in synchronization with the aforementioned safety measures.
- Revitalized the *Progress Development Review Process*. Capitalized on thorough human resource knowledge to review Personnel Evaluation Reports (PERs). Scrutinized copy for 70+ PERs assessing whether the content was consistent, the feedback was constructive and conducive to increasing employee productivity and morale.

Continued ⇨

Engineering Operations Manager. This candidate positions himself to work in the corporate world by either excluding or replacing military jargon with common terms. This strategy tones down the impression of power and control which can be intimidating to the civilian workforce.

KEVIN BEDAY

DEPUTY HEAD OF DEPARTMENT - COMBAT SYSTEMS ENGINEERING   2002 - 2003
Her Majesty's Canadian Ship REGINA
Selected to manage a 25-member technical team to meet the ships' daily corrective and preventative maintenance functions. Coordinated all staff/intern training, personnel reviews, administrative detailing, and external departmental communications. Held accountable for assessing damage and prioritizing repairs for mission requirements.

- Rational decision making capabilities handled overseeing the safety and security of the ship's company as *Officer of the Day* and was a *Force Protection Leader* in charge of repelling terrorist attacks, rules of engagement, and situation assessment.
- Conducted a technical investigation into an environmental spill. Identified the causal factor of the automated monitoring system failure. Generated detailed report to improve design.
- Hand picked by the Commanding Officer to spearhead the ships' deployment in preparation of the second Gulf War. Labour intensive, 7-month initiative. Granted autonomy to screen and train mission personnel, plan and conduct tests, trails and maintenance cycles. Guided HAZMAT spill clean up team. Designated as Liaison Officer for Hong Kong Port. Interfaced with Canadian/American Consulates, Chandlers, and Military/Hong Kong Police Forces. Undertook a pre-docking inspection. Flew to Hong Kong one week in advance to conduct meetings, coordinate security, assess threat potential and arrange key community events.
- Project managed the Annual Trials Program, totalling 100+ trials for more than 50 individual systems. Scope of responsibilities were comprehensive including the identification, coordination and completion of equipment testing. Generated schedules, monitored maintenance needs, and delivered impact statements to senior management identifying potential system shortcomings based the analysis of results.

COMBAT SYSTEMS ENGINEERING ASSISTANT   2001 - 2002
Her Majesty's Canadian Ship CALGARY
Achieved Officer of the Day (OOD) qualifications. For 24 hours, once a week, coordinated the activities of the entire ship including maintenance, emergency response, coordinating external resource coordination, radiation safety, hazardous materials spills response, engineering emergencies situations, internal communication systems and a 220-staff supervision.

- Solidified systems knowledge of Weapons, Communications, Command and Control, Sonar, Radar, Electronic Warfare, Navigation and Hydraulics by obtaining Naval Combat Systems Engineer Technical Qualification.

EDUCATION (See *Addendum* for complete listing)

BACHELOR OF ENGINEERING: ELECTRICAL ENGINEERING   1996 - 2000
Royal Military College of Canada

TECHNOLOGY: MS Office, Project, PeopleSoft, AutoCAD, IDEAS, Matlab, Visio, C, C++, Assembler

SPEAKING ENGAGEMENTS

(2003) *Overall Combat Systems Suite.* Addressed Ship's Company and 200 Sea training staff.
(Ongoing) Speak to entire Base Information Services Department on a monthly basis.
As Naval Officer, conduct group presentations ranging from safety, ship tours to technical briefs.

SIGNIFICANT RECOGNITION

Finalist for Lockheed Martin *Combat Systems Engineering & MacDonald-Dettwiler Head of Dept* Awards.
Received full scholarship to attend Royal Military College of Canada and *Alexander Rutherford.*
Awarded the *South West Asia Medal* (Afghanistan Bar) for Deploying on Operation APOLLO.

Marilyn A. Denholm

123 Augusta Avenue
Toronto, Ontario M1M 1M1
416 555 1212 • md@careerprocanada.ca

Executive Director – Healthcare

Dynamic and highly regarded Executive Director with 20+ years experience in not-for-profit healthcare. Innovative and divergent thinker with a track record for revitalizing organizations and implementing cutting-edge strategies to improve operations, visibility, fundraising, and long-term sustainability. Marketing and business savvy.

Exceptional speaker and relationship builder with the ability to create excitement around cause and represent the organization to all local and national media as a passionate and articulate spokesperson. Reputation for enlisting and leading executive and professional-level volunteers to donate expertise and create cutting-edge concepts.

Areas of Expertise

- Strategic Planning & Vision
- Campaign Management
- Donor Development & Stewardship
- Financial Oversight / Cost Control

- Board Governance
- Media Relations
- Advocacy
- Sustainability Strategies

- Innovative Fundraising Strategies
- Marketing Strategies
- Partnership Building
- Staff & Volunteer Management

Performance Milestones

Strategic Leadership

- Successfully turned around a national healthcare organization in the face of critical operational challenges – transformed the organization both strategically and administratively, revitalized core program and delivery details, and turned a struggling organization into a pioneering multi-service organization

- Developed both the strategic visions and business plans that turned fledgling organizations and development programs into dynamic, market-focused, and cost-effective enterprises

Fundraising & Development

- Doubled fundraising and sponsorship revenues for the AD Society of Augusta in less than 3 years

- Recently secured a $250,000 grant from the Ontario Trillium Foundation

- Doubled funding to $1.5 million for the Augusta Centre for Security

- Established two hospital foundations from scratch, conceived and introduced all fundraising initiatives, built governance and board structures, and quickly generated 6-figure fundraising revenues

Education and Advocacy

- Directed the creation of two education websites for the AD Society of Augusta that won Gold and Silver Awards against international healthcare education sites - www.ADKids.ca and www.ad.ca

- Key spokesperson for national, provincial, and community healthcare organizations – built strong media relationships and successfully represented the organization in live radio and television broadcasts

- Outspoken advocate on behalf of Canadians with AD on Health Canada's National AD Control Task Force and the Ontario Ministry of Health & Long-Term Care AD Advisory Committee

Executive Director. This non-profit executive has an extended track record, which demands 3 full pages. With such a full career, the "Performance Milestones" section is broken into the most critical functional categories for an Executive Director. This adds focus to her many accomplishments.

Professional Experience

AD SOCIETY OF AUGUSTA, Augusta, Ontario

Executive Director   1999 – Present
Brought in to revitalize a failing national organization and lead it through a complete strategic and operational restructuring. Challenged to rebuild the entire core operation, invigorate program offerings, rebuild reputation and exposure, increase funding, and bring energy back to the society, its staff, and volunteers.

Quickly developed a bold business plan to transform the organization into a more market-focused, business-minded enterprise that would enable the Society to grow in its ability to serve the Canadian AD community. Rebuilt the organization administratively, introduced new and innovative service delivery approaches, spearheaded new funding solutions and partnerships, and launched aggressive new marketing initiatives.

- Increased fundraising and sponsorship revenue from $600,000 to $1.2 million in less than 3 years.
- Introduced the Canadian AD Plan, an innovative delivery network designed to consolidate international and community resources and facilitate improvements in service and delivery.
- Secured a $250,000 grant from the Ontario Trillium Foundation to drive the development of program assessment tools and outcome measurement.
- Established collaborative relationships with other AD health bodies and professional associations across Canada, including the Canadian Network for AD Care and Health Canada.
- Drove the research, funding, planning, and development of the society's National AD Education Program Initiative, including the creation of two award-winning patient education websites – competing against the best health sites internationally for the World Wide Web Health Awards, www.ADKids.ca and www.ad.ca won the Gold and Silver Awards respectively for Patient Education.
- Established long-term, ethically-guided funding partnerships with leaders in the pharmaceutical industry.
- Assumed role as key spokesperson for the Society – generated increased media exposure locally and nationally, represented the society in all print media, and appeared regularly on live radio and television programs.

BIG SISTERS OF AUGUSTA, Augusta, Ontario

Director of Development   1994 – 1999
In the wake of the removal of all program funding, revitalized struggling development efforts and generated new fundraising and sponsorship initiatives.

- Planned and implemented innovative new fundraising strategies that increased private sector development revenues by 150%.
- Conceived and introduced the highly successful Big Sisters Race that netted over $100,000 in its first year and has grown every year as a part of the Augusta Children's Festival held every July.
- Targeted and secured key partnerships with fundraising volunteers in the investment sector.

AUGUSTA CENTRE FOR SECURITY, Pinehurst, Ontario

Director of Development   1990 – 1994
Directed the development efforts for a national "think tank" that raised funds, built awareness, and influenced government policymaking around issues of global and national security, including WMD non-proliferation, arctic and environmental security, security policy development in South Africa, and Military-Industrial Conversion in the former Soviet Union.

- Led a team of high-profile volunteers from the national and international business, diplomatic, and security communities.
- Doubled funds raised to $1.5 million, including over $500,000 through foundation funding – researched and approached foundations and worked with renowned researchers to develop successful RFP's.

LYNDSEY HOSPITAL, Rosemount, Ontario

Director of Development   1988 – 1989
Established the hospital's foundation from scratch and led all development initiatives to raise funds for clinical research into spinal cord injury and rehabilitation. Staffed the foundation's first Board of Directors and built its strategic and operational infrastructure, including all policies, databases, fundraising programs, and marketing strategies.

- In one year, brought fundraising revenue from $0 to over $300,000, and created the highly successful "Lyndsey Run" awareness campaign focusing on youth and spinal cord injuries.

BANFF GENERAL HOSPITAL, Banff, Alberta

Director of Development   1986 – 1988
Established the hospital's first foundation and fundraising program. Created all policies, established a donor database and patient donor program, hired staff and volunteers, spearheaded fundraising events and campaigns, and introduced initiatives for service club and local business involvement.

- Brought funds from $0 to $250,000+ in under 2 years, and successfully established relationships with the hospital trustees and doctors to encourage both corporate and individual giving.

AMOPHILA SOCIETY OF ONTARIO, Toronto, Ontario

Program Director   1982 – 1986
Managed a community office for the ASO and coordinated the development of education and support programs to patients and their families. Led a team of 6 hospitals in the successful application for funding from the Ontario Ministry of Health to support the emerging health epidemic within the community.

Previous roles include program development and management positions with the YWCA of Greater Augusta and Community Centre.

Professional & Volunteer Contributions

CANADIAN CENTRE FOR AD CARE
Director   1999 – 2003
Chair, Strategic Planning Sub-Committee on Needs Assessment   2002 – 2003
Member, Communications Committee   1999 – 2002

NATIONAL ASSOCIATION FOR HOSPITAL DEVELOPMENT (now AHP)
Received Certified Standing   1987
Chair, Communications   1986
Co-Chair, Sponsorship Committee, International Conference   1982

Education & Executive Development

APPLIED SCIENCE (HONOURS) – University of Augusta

Ongoing executive and non-profit development includes:

Business Management (Ongoing)	Scenario Planning for Managers and Executives
Marketing for Not-for-Profit Organizations	Professional Media Training
Priority Management	International fundraising and healthcare conferences

ROBERT FOSTER, MBA

55 Bay Crescent, Suite 555
Toronto, Ontario M1M 1M1
E-mail rfoster@careerprocanada.ca

Mobile (416) 555-2345
Residence (416) 555-1234
Facsimile (416) 555-3456

SENIOR BUSINESS EXECUTIVE

Dynamic Leadership ◆ Business Turnaround ◆ Revenue Generation ◆ Market Expansion

A seasoned general manager with extensive experience overseeing industry-leading organizations. An energetic visionary, restructuring operations and leading cultural change to deliver enterprise excellence. Demonstrated ability to turnaround underperforming operations and achieve unprecedented results. A dynamic leader and articulate communicator with a talent for developing highly motivated teams with the mutual goal of company growth and profitability. Top performer with a career-long record of negotiating complex customer relationships and closing multi-million dollar deals. Recipient of multiple sales, marketing, and organizational achievement awards.

Demonstrated achievements in:

▸ Strategic Vision & Planning	▸ Leadership & Team Building	▸ New Product Launches
▸ Profit & Loss Management	▸ Account Development	▸ Market Penetration
▸ Budgeting & Forecasting	▸ Relationship Management	▸ Feasibility Analysis
▸ Executive Presentations	▸ Strategic Partnerships	▸ Change Management

An exemplary career with the Leading Pharma Group of Companies
…with a track record of improving industry leadership position by consistently beating all targets.

	1996	1997	1998	1999	2000	2001	2002	2003
% vs Target	**108%**	**104%**	**112%**	**102%**	**108%**	**103%**	**101%**	**101%**

SELECTED ACCOMPLISHMENTS

▸ **Rebuilt Top Surgical Canada from the ground up** shifting from a clinical focus to a sales focus, which produced instantaneous results and achieved 24.0% gains in the first year to become the world leading franchise.

▸ **Launched into a new market within the medical devices and diagnostics sector**, and generated $49.2 million revenue, exceeding the income target by $1.2 million by focusing the sales force on highly profitable product platforms.

▸ **Rationalized the product line portfolio for a $52 million organization** by focusing on inventory capital, product marketability, and profitability; reduced the portfolio by 43 product lines and improved cash flow by $2.3 million.

▸ **Conceived and instituted a progressive operational plan**, re-engineered the product introduction process and implemented product life cycle management, ultimately reducing overall headcount, slashing returns by 83%, and increasing revenue by 30%.

▸ **Orchestrated a highly successful turnaround of the orthopaedics business in Canada** by revamping the sales and marketing organization, recruiting and hiring a talented sales team, and initiating an innovative marketing strategy.

▸ **Led the Strategic Planning Team and authored a revolutionary strategic plan** projecting the corporate vision and objectives through to 2010 for the complete medical devices and diagnostics sector in Canada.

▸ **Negotiated and signed a multi-million dollar suture contract** as part of corporate package with the largest teaching institution in Canada, producing one of the best wins that the organization has ever achieved.

Continued ▸

General Manager. The table on page one effectively highlights the candidate's consistent results and visually separates the profile from the body of the résumé. The résumé is rich in accomplishments – leading in with detailed stories, which are later supported by tight bulleted statements summarizing bottom-line achievements.

ROBERT FOSTER, MBA

CAREER HISTORY

Leading Pharma Group, Markham, Ontario   **1988-Present**

$42 billion world leader in health care products and services for the consumer, pharmaceutical, medical devices, and diagnostics markets.

General Manager, Leading Pharma Canada Group   2003-Present

Brought on board to turnaround, revitalize, and grow the troubled Canadian operation. Full P&L responsibility for sales, marketing, and operations. Member of the Management Board. Responsible to oversee 165 direct and indirect reports. Accountable to achieve a sales target of $52 million and manage a balance sheet including $3.5 million in capital acquisitions and $28 million in inventory.

Key business results:

▸ Revamped the marketing and sales organization and initiated a long-term strategy.

▸ Slashed the product line portfolio by 43 lines and improved cash flow by $2.3 million.

▸ Improved cycle time by 83% and increased revenue by 30%.

▸ Exceeded the business plan by 4.4%.

General Manager, Leading Pharma Inc.   2001-2003

Promoted to oversee the overall sales and marketing organization in Canada. Member of the Management Board. Accountable to oversee 45 reports. P&L responsibility of $48 million.

Key business results:

▸ Restructured the operation and instituted leadership changes.

▸ Achieved the $48 million business plan.

▸ Exceeded income targets by $1.2 million in the first year.

Director of Marketing and Sales, Top Surgical Canada   1999-2001

Aggressively promoted to revitalize the failing Canadian operation. Accountable to oversee 40 reports. P&L responsibility for sales and marketing with a target of $30 million.

Key business results:

▸ Developed and implemented the 2000 business plan.

▸ Exceeded previous year revenue by 24%.

▸ Over-achieved the business plan by 3.5%.

Director of Marketing, Top Surgical Canada   1998-1999

Brought on board to oversee the Canadian marketing organization. Accountable to supervise 5 reports and manage a $3 million marketing budget.

Key business result:

▸ Negotiated and signed largest suture contract in Canada.

Previous positions held

Business Director, Leading Pharma Inc.	1997-1998
Regional Director, Leading Pharma Inc.	1996-1997
Regional Sales Manager, Top Surgical Canada	1995-1996
Product/Procedure Manager, Top Surgical Canada	1992-1994
Sales Representative, Lab Services Inc.	1988-1991

Continued ▸

ROBERT FOSTER, MBA

FORMAL EDUCATION

University of Toronto   **1996**
Masters of Business Administration (MBA)

McMaster University   **1986**
Bachelor of Arts (BA) Economics, Minor Computer Science

Simon Fraser University   **1984**
Faculty of Business

PROFESSIONAL DEVELOPMENT

Actively committed to continuing education via various accredited courses and programs:
- Executive Development Program (e-Commerce)
- Advanced Manager Leadership Training
- Sales Management/Competency Development
- Emotional Intelligence Training
- Transitions Leadership Program for Executives
- Leadership in Action for High Potentials

TECHNICAL SKILLS

Proficient in a variety of software applications including:
- Microsoft Office Suite (Word, Excel, and PowerPoint)
- Corel Suite (WordPerfect, Lotus, and Harvard Graphics)

AFFILIATIONS & ACTIVITIES

- Toastmasters International, VP Education, Club and Area Champion, Youth Leadership
- TSN "Off the Record," 4 television appearances
- University of Western Ontario, Course Instructor
- United Way, Committee Member
- Rotary Clubs, Public Speaking

PERSONAL ACHIEVEMENTS

- Competed in New Zealand's 6 day Extreme Adventure Race (2001, 2003).
- Completed 2 Ironman Triathlons (1999, 2000).
- Captain of the McMaster University Varsity Football Team.
- Attended Simon Fraser University on a football scholarship.

Peter Yates, BA, CPGA

111 Gilbera Grove, Toronto, Ontario M1M 1M1
Phone: 416.555.1234 Email: pyates@CareerProCanada.ca

GENERAL MANAGER • HEAD PROFESSIONAL

"Peter is a pro's pro and a manager's manager; he handles the public with the patience of a saint while achieving the best result for the club and the member."

Highly respected, conscientious and reliable golfing professional with a strong business acumen dedicated to promoting golf. Energetic and passionate about steering the business to growth and optimizing new opportunities. Hands-on leader, motivator and coach, acknowledged by peers and clients for the outstanding ability to simplify golfing instruction to persons of all abilities. Sets and maintains high standards, strives for operational excellence, creates the strategic direction, builds the business into a reputable and profitable entity in a competitive environment. Core expertise includes:

- Golf Instruction
- Board of Director Liaison
- Pro-Shop Operations

- Financial Management
- Retail Golf Management
- Resource Management

- General Management
- Training & Development
- Facility Maintenance

Professional Experience

Modiva Golf Centre Inc., Toronto, ON   1989 - present
GENERAL MANAGER/HEAD PROFESSIONAL

- Recognized for extraordinary business development; the ability to drive revenue and deliver a quality environment in which to work and succeed.
- Appraised recently by the absentee owner - *"Peter undertook full operational and financial charge of our 18-hole golf course, driving range and pro-shop without direction or oversight from me, and carried our enterprise to a level of profitability that has outpaced the competition in the GTA. His management skills are deft and thoughtful. His instructional skill indisputable. His direct supervision of all staff reveal human resource strengths beyond the scope of our business."*
- Provide an exemplary level of customer service for the 50,000 annual visitors; generate interaction between persons of all backgrounds, cultures and levels.
- Hold full financial accountability for the 18-hole golf course, driving range, pro-shop and concessions, consistently outperform owner's expectations; accredited for operating at optimal performance with minimal expenditures.
- Designed and implemented the 'Learn to Golf' and 'Improve your Golf' programs. Strengthened the golf training plans, refined to a 7 to 1 ratio, resulting in unprecedented favourable responses from the clientele necessitating the development of an advanced program with a 4 to 1 ratio. Built a tremendous reputation based on referrals and limited advertising, attracting diverse child and adult patrons from a 50 kilometre radius.
- Elevated the revenue generated from golf training programs over a 2 year period by 210%, achieved after redesigning the lesson structure and recruiting additional Golf Professionals.
- Acknowledged for top performance teaching and motivational coaching leadership, with the ability to simplify golfing interactively through effective communication, delivering a succinct message to persons of all ages, cultures and skills.
- Accredited for motivating and helping 4 assistant professionals receive their Class A status from the CPGA.
- Conceived and negotiated a highly profitable partnership with the Town of Markham Parks & Recreation Department to administer and teach their golf camp, now recognized as their most popular camp and consistently overbooked.
- Designed and utilized various teaching aids to advance a student's expertise.
- Recruit, train and direct 2 Associate Professionals, 7 full and part-time employees in the pro-shop, 10 part-time golf range employees and the Golf Course Superintendent and his employees.
- Devise and monitor annual budget, control all financial transactions, approve purchases and renovations according to owner's requirements.

Golf Club General Manager. This professional utilizes an upscale design in both the border and the section headers. The wording in the headline quote positions him with a unique management style that clearly fits the golfing industry.

Peter Yates, BA, CPGA   **Page II**

Modiva Golf Centre Inc., continued
- Administer the daily, monthly and annual accounting and financial report preparation including overseeing the point of sale, payroll, receivables, payables, banking, credit card administration and government remittances (GST, gas tax refund, WSIB, retail sales tax and corporation tax) utilizing accounting software.
- Interact with golfing suppliers to purchase equipment for the pro-shop, ensuring an adequate inventory is maintained according to buying patterns.
- Work with the golf course superintendent to continually upgrade the facility, maintain a strong knowledge in turf management.
- Endorsed by the Markham Economist & Sun with the Readers' Choice Award for the "Best Driving Range" in 2000, 2001 & 2003.
- Actively involved in establishing a local community spirit, encourage participation from residents to be involved through a variety of initiatives and incentives in the game of golf.
- Tied for first place in the 2000 Ontario PGA Senior/Junior Pro Golf Tournament as the junior partner.

Riverdale Golf & Country Club, Brampton, Ontario   1987 – 1989
GOLF PROFESSIONAL
- Convinced the Board of Directors to establish a winter golf school located within the banquet facility to stimulate interest in golf and allow the course to generate revenue year round. Winter school proved to be highly successful and is still running.
- Displayed a sound knowledge of effective teaching, leadership and a passion for golf with the promotion to Head Professional after the existing Head Professional became Director of Golf. Acknowledged for elevating the standard of teaching at the club to a new level.
- Oversaw weekly payroll for 12 persons, accounts payable, cash flow projections and recruitment of golf professionals.
- Accountable for the maintenance and fuelling for a fleet of 36 golf carts.
- Facilitated golfing lessons to the members on the practice range and on the 18-hole golf course.
- Managed members' tournaments in partnership with the Men's and Ladies' Captains and assisted with the organization of outside tournaments hosted by the club.

Empire Golf Centre, Thornhill, Ontario   1985 – 1987
HEAD TEACHING PROFESSIONAL
- Held full accountability for all operations at the indoor golf facility including maintenance, golf tuition and professional club fitting.
- Assisted the store manager with the operations for a busy golf retail store and membership applications.
- Led a successful Blind Golfers' Clinic for the Canadian National Institute for the Blind, an exceptional learning experience.

Riverdale Golf & Country Club, Brampton, Ontario   1983 – 1985
ASSISTANT GOLF PROFESSIONAL

Education

Canadian Professional Golf Association, Acton, Ontario   1987
CLASS 'A' PROFESSIONAL

University of Toronto, Toronto, Ontario   1982
BACHELOR OF ARTS – Urban Planning

Strong proponent of continuously updating skills, frequently attend seminars hosted by the Ontario PGA.

Affiliations

Canadian Professional Golf Association   1983 – present

ROBERT KORTENAAR
CSP, CHME

11 Augusta Drive
Pinehurst, Ontario L1L 1L1

905.555.4455
robertk@careerprocanada.ca

SENIOR SALES & MARKETING EXECUTIVE
SPECIALIST IN DRIVING HOTEL & HOSPITALITY PROFITABILITY

Business Development / Strategic Planning / Key Account Sales & Management
New Market Development / Marketing Campaigns & Initiatives / Business Planning & Forecasting

---

Dynamic sales and marketing career driving consistent revenue gains in the hotel and hospitality industry throughout Canadian and U.S. markets. Comprehensive understanding of hotel operations, sales, and profitability. Achieved strong revenue, market, and profit growth through expertise in business development, executive-level sales, and creative marketing initiatives. Proficient in ACT!, Excel, and MS Word. Extensive expertise supported by professional certification in the following:

- National & Executive Sales Management
- Hotel Management
- Food & Beverage Controls
- Hospitality Marketing
- Travel & Tourism
- Dining Room & Catering Management

★ **CERTIFIED SALES PROFESSIONAL (CSP)** ★
★ **CERTIFIED HOSPITALITY MARKETING EXECUTIVE (CHME)** ★

PROFESSIONAL EXPERIENCE

CHOICE HOTELS INTERNATIONAL, Silver Spring, Maryland (Head Office)
(Largest franchise hotel organization worldwide with over 5000 locations internationally and sales in excess of US$1 billion.)

NATIONAL SALES DIRECTOR – WORLDWIDE SALES   2001 – Present
Selected to develop and manage key association and consortia accounts throughout Canada and the Midwest/Western U.S. Primary accountability for $60 million CAA/AAA account, the largest single revenue-producing leisure account in the company. Consortia accounts concurrently managed include American Express, Rosenbluth, World Travel, and Carlson Wagonlit.

Scope of responsibility includes all Canadian and U.S. regional sales and marketing initiatives, strategic sales and market planning, and the coordination of a team of Field Service Directors throughout Canada and the U.S.

- Exceeded annual revenue projection by $1 million within first 6 months.
- Developed highly successful joint marketing initiative between AAA Nebraska, AAA Colorado, and Alberta Motor Association (AMA) that increased gross roomnights by 81%, increased gross revenue by 77%, and secured largest market share (14.83%) of any hotel company with AMA.
- AAA/AMA joint marketing initiative nominated for 3 distinguished MARQ Awards – AAA Nebraska initiative recently awarded top prize in competitive SYC&S category.
- Created dynamic spring promotion for CAA/AMA that increased revenue from a 9.83% decline to a positive growth of 21.5%.
- Introduced and launched two successful national marketing events designed to recognize high performing CAA partners.
- Developed and produced all collateral marketing and training materials for Choice Hotels Canada.

CHOICE HOTELS CANADA, Mississauga, Ontario (Head Office)
(Largest hotel franchise organization in Canada, operating 250 locations nationally under 8 leading brands.)

NATIONAL SALES MANAGER – TRAVEL INDUSTRY & CORPORATE   1999 – 2001
Hired to spearhead introduction and development of new corporate and consortia account portfolio, while revitalizing growth of leisure accounts nationally. Coordinated all strategic sales and marketing initiatives, market analysis, incentive management, budget planning, and management of largest volume corporate account portfolio.

Hospitality Sales and Marketing Executive. This executive's profile draws attention to his industry and executive certifications. He breaks his experience into two sections to highlight his related experience and downplay inappropriate positions.

CHOICE HOTELS CANADA, continued

 ➢ Developed sales and marketing initiatives, promotions, and market education that assisted the licensee in increasing Revpar and developing yield management techniques.
 ➢ Personally secured 30 key corporate accounts from ground zero within 2 years.
 ➢ Grew major Quixstar/Amway corporate account by 2000% within 1 year.
 ➢ Generated exponential growth and dramatically improved product awareness within leisure market through aggressive sales and marketing strategies.

VACATIONS INTERNATIONALE, St. Catharines, Ontario
(Boutique holiday and travel business servicing high-end personal and corporate clientele throughout the Greater Niagara Region.)

PRINCIPAL / SALES & MARKETING DIRECTOR   1993 – 1999

Successfully built business from start-up into solid revenue generator within 2 years. Developed strategic direction, built infrastructure, and initiated marketing, image development, sales, and public relations directives.

 ➢ Identified and capitalized upon market trends through highly successful direct mail, presentations, and local promotional campaigns.
 ➢ Dramatically increased revenues by successfully targeting and penetrating lucrative corporate market.
 ➢ Grew sales from $0 to $1.5 million in less than 18 months, and quickly established position as industry leader throughout Niagara.

ADDITIONAL EXPERIENCE

HOUSEHOLD FINANCIAL CORPORATION, St. Catharines, Ontario
(US$Billion Fortune 200 financial services company with offices throughout Canada and the U.S.)

FINANCIAL ACCOUNT EXECUTIVE   1996 – 1997

Sold a diverse range of lending and credit instruments and services throughout Ontario market. Developed and managed a diversified account base of over 200 personal accounts valued at over $1 million.

 ➢ Awarded "Top Sales" Ontario wide, and ranked 11th across Canada.

WORLDWAYS CANADA LTD., Mississauga, Ontario - **IN-FLIGHT SERVICE MANAGER**   1985 – 1991
HERITAGE COLLEGE, St. Catharines, Ontario - **AIRLINE TRAINING INSTRUCTOR**   1988 – 1995

INDUSTRY CERTIFICATION & EDUCATION

Certified Hospitality Marketing Executive (CHME) – Hospitality Sales & Marketing Association	2002
Executive Program in Sales Management – Schulich School of Business, York University	2001
Skills for Sales Success – Canadian Professional Sales Association	2001
Certified Sales Professional (CSP) – Canadian Professional Sales Association	1999
National Professional Sales Manager Certification – Ontario Tourism Education Corporation (OTEC)	1998
Travel & Tourism – St. Catharines Business School	1983
Hotel Management: Food & Beverage Controls / Dining Room & Catering Management – Niagara College	1982

INDUSTRY AFFILIATIONS

Hospitality Sales & Marketing Association International (HSMAI)	2002
Canadian Hotel Marketing & Sales Executives (CHMSE) – Ontario Chapter	1998 – Present
Canadian Professional Sales Association (CPSA)	1998 – Present
Ontario Tourism Education Corp. (OTEC) – Hospitality Sales Manager Industry Evaluator	1998 – Present

RICHARD D. HUNTER, BSc, CHRP

12 Rathburn St., Edmonton, Alberta, T2T 2T2
Phone: (780) 555-1212, Cell (780) 555-1213
e-mail: hunter@careerprocanada.ca

HUMAN RESOURCES LEADER

Creating work environments where employees and organizations excel

Demonstrated Competencies:

Strategic Leadership

Organizational Development

Policies & Programs

Organizational Effectiveness

Downsizing & Restructuring

Recruitment & Selection

Succession Planning

Training & Development

Performance Management

Compensation & Benefits

Employee Relations

Labour Relations

Workers' Compensation

Health & Safety

Legislative Compliance

★ ★ ★ ★ ★

Recipient of Multiple Awards

Industry Leadership Award
Institute of HR Performance
2005

Gold Award
Canadian Council of HR Professionals
2005

Award of Excellence
Career Professionals Association
2004

Silver Award
Canadian Council of HR Professionals
2004

Silver Award
Canadian Council of HR Professionals
2003

An experienced professional with an extensive HR generalist background. Proven success in partnering with business leaders to optimize organizational effectiveness in union and non-union environments. Proficient in designing, implementing, and managing effective policies, programs, and processes. Well-developed decision-making skills combined with an open and accessible management style, emphasizing individual empowerment and team development. Excellent knowledge of employment legislation and practices in Canada and the U.S., bringing a strategic perspective to HR issues.

CAREER HISTORY

COMMIT INC., Edmonton, Alberta   **2001 - Present**

Leading global provider of outsourced environmental compliance solutions, with $70 million revenue and offices located across Canada and the U.S.

Director, Human Resources

Reporting directly to the CEO and President, overall responsibility for overseeing HR and payroll, supporting 4 business units with 300 employees across Canada and the U.S. Accountable to set and administer a $6 million HR and staffing budget.

- Restructured the organization's HR department to provide leadership and outstanding customer service to all business units, which directly resulted in a promotion to the Director role.

- Designed and rolled-out a comprehensive Employee Handbook, outlining corporate policies, procedures, and guidelines for both Canadian and U.S. operations.

- Initiated and instituted a wide variety of innovative programs covering employee relations, performance management, and succession planning to drive organizational performance.

- Established and proactively managed the international corporate compensation program and revamped the benefits plan, resulting in a 22% cost savings on annual premiums.

- Rolled-out a proactive health and safety program and culture change across the organization, resulting in a 20% reduction in reportable injuries and 36% cost savings in Workers' Compensation payments.

- Developed management strategies and led the Collective Bargaining, as chief spokesperson, achieving 2 Union Agreements in North America within a four-month period.

- Provided strategic guidance to the leadership team, including consultative advice regarding the interpretation of 3 Collective Agreements, which directly reduced the number of arbitration cases.

Human Resource Leader. A unique, upscale design incorporates the candidate's name and credentials. Accomplishments are bulleted separately from responsibilities to ensure that they stand out.

RICHARD D. HUNTER, BSc, CHRP

(780) 555-1212

Creating work environments where employees and organizations excel

CAREER HISTORY (CONTINUED)

ACADEMY HEALTH, Edmonton, Alberta   1999 - 2001

With over 5,000 employees in two locations, AH provides a long-standing tradition of healthcare, research, and education in the province.

Senior Corporate Human Resources Advisor (2000 – 2001)
Human Resources Manager (1999 – 2000)

Retained to lead the full scope of HR, supporting a client group of 1000 employees. Manage labour relations, recruitment, compensation, training and development, employee relations, and performance management. Represent the hospital in grievance and arbitration hearings. Lead special projects as required.

- Interpreted policies and procedures, relevant legislation, multiple collective agreements, and advised the management team, ensuring consistency across the organization and reducing grievances by 25%.

- Led the recruitment and selection cycle, guided managers through the process, and slashed the turnaround time in hiring effective candidates by 80%.

- Represented the hospital at step 3 grievance hearings; formulated and forwarded the employer's response to grievance hearings.

- Coached and mentored managers on the performance management cycle, resulting in continued employee growth and development.

FORMAL EDUCATION

Ryerson University   1999
- Certificate in Human Resources Management (CHRM)

Ryerson University   1995
- Diploma, Occupational Health and Safety

University of Toronto   1990
- Bachelors of Science Degree, Chemistry

PROFESSIONAL DEVELOPMENT

ABC Management Systems   2003
- Management Excellence Program

York University   1996
- Workers' Compensation Certificate

The Canadian Institute   1996
- Disability Claims Management Certificate

Professional Affiliations

Society for Human Resources Management (SHRM)
Certified Member in the U.S.

Human Resources Institute of Alberta (HRIA)
Certified Human Resources Professional (CHRP)

★ ★ ★ ★ ★

Computer Proficiency

Microsoft Office Suite
(Word, Excel, and PowerPoint)

Various HRIS Technology

★ ★ ★ ★ ★

"Richard Hunter has excelled in the field of Human Resources and provided exemplary leadership to our organization."
R. Mee, CEO, Commit Inc.

"Richard has provided a commendable service to the HR industry in Canada through his volunteer support."
L. Donald, Executive Director, HRIA

RONA REAM, BA, CHRP
12-34 Avenue E., Toronto, ON • M1M 1M1 • 416.555.1234 • ream@careerprocanada.ca

---

DYNAMIC, AWARD-WINNING HUMAN RESOURCE EXECUTIVE
With Excellent Leadership and Management Skills

INTERPERSONAL AND TEAMWORK SKILLS

- Collaborative, team oriented approach led to success with a range of positions & personalities
- Passion for work in various environments, i.e., complex, fast-paced, entrepreneurial
- Knowledge and continuous learning increased ability for working with diverse cultures

CHANGE MANAGEMENT SKILLS

- Developed vision and strategy to achieve diverse workforce in a global environment
- Collaborated on diverse global committees to develop and implement strategy
- Led management project teams to develop and implement employment equity

LEADERSHIP SKILLS

- Supervised diverse staff and promoted accommodation of individual needs
- Led employees in execution of progressive programs and policies
- Acted as role model to exemplify organizational values and resolve conflicts

CAREER ADVANCEMENT

HUMAN RESOURCES MANAGEMENT AND DIVERSITY SPECIALIST   2001-Present
HR-EXTRA COMPANY LIMITED

Retained to enhance the human resources services for clients and, as an advisor with an entrepreneurial spirit, to provide a range of human resources consulting services.

- Employment Equity and diversity consultations ensured successful self-identification audit
- Provision of HR counsel led to effective resolution of performance issues
- Development of compensation design and plan with salary ranges/grades also used for Latin America
- Job analysis and direction of evaluation committee launched new salary review program
- Strategic design and development of policy manual is used as an example for best practices
- Customization/facilitation of training for cultural change/staff development improved employee relations
- Coach for resume and interview process enhanced program results

PROFESSOR, FACULTY OF BUSINESS   2000 Winter
GENERAL COLLEGE

Contract as part time professor to design curriculum for two core courses within the faculty of business.

- Delivered presentations to students pending graduation
- Developed, researched and posted material for inclusion on website
- Managed Human Resources: HR law, policies, practices and global environment
- Performed Career Search and Planning: research, resume and interview techniques

Continued   ⇨

Human Resources Executive. A powerful headline captures the reader immediately. The profile structure combines skill categories into three key leadership areas to emphasize this professional's management style.

RONA REAM

MANAGER, WORKPLACE DIVERSITY 5 yrs; MANAGER HR 4 yrs; HR SPECIALIST 2 yrs.
123 COMPANY LIMITED   1990 - 2001

Initially joined the organization to provide employment services for eight divisions across Canada and an employee population of approximately 2,400. The complex organization structure included manufacturing, provision of wireless services and engineering software/hardware design and development. Promoted to management level positions from employment specialist and developed the company's reputation as a leader in the areas of best practices and diversity.

- Performed superb analysis of corporate policy and OD strategies led to major company recognition
- Led organizational change and human resources quality audits that passed requirements
- Championed online performance monitoring and major career development initiative
- Viewed as subject matter expert for diversity & human rights - featured cost preventative measures
- Developed & facilitated core training programs with above average evaluations
- Negotiated & implemented community funding with placement on Wall of Honour
- Integrated organizational principles within training programs that supported change agendas
- Achieved Outstanding Employer of Year Award for positive employment programs
- Conducted interviews for a range of positions up to executive level and surpassed quality of hiring
- Negotiated cost savings of $50K in temporary staffing
- Executed Six Sigma process for employment area with reduced cycle times and costs
- Presented & moderated teleconferences that resulted in enhanced public image for employer
- Demonstrated leadership in supervising diverse staff. Committee chair: health & safety representative

EDUCATION & TRAINING SPECIALITIES

Bachelor of Arts (Social Sciences) York University 1999
Certified Human Resources Professional, Human Resources Professional Association, 1990
Human Resources Management, Dean's Honour List 1987, General College
Certificate in Race, Culture and Empowerment, General College
Advisor Course, Workplace Discrimination & Harassment Prevention Unit, 123 Company Limited:

- Training Techniques for Field Managers
- New Employee Orientation
- Uncompromising Integrity
- Preventing Sexual Harassment
- The Art of Successful Negotiations
- Global Institute for Manager

TECHNICAL PROFICIENCY
HARDWARE: PC • Laptop • LCD • MAC
SOFTWARE: MS Office 2003 • Windows XP • EECRS • Email • Internet Research

VOLUNTEER SERVICES
Volunteer, St. John's Social Therapy Dogs
Volunteer, Canadian Cancer Society

COMMITTEE, PUBLICATIONS & SPEAKING ENGAGEMENTS
Available upon request

"Rona nurtures the achievements of her friends, associates and also the community she serves."
I. Beam, ABC Incorporated

Sam H. Ellis

1 Rue Deroches, Pointe Claire, Quebec H1H 1H1
Phone (514) 555-1212 ▣ Mobile (514) 555-1212 ▣ E-mail shellis@careerprocanada.ca

Top Performing IT & Software Development Manager

Team Leadership | Software Design | Application Development | Problem Solving | Customer Satisfaction

Versatile professional with outstanding experience in IT management and a proven record of accomplishment in hands-on application design and development. Expertise spanning the entire software development lifecycle (SDLC) in mission critical environments. Articulate communicator with the ability to convey technical feedback in user-friendly terms. Talented problem solver, resolving complex issues by uncovering the root cause and applying lasting solutions. A collaborative leader, with a passion for technical excellence, developing and empowering autonomous teams. Ready and willing to travel.

Demonstrated achievements in:

▣ Leadership & Team Building	▣ Project Management	▣ Disaster Recovery & Security
▣ Budget Administration	▣ Business Systems Analysis	▣ Technical Troubleshooting
▣ Policies & Practices	▣ End-User Requirements	▣ Network Administration
▣ Technical Documentation	▣ Object Oriented Programming	▣ Telephony Management

Technical Skills

Operating Systems	MS-Dos, Windows 95, 98, 2000, XP, and NT
Programming Languages	C#.Net, Delphi, VB, VBA, XML, SQL, and C++
Web Development	HTML, ASP, ASP.Net, FrontPage, and MS SourceSafe
Databases	SQL Server and MS Access
Internet	MS Outlook, Internet Explorer, and Netscape
Office Applications	Microsoft Office Suite (Word, Excel, PowerPoint, and Project), and Visio
Telephony	PBX and Nortel Switches

Career History

Essential Technology, Montréal, Quebec   **1999 – Present**

Service organization with 100 employees in 2 call centres, processing up to 150,000 insurance claims per year.

Executive IT Manager (2004 – Present)

IT Manager (2000 – 2004)

Intermediate Software Developer (1999 – 2000)

Promoted to oversee the full scope of IT, software development, networking, and telephony, reporting directly to the President. Train, mentor, and supervise a team of 4 technical employees. Create and manage a $90,000 capital expenditure budget. Develop a technology strategy and implementation plan. Recommend solutions to new business initiatives and technological advancements. Manage vendor contracts and relationships. Ensure 99.9% system availability.

▣ Spearheaded a $2 million re-build of a mission critical software as 'Chief Architect' and effectively implemented Microsoft best practices, design patterns, and object-oriented design in the one-year project.

▣ Conceived and created a network improvement strategy and oversaw a $150,000 upgrade, enabling the organization to expand with a more robust, scalable, and faster solution.

▣ Redesigned and implemented a formal backup and restore procedure, slashing administration costs by 75% while simultaneously improving access to data.

▣ Researched, implemented, and administered corporate-wide antivirus protection, successfully maintaining a 4-year 'virus-free' record.

▣ Facilitated a corporate programming language change from Delphi to C#.Net and trained all technical staff, improving department productivity considerably.

Information Technology Executive. With a recent promotion to the executive level, this IT professional outlines his *Value Proposition* in this power statement, which includes both leadership and hands-on technical skills.

CAREER HISTORY

Essential Technology (continued)

- Designed and implemented various business systems including an asset tracking system, employee time sheet tracking system, and backup scheduling software.

- Established a wide variety of departmental standards, policies, and best practices, which increased the productivity of software developers and maintained consistency in programming.

- Conceived and designed the corporate intranet site, providing easier access to shared information and improved productivity.

XYZ Telemanagement (now ABC Services), Milton, Ontario   **1998 – 1999**

Medium-sized telemanagement software company with 100 employees in two locations across Canada.

Software Developer (1997 – 1999)
QA Tester (1997)

Promoted to develop various applications related to corporate software products reporting to the IT Manager. Develop and maintain structured test plans and installation procedures. Organize quality assurance efforts of third-party developers, document issues, suggest improvements, and fix discrepancies.

- Worked cooperatively with outsourced developers, effectively ensuring adherence to corporate guidelines and project scope.

- Resolved discrepancies in Delphi and C++ applications and performed peer code reviews, resulting in higher quality output.

- Proactively assisted programmers with technology development issues, enabling the department to meet and exceed corporate expectations.

FORMAL EDUCATION

Humber College, Etobicoke, Ontario, 1998
Computer Programming Diploma, Graduated with Honours

PROFESSIONAL DEVELOPMENT

Learning Tree International, Toronto, Ontario, 2000
Management Skills for the I.T. Professional
Disaster Recovery Planning for the Enterprise

Team Leadership | Software Design | Application Development | Problem Solving | Customer Satisfaction

SAM H. ELLIS

1 Rue Deroches, Pointe Claire, Québec H1H 1H1
Téléphone : (514) 555-1212 ▦ Cellulaire : (514) 555-1212 ▦ Courriel : shellis@careerprocanada.ca

DIRIGEANT EN DEVELOPPEMENT DE LOGICIEL ET DE TI, PERFORMANCE EXCEPTIONNELLE

Direction d'équipes | Conception de logiciels | Élaboration d'applications | Résolution de problèmes | Satisfaction de la clientèle

Professionnel doué d'aptitudes diverses avec une expérience hors du commun en gestion des TI. Sa réputation est reconnue pour l'élaboration et la conception réussies d'applications pratiques. Son expertise couvre le cycle entier de développement de logiciels (SDLC) dans les environnements essentiels à la mission. Bon communicateur ayant la capacité de transmettre des informations techniques en termes faciles à comprendre. Doué pour résoudre les problèmes, il apporte des solutions durables aux problèmes complexes en découvrant la cause fondamentale. Dirigeant collaboratif ayant la passion de l'excellence technique, il sait composer et rendre les équipes autonomes. Disponibilité pour les déplacements.

Accomplissements confirmés dans les domaines suivants :

- Direction et création d'équipes
- Gestion du budget
- Pratiques et directives
- Documentation technique
- Gestion de projet
- Analyse de systèmes de gestion
- Programmation orientée objet
- Sécurité et reprise après sinistre
- Diagnostic de pannes techniques
- Administration du réseau
- Gestion de téléphonie

COMPETENCES TECHNIQUES

Systèmes d'exploitation	MS-Dos, Windows 95, 98, 2000, XP et NT
Langages de programmation	C#.Net, Delphi, VB, VBA, XML, SQL et C++
Création de pages Web	HTML, ASP, ASP.Net, FrontPage et MS SourceSafe
Banques de données	SQL Server et MS Access
Internet	MS Outlook, Internet Explorer et Netscape
Applications de bureau	Microsoft Office Suite (Word, Excel, PowerPoint et Project) et Visio
Téléphonie	Commutateurs Nortel et PBX

TRACE DE CARRIERE

Essential Technology, Montréal, Québec   **1999–Aujourd'hui**

Prestataire de services avec 100 employés dans 2 centres d'appels, traitant jusqu'à 150 000 demandes d'indemnité d'assurance par an.

Cadre dirigeant des TI (2004–Aujourd'hui)

Dirigeant TI (2000–2004)

Développeur de logiciel intermédiaire (1999–2000)

Promotion pour superviser les opérations complètes des TI, développement de logiciels, réseautique et téléphonie, relevant directement du Président. Formation, conseil et supervision d'une équipe de 4 employés techniques. Création et gestion d'un budget des dépenses en capital de 90 000 $. Élaboration du plan de mise en oeuvre et de stratégies technologiques. Recommandation de solutions pour les initiatives commerciales et les innovations technologiques. Gestion des relations et des contrats fournisseurs. Responsabilité de la disponibilité du système à 99,9 %.

- Direction d'un projet de reconstruction de logiciel indispensable de 2 millions de dollars en tant qu'Architecte en chef et mise en oeuvre réussie des conceptions orientées d'objets, des formes de conception et des meilleures pratiques de Microsoft dans ce projet d'un an.

- Conception et création de stratégies d'amélioration du réseau et supervision d'une mise à niveau de 150 000 $, permettant à l'entreprise de se développer avec une solution plus rapide, solide et évolutive.

Directeur en technologies de l'information. Avec une récente promotion au niveau de directeur, ce professionnel des TI met l'accent sur sa *proposition de valeur* dans sa déclaration de facultés, qui inclut à la fois ses compétences techniques pratiques et ses qualités de leader.

SAM H. ELLIS

TRACE DE CARRIERE (SUITE)

Essential Technology (suite)

- Restructuration et mise en oeuvre d'une procédure officielle de sauvegarde et de restauration des données, réduisant ainsi les frais d'administration de 75 % tout en améliorant l'accès aux données.

- Recherche, mise en oeuvre et administration de la protection antivirus de l'entreprise entière, tout en maintenant le record « sans virus » pendant 4 ans.

- Facilitation d'un changement de langage de programmation de l'entreprise, de Delphi à C#.net et formation de tout le personnel technique, améliorant considérablement la productivité du département.

- Conception et mise en oeuvre de plusieurs systèmes opérationnels y compris un système de suivi d'inventaire, de suivi d'emploi du temps des employés et un logiciel d'ordonnancement de sauvegarde.

- Mise en place d'un grand nombre de meilleures pratiques, de normes et de standards dans le département, améliorant la productivité des développeurs de logiciels tout en maintenant l'uniformité de programmation.

- Création et conception du site intranet de l'entreprise, donnant accès au partage de l'information et augmentant ainsi la productivité.

XYZ Télégestion (à présent Services ABC), Milton, Ontario   **1998–1999**

Entreprise de taille moyenne de logiciels en télégestion avec 100 employés dans deux bureaux au Canada.

Développeur de logiciel (1997–1999)
Vérificateur AQ (1997)

Promotion pour développer plusieurs applications liées aux produits de logiciels de l'entreprise, relevant du directeur TI. Création et maintenance de plans de vérification structurés et de procédures d'installation. Organisation des efforts d'assurance qualité des développeurs de tierce partie, documentation des problèmes, suggestions d'amélioration et réparation d'anomalies.

- Travail en coopération avec les développeurs impartis, s'assurant de manière efficace du suivi des directives de l'entreprise et de la portée du projet.

- Réparation des anomalies des applications en Delphi et C++ et conduite de l'examen du code par des pairs, ayant pour résultat une meilleure qualité finale.

- Assistance proactive des programmateurs avec les problèmes de développement de la technologie, permettant au département d'atteindre et de dépasser les attentes de l'entreprise.

ÉDUCATION

Humber College, Etobicoke, Ontario, 1998

Diplôme en programmation informatique, obtenu avec distinction

DEVELOPPEMENTS PROFESSIONNELS

Learning Tree International, Toronto, Ontario, 2000

Compétences en gestion pour le professionnel en TI

Planification de reprise après sinistre pour l'entreprise

Direction d'équipe | Conception de logiciel | Élaboration d'applications | Résolution de problèmes | Satisfaction de la clientèle

GEORGE CAMPBELL

#123 North Road
Oakville, ON L1L 1L1
Phone: 905-555-4567
Email: gcampbell@careerprocanada.ca

⊕ **INTERNATIONAL BUSINESS DEVELOPMENT**   ⊕ **SALES & MARKETING**   ⊕ **LEADERSHIP**

A diverse business professional who *"opens doors"* internationally to create results utilizing the following business development formula:

Client Needs + (Value-driven partnerships + Creativity + Enthusiasm + Business Savvy) = Client Solutions

NOTEWORTHY CAREER ACHIEVEMENTS

INTERNATIONAL BUSINESS DEVELOPMENT
•International & Diplomatic Protocol • Global Supply Chain Management •Start-up Venture •Strategic Planning & Alliances

- Designated by Malaysian consulate to spearhead the formation of the Malaysian Canadian Business Council, which facilitated international trade between Canada and Malaysia.

- Participated, as "think tank" representative for IMS Canada (Intelligent Manufacturing Systems), with leading global companies and researchers to develop next generation of manufacturing processes.

- Sourced, manufactured, and supplied a line of self-branded products, which met CGSB or ISO Standards, to various sectors of the Canadian healthcare industry.

- Responded to National Defence of Canada's urgent request for 150,000 special wound care units for troops in Afghanistan. Exceeded delivery and quality requirements.

SALES & MARKETING
•Sales Presentations • Product Research & Development   • Competitive Product Positioning • New Product Introduction

- Orchestrated and established the sales & marketing for self-branded healthcare products for various Canadian markets including federal/provincial/municipal governments, distributors/dealers, and hospitals.

- Developed and delivered several product and training presentations to private and public sector groups where audiences exceeded 500.

- Reduced sales force by 50% and increased sales by 20% within first seven months as National Sales Director.

- Acquired funding of $120,000 from National Research Council of Canada for continued research and development of a unique patented process.

- Marketed new technology for combustion engines to Harley Davidson, Kohler Engines, Ford Motor Company, and the United States Armed Forces.

International Business Development Leader. This candidate exudes creativity from top to bottom. The picture in the profile adds interest without losing a sense of professionalism. The business development formula in the profile offers a visual of the client's personality.

GEORGE CAMPBELL

LEADERSHIP
•Efficiency Improvement   •Relationship Focused   •Community Involvement   •Self-venture   •Chairman   •Shareholder

- Implemented, as an integral member of management team, *Just in Time* materials system for Ford Motor Company. Along with other creative innovations, reduced departmental workforce by 50%.

- Developed and implemented Occupational Health & Safety program for a 500-employee corporation. Within one year, reduced incidents by 83.7% and appealed to WSIB for re-classification; received credit of $650,000 and annual assessment premium savings of $60,000.

- Appointed as chairman for Hamilton Occupational Health & Safety Committee as acknowledged expert in health & safety field.

- Played an integral role in the development of over 200 residential homes as a 20-year shareholder and director of Tommar Construction Limited.

- Modelled life-long involvement in volunteerism and community initiatives.

- Led and sustained successful self-venture for over eight years.

CAREER HISTORY

ALETEC Inc: **DIRECTOR OF SALES & MARKETING**   **2000-Present**
Led team to establish international markets and sales activity for engineering process.

Bryant Medical Technologies: **NATIONAL SALES MANAGER**   **1999-2000**
Maintained and developed new sales in Ontario and Quebec within healthcare and industrial markets.

Pantel Products Limited: **OWNER**   **1991-1999**
Sourced and supplied international healthcare products to various markets in Canada.

Ford Motor Company: **MATERIALS MANAGEMENT SUPERVISOR**   **1984-1991**
Managed line feed drivers to ensure assembly parts were expedited to production line.
Accountable for process improvement, health & safety, labour issues, and employee training.

C.H. Williams Limited: **CANADIAN HEALTH & SAFETY DIRECTOR**   **1978-1983**
Developed and implemented Occupational Health & Safety policy and program for Canadian operations.

EDUCATION & PROFESSIONAL DEVELOPMENT

- Mohawk College, Hamilton, ON -- Civil Engineering Program

- Professional development/leadership courses:

  - Management Techniques
  - Sales & Marketing
  - Materials Management
  - Occupational Health & Safety

  - Leadership Development
  - International Business Development & Finance
  - Logistics, Supply Chain Management
  - Personal & Professional Enhancement

Martin Yao

123-456 Handy Lane
London, Ontario, N1N 1N1, Canada

Phone: 519 555-7654
E-mail: myao@careerprocanada.ca

MARKETING / NEW BUSINESS DEVELOPMENT / TRAINING AND DEVELOPMENT

Fluent in Mandarin and English / MBA Candidate

EXECUTIVE PROFILE

Highly successful executive experience in new business development and business system analysis including full P&L responsibility for creative sales, market penetration and expansion, communication, and staff training

Diversified corporate experience leading to the designation as one of the top 100 experienced marketing research project managers in China; highly skilled in budget controlling

Ability to multi-task and respond to rapidly changing client requirements in handling multimillion-dollar projects

Training and development expertise gained through effectively hiring, training, supervising, and motivating staff and management

EDUCATION

School of Business, London, Ontario, Canada   2004-2006

Master of Business Administration Candidate

    Focus on Marketing Management, top 10% in marketing course

    Vice President of Public Relations in the *Ivey China Business Student Club*

Beijing University, Beijing, China   1990-1994

Bachelor of Computer Science

    Recipient of Dean's Scholarship for two consecutive years / GPA 4.0 (90%)

WORK EXPERIENCE

Hi-Sci-Tech Co., Ltd, Beijing/Shanghai, China   2001-2003

A fast growing high-tech trading and consulting start-up company with $800,000 annual sales

Sales Director / Co-founder

- Established the marketing strategy and action plan for the company's core product—*First Choice digital recording systems*, and became the exclusive agent in China within four months.

- Developed and maintained solid business relationships with eighteen leading banks and the railway system, doubling the revenue in one year.

- Led a team of 20 engineers and 10 salespeople to triple the revenue in three years.

Marketing Executive. This candidate chooses to highlight his Chinese experience and language skills, rather than minimizing them. This strategy effectively targets marketing roles that require an expert with the ability to penetrate markets in China.

Martin Yao   **Page Two**

<u>HAPPY Marketing Research Co., Ltd</u>**,** Beijing, China   1999-2001

A marketing research start-up company with $500,000 annual sales

Executive Director / Co-founder

- Cultivated profitable business partnerships with three local leading advertising companies and six multi-national companies.

- Built a cross-functional team of eight, boosting annual revenue from $100,000 to $500,000 in three years.

- Set up a flexible training system for project-based training and administered it to 23 staff members, with the result of significantly stabilizing the service quality.

<u>JRHawthorne Ltd.</u>**,** Beijing, China   1994-1999

A multinational marketing research company with $20 billion annual sales globally

Senior Supervisor of the Operations Department / Project Manager

- Implemented, with an operations field work team of nine, more than 1000 projects: gained recognition of being one of the most experienced project managers in China.

- Reorganized the organizational structure, greatly improving customer response and quality; and reduced 35% of the expenses by creating an overtime control system.

- Received the highest *Performance Appraisal* score and advanced, in record time, from clerk to senior supervisor.

ADDITIONAL INFORMATION

Winner: *JRHawthorne Ltd. Outstanding Contribution Award, JRHawthorne Ltd. Demonstrating Core Values Award, JRHawthorne Ltd. Team Star Award*

Captain of the basketball team in high school and university

Chairman of the Staff Club at *JRHawthorne Ltd.*

Luca Davinci

100 Denby Ave ▪ Suite 1600 ▪ Toronto ▪ Ontario ▪ M1M 1M1 ▪ Canada
☎ 416-555-8765 (home) ▪ 416-555-7654 (mobile)   💻 lucadavinci@CareerProCanada.ca

MANAGEMENT / MARKETING
Results-driven with strong leadership and entrepreneurial work ethic

PROFILE

Multifaceted marketing experience: Over five years of sound experience in the areas of marketing research, campaign strategy, project management, strategic alliance building (through networking and negotiation), and effective cross-functional communication.

Technical service and products: Skilled in the development, management, and delivery of processing and facilitating all types of inquiries, new direct client marketing campaigns, and highly successful E-CRM databases tracking website visitor trends and buying patterns.

Advanced levels of computer and software expertise: Strong understanding and practical experience in commonly used web-based languages and development tools.

WORK EXPERIENCE

<u>Company Concern</u>, Toronto, Ontario, Canada   2003-Current
Ebay affiliated auction service
PARTNER/DIRECTOR OF MARKETING

Partner in a Toronto based *Ebay*-affiliated auction service responsible for compiling and organizing demographic and consumer market related data, developing the initial profitability research and ad campaign strategy, and managing the overall project:

- Led, motivated, and built a team of directors and IT database developers through the development of company infrastructure and goals.
- Built strategic business relationships with non-profit organizations capturing further low cost market access and exposure.
- Negotiated and made deals, acquiring significant discounts and allowances on various retail leasing agreements and other significant start-up capital costs.

<u>First Canadian Bank - Discount Brokerage</u>, Burlington, Ontario, Canada   2001-2003
LICENCED INVESTMENT REPRESENTATIVE

Processed and facilitated all client investment, trades, and financial product inquiries; managed client relationships and accounts; provided support and resources to local bank managers:

- Generated consistently high levels of commission, reaching levels of over $20,000 in one day.
- Updated and contributed several key portions of the bank intranet and database, resulting in easier and more efficient access to detailed investment information and procedures.
- Initiated, developed, and administered, as part of a select member team, new direct-client marketing campaigns resulting in significant dollar increases in assets under management.

<u>First Canadian Bank</u>, Toronto, Ontario, Canada   2000-2001
INVESTMENT ADVISOR ASSISTANT

Worked as an assistant to the Advisor; handled new business and light administrative duties:

- Developed business through targeted cold calling, networking, and referrals resulting in large increases in new business and total assets under management.

Marketing Manager. The candidate's use of icons visually directs the reader to the phone numbers and e-mail address. Bold lead-in statements within the profile succinctly outline this individual's area of expertise.

Luca Davinci **Page Two**

Harrison-Ford, Toronto, Ontario, Canada 1996-2000
MARKETING/WEB MANAGER

Conceptualized, developed, and implemented multiple marketing and promotional campaigns for a small-sized fast moving consumer goods retailer; controlled general website direction and development, as well as buying, placing, and overseeing all print materials:

- Implemented highly successful E-CRM databases tracking website visitor trends and buying patterns, gaining nearly 30% in business growth and profit in first year of implementation.

- Generated high levels of consumer awareness through targeted banner ad campaigns receiving mention on CNN and several other major online publications resulting in further increases in sales and web traffic.

- Utilized *Ebay* in separate marketing strategy which became highly cost-effective and grew sales by nearly 10%.

TECHNICAL SKILLS

High levels of expertise on both PC and Macintosh computer systems, with certification in *MS Office Word*, *Excel*, *PowerPoint*, *Outlook*, *Project*, and *Access*.

Strong understanding and practical experience in commonly used web-based languages and development tools such as *HTML*, *Java*, and *Flash Dreamweaver*.

Competency and familiarity with most Marketing and Graphical software titles including *Photoshop*, *Corel*, and *QuarkXpress*.

EDUCATION

York University, Toronto, Ontario, Canada 1995-1999
B.S.B.A. Marketing Major / Computer Science Minor

Canadian Securities Course (CSC) 2001

Investment Conduct and Regulatory Requirements Course (CPH) 2001

Options Licensing and Derivatives Fundamentals Course (OLT) (DFC) 2001

MINDY YO

123 FIRST DRIVE · OSHAWA · ON · L1L 1L1 · CANADA
TELEPHONE: 905 555-1234 · E-MAIL: YOMINDY@CAREERPROCANADA.CA

MARKETING RESEARCHER AND BUSINESS DEVELOPMENT EXECUTIVE
A Verifiable Record of Building Strong Relationships and Achieving Customer Satisfaction in Competitive Markets

QUALIFICATIONS SUMMARY

- Key Top-level Contacts
- Strategic Market Analysis
- Business Plan Development
- Regional Reputation

- Organizational Leadership
- Presentation and Training Skills
- Project Management
- Fluency in English and Mandarin

CAREER HISTORY

Strategic Solutions International, Shanghai, China   2000 – Present
Strategic Solutions International is a strategic marketing solutions-focused agency employing both qualitative and quantitative research methodologies to provide consumer insights, strategic advice, and direction.
Research Partner
Combine qualitative research with creative insights to holistically analyze consumer patterns and provide innovative solutions:

- Conduct marketing research projects—employing integrated research methodologies to cater to different research and brand needs—to provide unique analyses and solutions to such clients as *EA, Mattel, Coca Cola, Nokia, and Maxxium (Remy Martin).*
- Consolidate local consumer group insights and help each client identify and act upon their unique growth opportunities through expertise in analysis, report writing, and open communication.
- Teamed with three others to produce three major youth studies, generating research to enable clients to receive, select, evaluate, and integrate the information with their data and third-party information; and then apply the new information to specific business issues and situations.

ABC, Shanghai, China   1995 – 1999
ABC helps clients clarify and understand the complexities of the marketplace, so they can build the efficiency and productivity of their marketing and sales programs, increase revenues, and improve profitability.
Senior Research Executive (1995 – 1997)
Investigated the lifestyle, values, attitudes, and behaviours of different local consumer segments such as women and the "One-Child Generation" through a set of consumer-focused, customized research techniques including observation, home visits, interactive workshops, and focus groups:

- Designed and implemented 200 customized research studies to provide clients with opportunities and techniques to first examine the trends and understand the impact of the market forces that influence consumers' purchasing decisions and then link this purchasing information to specific demographics and motivational factors.
- Built and managed key long-term relationships, developing close client partnerships in order to design personalized services and help clients recognize their strategies and business objectives.

...2

Marketing Research Leader. A strong tagline focuses on this marketing researcher and business development executive's relationship management expertise.

MINDY YO

ABC, Shanghai, China (continued)   1995 – 1999
Research Executive (1995 – 1997)
Specialized in qualitative research to exploit consumer perception and attitudes, behaviours, needs, and motivations; addressed specific future marketing opportunities and issues such as new product development, product and brand concept development, consumer targeting and brand diagnosis, and brand equity review:

- Assessed and analyzed individual business situations and research needs through effective communication and superior research skills, resulting in more efficient, client-focused outcomes.
- Performed analysis and fieldwork services to provide clients with a range of options so they could evaluate and appreciate why marketing campaigns succeed or fail.
- Managed a trend pool of over 100 teenagers, young adults, and trend professionals (fashion magazine editors, fashion designers, hair stylists, and DJ's) across five Chinese cities to build up a broad database for *XYZ Pop*.

RELATED ACTIVITIES
Volunteer Forum Leader on BBS (Internet), exploring such topics as brand communication, consumerism, consumption psychology, and culture analysis

Volunteer for *Dreams Can Come True*, Mississauga, Ontario – Committee member and coordinator for *Can-Am Equine Emporium Event* and *Dreams Awareness Week*

Recipient of the 1999 *ABC* Outstanding Performance Award

EDUCATION
AAA University, Oakwood, CA, USA   1999 – 2000
Bachelor of Business Administration

Chinese University of Finance & Economics, Shanghai, China   1995 – 1996
Three extra courses for credit (*Social Psychology, Personality,* and *Cognitive Psychology*)

Chinese University of Finance & Economics, Shanghai, China   1993 – 1995
Associate's Degree in English for International Business

AJAZ J. KHAN, B.SC.

1234 Sandstone Road
Wolfville, Nova Scotia
B1B 1B1

Phone (902) 555-1234
Cell (902) 555-2345
E-mail ajkhan@careerprocanada.ca

INFORMATION TECHNOLOGY LEADER
Global Organizations ▪ Large-Scale Integrations ▪ Off-Shore Outsourcing ▪ Start-Up IT Operations

A strategic, results-oriented senior business and technical manager, with expertise instituting and overseeing global IT operations. Accomplished in major organizational transformations, mergers, and acquisitions with a proven record of achievements in large-scale project management. An inspiring leader creating superior work teams and optimal-performance work environments. Talent for building mutually beneficial relationships with business executives and external service providers. An innovative professional, effecting change in situations which present major challenges requiring creative, appropriate, and cost-effective technical solutions.

Core Competencies- Leadership & Business Management

Strategic Vision & Planning ▪ Budgeting & Forecasting ▪ Presentations & Negotiations
Team Building & Leadership ▪ Organizational Development ▪ Cross-Cultural Communications

Core Competencies- Project & Program Management

Global Best Practices ▪ Feasibility Analysis ▪ Strategy Deployment ▪ Change Management
Process Re-engineering ▪ Continuous Improvement ▪ Productivity & Profitability

Core Competencies- Technical

Business Systems Deployment ▪ Quality Assurance (QA) Methodology ▪ Capability & Maturity Modelling (CMM)
Infrastructure Development ▪ Application Development ▪ Networking Architecture

*** Two-time recipient of the Merit Award for Outstanding Achievement from Technica. ***

CAREER HIGHLIGHTS

- **Conceived and established an off-shore IT operation** in Singapore, resulting in a 45% cost savings and a 20% improvement in software development and maintenance lifecycle.

- **Directed four major European IT mergers and acquisition integration projects** covering Italy, France, Ireland, and the Czech Republic and completed the projects on schedule and under budget.

- **Formulated a comprehensive off-shore/near-shore sourcing strategy**, using the highly successful Singapore model as a prototype, and played a key role in instituting off-shore operations.

- **Orchestrated an IT operational restructuring in France and Switzerland** and reduced personnel 15%, which ultimately slashed costs 22% and improved customer satisfaction 10%.

- **Supported the successful start-up of a $50 million manufacturing operation** in Brazil, by establishing both in-house and outsourced IT functions well ahead of schedule.

- **Administered recruitment, development, and succession planning** of key positions in the Americas, Europe, and Asia, reducing dependency on expatriate posts and ensuring regional self-sufficiency.

- **Proposed and established a global support model** complete with education, knowledge transfer, change management, disaster recovery, and service level agreements.

- **Managed and supported network and office systems migration projects** for newly acquired locations in Mexico, Ireland, Wisconsin, North Carolina, California, and United Kingdom.

- **Launched strategies for e-business architecture, LAN/WAN, and global messaging,** and migrated 2500 users from a legacy system, in preparation for a projected growth to 40,000 employees worldwide.

Off-Shore Information Technology Leader. The comprehensive listing of key phrases is broken down into separate core competencies to improve readability. Each statement starts with a bolded phrase to ensure that the reader spots the accomplishments.

AJAZ J. KHAN, B.SC. ▪ Phone (902) 555-1234

PROFESSIONAL EXPERIENCE

Technica International Inc., Wolfville, Nova Scotia   **1998 - Present**
A world leader in electronics manufacturing services (EMS), with over 50 locations in Asia, Europe, and the Americas and revenue of $10 billion USD.

Senior Manager, Off-Shore Development (2003 - Present)
Reporting to Vice President of Strategic Solutions, responsible for establishing and overseeing the Singapore operation, supervising 20 employees, and managing an operating budget of $1 million. Accountable to design and implement various strategic business solutions and e-business infrastructure. Identify complementary operating locations, source off-shore service providers, establish the business model and communications strategy, and interface with local economic development boards.
- Implemented the Singapore operations from start-up, addressing global cost reduction initiatives, and achieved a 95% on-time delivery of projects with 93% resource utilization.
- Assisted in the execution of two world leading near-shore service providers in India and successfully slashed costs by 50%.
- Developed and deployed corporate governance and policies for off-shore activity including process model, services scope, performance metrics, and tracking system.

Senior Manager, Corporate Information Technology Integration (2001 - 2003)
Responsible for International IT operations management and large-scale project management, reporting to both the Vice President of Integration, and the Vice President of European IT Operations. Accountable to manage the France and Switzerland operations, customer accounts, and service delivery, with 12 direct reports and a $1.5 million operating budget. Project management responsibilities include large-scale merger and acquisition integrations in various European countries.
- Restructured the IT operations in France and Switzerland, which significantly reduced operational costs and enhanced customer service, ultimately achieving an exceptional customer satisfaction rating.
- Devised and instituted formal integration procedures for rapid infrastructure and applications deployment, resulting in shortened lead time for new customer introduction and seamless transfer to regional teams.
- Spearheaded the IT integration of various acquisitions including Motorola in Ireland, Sagem in Czech Republic, and Avaya in France, completing all projects on schedule and on average 15% below budget.
- Marshalled the integration of a $1.5 billion business in Italy, with a $12 million project budget and a team of 80 employees, and effectively amalgamated operations on-time and under budget.
- Played a key role as a core member of the global sourcing contract negotiation team, presenting recommendations to the Executives and contributing to the Request for Proposal (RFP) development.

Previous Positions Held:
Manager, Corporate Information Technology Strategy & Integration (2000 - 2001)
Information Technology Manager, Office Systems (1999 - 2000)
Team Leader, Integration (1998 - 1999)

University of Maine, Augusta, Maine   **1995 – 1998**
Manager, Data Centre Operations

FORMAL EDUCATION

Bachelor of Science in Electrical Engineering
University of Maine, Augusta, Maine, 1995

PROFESSIONAL DEVELOPMENT

Actively committed to continuing education via seminars, workshops, trade shows, and formal courses.

References available upon request

Stephen Bradley

1234 Ridge Point Path, Oakville, ON, L1L 1L1 Phone: 905.555.1234 Cell: 905.555.2345 E mail: sbradley@CareerProCanada.ca

Operations Manager ✗ *Distribution Manager* ✗ *General Manager*

Transportation ✗ *Warehousing* ✗ *Manufacturing*

Competent, decisive and dedicated senior executive with an extensive knowledge of distribution, operations and executive management. Hands-on leader, mentor and motivator; instils confidence in employees to succeed and deliver. Articulate; establishes profitable rapport with staff, peers, clients and suppliers; proactively works with unions to address issues and ensure smooth business operations. Visionary; recognized for conceiving and implementing numerous initiatives that elevate productivity and profitability. Understands operational excellence and the impact on the customer; committed to continuous improvement. Effective and efficient organizer and strategic thinker.

Professional Experience

Canadian Logistics Limited, Mississauga, Ontario   1976 – Present
Held the following progressively responsible positions:
GENERAL MANAGER – Mississauga Distribution Centre   1999 – Present
Accomplishments:
✗ Acknowledged for improving the following performance measures:
  ✗ *Delivery reliability* by 10% to 93% through employee involvement and using detailed process and activity sheets.
  ✗ *On-time deliveries* by 4% to 96% by involving and educating McDonald's Restaurants in the logistics of deliveries.
  ✗ *Warehouse Productivity* from 208 to 230 cph or 11%, recognized as the highest increase in the Canadian Logistics Distribution Network. Accomplished by warehouse layout redesign and a comprehensive workflow study.
  ✗ *Off load rate* from 178 to 228 cph or 28% by helping conceive and initiate a transparent delivery system using carts.
✗ Played the pivotal and leadership role in receiving the following awards:
  ✗ *"National Distribution Centre Special Achievement Award, 2000"*; for the cart delivery program rollout.
  ✗ *"National Distribution Centre Growth and Earnings, 2000"*; given for overall strict fiscal management, meeting budgets.
  ✗ *"McDonald's Supplier Excellence Award, 2000".*
✗ Recognized for consistently working below budgets and exceeding outside business revenue.
✗ Led the QCD Performance Management System implementation, attended QCD training and facilitated staff education programs. System elevated productivity, performance, staff motivation and management reporting.
✗ Instrumental in designing, initiating and training the cart delivery program, which improved delivery schedules, reduced driver workload, assisted McDonald's Restaurant staff with inventory management and increased turns of transportation assets.
✗ Restructured the warehouse layout, to permit greater flexibility and retrieval of inventory in shorter time frames and allow for more defined warehouse management.
✗ Conducted successful negotiations with the Teamsters Union to establish a labour contract within a strict budget; agreement achieved with no interruption of supply.
✗ Accountable for introducing Logistics Limited E-commerce strategy to the Mississauga Centre, which benefited the company and the vendors, saving thousands of dollars.
Responsibilities:
✗ Oversaw the daily operations of a 90,000 square foot warehouse, the largest and busiest in the Logistics Limited chain, with: 170 employees, 38 trailers, 24 tractor units, $9 million operating budget and generating $277 million in sales. Supplied 425 McDonald's Restaurants with 250 skus encompassing all products used in McDonald's Restaurant operations including perishables.
✗ Solidified the overall distribution centre operations through hands-on daily management of all business activities, empowering staff to meet or exceed high standards.

Operations and Distribution Executive. The five keywords listed in this headline concisely outline the candidate's area of expertise and industry.

FIELD SERVICE MANAGER, Vancouver, B.C.   1995 – 1999
- Recognized for conceiving, developing and implementing the CAD storage layout and the "Macsimizer" restaurant inventory control program for McDonald's Restaurants. Utilized at all new restaurant locations in British Columbia.
- Played a key role in selling the transparent delivery concept to McDonald's Executive Board; as a result, McDonald's and Logistics Limited companies invested in the manufacture of the carts and the delivery infrastructure including delivery ramps, reducing delivery time at each location.
- Initiated the successful restaurant replenishment project, tasked with instituting defined parameters and guidelines to level out deliveries while maintaining an even inventory.
- Selected as the Chair of the Job Evaluation Committee charged with reviewing job descriptions and pay equity for 700 employees.
- Acted as the Distribution Centre Instructor for the TQM Program.

TRANSPORTATION MANAGER, Vancouver, B.C.   1988 – 1994
- Major contributor to Logistics Limited's recognition as the "Centre of the Year" in 1989 and 1990 for exceeding financial targets and performance indicators.
- Coordinated the Manuguistics "Trucks" routing system, which allowed greater control of delivery schedules within a geographic area.
- Renowned as being the first Logistics Limited Transportation Manager to solicit and maintain new business outside the McDonald's contract. Schedules amended to carry zinc ingots and lumber.
- Implemented a rotating delivery system allowing the distribution centre to operate 24 hours per day, seven days a week, fully utilizing company assets and reducing deliveries by 30%.
- Devised and developed yearly operation and capital budgets, completed month-end results and maintained strict cost control on a daily and weekly basis.
- Recruited drivers, conducted road testing, acted as mediator between union and company; patiently and efficiently resolved grievances.
- Created delivery schedules for 110 restaurants and 25 drivers completing 3,000 routes and 9,000 deliveries per annum.

TRANSPORTATION SUPERVISOR, Vancouver, B.C.   1986 – 1987
- Accountable for daily dispatch and fleet operations.

WAREHOUSE LEAD HAND, Vancouver, B.C.   1983 – 1986
- Supervised 10 unionized personnel, tasked with productively picking, receiving and loading inventory in a shift environment.

DRIVER, Vancouver, B.C.   1980 – 1983
- Held an "AZ" Class 1 driving licence, drove tractor-trailer units delivering to McDonald's.

WAREHOUSEMAN, Vancouver, B.C.   1976 – 1980

Education

Canadian Institute of Traffic & Transportation **Certificate in Distribution**	1994
Industrial Accident Prevention Association **Safety, Health And The Law,** Level 1	1999
The Leadership Strategies Institute, Chicago, Illinois **Leadership Strategies**	1996
Justice Institute of British Columbia, B.C. **Certificate – Traffic Accident Investigation**	1990
McDonald's Institute of Hamburgerology, Chicago, Illinois **Basic Operations** **Performance Management** **Canadian Development Course**	1995 1989 1988

SEAN MURPHY
111 IRISH CORNER · CHATHAM · ONTARIO · N1N 1N1 · CANADA
☎(519) 555-4321 · SEAN.MURPHY@CAREERPROCANADA.CA

> **SENIOR-LEVEL OPERATIONS MANAGEMENT EXECUTIVE**
> NEW BUSINESS DEVELOPMENT / NEGOTIATION / INTEGRITY / ORGANIZATIONAL LEADERSHIP
>
> *A Verifiable Record of Building Growth and Profit in Competitive Markets*

CORE STRENGTHS
Proven Ability to Identify, Capture, and Build New Opportunities

Excellent Communication Skills · Networking and Strategic Contact Development Expertise · Visionary Leadership · Innovation · Risk Management · Negotiation · Team Building and Leadership · Staff Training and Development · Creative Problem-Solving

PROFESSIONAL EXPERIENCE

PowerPoint, Chatham, ON   1994 – 2006

PowerPoint, appealing to people of all ages, combines the classic games of tag and hide & seek with a high-tech spin.

Director of Operations

Advanced from the roles of General Manager and Area Manager to work in liaison with the VP Operations to direct the operations of a $45 M family entertainment business operating throughout the US and Canada; held direct responsibility for P&L results, pricing, new product creation, policies, and procedures:

- Increased ancillary revenues by approximately $115 K in the first year, by sourcing and implementing three new vending and confectionary contracts; managed contracts and successfully renegotiated contracts, with better revenue splits over the five year period.

- Created, developed, and spearheaded the largest *PowerPoint* tournament in the world (involving 75 seven-person teams of "members" from across North America) and the building block on which the "Members Program" was built.

- Co-created and implemented a universal system of executing a Party package, standardizing the largest business offering (35% of all bookings); provided for increased availability of this package during peak times by streamlining both the staging process and the party room accessibility.

- Created two packages of training materials and prepared two presentations for continent-wide training workshops; materials are still in use today.

- Teamed with three senior management executives to forecast and set company budget and performance targets; shared objectives with six area managers, training and motivating them to effectively meet the targets on time and on budget.

Collegiate Coupon Clipper, London, ON   1992 – 1994

Collegiate Coupon Clipper was an entrepreneurial venture which developed the first multi-campus coupon-based publication in the London area.

General Manager (Sole Proprietor)

Created business from scratch, building key alliances and partnerships to assess and meet customer needs:

- Controlled all operations, including Business Plan, P&L, and Accounts Receivable.
- Successfully negotiated, acquired, and managed 55 advertising contracts.

...2

Operations Director. Instead of a lengthy power profile, this executive opted for a headline that included key areas of expertise and a strong positioning statement outlining his employer's buying motivators.

SEAN MURPHY

Strictland Publishing, London, ON   1989 – 1992

Strictland Publishing published a domestic magazine which was distributed to 75,000 people in London and the surrounding areas.

Sales Account Manager

- Developed highly effective sales strategies, negotiated 70 advertising contracts, and effectively met targets.

The Cove Department Store, London, ON   1987 – 1989

*The **Cove Department Store** chain has over 500 stores and nearly 70,000 associates, and is located in every province in Canada.*

Sales Manager (promoted from Personnel Manager)

Oversaw the hiring, training, and disciplinary action for the 100 staff members in the soft goods (fashion) section; effectively met sales budgets, and supervised the bi-annual inventories:

- Successfully set up and executed all operations in the seasonal shops, despite tight time constraints.
- Developed and implemented promotional materials, on time and on budget, for the soft goods section.

SPECIAL RECOGNITION

PowerPoint Award of Excellence recipient ▪ *PowerPoint* Award of Growth recipient ▪ High School Valedictorian

EDUCATION

The University of Western Ontario, London, ON   1984 – 1987

B.A., English Literature

LST Institute for Behavioural Science, Human Interaction Lab, Atlanta, Georgia   2002

Certificate of Achievement

ISABEL ARTHUR, M.B.A.

12 Greenway Drive   Cell: (647) 555-1212
Toronto, Ontario, M1M 1M1, Canada   Fax: (416) 555-1212
Email: iarthur@CareerProCanada.ca

EDUCATION

Ph.D. (Organizational Behaviour), *School of Business, University of California*, LA, California   2003 - present
Dissertation: *Leadership and Distance*
Dissertation Chair: Sam Smith

M.B.A. (Strategy/Organizational Behaviour), *School of Business, Ontario University*, Sarnia, Ontario   1997

Bachelor of Arts (History/Political Science), *Montreal University*, Montreal, Quebec   1994

RESEARCH AGENDA

The underlying research theme is an investigation into the behaviours of leaders and perceptions, performance, and behaviours of followers whose relationship is impacted by the context of distance. This systematic research program investigates the elements of distance (such as physical, psychological, and interaction) and uses knowledge gained from existing theories of leadership to predict the nature of the relationships within these dyads, and examines how the relationships will impact some of the traditional workplace outcomes such as performance, organizational citizenship behaviour, and satisfaction.

TEACHING INTERESTS

- Organizational Behaviour
- Leadership

AWARDS AND GRANTS

- Winner, John A. Doe/Commerce Associates Doctoral Fellowship, 2005
- School of Business Doctoral Fellowship, *University of California*, 2002-2006
- Dean's List, School of Business at *Ontario University*, 1995-1997

JOURNAL ARTICLES

Arthur, I. and Smith, S.S., (2004). "A contingency approach to SHRM: Links between human resource practices and firm strategy." *Under review at Human Resources Management.*

WORK IN PROGRESS

Arthur, I. (2005). "A multidimensional taxonomy of organizational distance: The leadership case."

Arthur, I. (2005). "How far does leadership travel?"

CONFERENCE PRESENTATIONS

Arthur, I. (2005), "The multidimensionality of leadership distance," Western Management Academy, Phoenix, 2005.

Facilitator, *Leadership: Mentoring (PDW)*; Management Academy, Waikiki, 2005.

Facilitator, *Politics and Perception*; Management Academy, St. Louis, 2004.

Organizational Behaviour Consultant. This Ph.D. candidate opted for a formal curriculum vitae format, which displays her outstanding educational and research background appropriately for an academic role.

PUBLISHED CASES

"ABC Applied Systems (A)" and "ABC Applied Systems (A)" Teaching Note *School of Business Case Number 123456*, co-authored with Janet M. Hoskin

"ABC Applied Systems (B) - The Red Team Enters" and "ABC Applied Systems (B)" Teaching Note *School of Business Case Number 234567*, co-authored with Janet M. Hoskin

"ABC Applied Systems (C) – Aftermath … Business As Usual" and "ABC Applied Systems (C)" Teaching Note *School of Business Case Number 345678*, co-authored with Janet M. Hoskin

"ABC Applied Systems – Anna's Challenge" and "ABC Applied Systems – Anna's Challenge" Teaching Note *School of Business Case Number 456789*, co-authored with Janet M. Hoskin

TEACHING EXPERIENCE

INSTRUCTOR, *Leading Organizations*
School of Business, University of California, LA, CA
Taught a required course in Organizational Behaviour, with 30-35 students per section
- Designed and facilitated experiential activities as well as classroom lesson plans on a weekly basis
- Achieved an average Teaching Rating of 4.4/5.0 (Fall 2004: 2 sections/Spring 2005: 4 sections)

AD HOC REVIEWER

Management Academy, Organizational Psychology and Communication/Information Systems divisions

PROFESSIONAL MEMBERSHIP AND SERVICE

Management Academy
- Logistics Chair, 2005 New Doctoral Student Consortium
- Logistics Committee, 2004 New Doctoral Student Consortium

Western Management Academy
- Presenter

PROFESSIONAL DEVELOPMENT

Case Teaching Workshop, *School of Business, University of Ontario*, Sarnia, ON		2004
Case Writing Workshop, *School of Business, University of Ontario*, Sarnia, ON		1996

RELATED EDUCATIONAL EXPERIENCE

SCHOOL OF BUSINESS, Ontario University**,** Sarnia, ON   1996 - 1998

The second largest producer of cases in North America and ranked in Financial Times' "Top 20" MBA Programs
Research Associate/Case Writer
- Performed research and interviews; evaluated survey responses for a major study on Champions.
- Developed teaching materials, including cases and teaching notes; marked 240 MBA1 exams.

LEADER, Ontario University, Sarnia, ON   1995 - 1997

A student-initiated and managed project of 45 business students to expose interested students in the former Soviet Republics to introductory free-market business concepts
Site Manager/Instructor
- Developed/collected training materials for three-week case-based course; liaised with partners in Lutsk, Ukraine, and Nizhny Novgorod, Russia; coached and managed group of four instructors.

ISABEL ARTHUR, M.B.A. 2 of 3

BUSINESS EXPERIENCE

ABC ONE-ON-ONE REVIEW, Los Angeles, CA   2001 – 2002

An SAT tutoring company providing home-based preparation for college entrance exams
Vice President, Marketing
Directed the overall marketing efforts, including direct and online marketing as well as brand positioning and product development for the launch of this new company.

- Designed the marketing message, materials, and press kit for ABC to present to potential investors, clients, and partners – schools and counsellors.
- Researched the initial competitive analysis (using secondary sources, surveys, and focus groups) used to launch the business.

123 CORPORATION, Los Angeles, CA   2001

An advanced decision-support software company converting knowledge from leading professional service firms
Manager, Knowledge Products
Created interactive software modules to assist senior financial executives in decision-making by interviewing industry and professional services experts.

- Authored five interactive modules on foreign exchange risk management and compensation strategy by working with experts and using their knowledge as a basis for assessment tools, insight, and results.
- Conducted research on market size and segments to support investor materials for both the core and custom product lines of business.

#1, Los Angeles, CA   1999 - 2001

An internet previewing company
Director, Business Strategy (September 2000 – January 2001)
Analyzed all aspects of the business at top and departmental levels; surveyed the market to determine viability of the business model and understand all players in the market.

- Presented introduction to streaming media syndication, detailing competitive landscape and identifying key priorities and targets to executive management and board of directors.

Director, Affinity and Member Services (October 1999 – September 2000)
Conceptualized and implemented *#1 Rewards* – a private label loyalty program; initiated and supervised all member communications and directed primary research.

- Increased member visits as a portion of total visits 215%, number of previews 874%, and preview revenue 456% by launching *#1 Rewards*.

DNY ONLINE, Los Angeles, CA   1999

The online division of the largest U.S. entertainment and media company
Marketing Analyst – Market Research
Compiled and disseminated primary and secondary research findings; addressed individual questions within *BV Internet Group*, *DNY Online*, and other *DNY* units for research support.

- Initiated bi-monthly market research newsletter with distribution base of 90, reflecting the most current information about research and trends in online space.
- Oversaw all relationships with secondary/syndicated research suppliers and disseminated that information throughout the organization; developed online surveys.

AAA LTD., Toronto, Ontario   1997 - 1998

An international strategy consulting firm with more than 60 worldwide offices
Associate Consultant
Engaged to improve business performance of *Fortune 100* companies; researched new concepts for *AAA* to take to market; played lead role in recruiting efforts.

- Devised marketing materials to win three new clients by executing research in "Successful Growth" of both revenues and market capitalization with an international team.

ISABEL ARTHUR, M.B.A 3 of 3

JOHN W. WILLIAMS
SENIOR EXECUTIVE • STRATEGY • LEADERSHIP

100 Main Avenue • Oakville, Ontario L1L 1L1
Office: 905 555 1234 • Mobile: 416 555 6789

DOMESTIC & INTERNATIONAL BUSINESS DEVELOPMENT
- Pharmaceutical & Biotechnology Sectors -

HIGH-PERFORMANCE EXECUTIVE credited with driving the domestic and international business development initiatives that have consistently increased bottom-line profitability. Fearless business leader with award-winning track record for consistently producing results. Combines creative business acumen with exceptional leadership qualities attracting and inspiring top-quality teams.

Executive sales and marketing strategist and tactician with international success and a global network of contacts. Exceptional communication, negotiation, and strategic partnering skills in all cultures and at highest corporate levels internationally. Creative problem solver with both traditional and Internet marketing success. Areas of excellence include:

Strategic Planning • Growth Strategies • Competitive Market Positioning • New Market Development • e-Marketing
Brand Development & Management • Competitive Analysis & Positioning • New Product Development
Pricing Strategies & Structures • Joint Ventures & Strategic Partnerships • Leadership & Mentoring

PERFORMANCE MILESTONES

- Developed new revenue stream for Previa International, currently generating $18 million in annual sales and representing 50% of the total corporate volume.

- Opened up new international markets in Japan and Brazil and expanded business to a total of 25 countries internationally, growing company from $1 million to over $9 million in annual sales.

- Led the revolutionary redesign of a global pharmaceutical company's sales and marketing strategy – put forward 175 recommendations and spearheaded industry-leading changes to marketing processes and strategies.

- Personally secured or positioned companies to secure multi-million accounts with industry leaders such as AstraZeneca, Lilly, Searle, Millennium, Amgen, Genentech, Seagrams, and Olympia & York.

PROFESSIONAL EXPERIENCE

PREVIA LTD (division of ABC Consulting Group; formerly ABC/Previa)
US$21 million communication and information solutions provider for the global pharmaceutical industry

President, Nuvis International
1998 to Present

Under the new Previa brand, led the aggressive expansion of all Internet-based services globally. Primary driving force behind all strategic and tactical undertakings with full P&L accountability and management of international operations in Europe, Japan, US, and Latin America. Recruited and direct an 8-person international team.

Drove the strategic change of focus from small international markets to larger global accounts, built and manage an extensive global distribution network, assembled an international team of representatives, and led all major business development and key account management.

Bottom Line Results
- Generated a 6-fold growth in sales from $1 million to $6 million USD within the first 2 years in position.
- Grew business to account for almost 50% of Previa Ltd. sales and 25% of the corporation's total business.
- Generated revenues of $9 million USD for 2003, an increase of 100+% over the previous fiscal year.
- Personally responsible for closing over $2.8 million USD in 2003, projected at over $3 million USD for 2004.

...2

Pharmaceutical Business Development Executive. The "Performance Milestones" section on page one creatively summarizes this executive's impressive record of accomplishments spread over his career. To maximize impact, he categorizes his current position's results under three headings – "Bottom Line Results," "Business Growth," and "Leadership."

Business Growth

- Expanded international business to currently hold operations in 10 countries with services operating in 25 countries.
- Conceptualized and launched PreviaPress (www.previapress.com), a highly profitable information resource leveraging "thought leaders" in the medical industry – service launched in all major markets and currently generates $18+ million USD annually, representing 50% of the total corporate business volume.
- Expanded and currently manage the global distribution network of Value Added Partners throughout Europe, Japan, the US, and Brazil with a focus on adding new distributors in Australia and Mexico by Q4 2004.

Leadership

- Attracted, hired, and currently direct a talented team of business development representatives in each major international market (Brazil, Canada, Europe, Japan and the US) – successfully managed HR and corporate issues in all markets.
- Over past 12 months, led team to secure over $4.5 million in major deals with industry leaders AstraZeneca, Lilly, Millennium, Amgen, and Genentech.
- Assisted in the development of new corporate identities to properly manage sales and assets in new global markets.

Executive Vice President, ABC/Previa

1996 to 1998

Executive sales management position responsible for growth in Canadian and US-based International and domestic markets. As key member of the Executive Committee, contributed to the strategic direction of the company and heavily involved in the development, marketing, and sales of new services.

- Grew annual revenues by over 500% from $650,000 to $4 million USD.
- Secured the first million-dollar sale in company history with a major pharmaceutical company.
- Personally conceived, developed, and launched the highly successful Physicians Guide (www.physicianguide.ism).

Executive Vice President, ABC Consulting Group Inc.

1994 to 1996

Recruited to manage P/S/L's syndicated market research service in Canada. Responsible for all strategic growth, introduction of new services, and key account management. Full P&L accountability

- Increased business to represent 60% of the company's total revenue.
- Introduced 3 new services in less than 24 months, including groundbreaking e-marketing research services in the earliest stages of the Internet.

ONTRACK CANADA INC., Oakville, Ontario

Process Reengineering Team Leader

1992 to 1994

Concurrent with role as Group Marketing Manager, assigned to spearhead the complete redesign of OnTrack's marketing strategy and introduce revolutionary new approaches to pharmaceutical marketing. True "green field" opportunity with responsibility for assembling a multifunctional team, conducting upfront research, and leading the strategic and tactical introduction of all new recommendations.

- Coordinated and participated in the *Circle of Excellence*, an intensive 3-day "think tank" to re-engineer the sales and marketing process.
- Developed 175 recommendations for changing or improving existing processes – prioritized and implemented the most important 20% resulting in a revised sales training program, a change in customer identification and recognition, direct savings of over $1 million, a redesign of market research priorities and the introduction of "social marketing".
- Introduced a new "vision" for the sales force, improving customer service ranking from 12th to 3rd in less than 2 years.

Group Marketing Manager

1992 to 1994

Managed the growth and profitability for a group of 6 key brands with combined revenues exceeding $45 million (Isopill SR, Lemuden, Molitil, Danatone, Teracidie, and Pantone CR). Member of senior management team.

- Successfully maximized brand profitability by developing new strategies to renew brand enthusiasm, improving team capabilities, and effectively managing strategic alliances.
- Took a stagnant brand and increased sales by $4 million CAD, the highest level of growth in 3 years.

...3

Marketing Manager   1991 to 1992

Established new brands Tykopec, Lemuden and Molitil to generate over $20 million in revenue. Developed new sales processes and introduced new launch strategies that generated year-over-year growth for new brands and improved results on declining brands.

- Developed and implemented creative marketing strategies, including the successful *Bookends* educational program which resulted in 20% growth over previous year.
- Took a brand with declining NRx and increased share from 18 to 32%.

District Sales Manager   1987 to 1991

Top district performance for 3 consecutive years and the only manager to ever win 3 Summit Club Awards for outstanding district sales performance (1988, 1989, 1990), achieving the highest percentage for exceeding targets.

Training Manager   1986 to 1987

Developed the first comprehensive distance training program for the launch of Isopill SR, the most successful launch in company history.

- Created a curriculum of 3 learning modules and 8 hours of training, trained 80 sales and sales management personnel across Canada over a 4-week period, and introduced mentor programs, field trainers, and positive learning techniques.

*Previous roles include award-winning sales and sales management positions in the pharmaceutical and technology/training industries. "Salesman of the Year" for 1986 for consistent sales overachievement and demonstrated superior presentation and closing skills by winning top-level contracts with **Seagrams** and **Olympia & York**.*

SPEAKING ENGAGEMENTS

Spoken at international events and industry conferences throughout Canada, the US, Europe, Japan, and Buenos Aires. Topics include **Reengineering Marketing Processes**, **Regional Marketing**, **Internet Marketing**, and **Marketing & Patient Compliance**

EDUCATION & EXECUTIVE TRAINING

Strategic Marketing Management Program	University of Toronto
Leadership Training	Di Bianca Berkman
Strategic Presentations Workshop	Dale Carnegie
Searle Management Development Program	Searle Canada
Performance Management	Searle Canada
Persuasive Communications	Garfield / Rega and Associates
Instructional Technique	Freisen, Kay and Associates
Facilitation Skills	A.T. Kearney
APMR *(Accredited Pharmaceutical Manufacturing Rep)*	Pharmaceutical Manufacturers Association of Canada
B.Sc. (Chemistry) Program	McMaster University

DR. LESLIE R. TENNISON

PHD BIOCHEMISTRY • MSC CHEMISTRY • DIPMNGT

20 Calderhall Avenue, Toronto, ON M1M 1M1 • Tel: 416.555.1234 • lrt@careerprocanada.ca

Dedicated scientist with executive managerial experience.

Diverse background in chemistry and biochemistry. Worked with and for national and international companies and agencies. Led teams of multi-disciplinary groups, including biochemists, microbiologists, geologists, researchers, oil well operators and pollution control experts.

Extensive education includes recent post-doctoral research and degrees in Chemistry and Biochemistry involving petrochemical and medical research. Highly experienced in laboratory work, simulated field conditions and field work under adverse conditions.

EDUCATION

Post-Doctoral Research Work – University of Toronto, Ontario, Canada *(2003)*

DipMngt (Diploma in Management) **–** School of Economics, London, England *(1992)*

PhD in Biochemistry – Lakehead University, Alberta, Canada *(1989)*

MSc in Chemistry – Lakehead University, Alberta, Canada *(1978)*

ADVANCED COURSES

- Chemistry and Cementation Techniques of High-Temperature High Pressure Oil Wells
- Oil Field Pollution and Their Solutions
- Hydrogen Sulphide Detection
- Off-shore Management and Maintenance of Water Quality
- Application of Microbiology in Petroleum Exploration

CAREER

Post-Doctoral Researcher
Toronto Institute of Biotechnical Sciences, Cecil Centre
University of Toronto, Ontario, Canada

June 2003 – Present

Microbiological and Immunological studies (Department of Immunology): Research on the native microflora in the water injection system.

- Evaluated the affectivity of different biocides for the effective control of aerobic and anaerobic bacteria.

May 2000 – June 2003

Bio-mass and Bio-fuels (Fuel Research Group): Studied generation and comparative yields of bio-diesel from biomass samples (tundra vegetation).

- Developed the techno-economic feasibility report for mass production of bio-fuels.
- Researched universal characterization of coke structures.
- Conducted study of Catalysis in Fluidized Catalytic Cracking and Microactivity Test Reactor.

Achievements

- Modelled stripping process and evaluated Microactivity Test Reactor performance.
- Discovered a new approach to catalyst regeneration using hydropyrolysis.
- Characterised hard and soft solvent coke structures.

Page 1 of 2

Researcher. This researcher transitioning into a management role chooses a comfortable mix of personality and experience for his profile rather than just listing scientific data. The résumé includes his "Professional Memberships" to show that he is well connected with contacts in both industry and academia.

CAREER CONTINUED

Director – Chemical Division
National PetroGas, Fort William, Alberta, Canada
December 1985 – April 2000

Decision-making on crucial technical and financial issues for this Fortune 500 company with a turn-over of more than $3.5 billion. Led teams of scientists involved in both Research & Development and Field Operations in various projects throughout western Canada, including:

2000   **Water Quality Studies** – Research Institute Project (3 months)
Senior Scientist in charge of a team of ten scientists involved in ISO-9001 certified project. Monitored and determined oil contents and pollution parameters of waste water. Resolved saturates and mono/dia/triaromatics.

1997 – 2000   **Geochemical and Pollution Studies** – Tar Sands Project
Led a 15-member team of scientists and drilling operators working on effluent water studies, gas analysis, design of cement slurries, drilling fluids properties, activated production systems and drilling high-temperature/high-pressure well. Awarded commendation for dedication and excellent results.

1992 – 1997   **Microbial Enhanced Recovery** – Pilot Project
Headed 7-member scientific team. Initiated and designed project and successfully implemented it in the field. Isolated, screened and identified suitable cultures. Evaluated desirable metabolites. Developed thermophilic cultures. Designed biocide treatment for water injection schemes and prepared follow-up studies. Controlled populations in sulphur recovery units and developed sulphur oxidizing bacteria to meet pollution control specifications.

1986 – 1992   **Research & Development / Operational Chemistry** – Alberta Project
Team leader of 10-member scientific/production/drilling operations team. Planned and designed drilling and monitored and maintained drilling fluids. In charge of research and development on effluent treatment plant and scale inhibitors. Monitored operational set-ups modified on the basis of studies of demulifiers.

PROFESSIONAL MEMBERSHIPS

PetroGas Institute (Canada)

Institute of Oil and Gas Production Technology (UAE)

The Institute of Petroleum (UK)

Society of Petroleum Engineers (University of Toronto, Ontario, Canada)

DALE EVANS

111 Wilson Lane, Toronto, Ontario M1M 1M1
Home: 416.555.1234 Cell: 416.555.2345
Email: devans@CareerProCanada.ca

SENIOR SALES EXECUTIVE

Industrious, tenacious, challenge-driven senior sales professional with strong business acumen; acknowledged for working diligently with cross-functional personnel to provide optimum results. Inspirational team builder; provides the motivation and tools for staff to deliver and excel. Loyal, ethical, flexible; interacts well with all levels, thrives in a fast-paced environment of ongoing change. Resourceful, project driven, highly organized and efficient. Articulate communicator and negotiator; exudes energy and confidence to sell. Visionary; predicts future needs, in response to new product development and buying patterns. Core business expertise includes:

- Business Development
- Life Cycle Development
- Conflict Management
- Sales & Marketing
- Relationship Management
- Contract Management

PROFESSIONAL EXPERIENCE

Dysco Canada Limited, Toronto, Ontario   1999 - present
VICE PRESIDENT, BUSINESS DEVELOPMENT
Dysco Canada offers a face-to-face sales force to generate business-to-business or business-to-consumer sales. Dysco clients pay commission on the sales produced. On a local, North American and International scale, Dysco specializes in gaining a fast and measurable advantage for clients particularly in the telecom, retail energy, office products and financial sectors.
- Charged with sourcing and securing new accounts from potential clientele around the world requiring Dysco's unique and exemplary services.

Key accomplishments have included:
- Recruited to expand business operations and replicate the successful U.K. charity business operations. Process included: Conducting an appraisal of the legalities and sales strategies in a sensitive and competitive charitable giving environment.
- Conceived and developed viable and adaptable strategies to apply the process to the North American market.
- Actively researched prospective new clients in the not-for-profit sector. Captured all the initial 7 targeted potential clients including the following prestigious clients to commence charity operations in Canada: The Hospital for Sick Children, The Cancer Society, Arthritis Society and Reach for the Stars.
- Accredited for producing the following outstanding results:

Year	# of new monthly donors	Average monthly donation	Yearly value for charity
2002*	8,525	$5.13	$524,799
2003	24,049	$10.37	$2,992,657
2004	37,995	$14.07	$6,415,075
2005**	36,433	$17.73	$7,751,485

* Partial year testing phase   ** Actual Jan-Sept estimates from Oct – Dec

- Approached Office Supplies with a proposal to outsource sales of various products to the Dysco sales teams located in Vancouver, Toronto and Sweden. Worked with diverse personnel from Office Supplies and Dysco to develop the financial modelling, and define sales strategies to entice prospective clients into long term contracts versus a trial contract with a high churn rate. Sales program expanded into Sweden in November 2003 in partnership with The Tiger Group.
- Worked with diverse energy suppliers across North America after deregulation to act as their acquisition agents. Secured over 100,000 new gas and electricity clients for suppliers since 2000.
- Facilitate interactive presentations utilizing PowerPoint at the Board level.
- Control 30 independent sales offices across North America each with 10 to 40 staff.

Sales and Business Development Executive. This executive tightly focuses his résumé on sales and business development. The Dysco story unfolds with a strong company context clarifying the purpose of the organization and the individual's role, which seamlessly lead into tangible accomplishments.

DALE EVANS |

Dysco, VICE PRESIDENT, BUSINESS DEVELOPMENT...continued
- Co-conceived, co-designed and co-implemented the "Save & Play" (www.saveandplay.com) fundraising product generating sales in excess of **$1.5 million** per month providing **$6 million** to charity partners since 2000.
- Conduct extensive reviews into trends within the core industries; analyze giving and buying patterns and the impact on revenue in the different European and North American cultures.
- Oversee the development, marketing material, printing and third party verification.

Tilest Brokers Ltd., Toronto, Ontario   1988 - 1999
Held the following progressively responsible positions:
VICE PRESIDENT & MANAGER, DERIVATIVE PRODUCTS   1996 - 1999
- Recognized for capturing Tilest's largest trade from a major Canadian Chartered Bank through patiently and methodically working to define their needs, building sound rapport and gradually increasing trades, generating $69,000 in one trade.
- Increased desk revenue by 38%, developed business relationships with existing customers.
- Managed a busy, deadline-driven derivative desk, including future rate agreements, interest rate swaps, caps, floors, swaptions and bonds.
- Acted as the key intermediary with the Investment Dealers Association.

VICE PRESIDENT & ASSISTANT MANAGER, DERIVATIVE DESK   1992 - 1996
- Acknowledged by peers for outstanding work with the promotion to V.P. level within 2 months of appointment as Assistant Manager.
- Successfully co-led a merger between 2 separate operating entities within the parent company.
- Played a key team member role tasked with creating and implementing the employee "Mentor" program, assisting several new employees through the initiative.
- Selected by senior management for promotion to run the Derivatives Desk while continuing to be responsible for bond trades.

SENIOR BROKER, SHORT BOND DESK   1991 - 1992
- Accountable for covering large domestic and international bond trading accounts, successfully executing their bond trading strategies.

INTERMEDIATE BROKER, SHORT BOND DESK   1990 - 1991
- Covered the medium-sized domestic and international banks and investment dealers, executed their trades through the Tilest system.

OPERATIONS CLERK/TRAINEE BROKER/JUNIOR BROKER   1989 - 1990
- Learned all aspects of the Canadian bond market in a deadline-driven and hectic environment.

Newmarket Honda, Newmarket, Ontario   1987 - 1988
SALES EXECUTIVE
- Accredited for selling 20 new and used vehicles in 9 months.

EDUCATION |

Euromoney International, Toronto, Ontario   1992
DERIVATIVE FUNDAMENTALS

Canadian Securities Institute, Toronto, Ontario   1989
CANADIAN SECURITIES COURSE

York University, Toronto, Ontario   1987
BACHELOR OF ARTS - Economics

VERNON P. DODD, BBA

123 Mulberry Avenue
Vancouver, British Columbia V1V 1V1
E-mail vpdodd@careerprocanada.ca

Phone 604 555-1234
Mobile 604 555-2345
Facsimile 604 555-3456

HIGHLY ACCOMPLISHED SALES & MARKETING MANAGER

Revenue Generation ◇ Market Expansion ◇ Profit Growth ◇ Bottom-Line Results

Top-performing professional with extensive experience and verifiable achievements in the full scope of business-to-business sales and marketing. Talent for identifying and maximizing new business opportunities. Outstanding presenter and negotiator with the demonstrated ability to sell ideas, concepts, and programs to senior-level executives. Expert at developing superior relationships with multi-million dollar clients and service providers. Solid expertise leveraging various media to produce unprecedented results. A collaborative leader, trainer, and team builder, producing top performing employees and teams. Ready and willing to travel. *Demonstrated achievements in:*

◇ Budgeting & Forecasting
◇ Price & Contract Negotiation
◇ Organizational Leadership
◇ Customer-focused Service

◇ New Business Development
◇ Cold Calling & Prospecting
◇ Client Needs Assessment
◇ Solutions Selling

◇ Key Account Management
◇ Relationship Development
◇ Sales Management
◇ Network Development

An impeccable track record of consistently generating year-over-year increases in revenue and profit...

	1997	1998	1999	2000	2001	2002	2003	2004
% vs. LY	266%	167%	250%	120%	125%	113%	103%	114%

CAREER HISTORY

ABC Winning Strategies, Vancouver, British Columbia   **1999 – Present**

Start-up business-to-business marketing communications agency with 4 employees, servicing information technology, travel, airlines, financial, fashion, and health sectors.

Director, Sales & Marketing

Responsible for new business development, sales, and marketing of the organization with a revenue target of $1 million. Hire, train, and oversee 3 employees. Solicit new business through referrals and network of contacts. Manage existing clientele. Develop proposals. Prepare and perform presentations. Negotiate agreements with clients. Resolve technical issues and provide exceptional ongoing customer service.

◇ Created the organization from the ground up and exceeded all revenue targets by personally bringing in 4 multi-million dollar clients in the first year alone.

◇ Hired and trained employees providing them with appropriate leadership and support, producing a highly committed, top-performing team.

◇ Aggressively pursued and won major accounts including a national airline and a high-end Swiss watch manufacturer, doubling revenue and profits for 5 consecutive years.

◇ Negotiated, closed, and coordinated a catalogue development, design, and printing project for an international high-end client for bath and beauty products.

◇ Performed market research and ensured appropriate pricing and positioning, producing the best solution for each individual client, while increasing the profit margin 20%.

◇ Developed strong ongoing relationships with key clients and marketing agencies including American Express, Air Canada, Marketel, and various tourist boards, creating a viable and sustainable organization.

Sales and Marketing Director. The chart effectively divides the power statement from the body of the résumé, while highlighting consistent year-over-year increases in revenue.

VERNON P. DODD, BBA

CAREER HISTORY (CONTINUED)

XYZ Solutions Ltd., Helsinki, Finland   **1995 – 1998**

Start-up marketing agency with 5 employees supplying promotional products to corporate clients.

Director, Sales & Marketing

Retained to grow the organization reporting directly to the President and CEO. Performed new business development and oversaw existing accounts. Managed and budgeted the full scope of client projects; determined client campaign needs and researched suitable products. Primary contact for customer relations.

◇ Implemented promotional campaigns for major corporations such as the Finland Post, several banks, and insurance companies, bringing success and visibility to these organizations.

◇ Developed Requests for Proposals (RFP) and performed client presentations, exceeding all targets by generating $600k revenue.

◇ Established an exemplary reputation for the organization, successfully positioning it for purchase by a major marketing agency.

Previous Position Held

◇ Mecca Insurance Co., Insurance Inspector, Recipient of Various Sales and Marketing Awards

FORMAL EDUCATION & PROFESSIONAL DEVELOPMENT

Ryerson Polytechnic University, Toronto, Ontario   **1999**

◇ Business Management

Helsinki School of Business, Helsinki, Finland   **1992**

◇ Bachelor of Business Administration (BBA)

COMPUTER SKILLS

Proficient in a variety of software applications including:

◇ Microsoft Office Suite (Word, Excel, PowerPoint, and Publisher)

◇ Desktop Publishing (Adobe Photoshop, Illustrator, PageMaker, Acrobat, and Quark)

PROFESSIONAL AFFILIATIONS

◇ Canada Finland Chamber of Commerce (CFCC), Member of the Board of Directors, Chair

◇ European Union Chamber of Commerce in Vancouver (EUCOCIV), Member

Revenue Generation ◇ Market Expansion ◇ Profit Growth ◇ Bottom-Line Results

NORMAN ROGERS

111 Sunnyvale Circle Burlington, Ontario L1L 1L1, Canada
Phone: 905-555-1234   E mail: n.rogers@CareerProCanada.ca

SALES & MARKETING

Highly efficient and effective, "results and challenge driven" executive. Strong business acumen and diverse knowledge encompassing a number of critical business areas, with an emphasis on sales and marketing. Recognized for tackling and resolving hard issues affecting business operations; patient and methodical, task oriented – consistently exceeds expectations. Visionary and strategic thinker; critically analyzes issues before making decisions. Works judiciously to become an expert in all assigned projects; sets and maintains high standards. Exudes energy and confidence to excel and deliver. Articulate and effective presenter and negotiator; builds synergy and rapport with persons of all levels and backgrounds. Core business expertise includes:

- Business Development
- Cross Matrix Operations
- Systems Integration
- Strategic Planning
- Client Relations & Retention
- Project Management
- Change Management
- Technology Transfer
- Resource Management

PROFESSIONAL EXPERIENCE

Core Engineering Inc., Hamilton, Ontario, Canada   1999 – Present
SALES & MARKETING MANAGER – Network Management, Utilities
- Conceived and developed, in collaboration with Engineering Manager, a financial business model to realign financial strategies and meet annual targets in a very difficult and turbulent economy with numerous competitors. Adjustment resulted in reducing sales and administration costs by 10%, increasing cost recovery by 15%, improving cash flow by 25% and elevating the scope of work on one key project by 400%. Success led to presentation of paper "Use of Automation to Maximize Asset Productivity" at 3rd party executive seminar.
- Played a pivotal role in negotiating diverse contracts, co-ordinated with the corporate centres of excellence in Houston, Raleigh, Frankfurt, Moscow, Sydney, Oslo and Helsinki, to prepare contracts; met with clients to define needs and worked judiciously to match their specific requests and budgets.
- Appointed by the Vice President Automation as the executive sponsor to prepare a scope of work document for a vital project for Toronto Power; project realized $250,000.
- Directly attributed with the following statistics for 1999 - 2002:

Retained clients	New account growth	Sales & Admin costs	Recovered operational costs	Cash flow improvement	Largest scope of work change
100%	150%	(10)%	15%	25%	473%

- Accredited with selling the first wireless/solar powered application, a dam breach safety system to Ontario Hydro, valued at $300,000. Sale leveraged by utilizing Ontario Hydro contacts.
- Interacted with diverse, cross-functional decision makers within the Ontario, Alberta and Latin America supply and demand side electrical deregulation markets to outline the transition of operations and services and to capture possible business opportunities.
- Led a front-end engineering and design project for a $1 million modernization and power generation upgrade for Clayboss. Project included: cost and benefit analysis on new technology, end-user training, construction and replacement resources.

Buckle McLean Inc., Burlington, Ontario, Canada   1980 – 1999
Held the following five progressively responsible positions prior to acquisition by Core Engineering Inc.:
GENERAL MANAGER   1996 – 1999
- Seconded by Vice President, Sales and Service, Canada, to St. John's, Newfoundland to establish Buckle McLean's presence in the growing oil and gas industry and to initiate a joint venture with Buckle SEA (Nfld.) Limited.
- Spearheaded venture to secure a $12 million contract with Smith and York to supply engineering support services for Hibernia during the capital and operations phase. Led negotiations, won contract in a fiercely competitive market, reviewed specifications, wrote responses and provided all business support and guidance to assigned team.
- Recruited and hired skilled professionals including engineers, software developers and administration personnel to ensure Buckle SEA was able to deal with a diverse corporate culture; cross-trained employees and developed the first off-shore compensation plan for Buckle SEA to meet clients' criteria.
- Conducted a comprehensive operational design for a $2 million asset management system for Terra Nova.

Sales and Marketing Executive. Innovative layout of the candidate's contact information incorporates his target area of expertise. All section headers display a graphic design that is consistent with original contact information motif.

NORMAN ROGERS

- Acted as Project Manager, automation systems installation for the first Canadian transshipment terminal, a brand new facility designed to expedite cargo from shuttle tankers to ocean going tankers.
- Accountable as the company's leader in St. John's for directing Buckle SEA's growth, evidenced by the following statistics:

Year	Revenue	Annual	Retained clients	New Clients	Service revenue/employee	Chargeable time recovered	Profit (cap)
1999	$14,000,000	280%	100%	100%	$202,188	97.8%	10%
1998	$10,000,000	250%	100%	150%	$195,919	101.1%	10%
1997	$4,000,000	5000%	100%	200%	$189,476	95.1%	10%
1996	$80,000						

- Partnered with Memorial University of Newfoundland and College of the North Atlantic to assist them in graduating students proficient in current industrial market trends and skill sets. Worked with academia to strategize and execute new methods to secure government funding.
- Acknowledged for a 100% incident free safety and environmental record.

BUSINESS DEVELOPMENT MANAGER   1993 – 1996

- Recognized for instilling confidence and motivation in staff to succeed and deliver, achieving sales in the nuclear utility installation business sector, despite a rationalization program.
- Consistently exceeded sales quotas by 12% across the diverse industrial and manufacturing markets.
- Introduced the executive account manager role, tasked with targeting clients within defined business opportunity areas, resulting in an unprecedented 200% increase in revenue at a 25% profit margin.
- Acknowledged for patiently and methodically working to successfully acquire a contract in a new market segment for a gas turbine governor system sold to Alberta Power for $1 million.
- Played the key role in initiating a new service for Bowmar Inc., providing engineering design and service support for the client's Fort Francis plant, elevating plant efficiency and increasing client's revenue by $500,000, reducing sales and marketing costs and lowering liabilities.

Year	Bookings	Annual	Retained clients	New clients
1996	$10,800,000	108%	100%	110%
1995	$10,000,000	105%	94%	112%
1994	$9,500,000	106%	100%	107%

SENIOR ACCOUNT MANAGER   1987 – 1993

- Assigned by Regional Manager to augment underperforming sales staff, leading to a full-time direct sales position.
- Responsible for preparing and delivering a proposal to capture business from a competitor in the pulp and paper industry; won $400,000 contract at a 30% premium over incumbent. Contract resulted in numerous additional projects.
- Researched and identified profitable new business opportunities throughout the northern Ontario pulp and paper industry. Obtained several lucrative contracts through patiently and diligently working with prospective clients to meet their requirements.

REGIONAL ENGINEER – PROJECT DEVELOPER   1980 – 1987

- Selected to present a paper at the IEEE annual convention, 1986, resulting in a substantial business partnership with Jamesbark Consulting. Alignment with Jamesbark resulted in five $1 million projects.
- Prepared engineering and costing specifications for sales staff, acted as the technical support during sales negotiations.

EDUCATION

New Brunswick Community College, Saint John, NB   1980
DIPLOMA – Electronic Engineering Technology

Strong proponent of continuing education and updating skills. Selected courses, workshops and seminars include:

- Open Market Competitiveness
- Managing for Success
- System Integration
- Psychology of Selling

- Process Variability Reduction
- Team Building
- Regional Economic Partnering
- Target Marketing

- Alliance Responsibilities
- Frontier Industry Growth
- Process Optimization
- Emergency Preparedness

DENNIS G. HARRIS

111 Oak Tree Court, Ottawa, Ontario K1K 1K1
Phone: 613.555.1234 Office: 613.555.2345   E mail: dharris@CareerProCanada.ca

VICE PRESIDENT SALES

Dynamic, bilingual, challenge and results-driven senior sales executive with an exemplary background of elevating revenue and market share and capitalizing on business opportunities for profit and growth. Drives competitive advantage; visionary, thinks outside the box; acknowledged for consistently exceeding sales quotas and expanding company horizons. Articulate, tactful and diplomatic communicator and negotiator; proactive leader, charismatic team builder who motivates and empowers staff to succeed and deliver; manages and recruits sales teams across North America. Understands operational excellence; strong business acumen, exudes energy and confidence to excel and deliver. Core business competencies include:

• Channel Management	• Driving Growth
• Contract Negotiations	• Dealer Relationships
• North American Sales	• Marketing & Advertising
• Strategic Business Development	• Team Development & Leadership

PROFESSIONAL EXPERIENCE

CA TelNetCom (Canada) Inc., Ottawa, Ontario   2000 – Present
DIRECTOR – SALES, NORTH AMERICA
- Recruited as the company's first Canadian employee, acknowledged for developing the Canadian marketplace into an integral and profitable entity within the overall company infrastructure.
- Accountable for boosting the market share in Canada by 6% from $5 million revenue to $12 million U.S. within 18 months.
- Selected by President, CA TelNetCom, due to extraordinary work record and sales accomplishments to assume control of the U.S. sales operations in addition to responsibility for Canadian operations.
- Accredited with playing the leadership role in CA TelNetCom, achieving the following impressive results:

Fiscal Year	Forecast USD	Achieved USD	Variance +/- USD	Percent	New Market Share	Previous Year
CA TelNetCom Inc. (Canada)						
2002	$5,000,000	$5,150,000	$150,000	3.0%	31%	31%
2003	$5,750,000	$7,745,250	$1,995,250	34.7%	34%	31%
2004	$8,500,000	$10,786,500	$2,286,500	26.9%	37%	34%
2005	$12,000,000	$13,056,000	$1,056,000	8.8%	39%	37%
CA TelNetCom Inc. (United States of America)						
2004	$60,000,000	$61,020,000	$1,020,000	1.7%	43%	42%
2005	$69,000,000	$69,690,000	$690,000	1.0%	44%	43%

- Source Distributors through research and extensive networking; qualify, project annual turnover, work in partnership with them to build, develop and exceed forecasts and create unique marketing strategies aimed at targeted end users.
- Worked with U.S. based senior executives to recognize Canada as a viable and expanding market, convinced team to finance marketing strategies. Created and implemented aggressive marketing campaigns designed to elevate presence in a competitive industry.
- Direct recruitment for sales staff; manage, train, mentor and monitor 3 Regional Sales Managers in Canada and 8 in U.S. Manage the Toronto Service Centre with 5 technicians, 1 supervisor and 1 shipper.
- Attributed with leading all of the Canadian sales staff to become recipients of the "President's Club" award for exceeding sales by 125%.
- Represent CA TelNetCom at trade and vendor shows across North America, provide sound advice and interactive product presentations to prospective clients.

Sales Director. The tables on this résumé successfully highlight year-over-year results in a visual manner.

DENNIS G. HARRIS
Page Two

Canadian Tire Acceptance Ltd., Welland, Ontario   1994 – 2000
NATIONAL SALES MANAGER
- Recognized for boosting the Canadian Tire credit card's presence in store through negotiating agreements with the Canadian Tire Owners Association to be more proactive in its approach to having sign up booths close to front doors. Profitable working relationship with owners to partner with them resulted in propelling in-store booths from 100 to 325.
- Supervised, trained and motivated 5 Outside Sales Representatives, 2 Inside Sales Support staff.
- Assigned to oversee the negotiations with owners to install ING ATM machines in selected stores. Facilitated presentations to store owners across Canada, secured support to install 258 ATMs, a major accomplishment and concession by owners resistant to change.
- Achieved the following unprecedented elevation in Canadian Tire card acquisition:

Fiscal Year	Forecast	Achieved	Variance +/-	Percent	New Market Share	Previous Year
NEW Canadian Tire Acceptance Retail Card Acquisitions						
1995	410,000	466,990	56,990	13.9%	30%	28%
1996	480,000	566,880	86,880	18.1%	32%	30%
1997	590,000	709,770	119,770	20.3%	33%	32%
1998	715,000	890,890	175,890	24.6%	36%	33%
1999	930,000	1,129,950	199,950	21.5%	37%	36%
2000	1,120,000	1,408,960	288,960	25.8%	39%	37%
Canadian Tire Options Master Card (Canada Only)						
1995	125,000	137,500		10.0%	0%	0%
1996	150,000	174,600		16.4%	0%	0%
1997	275,000	333,850		21.4%	0%	0%
1998	400,000	451,600		12.9%	0%	0%
1999	450,000	515,700		14.6%	4%	2%
2000	510,000	579,870		13.7%	6%	3%

Bell Mobility Paging, Barrie, Ontario   1992 – 1994
REGIONAL DEALER MANAGER – Central Ontario
- Recruited to expand the paging business in an underperforming area, Central Ontario.
- Sourced and signed 90 new dealership agreements, generating an extra $1 million in revenue.
- Exceeded sales quotas by 45.3%, realizing the maximum annual bonus.

Cantel Paging, Truro, Nova Scotia   1991 – 1992
SALES/APPROVED AGENT REPRESENTATIVE
- Recruited to develop untapped territory, increased dealers from zero to 75 within one year.

Canadian Armed Forces   1984 – 1989
MILITARY POLICE OFFICER

EDUCATION

Algonquin College, Ottawa, Ontario   1984
DIPLOMA – Law & Security Administration.

Strong proponent of continuing education. Successfully completed numerous courses in the following:

Executive Leadership	Business Relationship Management	Team Building
Negotiation Skills	Sales Techniques	Front Line Leadership

DENNIS BROHMAN

31 Augusta Road S.W.
Toronto M1M 1M1

dbrohman@careerprocanada.ca

Phone: (416) 333-4444
Cellular: (416) 555-7777

SENIOR SALES EXECUTIVE
Specializing in High-Tech Business Development & Key Account Management

★ RECIPIENT OF OVER 28 AWARDS FOR EXTRAORDINARY SALES PERFORMANCE ★

TOP-PRODUCING SALES EXECUTIVE with career expertise managing key accounts and generating outstanding revenue gains in the IT industry. Combines outstanding customer needs assessment and solutions selling skills with advanced negotiation and relationship management capabilities. High-level understanding of complex systems management, networks, databases, mainframe, and distributor products and software. Outstanding leadership, communication, and presentation skills. Fluent English and French.

SALES ACHIEVEMENTS

➤ **9 "GOLDEN SALES" AWARDS, granted to top 10% for extraordinary sales achievement and leadership**
➤ **19 "100% TEAM" AWARDS for sales results above quota**
➤ *Recent sales results include*:

YEAR	% OF QUOTA	YEAR	% OF QUOTA
2005	**145% YTD**	2001	**177%**
2004	**271%**	2000	**189%**
2003	**152%**	1999	**168%**

PROFESSIONAL EXPERIENCE

SOLOTECH CORP.
Exemplary career in the sales and marketing of IT solutions across a wide variety of hardware and software lines. Rapid advancement through increasingly responsible sales account, executive, and leadership positions on the strength of solid relationship building skills and consistent ability to exceed revenue targets.

CONSULTING SALES EXECUTIVE – Copernicus Systems Inc., Toronto, Ontario   2000 – Present
Copernicus Systems Inc. is a wholly owned SoloTech subsidiary marketing integrated IT Systems Management software solutions.

Charged with the sale and account management of multi-million dollar enterprise IT solutions to key corporate accounts across financial, insurance, and telecommunications industries. Promoted through Sales Executive (2000) and Senior Sales Executive (2001) positions. Scope of responsibility includes account ownership, business development, strategic sales planning, team leadership (10 direct reports), consultation on client business casing, and negotiations.

• Successfully built entire client base from scratch by establishing solid relationships with client executive team, selling expertise, and delivering powerful multimedia presentations on Copernicus' integrated solutions.
• Established key business relationships with SoloTech Business Partners and SoloTech Global Services to deliver complimentary services and technology components.
  ➤ **Within first year, single-handedly sold key corporate accounts and effectively realized 148% of sales targets**
  ➤ **Continued to over-achieve all targets in subsequent years – 271% (2003), 145% YTD (2004)**

...2

Sales Executive. This executive boasted an award-wining career with fantastic sales results. He highlights his impressive number of sales awards upfront. His results are impressive and consistent enough for him to showcase them in a chart.

SOFTWARE ACCOUNT MANAGER, Toronto, Ontario   1998 – 2000

Managed all sales, sales strategy, and account management of enterprise database and applications development software products (DB2, Java). Responsible for negotiating complex software solutions and supporting services to major players in the financial services industry. Focused on the development of solid client relationships and assistance with business case development to correctly identify specific client architecture, resource, and service requirements. Assembled and led a team of 6 Technical Specialists.

➢ **Achieved sales results of 168% (1998) and 189% (1999)**

PROGRAM MANAGER, NORTH AMERICA – Software Development Labs   1997

Specifically recruited to manage internal sales and marketing of new Database and AS/400 software applications throughout U.S. and Canadian markets. Developed and delivered highly effective sales presentations promoting software capabilities and illustrating sales potential.

➢ **Introduced creative incentive program resulting in a significant sales increase across market.**

BUSINESS DEVELOPMENT MANAGER, Quebec City   1992 –1997

Promoted to run Quebec SoloTech branch, focusing on the management and development of all mainframe and associated software sales to key government ministry accounts. Unique client group required patience, persistence, high degrees of creativity, and solid relationship building, negotiation, and business casing skills. Success hinged on ability to recognize and market to unique government requirements, anticipate and work within strict budget restrictions, and negotiate creative leasing/financing options. Full management and leadership responsibilities for team of 10 System Engineers and 6 Sales Representatives.

➢ **Consistently exceeded sales targets, averaging 128% over six years.**

ACCOUNT MANAGER, Vancouver, British Columbia   1986 – 1992

Recruited to take over mainframe sales and manage multi-million dollar financial and commercial accounts. Responsible for all front-end sales, relationship building, and account management.

➢ **Consistently exceeded targets, averaging 148% over six years.**

Previous experience produced exceptional sales results in the following positions:

Account Manager (251%)	Senior Sales Representative (194%)
District Marketing Specialist (110%)	Sales Representative (245%)
Sales Manager (112% avg)	

PROFESSIONAL DEVELOPMENT

• SoloTech Management Series – Levels I & II	• Negotiation & Soft Selling
• CRM Practices	• Selling E-Business
• Solutions Selling Process	• Messaging and Collaboration Sales – Lotus
• Advanced Selling Methodology	• IT Systems Management Principles

PERSONAL ACHIEVEMENTS / ACTIVITIES

➢ Private Pilot Licence – over 5000 flying hours
➢ Skydiving – over 350 jumps
➢ Additional interests include rock climbing (indoor and outdoor), equitation, mountain biking, and boating.

Outstanding professional references available upon request.

Jason Mao

#111 -1234 Richmond Street • London • ON • N1N 1N1 • CANADA
Tel: 519 555-1212 • Email: jmao@CareerProCanada.ca

SATELLITE ENGINEERING / MULTI-SITE MANAGEMENT / INNOVATION / CHANGE MANAGEMENT / TRAINING & DEVELOPMENT

Results-driven Satellite Engineer with comprehensive experience in Technology, Team Leadership, Training, and Management • Proven ability to troubleshoot and manage multi-site operations, using creative and innovative solutions • Capacity to increase performance and efficiency through resourceful Change Management • Experience across diverse corporate cultures • Fluency in English and Mandarin

EDUCATION

School of Business, London, Ontario, Canada   2004 – 2006
Master of Business Administration – Candidate 2004
    General Management Concentration, Member of Soccer and Consulting Clubs

Institute of Technology, China
Master of Aerospace Engineering – Top 5%   1999
Bachelor of Science in Engineering – Top 10%   1994
1st Rank People's Scholarship (highest academic award in China), Student Union President

PROFESSIONAL EXPERIENCE

Chinese Space Institute, Beijing, China   1997 – 2003
CSI is China's sole spacecraft designer, manufacturer, and launcher
Senior Director of Technology Management & Training Centre
Supervised three technology training programs, each of which provided training on updated technology developments to 500 space scientists and engineers per year; analyzed strengths and weaknesses in company technology and status updates for big contract bids; recommended strategies in technology development to senior management, and collaborated with University of Florida, Alabama University, and two US space centres:

- Successfully managed 89 staff members in 14 branches, based in five cities.
- Developed an Internet database (which was adopted by the Chinese Aerospace industry) to collect and update necessary information for company technology training.
- Negotiated contracts with China TV, Film and Radio Broadcast Department; initiated and maintained long-term relationships with DEC, IBM, CISCO, HP and other local suppliers.

Peking Academy of Space Engineering and Technology, China   1994 – 1997
PASET is a subsidiary of CSI and responsible for spacecraft design
Chief Engineer, Satellite Thermal Control Designing Group
Managed the design process, drafted the work plan, delegated tasks, negotiated with clients, and supervised quality control:

- Led a 10-member team to successfully design two satellites' thermal-control designs for FH-1 & BD-1 satellites, ultimately saving $2M US per design.
- Worked with a team of six engineers to develop the method of *Satellite Thermal Control Designing*; successfully designed and conducted large thermal-control design testing experiments, which resulted in $400,000 US per design.

OTHER

Proficient in Internet research, *MS Word, Excel, MS Project, AutoCAD,* and *Windows XP*
Member of Project Management Institute (PMI)

Satellite Technology Leader. This concise résumé works for an experienced senior level technical professional transitioning into Canada. The out-of-country experience and gap in work experience are minimized by outlining his strong educational qualifications first.

Elizabeth A. Howard, MBA

444 Main Street
London, Ontario
N1N 1N1

H: 519.555.1234
B: 519.555.6789
eah@careerprocanada.ca

STRATEGIC MARKETING EXECUTIVE
Specialist in B2C Marketing

Idea-oriented executive credited with leading the strategies that have successfully opened new markets and channels, and generated consistent profitability and market share growth. Balances a strong entrepreneurial and conceptual mindset with a focus on optimizing efficiency and productivity. Diagnostic ability to match products to markets, create the vision, and lead teams through deployment and growth. Adept at leading initiatives within complex organizations and a recognized expert in internal and external communications. Effective business manager with proven P&L, operational and staff management skills.

AREAS OF EXPERTISE

- Strategic Planning & Positioning
- Brand & Reputation Management
- Unit & Budget Management
- Business Development
- Assessments & Reviews
- Communications & PR
- Leading New Initiatives
- Channel & Sales Management
- Staff & Stakeholder Leadership

MARKETING HIGHLIGHTS

- Key strategic player in the emergence of Premiere Trust following deregulation in 1992 – orchestrated the entire go-to-market plan for this new line of business; led it to **gain $1 billion in assets a full year ahead of schedule**

- Helped conceive and manage Canada's first major Estate Management channel for Premiere Finance – realized a **200% increase in volumes in first year**, with portfolio eventually growing to **exceed $3 billion**.

- As a Principle with Waterdown Consulting, aided major corporations in new channel assessment and development, exit and growth strategies, product launches, and e-marketing campaigns – clients include **Bank of Ontario**, **Big Box Retail**, and the **Canadian Finance Institute.**

- Currently teach leading-edge communications strategies to MBA and Executive MBA candidates as a faculty member at the Jonathan Riley School of Business (University of Ontario) – **ranked #2 as most quoted academic in the media throughout the university, and #16 in Canada.**

- Author of *E-mail: Managing Your Inbox* (2003, Sanford & Sons U.S.) and recognized expert in email management and communications – book chosen for review by Globe and Mail, National Post, and CA Magazine; routinely consult for clients that include **Inco, Hydro One**, and the **Federal Government.**

PROFESSIONAL EXPERIENCE

JONATHAN RILEY SCHOOL OF BUSINESS, University of Ontario

Professor / Lecturer – Management Communications   1999 – Present

Appointed to design and deliver a series of improved business communications courses for the MBA and Executive MBA programs. Focusing on injecting more real world applicability into the program, developed practical curricula that focus on both internal and external communication strategies, channels, and planning processes that demonstrate how to market to customers, control risk, manage media, create compelling presentations, and enhance overall organizational performance.

- Developed 20 case studies and technical notes currently sold worldwide through the university's publishing arm.

- Created the new Media Relations & Public Affairs course providing hands-on approach to media and crisis communications training.

- Initiated first-ever applied research into email in the workplace and quickly gained global reputation as industry expert in unproductive email practices, root causes, and profitable corporate solutions.

...2

Strategic Marketing Executive. By culling together major marketing achievements and showcasing them up front in the "Marketing Highlights" section, this executive successfully takes the focus away from her most recent faculty position at a well-known university.

WATERDOWN CONSULTING, Toronto, Ontario

Principle, Strategic Consulting   1998 – 1999

Senior consulting role servicing the financial services industry group in the Strategic Change unit. Provided strategic marketing and business development support for high-profile retail, corporate, and financial organizations. Scope of engagements included exit and build/grow scenarios, new business planning, business assessments, e-commerce marketing campaigns, and new channel development. Projects included:

- **Bank of Ontario** – helped develop new multi-million dollar online insurance product line and e-marketing strategy

- **Canadian Finance Institute** – facilitated new strategic visioning and business planning processes

- **Big Box Retail** – consulted on channel marketing initiative to provide selected financial services as part of their existing loyalty program

PREMIERE FINANCE, Toronto, Ontario

General Manager, Marketing – Premiere Trust   1990 – 1997

Selected to lead marketing and distribution strategies for new investment management business lines in anticipation of deregulation. Determined product market, opened up new channels, and helped guide the business from zero sales to breakthrough growth nationally, exceeding $1 billion in assets one year ahead of schedule and consistently exceeded new growth targets by 18-23%.

- Within 3 months, developed and secured immediate approval for the go-to-market plan, including channels, products, opportunities, challenges, pilot program, and launch.

- Re-branded Toronto and Montréal (existing locations purchased from another company) post-deregulation, then co-ordinated rollout to 40 new sales territories across Canada.

- Successfully systematized the channel and branding, becoming the first Premiere subsidiary to successfully manage the referral process from the branches.

- Created innovative new CRM and measurement systems that monitored most profitable clients, sales volumes for 1,200 branches, and tracked both asset migration and cannibalism from competing products – 65% of businesses booked were new assets.

- Recognizing opportunity, successfully commoditized "estate management" – created entirely new channel modelled on best practices in US and UK to become the first multi-million dollar estate business line in Canada.

- Over last 18 months, assumed line of business role focusing on increasing profitability within existing structure – managed P&L across 16 branches nationally with over 300 employees and a $20 million operating budget.

Senior Manager – International Private Banking   1987 – 1990

Promoted into new consulting role charged with enhancing financial operations across 7 global Premiere locations – Hong Kong, Cayman Islands, Singapore, Channel Islands, Bahamas, Bahrain, and London. Integrated global units into Premiere's organizational structure and educated Head Office on how to serve remote units more effectively.

- Consulted with remote locations on reporting and audit functions, local area marketing efforts, market/product assessments, internal process improvements, and HR allocations and expatriate recruiting.

- Overhauled operations in the Cayman Islands location facing record cash losses and security issues – within 6 weeks, systematically eliminated new cash losses, reconciled & recovered 60% of booked losses, eliminated processing bottlenecks, and reorganized the banking division (staff of 45).

Manager – Branch Banking   1981 – 1986

Managed four high-volume branches serving the wealthy, mass/affluent, and commercial segments, including flagship locations at Commerce Court and the Toronto Eaton Centre. Managed an average book of $100 million funds with staff of up to 67. Coordinated all business growth, marketing, sales, and retention strategies for the branch.

- Selected as best qualified Manager to pilot new branch banking system – seamless pilot and conversion encouraged bank to invest $150 million in system that dramatically improved service levels across the organization.

...3

BOOKS, COLUMNS, & SPEAKING ENGAGEMENTS

- **Book Author** – *E-mail: Managing Your Inbox*, Sanford & Sons, New York, 2003
- **Columnist** – "Your E-mail Inbox", *Globe & Mail*
- Quoted in the *National Post, Wall Street Journal, Financial Times (London), Asia Inc., ABCNews.com, Chicago Tribune, L.A. Opinion, Greenville News, Birmingham News*
- Appearances and speaking engagements include *Canada AM, CBC Newsworld, CBC Radio (live interviews and call-in shows), International Association of Business Communicators, Canadian Public Relations Society, Canadian Bankers Association, Human Resources Professional Association of Ontario, Carnegie-Mellon University, University of Arizona*
- Used as media source for **Microsoft Canada's** Office 2003 advertising program

INDUSTRY & COMMUNITY CONTRIBUTIONS

Editorial Board – Business Communication Review   2003 – Present
- Peer-reviewed critique of submissions for publishing, article submissions, and monitoring relevance and direction of this U.K. based publication

Board, Strategic Planning Committee – Wellness Ontario, London, Ontario   2000 – 2003
- Provide strategic marketing assistance to help position and grow this not-for-profit organization operating cancer support (Wellspring) and a 171-bed long-term care facility

Music Committee – Arts & Letters Club of Ontario   1997 – Present
- Contributions to organizational planning, concert events, and other initiatives supporting and enriching music through the organization

Executive Committee, Business Development – Women Entrepreneurs   1998 – 1999
- Led this interdisciplinary association of women entrepreneurs and executives through a strategic planning process

Mentor & Keynote Speaker – "One Step Ahead" Mentoring Program   1999
- Volunteered with mentoring program targeting and supporting women entrepreneurs

EDUCATION

MBA – General Management, University of Western Ontario   1995
Fellow – Institute of Canadian Bankers   1992

MARC BEAULIEU, B. COMM., C.A., C.M.A.

55 Regency Drive
Toronto, Ontario
M1M 1M1

Phone (416) 555-1234
Mobile (416) 555-2345
E-mail m_beau@careerprocanada.ca

TOP PRODUCING SALES, MARKETING & OPERATIONS EXECUTIVE

Dynamic Leadership | Revenue Generation | Market Expansion | Profit Improvement | Bottom-Line Results

Highly accomplished general manager with proven experience accelerating revenue growth, market share, and profitability for a multi-million dollar industry leader. Exemplary academic credentials, bringing a unique combination of business acumen, financial expertise, and common sense to produce both top-line sales and bottom-line results. Energetic relationship builder, with a career-long record of negotiating and closing complex agreements with leading retailers, distributors, and suppliers. An ethical and trustworthy professional, with the uncanny ability to connect with individuals at all levels by engendering trust, confidence, and respect. Bilingual in English and French. Willing to Travel.

Areas of Expertise:

- Profit & Loss Management
- Strategic Business Planning
- Infrastructure Development
- Competitive Market Positioning
- New Business Development
- High-Level Negotiations
- Strategic Partnerships
- Relationship Management
- Entrepreneurial Leadership
- Management & Team Building
- Organizational Development
- Customer-Driven Management

Demonstrated ability to achieve unprecedented results: Doubled revenue to over $250 million in 4 years while maintaining overhead costs and producing year-over-year increases in bottom-line profitability.

CAREER HISTORY

Media Giant Canada, Toronto, Ontario   **2003 - Present**

Canadian Subsidiary of $12 billion International Media Giant, with 5000 employees and global operations encompassing the production, development, and distribution of entertainment technologies in 60 countries worldwide. The Home Entertainment division is the most profitable in International Media Giant.

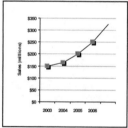

General Manager, Vice President, Canadian Operations

P&L responsibility for the overall operation of the Canadian organization encompassing sales, marketing, and operations. Member of the Board of Directors. Oversee 20 direct reports with offices in Toronto, Montreal, and Vancouver. Develop and achieve an annual sales target of $240 million. Create and execute strategic plans, open new markets, negotiate key client contracts, and service retailers and distributors nationally.

- Converted the operational focus from 'rental' to 'packaged goods' and opened up unconventional markets for DVDs, increasing sales from $150 million to over $250 million in 4 years.

- Crafted a formal business plan for the Canadian office and established an efficient business model focusing on highly effective product lines and strategies, producing outstanding sales and profit margins.

- Restructured organizational responsibilities and streamlined work processes, enabling the organization to decrease overall headcount by 16% while simultaneously doubling revenue.

- Executed comprehensive financial analysis of pricing sensitivity and, as a result, instituted competitive market pricing nationally.

- Established outstanding executive-level relationships with key retailers and distributors in Canada including Wal-Mart, FutureShop, and Shoppers Drug Mart.

- Acquired top 'in-stock' levels in Zellers (in excess of 98%), beating all competitors within the category and ultimately producing both lower merchandising costs and increased sales.

- Instituted extensive revenue sharing deals with Blockbuster and Rogers, enhancing customer satisfaction and boosting top line revenue by 20%.

Continued ➡

Subsidiary General Manager. A strong *Value Proposition* is strategically repeated in the headline and footer of the résumé. The Canadian subsidiary's quantifiable results are listed throughout the résumé drawing the reader in.

MARC BEAULIEU, B. COMM., C.A., C.M.A.

CAREER HISTORY

Media Giant Canada *(continued)*

➡ Attained innovative space deals to create exclusive permanent racking within major players including Best Buy and HMV, generating incremental sales increases of catalogue product.

➡ Scrutinized organizational costs, minimized travel and entertainment expenses, and reduced product returns, which slashed overhead costs and further increased bottom-line profitability.

➡ Spearheaded the formal monitoring and auditing of titles across Canada, which directly resulted in minimizing cross border shipments of product.

➡ Negotiated a new facilities leasing program with a more effective payment structure, saving on average $50,000 in fees.

➡ Oversaw 3rd party logistics supplier processes and activities, ensuring the effective production and distribution of product through various channels.

Top Capital Funds, Toronto, Ontario   **1999 - 2003**
Canadian company providing sophisticated investments in the form of mutual funds and tax shelter deals for high net-worth investors, with revenue in excess of $100 million.

Vice President, Sales

Oversee sales and marketing functions, reporting directly to the President. Deal with a wide range of financial planners and brokers. Preside over sales and communication functions with mutual fund distributors. Plan, develop, and implement viable strategies for the company's investments.

➡ Wrote the business plan, developed the financial model, and created all marketing materials for the company's first mutual fund.

➡ Launched the new publicly traded company specializing in US based mutual funds, successfully positioning it for purchase by the Investment Planning Council of Canada.

➡ Developed highly successful relationships with customers, stockbrokers, and financial planners by performing seminars across Canada, which created new business throughout the brokerage network.

FORMAL EDUCATION, PROFESSIONAL CERTIFICATIONS & AFFILIATIONS

Bachelor of Commerce (B.Comm.), Concordia University, Montréal, Quebec
Diploma in Accountancy, McGill University, Montréal, Quebec
Chartered Accountant (C.A.), CA's of Ontario, Member
Certified Management Accountant (C.M.A.), CMA's of Ontario, Member
Awarded 1st Place in Quebec for the 'Case Portion' of the formal CMA Exam

TECHNICAL SKILLS

Proficient in a wide variety of software applications including:
Microsoft Office Suite (Word, Excel, and PowerPoint)

LANGUAGES

Fluent in English and French.

Dynamic Leadership | Revenue Generation | Market Expansion | Profit Improvement | Bottom-Line Results

GERALD BAKERFIELD

111 Echo Avenue, Toronto, Ontario M1M 1M1
Phone: 416.555.1234   E mail: gbfield@CareerProCanada.ca

Global Financial Perspective

Executive Management • Money Market • Foreign Exchange
Asset Liability Management • Retail Banking

Competent, decisive and dedicated senior financial executive with an extensive knowledge of the global economy. Considered a leader, mentor and motivator; recognized for proactively and efficiently directing a team to deliver results during variances in the economy. Visionary, strategic and conceptual thinker; able to generate new ideas and initiate change. Results driven; works judiciously and methodically to achieve and exceed company mandated goals. Thrives on a challenge; critically scrutinizes and evaluates fiscal statements, liabilities and responsibilities. Combines sophisticated financial expertise with the tactical execution of global, bank wide initiatives to enhance customer service, bank operations and bottom line performance. Culturally sensitive; effective communicator and negotiator; develops profitable rapport with all levels. Unique perspective of the Canadian political environment with respect to the Province of Quebec.

PROFESSIONAL EXPERIENCE

Banca Commerciale Italiana of Canada, Toronto, Ontario   1984 – Present
Held the following progressively responsible positions:
VICE PRESIDENT – TREASURY   1998 – Present
Tasked with proactively contributing to the Bank's objectives by efficiency, expediency and profitability in the Treasury Department through proficient money market, and foreign exchange desk management.
Accomplishments

- Played an active role with the Project Management team in facilitating a relocation of the trading room. Process involved comprehensive needs and facility assessment, staff recruitment and computer systems research, tendering, purchasing and installations. Project completed within budget and strict time schedule.
- Launched a unique Treasury System delivering real time positions, since recognized and installed by bank's Italian head office and other foreign units. System permits an error free capability, increased productivity and more succinct position keeping.
- Contributed to the bank reaching the $2 billion asset level, a first for the Canadian branch. Managed the asset liability portfolios including liquidity, FX and interest rate risk.
- Met the majority of company-defined profit targets during tenure throughout a fluctuating economy.
- Worked with I.T., Risk Management and a Reuters consultant to upgrade the KONDOR+ system from version 1.8 to 2.0. Process involved regressive testing to ensure stable data transfer.

Responsibilities

- Played an active and critical role in the 6 member senior management team. Acted as treasury representative and at times reported in person to Board of Directors.
- Travelled to key Global financial centres ensuring liquidity and to find new financial partners.
- Oversaw all money market and foreign exchange dealing and corporate dealing desks. Monitored market information, variations, bank traders, Reuters News, Dow Jones and print, T.V. media and trade journals.
- Controlled Canadian, U.S. dollar and Euro cash management. Checked the cash position, manipulated cash flow to maintain profitability.
- Managed the treasury's statutory and OSFI, CDIC compliance.
- Administered the Euro currency conversion including pricing and changing FX system from legacy currency consolidations.
- Supervised 10 staff, including Treasury Services, Money Market and Foreign Exchange Managers. Responsible for all human resource issues, recruitment, scheduling, appraisals, budgeting and profit target issues.
- Developed the Y2K Liquidity Contingency Plan in partnership with other departments.
- Liaised with Italian Head Office Departments and Branches, Credit International and Securities and Syndications.
- Handled the $5 million defined benefit plan for the bank's Canadian operations.

Treasury Executive. The distinctive structure within the body of the résumé draws attention to this finance executive's stellar accomplishments by listing them prior to his responsibilities.

GERALD BAKERFIELD

ASSISTANT VICE PRESIDENT – TREASURY   1996 – 1997
Accomplishments
- Oversaw the introduction of the KONDOR+ system which significantly improved accountability, instant market analysis, pricing of products and maintenance of positions. Recognized by the senior management team as an integral component of productivity by reporting improvements and streamlining operations.
- Actively addressed a critical business development issue by leading a team tasked with designing and building a new trading room. Completed on time and within strict budget.

Responsibilities
- Worked judiciously in partnership with Executive Vice President to support the department operations, priorities, objectives and tactical plans.
- Guided the policy and procedure development to support the regulatory authority requirements.

SENIOR DEPARTMENT MANAGER   1989 – 1996
- Promotion recognized as the first Canadian management position to be filled by a non-Italian citizen.
- Selected by senior banking peers to fulfill the Director, Financial Markets Association of Canada (formally FOREX of Canada) position for one year.
- Facilitated the complex centralization of the corporate currency exchange eliminating the retail responsibilities and permitting better management over the foreign exchange and money market clientele.
- Instrumental in raising the Canadian asset level to $1 billion for the first time.
- Implemented the Bank of Canada zero reserve environment.

MONEY MARKET TRADER/FX TRADER   1984 – 1989
- Actively managed the asset and liability gap positions, developed trading relationships to provide access to liquidity.
- Handled customer activity providing information and booking Money Market/FX transactions.

Continental Illinois of Canada, Toronto, Ontario   1981 – 1984
Held the following two positions:
POSITION KEEPER/TRADER
AUDIT OFFICER

Royal Canadian Mounted Police, Regina, Saskatchewan   1981
CONSTABLE
- Successfully completed initial training. Posted to Maple Ridge, British Columbia.

EDUCATION

Strong proponent of continuing education. Relevant financial courses include:

• Canadian Treasury Functions	• Bank of Montreal, Toronto
• Treasury Functions	• Banca Commerciale Italiana, Milan
• Futures	• Dean Witter (Carr Futures), Toronto
• Asset Liability Management	• Risk Conferences Limited

Sheridan College, Oakville, Ontario   1981
CERTIFICATE – Business Administration
Accounting and Finance Major

COMMUNITY INVOLVEMENT

Participated in the Terry Fox Run for 17 of the last 21 years. Raised $15,000 in total, $3,500 in highest year.

Best Cover Letter Samples

KATE BELLERA, BEng.

1-11 Hopewell Circle
Brampton, Ontario • L1L 1L1
(905) 555-0123 • kbellera@careerprocanada.ca

June 15, 2007

Mr. Frank B. Islesworth
President & COO
Recruiters International
111 Yonge Street
Toronto, Ontario M1M 1M1

Dear Mr. Islesworth:

Mr. Islesworth, I was speaking recently with your colleague, John Power, who mentioned that your firm is in need of a reliable professional capable of delivering accurate administrative assistance. In my accompanying résumé, there is verifiable information concerning my ingenuity, efficiency, and accuracy with regard to all aspects of my work performance. I'm a dedicated customer service provider with excellent computer and data management skills. I can be counted on to meet and exceed deadlines, even while juggling a number of tasks at one time.

Prior employers have been impressed with the precision and problem-solving style that I apply to every situation. I have solved numerous concerns, from time planning to process improvement needs. Focused on the end result, I am proficient at researching solutions on the web and in relevant reports and publications.

My technical and service orientation would serve your busy enterprise well. I possess a positive, calm demeanour, which is reassuring to peers and clients alike. These features are enhanced by my complete involvement with, and support for, team and business objectives.

In one company in particular, I was responsible for meeting challenges where there were communication and training issues for personnel with a limited foundation in English. Through a tenacious, careful approach, and active involvement of all employees, I designed manuals and created laboratory-testing records, which incorporated simple points and logical flow. These projects resulted in forms that were valued tools for both staff and management.

In 1999, I completed my Bachelor in Engineering degree. I am proud of this achievement, not only for the education I gained, but also because I followed through on this with determination and perseverance. I have since recognized that my talents for observation, creativity, and detail would be better applied in more direct customer interaction and administrative situations.

Mr. Islesworth, I am able to accept a permanent, full time position starting immediately and would welcome the opportunity of a personal interview. I can be reached at your convenience at the number above or by email. I will make a follow-up call in a week to ensure you have had an opportunity to review my résumé. Your time and consideration of this is appreciated.

Sincerely,

Kate Bellera

Enc. Résumé

Administrative Assistant. The lead-in to this letter identifies a colleague who has referred the individual to the firm. This technique leverages the mutual acquaintance for that all-important interview.

TAYLOR RED

123 A Street North ▪ Saskatoon ▪ Saskatchewan ▪ S1S 1S1
(Home) 306.555.1234 ▪ ired@careerprocanada.ca

June 1, 2007

Martensville Animal Control Agency
1234 Ontario Avenue
Martensville, Saskatchewan S1S 1S1

Re: Dispatcher for Animal Control Officers

I am writing in response to your ad in the Saskatoon Phoenix News for a dispatcher to the animal control officers in your company.

My background is a diverse one, which includes many roles as an exceptional client service representative. You will find me to be an enthusiastic, understanding person who enjoys many challenges. For many years, I have watched documentaries depicting the tragic situations or deplorable conditions in which animal control professionals have discovered animals. It would be an honour to work for an organization that performs such necessary rescues and works with our Humane Society to further awareness of the plight of so many creatures.

My personal and work experiences have showcased my excellent organizational skills. I am a proactive and engaged team player, able to focus on goals and set priorities. Clientele and colleagues alike have commented upon my calm demeanour and tact in defusing sensitive situations. Whether dealing with animals (my own or others) or with people, this latter capability has proven valuable in many situations.

After purchasing a PC and teaching myself Internet searching, e-mail systems and word-processing, I have discovered an aptitude for computer technology. I'm known for my ability to quickly assimilate new accountabilities, and noticed for my accuracy and attention to detail.

With my love and respect for animals, being associated with the Animal Control agency in any capacity would be welcome. I am confident that my experiences and abilities, combined with my enthusiasm, will serve your firm well. I look forward to meeting with you at a mutually convenient time to further discuss my qualifications.

Sincerely,

Taylor Red
Encl.

Animal Control Dispatcher. In paragraph two, the candidate displays her interest in current issues related to animal control, while concurrently demonstrating her respect for the organization and its work.

COURTNEY TRAIN

55 BROOKWOOD DRIVE, APT. 555
DON MILLS, ONTARIO
M1M 1M1

TEL: (416) 555-5555

Bartender / Server

For: A nightclub or hospitality establishment

Please consider this letter of introduction as an expression of my interest in exploring employment opportunities with your organization. I have attached my résumé for your review, citing a detailed overview of my strengths including customer service and my ability to communicate well with the public and staff members.

I believe I can add value as a team member and perform my responsibilities in a professional and timely manner. My experience consists of the ability to prepare accurately measured cocktails, hands-on expertise with the Pro Bar System, knowledge of domestic and imported beers, and the ability to match the type of drink with the type of glass used.

Ultimately, I firmly believe that I am a candidate whom you can come to depend on. I have much to offer and feel that I will benefit a company where I can make a significant work ethic contribution to profits as a resourceful and results-oriented individual. My goal is to work full time on a long-term basis. To date, I have worked in smaller establishments and, at this time, nothing would please me more than to join a larger team of people as I move forward in my working experience.

I very much look forward to hearing from you so that we can schedule an interview to talk about your expectations and the possibility that my abilities are similar to those you are currently seeking to fulfill.

Yours very truly,

Courtney Train

Attachment: Résumé

Bartender. This individual took an interesting approach that does not include any recipient addressing information. As a result, the candidate can easily drop off a copy of the letter and résumé at various nightclubs and other locations in one swift run.

MARK T. HARRINGTON, MBA

12 Top Lane
Toronto, Ontario
M1M 1M1

Phone (416) 555-1212
Cell (416) 555-1234
E-mail mth@careerprocanada.ca

Via e-mail

January 5, 2007

George Main
Executive Recruiter
Recruit Thru Us
123 Main St.
Toronto, Ontario M1M 1M1

Re: Government Services Director – Reference 123

Dear Mr. Main,

As a seasoned Government Services Director with a stellar record of producing results, I can offer the vision and direction required to lead your client to the next level. Anticipating your need for such leadership, I am enclosing a résumé summarizing my qualifications for your review.

As the current Director of Corporate Services within the Northern Ontario Community Centres, I have developed a thorough understanding of the government sector. My core competencies include leading the full scope of financial, human resources, administrative, systems, and facilities management units.

My proven ability to develop effective solutions to complex business challenges sets my performance apart. In my present position and throughout my career, I have played a critical role in leading organizations through a variety of major transformations. By building consensus in supporting the organization's strategic directions and effectively managing change, I have earned a verifiable reputation for consistently converting corporate strategies into tangible results.

Following are some brief highlights of the strengths and experience that I bring to the table:

- Spearheading large-scale corporate mergers and reorganizations to improve operational effectiveness.
- Working closely with Boards and Committees to identify needs and surpass all expectations.
- Understanding and acting on government agenda to obtain funding and service opportunities.
- Coaching, mentoring, and developing employees to instil a team spirit and focused direction.
- Fostering strong alliances with internal and external stakeholders to ensure customer satisfaction.
- Improving financial budgeting, reporting, and controls to effectively contain costs and manage risk.
- Streamlining business processes and utilizing appropriate technology to produce corporate efficiencies.

The key to my success is a collaborative management approach. My colleagues have characterized me as a dedicated and dependable professional with the versatility and flexibility to work effectively with diverse environments and management styles. Finally, my ongoing dedication to professional development is evident as I hold an MBA augmented by university studies in Executive Leadership, Strategic Change, Human Resources, and Information Systems.

Although my present position has been stimulating and fast-paced, at this point in my career I am confidentially exploring a new and interesting challenge where my broad expertise can be fully utilized.

I welcome a personal meeting and will contact you during the week of January 12, so that we can discuss your requirements and my background further.

Thank you for your interest and consideration.

Sincerely,
Mark Harrington

Enclosure

Chief Administrative Officer. This letter clearly indicates the job title and reference number posted by the recruiter. The opening aptly addresses the recruiter by referring to his client. The closing offers a clear date when the candidate will be following up with the recruiter.

MATALADO MACHADO, MBA

1234 Winding River Road
Oakville, Ontario L1L 1L1

Residence: (905) 555-1234
mmachado@careerprocanada.ca

June 15, 2007

Mr. Frank B. Islesworth
President & COO
Recruiters International
111 Yonge Street
Toronto, Ontario M1M 1M1

Dear Mr. Islesworth,

This letter is in response to your search for an executive with proven expertise in varied upper management roles in both the Finance and IT sectors. My experience and verifiable accomplishments match those mentioned and more. As detailed in the enclosed résumé, I have held positions from Senior Management and Vice President through Chief Operating Officer encompassing Human Resources, IT and Finance departments. My successes range from projects of significant proportions saving companies millions of dollars to guiding organizations through mergers and complete corporate restructurings.

The results I drive are accomplished with thorough planning, teamwork, conflict resolution, sensitivity, empathy and the capability to remain calm during intense crises. With a foundation of indisputable ethics and empathy for the concerns and fears in the face of immense change, I engage personnel and clients alike with sincerity and respect, employing humour appropriately to diffuse tension.

Boards of Directors, peers and company employees appreciate my efforts in addressing the human element while ensuring organization-wide revitalization with systems integration. Vigorously, and with utmost integrity, I champion change processes for optimal results in the tightest of time frames. Meeting problems head on and through consensus building, I have launched such enterprising solutions as:

- Order entry websites including online credit card processing, fraud prevention and freight quoting
- International employee benefits programs
- Transborder logistics service
- Employee performance management system and recruiting strategies

At the moment, my salary is in the $150K range. I am flexible on the actual figure of my next role, depending on the total compensation and remuneration offered.

Mr. Islesworth, I have the ability to positively affect any endeavours or substantial changes, which the company in question may be facing. I look forward to an interview, which will allow me to share my background in greater detail and to discuss how I can be a positive force in any organization. I can be reached at my home most evenings. If I have not heard from you within the next week, I shall contact you to arrange the next steps in this process.

Sincerely,

Matalado Machado

Enc. Résumé

Chief Operating Officer. In the fourth paragraph, the candidate reveals his current salary in response to a request in the advertisement. He uses this tactic rather than offering his salary expectations. To invite an interview, he opts to suggest that he is flexible regarding the compensation.

DAVID CHANG

123 Melrose Place, Beverley Hills, California 12345   dchang@careerprocanada.ca   916.555.1234

Great Entertainment Inc.   February 23, 2007
Suite 111, 123 Main Street
Vancouver, British Columbia   V1V 1V1

Attention: Ms. Ruth President
Re: **In-house Corporate Counsel** employment opportunity

Dear Ms. President:

I am an experienced, senior Attorney who has spent over twenty years getting to know the interactive video entertainment industry. I balance an assertive attitude with a sincere desire to mentor my staff to achieve outstanding results on the issues we address. My solid combination of legal insight and negotiation skills has enabled me to handle many different problems confidently, and to provide sensible advice to my clients. When I first spotted the In-house Corporate Counsel opportunity on the Internet, I immediately thought, "This job would be exciting, challenging – a great opportunity to further improve my skills and knowledge in the video entertainment industry."

With a long history of experience in all of the requisite areas, I have a solid grounding in the essential skills that you expect from your In-house Corporate Counsel. I would bring to International Entertainment Inc. the following key strengths:

- A penchant for leadership.
- A passion for constant, continual learning.
- A talent for building harmonious, "win-win" relationships in an adversarial environment.
- Superior communication skills.
- A conscious sense of respect for everyone's efforts in the legal arena.
- The energy required to juggle high-pressure, simultaneous projects.

Although I am currently an American citizen, under NAFTA I qualify for an annually renewable Canadian work permit. I am eligible to receive a permit to act as a Foreign Law Practitioner in British Columbia and, as such, I would be licensed to advise on California and U.S. federal law. Also, I will soon be receiving a Certificate of Qualification (from the National Committee on Accreditation at the University of Ottawa) verifying that I am the equivalent of a Canadian law graduate and, ultimately, eligible to join the Law Society of British Columbia.

Thank you for reading my curriculum vitae. I am very excited to begin discussing how I could use my substantial legal expertise in service of Great Entertainment Inc., willing to travel on business (when necessary), and happy to relocate to Greater Vancouver for the right opportunity. I will contact you in one week to discuss the status of my application; in the meantime, please feel free to call me at any time. I look forward to meeting with you soon!

Sincerely,

David Chang

Enclosures 2 (résumé, list of representative transactions)

Corporate Counsel. After going through bulleted strengths, this letter explicitly addresses the candidate's Canadian qualifications and employability. The strategy alleviates concerns that this expatriate Canadian attorney might have difficulty being legally entitled to work in Canada.

Frieda Rothman

1-111 Cousins Drive ● North York, Ontario ● M1M 1M1 ● (416) 555-2345

April 23, 2007

Hiring Committee
Bank of Ontario
21 Wellington Street East
Toronto, Ontario
M1M 1M1

REF: KY001-0002 – Full-Time – Level 7 or G

It is with great interest that I apply for the position of **Learning Coach / Facilitator** as posted online.

I began my career with the Bank of Ontario in 1991 and regularly earned promotions that carried increasing levels of responsibilities. I am completely familiar with the Bank's wide range of credit services, investment commodities, and deposit products with specific expertise in Small Business and Financial Consulting. In my current role as Small Business Advisor, I exceeded sales targets and improved branch profitability by encouraging client usage of Web dealing, Investor's Edge, and Telephone Banking.

You mention in your posting that the successful candidate must have:

● BCO, Mutual Funds, CSC, and PFP accreditations	**I do**
● very strong communication skills in order to effectively facilitate through various media	**I do**
● solid facilitation skills using various approaches (online, telephone, classroom)	**I do**
● familiarity with standard technology tools such as MS Office Suite	**I do**
● experience in e-learning	**I do**

Currently, I am enrolled in the Professional Coaching Program at the Raymond School of Professional Coaching where my studies concentrate on unlocking individual employee potential. The subjects I am taking stress the importance of staff teamwork, overall job satisfaction amongst employees, and better working relationships between staff, management, and clients.

It is my wish to apply these exciting theories and deliver quantifiable results for the Bank of Ontario – in the form of increased productivity, strong and sustainable performance, and enhanced service levels.

I look forward to the prospect of further conversations in a personal interview.

Yours very truly,

Frieda Rothman

Enclosure – Résumé

Corporate Trainer. This letter outlines the candidate's experience within the company and extensive knowledge of the organization, its products, and its services. The bulleted points specifically address the employer's *buying motivators* outlined in the job posting.

Elise Sutton

111 Ledge Street ▪ Nepean, ON K1K 1K1 ▪ 613.555.1234

October 25, 2007

Dr. Martin
Dr's Offices
123 Health St.
Nepean, ON K1K 1K1

Dear Dr. Martin:

After three years in the United States, I have returned home to Ottawa. The city has seen explosive growth in the last five years, and I see great opportunities in helping you grow your dental practice.

I have extensive experience as a Dental Receptionist/Treatment Coordinator. As you are well aware, Ottawa has seen several practices establish themselves in the last few years. Patients have a choice, and service above the norm will keep them coming. To provide first-class patient care, a practice must work as a team, be well organized, and have excellent communication. To that end, my strengths include:

♦ Knowledgeable in dental procedures, which facilitates patient communication—able to educate them on the treatments required, and answer any of their concerns.
♦ Ability to schedule patients for maximum productivity.
♦ Experienced in helping a new practice become established.
♦ Leadership skills, organizational skills, and the capability to excel in a stressful environment.

Given my background, I am confident I can contribute to the continued growth of your practice. My enclosed résumé will provide you with details of my experience.

I will call you in a couple of days to see if we can schedule an interview, and explore this mutual opportunity.

Sincerely,

Elise Sutton

Enclosed: Résumé

Dental Receptionist. This letter leads in with a solid explanation that succinctly addresses a small gap in employment. It follows this up by outlining the candidate's strengths in bullet form.

EMILIO COSTAS

11 The Glen, Delta, BC V1V 1V1   ecostas@careerprocanada.ca   (604) 555-2222

SafeSavers   May 30, 2007
123 Northern Pike Road
Edmonton, AB   T1T 1T1

Attention: Mr. Joseph Whiteside, Employee Services
Re: **Employment opportunities in ER (Emergency Response)**

Dear Mr. Whiteside:

The events of the last few years have reaffirmed the fact that the world will likely never be the safe place that it ought to be. We have seen corporate, government, and public security become increasingly threatened by the emergence of emboldened terrorist groups operating far abroad from their traditional home bases. We have seen software and equipment malfunctions continue to cause disasters, despite recent advances in technology. And we know that we will continually be challenged in our ability to predict, prepare for, and respond to natural disasters such as earthquakes and fires.

I specialize in helping organizations to prepare for and mitigate the consequences of any such unforeseen emergencies - to be ready to respond, and to demonstrate to the marketplace that they are a safe bet for doing business. As the Emergency Planning Manager for a mid-sized Edmonton-based airline (NorthAl Airways), I single-handedly created and currently operate the company's entire ER function. The ER opportunity with SafeSavers is just the type of work that I excel in, and if brought on board, I can envision bringing immediate improvements in safety to your organization. Here are a few things I would bring to SafeSavers:

➢ **Proven leadership in Emergency Response**… The comprehensive program that I developed and operate for NorthAl Airways is a model of excellence, and it includes an ER Centre, ER Plan, ER Training Program, and a Bomb Threat Training Program.

➢ **Outstanding communication skills**… A skilled writer, I have written (both solely and as part of a team) several large documents for my airline employers, including an 800-page ER Manual, a Flight Attendant Manual, and several ER and Flight Attendant training programs. An experienced presenter and trainer, I have trained thousands of airline employees and have more recently given speeches to numerous groups on ER preparedness.

➢ **First-hand understanding of how businesses run**… I spent several years as the owner/manager of a busy ice cream shop and, more recently, was one of a small group of individuals that started NorthAl Airways from scratch.

➢ **The character and the drive to make things happen**… Many different challenges (both as an employee and as a volunteer) have made me able to work well with others, especially with difficult personalities in stressful circumstances. I perform well both on solo assignments and when coordinating activities with others. My highly organized, detail-oriented, quality-focused approach has consistently brought positive results.

Thank you for reading my résumé. I would really like to share with you my ideas about how I could build a top-notch ER function that protects SafeSavers well into the new millennium. Let's book an in-person meeting for sometime in the next two weeks. I will set some time aside on my calendar for this purpose. In the meantime, if I may answer any questions you might have, I'm only a phone call away.

Sincerely,

Emilio Costas
Enclosure (résumé)

Emergency Response Manager. The letter effectively outlines real-life issues in security that concern employers today and how the candidate can address them. The bulleted section delineates pertinent examples of the candidate's specific emergency response qualifications.

Mario Beaumont
11 Buckhorn Ave, Richmond Hill, ON L1L 1L1
Phone: 905-555-1212   Email: mbeaumont@careerprocanada.ca

January 12, 2007

Markham Fire Department
40 Winter Street
Markham, ON L1L 1L1

Re: Probationary Firefighter

Dear Hiring Manager,

I am submitting my resume for consideration in the position of Probationary Firefighter with the Markham Fire Department. With a General Business Diploma, a Health and Fitness Management Diploma, extensive experience in the health and fitness industry, and commitment to community service, I feel that my qualifications meet the requirements for the Firefighting position.

With seven years of experience in the fitness industry, I have built a strong clientele in the community giving me exposure to people from diverse backgrounds. Passionate about helping people, I have negotiated and problem-solved fitness and health challenges, improving many lives by helping people to lose weight and become motivated to maintain healthy lifestyles. Teaching fitness one-on-one and in groups has allowed me to work exceptionally well with the public and develop superior skills in the area of public relations.

Since the age of 15, I have led a healthy lifestyle by including daily exercise and a sensible eating regimen. This has helped to improve my mental and physical strength, which I feel are strong qualifications for the Firefighter position. Finally, to prepare my application for this position, I have acquired the CPR and First Aid credentials.

I am a highly self-motivated and active person who possesses a strong interest in serving my community. I have demonstrated this commitment when I worked with a hearing-impaired teenager for over 5 years. Having worked with all types of individuals, including young children, seniors, and persons with disabilities, has enabled me to adapt to all types of situations.

As an outstanding team player, my ability to get along with my team-mates on hockey teams, an arm wrestling team, and a weightlifting team is evident. Additionally, I have demonstrated commitment by organizing a power lifting competition with my group members.

Firefighting will allow me to satisfy my passion to serve others and contribute to a team environment. With an uncle as Captain of the Toronto Fire Department, I understand the commitment and dedication required from individuals who have selected this as a career.

Thank you for your time and consideration. Please do not hesitate to contact me for further information. I can be reached at 905-555-1212.

Sincerely,
Mario Beaumont

Enclosure

Firefighter. This letter effectively ties the individual's experience in the fitness industry with his passion for firefighting.

Luca Davinci

100 Denby Ave ▪ Suite 1600 ▪ Toronto ▪ Ontario ▪ M1M 1M1 ▪ Canada
☎ **416-555-8765 (home) ▪ 416-555-7654 (mobile)** 🖳 **lucadavinci@careerprocanada.ca**

January 29, 2007

Ms. Sandra Cummings
Hiring Manager
B2B Canada
222 Back Street
Toronto, Ontario M1M 1M1
Canada

Dear Ms. Cummings:

When I discovered the position of **On-line Direct Marketing Manager** on the *B2B* website, I wasted no time in applying. This position appears to be a perfect match for my skill set. I am a confident, sharp individual with experience in successful market strategy conceptualization and implementation. Please accept my enclosed résumé and this letter as my application for the position of **On-line Direct Marketing Manager.**

My attached résumé outlines my academic and work history. As a result of these experiences, I can offer you the following qualifications:

- Ten years of direct On-Line Marketing experience
- Proven leadership, problem-solving, and decision-making skills
- Experience in tracking and analyzing consumer and client behaviour
- In-depth understanding of, and experience with, *B2B* and its service offerings
- The ability to create highly cost effective e-CRM marketing systems
- Solid technical expertise in the areas of computer/Internet development software and design.

Given my experience and drive, I would quickly use my creative and intuitive approach to directly enrich my team while contributing to *B2B's* profit. Throughout my career, I have demonstrated an uncompromising attitude and a work ethic that stands alone, and I go far beyond the "9 to 5" work mentality.

I look forward to meeting with you soon, to further discuss how I can contribute to the ongoing success of *B2B*.

Sincerely,

Luca Davinci

Enclosure: Résumé

Marketing Manager. The bold job title quickly directs the reader to the position for which this individual is applying.

DR. SABRINA ALI

11 Lima Place, Oakville, Ontario, L1L 1L1, CANADA (905) 555-1234
dr.ali@careerprocanada.ca / www.dr.ali.careerprocanada.ca

January 15, 2007

IMG-Ontario
111 Bay Street, Suite 11
Toronto, ON M1M 1M1, CANADA

Attention: IMG-O Program Director

Please accept this letter as a formal application to the *International Medical Graduates Program* in Ontario, within the Family Medicine Stream. I have enclosed my Curriculum Vitae for your consideration.

I am a dedicated Primary Health Care Physician from Cairo, Egypt with more than 15 years of experience in both private and clinical practice. Delivering essential accessible heath care to vulnerable populations, especially the elderly and terminally ill, is a personal priority. I am committed to providing a balanced approach to preventative medical care that includes promoting wellness and the timely diagnosis and treatment of illness. Overly extensive workups stress both the patient and health resources. By taking good medical histories, I am able to diagnose potential health issues and to order only those diagnostic procedures that are necessary.

As you will read in my Curriculum Vitae, my skills are well-suited to delivering medical services in underserved areas and I welcome the opportunity to do so in Ontario. I believe my personal attributes of honesty, skill, compassion, and ethics would enhance my performance in the role of a medical practitioner in Ontario. To date, I have been recognized with several nominations, honours, certificates, and scholarships, and I intend to practice with the same degree of integrity in Ontario.

I received my LMCC in June 2004 and am ready and willing to relocate anywhere in Ontario. As a Canadian citizen and Ontario resident, I have had the opportunity to become familiar with the many community resources that are available in Ontario. I am committed to the Canadian Code of Ethics, and I strongly identify with the Health Promotion Strategies concept.

I trust that you will find all of the documents presented with this application complete and in good order, so that I may continue to move smoothly through this process. I look forward to working as a Family Physician, and I am ready to serve the people of Ontario.

Sincerely,

Sabrina Ali, MD

Enclosure: Curriculum Vitae

Medical Practitioner. The opening paragraph offers a clear explanation of the reason for the letter. In this concise document, Dr. Ali provides ample information about her background and directs the reader to her curriculum vitae for further details.

Samantha Knight *BScN*

1234 New Grad Avenue
Nepean, ON K1K 1K1

(613) 555-1234
(613) 555-0123
sam@careerprocanada.ca

May 26, 2007

Dorothy Hart
Human Resources Director
Grace Hospital
1234 Health St.
Nepean, Ontario K1K 1K1

Dear Ms. Hart:

An unselfish desire to care for others is an important quality for anyone entering the health and medical field. This genuine desire led me to pursue a Bachelor of Science Degree in Nursing. Having recently graduated, I am now armed with the knowledge and skills required to excel at my chosen profession.

While earning my degree, I built a solid background of transferable skills to the health and medical field. The enclosed résumé will give you a brief overview of those skills. Here are some of the highlights:

Nursing: ER and Mayo Clinic Special Care Unit experience taught me to handle stressful situations with poise and professionalism. Interacted directly with patients and their family, which enhanced my nursing skills. Received academic honours and scholarship. What this means to you is that I can take my share of the patient load, and relieve your overworked nursing staff.

Human Relation: Relevant experience developed leadership skills and expanded my commitment to helping others. Many patients have complimented me on my great bedside manners; when patients are well taken care of, they will not be as demanding, and stress is reduced for all nurses. What you get is a contributing team player, able to provide excellent patient care while holding her own.

Given the opportunity, I am confident that I can become a valuable part of your team. I have exceptional academic credentials, solid experience, and a profound devotion for helping people in need. Nursing is not just a job; it's a big part of who I am.

I am available to start immediately, and would like to schedule an interview with you at your earliest convenience. I look forward to hearing from you soon.

Sincerely,

Samantha Knight

Enclosure: Résumé

Nurse. Two strongly bolded qualifying areas demonstrate that this candidate will be a productive team member from the start. The letter ends with a reminder that she is available to start right away.

January 10, 2007

Mr. Seymour Rapp
Vice-President, Operations
Atlantic Packaging Products Ltd.
444 Atlantic Park Drive
Scarborough, Ont. M1M 1M1

Dear Mr. Rapp:

I would like to be your next **Director of Operations,** a position I saw advertised on January 5 in the *Toronto Star*. The attached résumé documents 8 years' managerial and related employment, including 5 years' packaging experience. My résumé shows how I:

CHARLES IRVING GALLAGHER

One Concentric Circle

Richmond Hill, Ont.

L1L 1L1 Canada

(905) 555-1234

- Increased profits by researching costs and negotiating with customers.
- Slashed expenses by automating manual tasks.
- Motivated staff to work harder and better.
- Liaised with senior managers and executives of major corporations.

In this letter, I would like to give you an idea of the kind of person I am and how it affects the way I work. For example, when I prepared a catalogue for Bell Canada Enterprises, I liaised cooperatively with several staff, including an artist. Because the catalogue was my idea, I had supervisory responsibility; but, I determined quickly that the artist was both talented and trustworthy. After letting him know what I expected of him, I gave him lots of freedom, knowing that if he had ownership in the process, he would do a much better job.

The more I observed, the more my initial impression was confirmed. My faith in the artist drew out his abilities, and both of us had the satisfaction of watching him produce excellent graphics.

This team-oriented approach is not only typical of my behaviour as an employee, but predates my entry into the work force. I started training as a hockey player when I was only 12. My coaches impressed upon me the importance of putting the team ahead of personal aggrandizement. As a result, I focused on passing and setting up goals, instead of scoring. I thus earned the respect of not only my teammates and fans but also many opponents.

I am convinced this attitude was an important factor in enabling me to win several awards, including the Canadian *Order of Merit,* and to participate on several award-winning teams. It is in this spirit that I seek to join your highly-reputed organization. Please call to set a convenient time to meet, so that we can discuss how I might best serve your enterprise.

Sincerely yours,

Charles Irving Gallagher

Operations Director. Innovative design and layout garner interest for this candidate. Short bulleted items attract the reader's eye and succinctly summarize relevant achievements. The letter also capitalizes on the individual's sports-related achievements by showing how his team-oriented approach propelled him towards success.

Martin Yao

123-456 Handy Lane
London, ON, N1N 1N1, Canada

Phone: 519 555-7654
E-mail: myao@careerprocanada.ca

March 15, 2007

Ms. Annette Smithson
Hiring Manager
Executive Enterprise
123 South Road East, Suite 321
Burlington, ON, L1L 1L1, Canada

Dear Ms. Smithson:

Please accept this cover letter and the attached résumé as my application for the **Management Process Consultant** position with *Executive Enterprise*, as posted in the *Lite Business School* Career Centre.

I am interested in this position because my passion lies in the consumer goods industry. The posted position matches my skill areas in the following three ways:

- As an experienced Project Manager, I consistently met clients' expectations and finished projects before their deadlines, while simultaneously handling several projects in different cities.
- As an Account Manager and Senior Sales Director, I learned to be outstanding at establishing and maintaining client relationships and delivering presentations.
- As a co-founder of two successful start-up businesses, I tactically honed my strategic planning and self-motivating abilities.

I strongly believe that my proven leadership, communication skills, and management experience, along with my desire to contribute as an executive and a project manager, will bring value to your organization. I have performed the analytic and marketing functions in over 1000 marketing research projects, priming me to meet – and often exceed – deadlines under great pressure, and I look forward to the challenges of the **Management Process Consultant** position at *Executive Enterprise*.

I am looking forward to meeting you so that we can discuss my suitability in further detail.

Thank you for your consideration.

Sincerely yours,

Martin Yao
Enclosure: Résumé

Process Consultant. The candidate carefully selected his points in this letter to match the posted requirements. The individual focuses his bullets on listing his previous positions that fit each requirement.

KATHARINE PATTERSON

1234 East 56th Avenue, Vancouver, BC V1V 1V1   katpat@careerprocanada.ca   (604) 555-1234

Retailing Is Us   May 30, 2007
4567 Main Street
Vancouver, BC   V1V 1V1

Attention: Mr. John Doe, General Manager
Re: **Retail store management opportunity - Vancouver**

Dear Mr. Doe:

The challenges of large retail store management are numerous, ongoing, and complex. They demand an experienced, proven leader who is motivated, organized, focused, and skilled at managing both the valuable assets and the many processes that typify a large operation. As one such leader, I would like to meet with you to discuss opportunities with the Retailing Is Us team.

I bring to you:

> ➢ Fourteen years of experience with a major grocery chain - culminating in my current senior management position – during which I became recognized and awarded for bringing outstanding results.

> ➢ A record of consistently achieving a broad spectrum of financial and non-financial objectives through long-term visionary, medium-term strategic, and short-term tactical activities.

> ➢ A total commitment to recognizing the value and the efforts of my staff, promoting a harmonious workplace, and ensuring top-notch customer satisfaction.

I would love to discuss the opportunity to manage a mid to large-sized retail operation for your company. I am certain that my long record of successes in this field would be a tremendous asset to your organization.

Thank you for receiving this letter and résumé. I will contact you in one week to discuss the status of my application. In the meantime, please don't hesitate to get in touch with me if I may provide any further information. I look forward to talking with you soon.

Sincerely,

Katharine Patterson
Enclosure (résumé)

Retail Store Manager. This manager has only worked for one employer. She capitalizes on this by highlighting her progressive experience and awards in the first bullet. She deemphasizes her lack of education by focusing her other bullet points to address the employer's buying motivators.

Mary-Anne Stevenson

110 Rowntree Gardens
Hamilton, ON L1L 1L1
Tel: 905.555.1234

December 17, 2007

Julie Adams
Recruitment Manager
Littlewood Primary School
Littlewood, ON L1L 1L1

Re: Position of Teacher Assistant

Dear Mrs. Adams,

It is with great interest that I apply for the above position. With three years of classroom experience, a Diploma in Teaching, and office experience, I am well prepared for the role of supporting a teacher in the classroom.

The enclosed résumé outlines my broad range of experience in working with children. In the classroom, I have successfully helped young people reach their academic goals by creating an environment that is conducive to learning. As a community volunteer, I provided counselling, guidance, and health education. In particular, I bring the following strengths:

- **Supervising and communicating with children** – experience in the classroom, in the schoolyard, at community events, and as a parent. Particularly sensitive to the special needs of children with varying abilities.

- **Evaluating students' performance and progress** – 3 years of classroom experience.

- **Administrative procedures and office skills** – gained through 5 years of administrative work experience and education (Certificate in Personnel Administration).

- **Professional attitude** – fully appreciate the responsibilities of this supporting role.

After taking a 7-year career break to care for my family, I am enthusiastic about resuming my teaching career through employment and via further education to upgrade my qualifications.

Thank you for considering my application. At your convenience, I am available for an interview and would welcome the opportunity to discuss how I would make a positive contribution to Littlewood Primary.

Sincerely yours,

Mary-Anne Stevenson

Enclosure: Résumé

Teacher's Assistant. Bullet points clearly address the essential job criteria as described in the advertisement. The letter also explains a 7-year gap in the candidate's work experience in a way that is understandable and commendable.

APPENDICES

APPENDIX A — 100 WORDS THAT ARE COMMONLY MISSPELLED IN CANADIAN RÉSUMÉS

✔ Correct Spelling	✗ Incorrect Spelling
Accept (agree)	Except
Accessible	Acessible/Accessable
Accommodate	Acommodate/Accomodate
Acknowledgement	Acknowledgment
Acquire	Aquire
Analyze	Analyse
Authorized	Authorised
B.Sc. (Bachelor of Science in Canada)	B.S.
Behaviour	Behavior
Benefited	Benefitted
Calibre	Caliber
Cancelled	Canceled
Capital (city)	Capitol
Capital (money)	Capitol
Capitalize	Capitalise
Catalogue	Catalog
Categorize	Categorise
Centimetre	Centimeter
Centralize	Centralise
Centre	Center
Centred	Centered
Characterize	Characterise
Colour	Color
Computerize	Computerise
Correspondence	Correspondance
Counselled	Counseled
Counsellor	Counselor
Customize	Customise
Defence	Defense
Demeanour	Demeanor
Dual (double)	Duel
Elicit (bring about)	Illicit
Emigrate (leave a place)	Immigrate
Endeavour	Endeavor
Enrol	Enroll
Enrolment	Enrollment

APPENDIX A — 100 WORDS THAT ARE COMMONLY MISSPELLED IN CANADIAN RÉSUMÉS

✔ Correct Spelling	✗ Incorrect Spelling
Except (exclude)	Accept
Familiarize	Familiarise
Fervour	Fervor
Finalize	Finalise
Focused	Focussed
Fulfill	Fulfil
Grey	Gray
Harmonize	Harmonise
Honour	Honor
Honoured	Honored
Illicit (unlawful)	Elicit
Immigrate (enter a place)	Emigrate
Initialize	Initialise
Instalment	Installment
Kilometre	Kilometer
Labelled	Labeled
Labour	Labor
Labourer	Laborer
Levelled	Leveled
Liaise	Liase
Licence (a certificate)	License
License (to allow)	Licence
Litre	Liter
Manager	Manger
Manoeuvre	Maneuver
Metre (unit of measurement)	Meter
Minimize	Minimise
Mitre	Miter
Mobilize	Mobilise
Modelled	Modeled
Mould (to shape something)	Mold
Neutralize	Neutralise
Occasional	Occassional
Occurrence	Occurance
Offence	Offense
Organization	Organisation

APPENDIX A — 100 WORDS THAT ARE COMMONLY MISSPELLED IN CANADIAN RÉSUMÉS

✔ Correct Spelling	✗ Incorrect Spelling
Organize	Organise
Paycheque	Paycheck
Practice (a place)	Practise
Practise (to rehearse)	Practice
Premier (first)	Premiere
Premiere (grand opening)	Premier
Principal (head of an organization)	Principle
Principal (money)	Principle
Principle (basic truth)	Principal
Prioritize	Prioritise
Privilege	Priviledge
Realize	Realise
Recognize	Recognise
Reflection	Reflexion
Résumé	Résume/Resume
Rigour	Rigor
Scrutinize	Scrutinise
Separate	Seperate
Specialize	Specialise
Stabilize	Stabilise
Than (comparing something)	Then
Then (time)	Than
Travelled	Traveled
Unionized	Unionised
Utilize	Utilise
Visualize	Visualise
We're (we are)	Were
You're (you are)	Your

APPENDIX B — 300 ACTION VERBS TO ADD IMPACT TO YOUR RÉSUMÉ

A

Accelerated
Accompanied
Acquired
Acted
Activated
Actuated
Addressed
Adhered
Adjusted
Administered
Admitted
Adopted
Advanced
Advertised
Advised
Allocated
Amended
Amplified
Answered
Anticipated
Applied
Appointed
Appraised
Approached
Approved
Architected
Arranged
Assembled
Assessed
Assigned
Attained
Attended

B

Bargained
Benchmarked
Boosted
Borrowed
Bought
Briefed
Broadened
Brought
Budgeted

C

Calculated
Checked
Clarified
Coached
Co-founded
Collaborated
Collected
Commended
Commissioned
Committed
Communicated
Concluded
Condensed
Constructed
Consulted
Contracted
Contributed
Controlled
Converted
Convinced
Coordinated
Corresponded
Counselled
Crafted

D

Delivered
Demonstrated
Demystified
Deployed
Designed
Detected
Developed
Diagnosed
Directed
Disciplined
Dispatched
Dispensed
Documented
Doubled
Drafted
Drove

E

Earned
Edited
Educated
Effected
Eliminated
Emphasized
Enabled
Encouraged
Energized
Enforced
Engaged
Enhanced
Enlisted
Eradicated
Evaluated
Examined
Exceeded
Exchanged
Executed
Exempted
Exercised
Expanded
Explained
Extracted

F

Fabricated
Facilitated
Familiarized
Figured
Finalized
Financed
Focused
Forecasted
Formalized
Founded
Framed
Fulfilled
Functioned
Furnished

G

Gained
Gathered
Generated
Graduated
Granted
Grouped
Guided

H

Handled
Headed
Hypothesized

I

Identified
Ignited
Illuminated
Implemented
Imported
Improved
Inaugurated
Increased
Indoctrinated
Induced
Instigated
Instructed
Insured
Integrated
Interpreted
Inventoried
Investigated
Involved
Issued

J

Joined
Judged

L

Landed
Launched
Lectured
Leveraged

Licensed
Lightened
Litigated
Lobbied

M

Maintained
Managed
Manipulated
Marshalled
Masterminded
Maximized
Measured
Minimized
Mitigated
Modeled
Moderated
Multiplied

N

Named
Narrated
Navigated
Negotiated
Nominated

O

Observed
Obtained
Offered
Officiated
Opened
Operated
Optimized
Orchestrated
Ordered
Organized
Overhauled

P

Partnered
Partook
Passed
Patterned

APPENDIX B — 300 ACTION VERBS TO ADD IMPACT TO YOUR RÉSUMÉ

Penalized
Penetrated
Perceived
Performed
Permitted
Persuaded
Phased
Planned
Prepared
Presided
Prevented
Promoted
Prompted
Proposed
Proved
Provided
Publicized
Published
Purchased
Pursued

Q

Quantified
Queried

R

Raised
Ranked
Realized
Reasoned
Recaptured
Redesigned
Reduced
Re-engineered
Re-evaluated
Referred
Refinanced
Refined
Refocused
Refurbished
Remedied
Removed
Reorganized
Repaired
Replaced
Replicated
Reported
Repositioned
Resolved
Re-staffed

Restored
Restricted
Restructured
Resulted
Retained
Re-tooled
Retrieved
Revamped
Revealed
Reversed

S

Safeguarded
Salvaged
Sanctioned
Satisfied
Secured
Separated
Served
Serviced
Settled
Simplified
Simulated
Slashed
Solidified

Solved
Sorted
Sourced
Spearheaded
Specialized
Staged
Standardized
Started
Steered
Stimulated
Streamlined
Strengthened
Stressed
Structured
Studied
Submitted
Substantiated
Substituted
Suggested
Summarized
Supported

T

Tackled
Tightened

Tracked
Trained
Transcribed
Translated
Transported
Trimmed
Tripled
Troubleshot

U

Upgraded
Upheld
Utilized

V

Validated
Valued
Verbalized
Verified
Viewed

W

Worked
Wrote

APPENDIX C — 300 KEY WORDS THAT EMPLOYERS VALUE

ENTRY-LEVEL

Accounts Payable (A/P)

Accounts Receivable (A/R)

Administrative Assistance

Administrative Support

Back Office Operations

Billing Procedures

Bookkeeping Support

Business Writing

Canadian Legislation

Cash Control

Cash Management

Cash Register Operation

Clerical Support

Client Communications

Client Invoicing

Communications Writing

Computerized Billing

Conference Arrangements

Conflict Resolution

Correspondence Writing

Customer Liaison

Customer Needs Assessment

Customer Satisfaction

Customer Service

Customer Support

Data Analysis

Database Administration

Database Entry

Database Maintenance

Department Liaison

Departmental Liaison

Desktop Publishing

Document Management

Document Writing

Editing

Employment Equity

Employment Insurance

Event Coordination

Executive Support

Federal Legislation

Front Office Operations

General Maintenance

GST/PST/HST Planning

Inventory Control

Inventory Counting

Laboratory Assistance

Lead Generation

Loss Prevention

Machine Operation

Mail Management

Maintaining Client Files

Management Support

Marketing Support

Mechanical Repair

Meeting Set-up

Merchandising

Microsoft Office Proficiency

Occupational Health & Safety

Office Management

Office Supply Control

Operating Office Equipment

Operations Manual

Operations Support

Order Processing

Organizational Skill

Organizing Events

Package Handling

Packaging & Mailing

Pay Equity

Petty Cash Control

Post-Sales Support

Pre-Sales Support

Problem Solving

Proofreading

Provincial Government

Provincial Legislation

Record Keeping

Records Management

Regulatory Reporting

Relationship Building

Report Writing

RRSP & Tax Planning

Sales Administration

Sales Tracking

Secretarial Support

Shipping & Receiving

Sorting & Filing

Store Opening & Closing

Supply Purchasing

Technical Support

Telemarketing

Telephone Reception

Telephone Support

Temporary Staff Supervision

Time Management

Travel Arrangements

Warehouse Management

Word Processing

Workflow Management

Workflow Planning

APPENDIX C — 300 KEY WORDS THAT EMPLOYERS VALUE

MID-LEVEL

Account Retention

Asset Management

Benefits Administration

Brand Management

Budget Administration

Business Development

Canadian Legislation

Capital Budgeting

Cash Flow Optimization

Category Management

Change Management

Channel Distribution

Client Needs Assessment

Client Retention

Collective Bargaining

Competitive Benchmarking

Consensus Building

Consultative Selling

Continuous Improvement

Contract Negotiation

Corporate Taxation

Cost-Benefit Analysis

Customer Training

Demonstrations & Presentations

Direct Mail Marketing

E-Commerce Implementation

Efficiency Improvement

Employee Coaching

Employee Empowerment

Employee Orientation

Employee Supervision

Employment Equity

Employment Insurance

Employment Standards Legislation

Expense Control

Facilities Management

Feasibility Analysis

Federal Legislation

Financial Analysis & Reporting

Government Liaison

GST/PST/HST Planning

Health & Safety

Human Resource Management

Innovative Training

Internet Recruiting

Inventory Optimization

Investment Portfolio Management

ISO Implementation

Key Account Management

Knowledge Management

Labour Relations

Legislative Compliance

Liability Management

Logistics Management

Management Support

Margin Improvement

Market Expansion

Market Positioning

Multi-channel Distribution

Multi-media Campaigns

Needs Assessment

Network Development

New Business Development

New Product Launches

Occupational Health & Safety

Organizational Development

Pay Administration

Pay Equity Implementation

Performance Management

Policy & Procedure Implementation

Process Improvement

Product Positioning

Productivity Improvement

Program Development

Project Engineering

Project Management

Proposal Development

Provincial Legislation

Quality Improvement

Recruitment & Selection

Relationship Management

Revenue Generation

Risk Management

RRSP & Tax Planning

Sales Presentations

Senior Management Liaison

Solutions Selling

Staff Training

Statistical Reporting

Tactical Planning

Team Leadership

Technology Implementation

Territory Management

Total Quality Management (TQM)

Trade Show Representation

Training & Development

Trend Analysis

Vendor Selection

Web Content Development

WSIB Claims Management

APPENDIX C — 300 KEY WORDS THAT EMPLOYERS VALUE

SENIOR-LEVEL

Acquisitions & Integrations

Alliance Development

Banking Relations

Bankruptcy Turnaround

Board of Directors Interface

Budgeting & Forecasting

Building Visibility & Awareness

Business Development

Business Process Optimization

Business Re-engineering

Business Turnaround

Capital Projects

Cash Flow Financing

Change Management

Channel Strategies

Competitive Market Positioning

Consensus Building

Continuous Quality Improvement

Corporate Communications

Corporate Development

Corporate Governance

Corporate Mission & Vision

Corporate Revitalization

Cross-Cultural Communications

Cross-Functional Leadership

Customer-Driven Management

Efficiency Improvement

Emerging Markets

Executive Compensation

Executive Presentations

Financial Planning

Financial Restructuring

Global Best Practices

Global Business Development

Global Manufacturing

Global Market Expansion

Global Operations

Government Relations

Growth Strategies

High-Level Negotiations

Influential Leadership

Infrastructure Development

Initial Product Offering (IPO)

International Business Expansion

International Logistics

Investor Relations

Joint Ventures

Leadership & Team Building

Leadership Development

Leading Edge Strategies

Legislative Compliance

Long Range Planning

Management Development

Margin Improvement

Market Development

Market Expansion

Market Positioning

Market-Driven Management

Matrix Management

Mergers & Acquisitions

Multi-Channel Management

Multi-Site Management

New Business Development

New Product Launches

Organizational Culture Shifts

Organizational Development

Organizational Leadership

Outperforming Competition

Outsourcing Operations

Paradigm Shifting

Participative Management

Performance Improvement

Performance Revitalization

Pioneering Technologies

Policy Development

Price & Contract Negotiation

Process Reengineering

Productivity Improvement

Profit & Loss (P&L) Management

Profit Growth

Profit Revitalization

Public Speaking

Relationship Optimization

Reorganization

Resource Planning & Management

Return on Assets (ROA)

Return on Equity (ROE)

Return on Investment (ROI)

Revenue Generation

Risk Management

Sales Force Development

Sound Financial Compliance

Start-Up Ventures

Strategic Business Planning

Strategic Partnerships

Strategic Vision

Team Development

Transition Management

Turnaround Management

Visionary Leadership

APPENDIX D — LIST OF CONTRIBUTORS

Sharon Graham, CRS, CIS, CCS, CPRW, CEIP
(905) 878-8768, (866) 622-1464
Career Professionals of Canada
info@CareerProCanada.ca
www.CareerProCanada.ca
Graham Management Group
www.GrahamManagement.com
info@GrahamManagement.com
See pages 48-49, 64-65, 74-75, 96-97, 104-5, 108-13, 116-17, 132-33, 146-47, 164-67, 185-87, 192-93, 196-99, 208-9, 224-25, 236-37, 245

Paul Bennett, B.Comm, CPRW
TARGET Career Services
(604) 876-9980, (888) 782-7438
paul@choosetarget.com
www.choosetarget.com
See pages 138-39, 247, 250, 257

Marian Bernard, CPS, CPRW, JCTC, CEIP
The Regency Group
(905) 841-7120, (866) 448-4672
marian@neptune.on.ca
www.resumeexpert.ca
See pages 50-51, 66-67, 101, 136-37, 140-41, 248

Martin Buckland, MRW, CPRW, CJST, CEIP, JCTC, CPBS
Elite Resumes
(905) 825-0490, (866) 773-7863
martin@aneliteresume.com
www.aneliteresume.com
See pages 38, 78-79, 114, 150-51, 162-63, 172-73, 188-89, 210-11, 222-23, 226-29, 238-39

Denyse Cowling, CIS, CPC, RPR
Career Intelligence Inc.
(905) 466-2034
dcowlings@cogeco.ca
See page 39

Annemarie Cross, CPRW, CEIP, CECC, CCM, CRW, CPCC
Advanced Employment Concepts
success@aresumewriter.net
www.aresumewriter.net
See pages 152-53

Theresa Dowsett, CHRP, CPCC, CCS, CRS
Career Acceleration Inc.
(705) 458-0101, (877) 241-8253
info@excelyourcareer.com
www.excelyourcareer.com
See pages 170-71, 178-79

Heather Erskine, RN, BA, CPRW, CRS, CIS, CCS
Erskine & Associates Inc.
(519) 642-1581
heather.erskine@gmail.com
See pages 60-61, 202-7, 212-16, 232, 252-53, 256

Audrey Field, CRW, BA, BEd.
Résumé Resources
(905) 857-6291, (877) 204-9737
info@resumeresources.ca
www.resumeresources.ca
See pages 40-43, 46-47, 58-59, 82-85, 98-99, 122-23, 130-31, 154-57, 180-81

Howard Earle Halpern, MA, CPRW
Résu-Card ®
(416) 410-7247, (877) 866-5454
halpern@sympatico.ca
www.NoBlock.com
See page 255

François Houle, CPRW
iWrite Business Services
(613) 843-8077
career@iwritebusinessservices.com
www.iwritebusinessservices.com
See pages 52-53, 56, 70-71, 88-89, 115, 128-29, 144-45, 148, 249, 254

Ingrid Jain, BA, MBA
IMJ Services (Résumé & Technical Translation)
(416) 502-9611
info@imjservices.com
www.imjservices.com
See pages 112-13, 198-99

APPENDIX D — LIST OF CONTRIBUTORS

Brenda Jean Lycett, BA, CHRP, RGR
Lycett 4CHANGE & Associates
(416) 498-4901 (Voice/TTY), (866) 601-7130
bjlycett@4change.biz
See pages 194-95

Ross Macpherson, MA, CPRW, CEIP, CJST, JCTC
Career Quest
(905) 438-8548, (877) 426-8548
ross@yourcareerquest.com
www.yourcareerquest.com
See pages 57, 62, 90-95, 100, 102-3, 134-35, 158-59, 168-69, 176-77, 182-84, 190-91, 217-19, 230-31, 233-35

Debra Mills, CPRW
Pro-CV Writing Service
dmills@pro-cv.co.uk
www.pro-cv.co.uk
See pages 72-73, 81, 149, 220-21, 258

John M. O'Connor, CRW, CPRW, CCM, CFRW, MFA
Career Pro Résumés
(919) 787-2400, (866) 717-2400
john@careerproresumes.com
www.CareerProResumes.com
See pages 54-55

Lynda Reeves, BA, ACS, CRS, CCS
Added Value Résumés
lyndare@sympatico.ca
www.addedvalueresumes.com
See pages 36-37, 86-87, 174-75, 242-43, 246

Linda Schnabel, PCC, CRS, CIS, CCS, JCTC
Career Works
(905) 523-4281
info@careerworks.biz
www.careerworks.biz
See pages 68-69, 120-21, 126-27, 142-43, 200-201

Karen Ruth Shane, BA, CPRW
Business Writing Network
(416) 226-0460
writinghelp@rogers.com
www.ohsofast.net/express
See page 244

Marlene Slawson, CRS, CPRW
Seneca College
416-491-5050
marlene.slawson@senecac.on.ca
www.senecac.on.ca
See pages 44-45, 106-7, 118-19, 251

Chris Starkey, BA CPRW, CEIP
KeyRidge Résumé Services
(709) 368-1902, (877) 968-1902
resume@resumechoice.com
www.resumechoice.com
See page 80

Daisy Wright, CDP, BA
A Wright Career Solution
(905) 840-7039
daisy@thewrightcareer.com
www.thewrightcareer.com
See pages 76-77, 124-25

APPENDIX E — INDEX OF SAMPLES

APPENDIX E — INDEX OF SAMPLES

APPENDIX E — INDEX OF SAMPLES

APPENDIX E — INDEX OF SAMPLES

ABOUT THE AUTHOR
Sharon Graham
CRS, CIS, CCS, CPRW, CEIP

Sharon Graham is a prominent Canadian professional résumé writer and career consultant. With a passion for supporting the career development industry in Canada, she has made it her personal goal to enable Canadian job seekers, résumé writers, and employment practitioners to achieve career and business success.

In 2004, Sharon founded Career Professionals of Canada – an organization with a mandate to enable Canadians to achieve their career, business, and organizational development goals by promoting quality, ethics, and expertise within the industry. With certifications in résumé, interview, and career strategy, Sharon also operates Graham Management Group, a leading executive résumé writing and career management firm.

Over the last 15 years, Sharon has contributed her services as a senior executive and consultant to a wide variety of individuals and organizations. An industry pioneer, she has been featured in leading Canadian media including Report on Business Television, the Globe and Mail, and the Toronto Star. A civic-minded individual, Sharon constantly endeavours to make a difference through her charitable and volunteer work for assorted causes.

Today, having built a reputation for integrity, philanthropy, and superior customer service, Sharon's business is largely referral based. It is her sincere wish that the strategies, information, and resources in this book will enable Canadians and others throughout the world to achieve their career goals.

Career Professionals of Canada

"working together for career success"

Where can you
research career professionals,
build your job search skills,
and improve your career prospects all in one place?

Career Professionals of Canada
www.CareerProCanada.ca

Career Professionals of Canada is an innovative organization with a mandate to support Canadians in their quest for career and business success.

Our professional members are leading Canadian résumé writers, employment consultants, and a wide variety of other career professionals. Working together, we provide quality services, comply with a strict ethical standard, and offer career expertise to enable individuals across Canada to achieve their goals.

If you are a job seeker, we are your best source for expert advice and assistance. We empower you with the most current information and resources that will move your job search forward!

FREE Directory of Career Professionals

Our website provides a FREE searchable listing of résumé writers and career consultants. Look up career professionals by connecting to www.CareerProCanada.ca. You can easily research organizations, compare offerings, and select the service that suits your individual needs. Our professional members will assist you in achieving your career goals.

FREE Career Connections Newsletter

You can subscribe to the FREE Career Connections e-newsletter designed as a resource for savvy job seekers, workers, and career professionals. Subscribe by sending an e-mail to info@CareerProCanada.ca. Or, if you prefer, connect to the Career Connections section of our site and read informative feature articles written by industry leaders.

Connect to Career Professionals of Canada today
to take advantage of this great new resource!

Partnering with a career professional is an investment in your future.
Our members enable you to outperform other qualified candidates!

(905) 878-8768 ◆ (866) 622-1464 ◆ info@CareerProCanada.ca ◆ www.CareerProCanada.ca

Other Books by Sentor Media

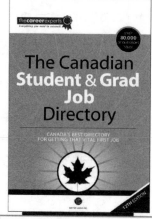

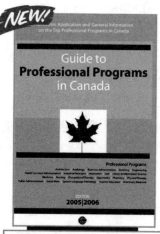